Preliminary Reports of
ASOR-Sponsored Excavations 1982–85

BULLETIN
of the
AMERICAN SCHOOLS of ORIENTAL RESEARCH

Supplement No. 25

PRELIMINARY REPORTS
of
ASOR-SPONSORED EXCAVATIONS
1982–85

Edited by

WALTER E. RAST

Assisted by

MARION ZEIGER

Published by

THE JOHNS HOPKINS UNIVERSTIY PRESS

for

THE AMERICAN SCHOOLS OF ORIENTAL RESEARCH

Published by

THE JOHNS HOPKINS UNIVERSITY PRESS

for

THE AMERICAN SCHOOLS OF ORIENTAL RESEARCH

Preliminary Reports of
ASOR-Sponsored Excavations 1982–85

Library of Congress Cataloging-in-Publication Data

Preliminary reports of ASOR-sponsored excavations, 1982–85.

  (BASOR supplement, ISSN 0003-097X; no. 25)
  Bibliography: p.
  1. Jordan—Antiquities. 2. Excavations (Archaeology)—Jordan.
3. Turkey—Antiquities. 4. Excavations (Archaeology)—Turkey.
5. Israel—Antiquities. 6. Excavations (Archaeology)—Israel.
I. Rast, Walter E., 1930– . II. Zeiger, Marion. III. American
Schools of Oriental Research. IV. Series: Bulletin of the American
Schools of Oriental Research. Supplemental studies; no. 25.
DS41.A55   no. 25   [DS153.3]   939'.4   87-35829
ISBN 0-8018-3697-2

The Johns Hopkins University Press
Journals Division
701 W. 40th Street, Suite 275
Baltimore, MD 21211

CONTENTS

The 1984 Explorations of the Ancient Harbors of Caesarea Maritima, Israel

ROBERT L. HOHLFELDER
Department of History
University of Colorado
Boulder, CO 80309

The 1984 season of field work in the ancient harbors of Caesarea Maritima added considerable information to our understanding of this important Levantine metropolis. Along the inner or southern face of the northern breakwater of the outer harbor, underwater excavations uncovered evidence of extensive renovation from the Byzantine era. This installation appears to have been restored as a rubble breakwater without the specialized support buildings of the original Herodian structure.

Land and underwater excavations around the inner harbor indicate that this fortified basin originally was part of Straton's Tower, constructed perhaps late in the second century B.C. by the tyrant Zoilus. It appears that this Hellenistic settlement reached its zenith at that time and that its extensive walls, probably constructed or completed during that period, protected the anchorage. Remains of the fortifications and the harbor itself may have induced Herod to locate Caesarea on the site.

Land and underwater explorations were conducted from 21 May to 30 June 1984, at Sebastos, the ancient harbor of Caesarea Maritima, a site that today is located on Israel's Mediterranean coast between Tel Aviv and Haifa (Oleson 1984: 9–11; Raban 1984a: 246–52; 1984b: 274–76; fig. 1).[1] Herod the Great constructed Caesarea between ca. 22 and 10 B.C. His aims were threefold: to challenge Alexandria as the major international seaport in the eastern Mediterranean, to glorify his own name and reign, and to pronounce in a grand manner his loyalty to his patron and emperor of Rome, Caesar Augustus (Hohlfelder 1982: 42–47). The most impressive feature of his new city was Sebastos, its massive harbor complex (Hohlfelder *et al.* 1983: 133–43; Raban and Hohlfelder 1981: 56–60). The four harbors of Caesarea assured this city an immediate and major role in the history of Palestine and the Levant and in the affairs of the Roman world. In fact, for the next six centuries the port functioned as one of the economic, political, religious, and intellectual centers of the eastern Mediterranean.

The 1984 excavations marked the final season of field work of the first five-year plan for general explorations of all the harbor facilities of Sebastos. In previous seasons, the Caesarea Ancient Harbour Excavation Project (CAHEP) had uncovered evidence for the design of the main artificial enclosing arm (the southern breakwater) of the great outer basin (ca. 200,000 m²) and for the construction techniques employed in its building (fig. 2). In addition, a small inner basin (ca. 10,000 m²) connected to the outer one (fig. 3), a large southern fair-weather mooring (more than 100,000 m²) (fig. 4), and a northern roadstead of as yet undetermined size have been found (fig. 5). All of these were components of the original building program for Herod's Sebastos (Oleson *et al.* 1984: 281–305). The 1984 land and sea explorations were intended to answer specific questions regarding

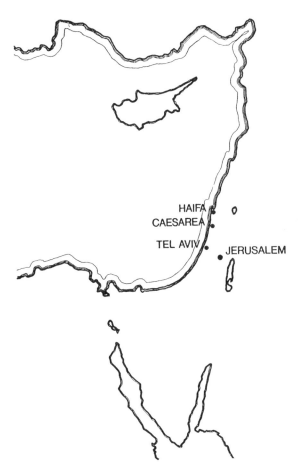

Fig. 1. Location of ancient Caesarea Maritima in relationship to Tel Aviv, Haifa, and Jerusalem.

chronology and design of other select features of the maritime structures of Sebastos in preparation for the 1985 study season, which was to be followed by final publication of the results of the first five years' work.

The major underwater excavations occurred along the inner face of the northern breakwater (Area H; fig. 6). Previous explorations along its southern counterpart had revealed considerable data relating to construction techniques and breakwater design features (Oleson 1985: 165–72). CAHEP's two probes were the first effort to see if the northern breakwater—which has puzzled investigators because of its very regular configuration vis-à-vis the badly damaged remains of the southern breakwater—was constructed in a similar fashion (fig. 2).

Efforts to reach the original face of the breakwater in two trenches opened in Area H were

thwarted by a heavy overburden of fallen rubble piled steeply along its southern side (figs. 7, 8). Excavators could not penetrate this overburden. As a result, no identifiable structural remains were uncovered. It is clear, however, that the rubble concentration was heaped on the breakwater at some time during its use; it was not part of the original design of this installation. This dumpage dates from a general harbor repair that Emperor Anastasius I (A.D. 491–518) undertook, sometime after 502 (mentioned by Procopius of Gaza, *Panegyricus*, xix in *PG*, 87.3.2817–2818).

Although this sixth century rehabilitation project accounts for the breakwater's relative structural integrity today, it obliterated the Herodian configuration of the breakwater. While it originally may have mirrored its southern counterpart's design with a loading quay, warehouses, seawall, etc., its function after Anastasius's renovation was much simpler. Following the repair, the breakwater was devoid of any specialized support buildings and appears to have served only as a rubble enclosing arm for the Byzantine anchorage (Hohlfelder 1985: 179–84).

The rubble overburden protected various artifacts from earlier periods of the harbor's use. A huge quantity of Roman pottery from the Imperial period (first through third centuries A.D.) was uncovered. Surprisingly, most of these finds shared a western provenience. Unlike most other pottery *corpora* from Levantine sites, many of the ceramic finds from Sebastos were imported.

This discovery, along with artifactual data from previous seasons in other areas of excavation, confirms the city's western orientation throughout its six-century existence as a classical city and seaport. The harbor facility was originally conceived as an international entrepôt. The foreign origin of so many of its artifacts suggests that it did serve such a role for all of its history, until the coming of the Arabs (ca. 640/1).

The excavations in Area H also revealed a small deposit of mid-fourth-century copper coins. The wide selection of mints represented in the finds suggests that this concentration may have been a sailor's purse dropped into the sea and not recovered. The Anastasian repairs later protected the find-site from any further damage from scouring by shifting sands. The coins are in reasonably good condition, unexpected for copper coins lost in an ancient harbor.

Excavations were undertaken in the entrance of the outer basin of the main harbor in an attempt

Fig. 2. Outer Basin of Sebastos looking north. The submerged southern breakwater is more irregular in shape than its northern counterpart owing to its vulnerability to storms. (Photograph courtesy Bill Curtsinger, National Geographic Society)

Fig. 3. Location of the inner basin looking west. This facility had fallen out of use by the Byzantine era. Today a mosque from Caesarea's Bosnian occupation in the late 19th century to 1940, tourist shops, and restaurants are atop the ancient harbor. (Photograph by R. L. Hohlfelder)

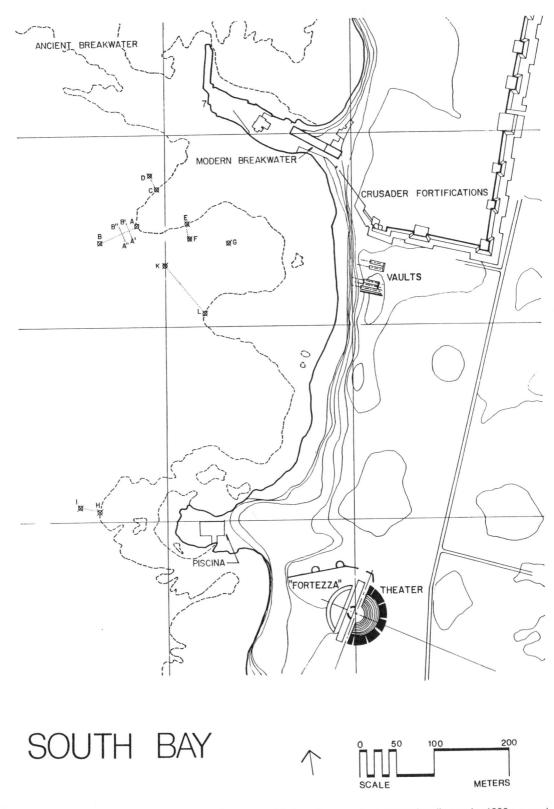

SOUTH BAY

SCALE

METERS

Fig. 4. The south bay served as a fair-weather anchorage well before Caesarea's construction (in use by 1200 B.C. and perhaps earlier), during the port's prominence as an international emporium, and probably after its demise under Arab rule.

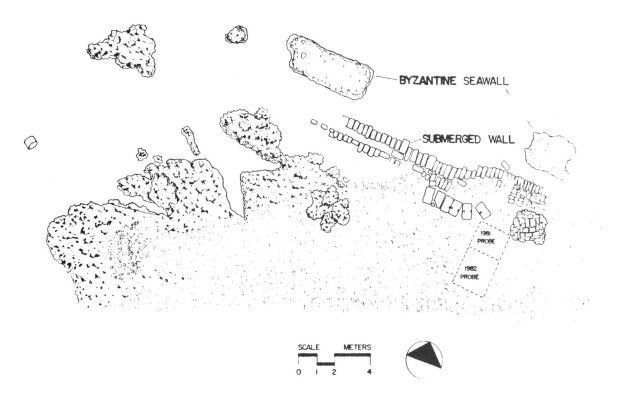

Fig. 5. CAHEP's Area J: The northern harbor area. The "submerged wall" dates from Hellenistic times and is similar in construction to seawalls found at Acco and Athlit.

to define the width of the channel (Area D; fig. 6). Previous attempts in 1982 to reach the inner face of the western channel line had failed (Oleson *et al.* 1984: 296). Efforts in 1984 were unsuccessful as well, because a huge volume of rubble obscured this segment of the original entrance (figs. 9, 10). It is now certain, however, that the ancient harbor mouth was at least 30 m wide and possibly as wide as 50 m. The breadth of the opening, comparable to Ostia and other great Imperial harbors such as Leptis Magna (80 m, Casson 1971: 368), would have certainly facilitated ship movement into and out of the basin but would have increased the likelihood of siltation and lessened the protection afforded ships moored within it.

A third underwater excavation was conducted along the southern face of a round tower that guarded the entrance to the inner harbor of Herod's Sebastos (Area T, fig. 6) (Oleson *et al.* 1984: 300). This exploration was undertaken to find diagnostic artifactual material to establish a date for the building of the tower and thus the

associated basin. The trench quickly reached the bedrock foundation on which the tower was constructed, at ca. 2.6 m below present sea level. Ceramic finds, as well as the design of the tower itself, suggest a construction date late in the second century B.C.

It seems that this round tower and the basin it protected were in existence before Caesarea. Therefore, they must have been associated with an Hellenistic settlement on the Palestinian coastline where Caesarea would later stand (Hohlfelder 1983a: 67–68). This guard tower was located in the lee of a natural promontory that defined the other, or southern, side of the entrance channel (fig. 11). It seems likely that a lighthouse stood on this promontory to mark the location of the landlocked harbor. Such a structure may have provided the actual name for this Hellenistic city, Straton's Tower.

The other major underwater project was the completion of a series of section lines drawn over both the northern and southern breakwaters

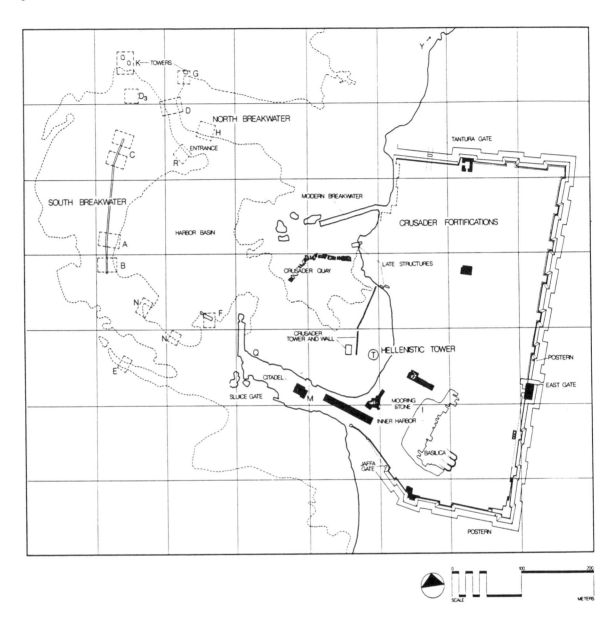

Fig. 6. Areas of CAHEP's excavations through 1984.

(Oleson *et al.* 1984: 291–93). Data from these systematic surveys will allow reconstruction of the arrangement of various building materials found on the breakwaters and will permit an estimate of their original size. In the final reports, it will be possible to collate this information with other survey reports and with a detailed study of aerial photographs of the submerged remains to create various reconstructions and sections of the ancient breakwaters.

No additional excavation was possible on the Roman shipwreck that had been identified as a major project for 1984 (Oleson *et al.* 1984: 302; fig. 12). Weather conditions were too extreme during CAHEP's entire season to permit uncovering this fragile but important find. It will be the

Fig. 7. Two CAHEP divers attempt to penetrate the rubble overburden in Area H using picks and an air lift. (Photograph by Mark Little)

Fig. 8. (Right) Rubble piled on the northern breakwater in the early sixth century sealed pottery and other artifacts beneath the dumpage. (Photograph by Mark Little)

Fig. 9. (Below) Divers slowly cut a probe trench through the rubble spill that obscured the entrance channel to the outer basin, CAHEP's Area D. (Photograph by Mark Little)

Fig. 10. Larger rocks in Area D are removed with a lift bag. (Photograph by Mark Little)

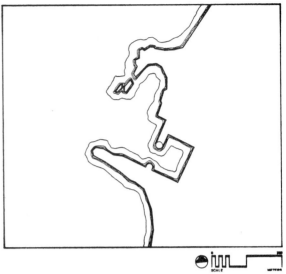

Fig. 11. The small enclosed basin, depicted here in the lee and north of the promontory, and the northern harbor (fig. 5) were both part of the Hellenistic settlement of Straton's Tower.

Fig. 12. Divers search wreck site for metal objects. Hull remains suggest the ship was a merchantman dating from the first century B.C. or A.D. (Photograph by Mark Little)

focus of future field work planned for phase II of excavations to begin in 1986.

CAHEP carried out extensive land excavations at the eastern seawall of the inner harbor associated with the guard tower (Area I: 1 & 2; figs. 6, 13). Earlier probes uncovered a mooring stone *in situ* in a loading quay west of the podium of the great temple of Rome and Augustus, which Herod had constructed (fig. 14); but there is no evidence thus far that dates the construction of the basin itself (Oleson *et al.* 1984: 299–301). Working with pumps to remove fresh water from this trench, excavators were able to go below a pavement of large blocks dating from a Byzantine reuse of the basin to find the original harbor floor (fig. 15).

It appears that the ancient builders of this harbor had cleared sand and debris down to bedrock and then hewed a deeper depression into the rock itself. At the time of this construction, the area had been closed to the sea. After a basin

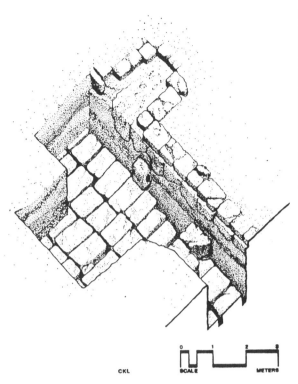

Fig. 13. Mooring stone *in situ* with Byzantine pavers beneath it.

Fig. 14. Mooring stone from inner basin. (Photograph by R. L. Hohlfelder)

had been hollowed out, a channel to the open sea, defined north and south by the guard tower and promontory respectively, was cleared allowing the sea to fill the protected anchorage. This manner of harbor construction, building into the land rather than out into the open sea, is more characteristic of a time before Herod.

Unfortunately, convincing evidence for the date of this impressive installation was not uncovered in the Area I excavations. The only definite datum was a coin of Nero with a later overstrike (post-69 A.D.), found above the bedrock floor along with a few late first century B.C. and early first century A.D. sherds. Its presence does not date the facility but only suggests that it was in use in the first century A.D.

Lacking significant artifactual or stratigraphical data relating to the origins of the inner basin, it is only possible to speculate regarding its construction date. It was probably hollowed out of the coastal bedrock at the same time the guard tower was constructed. Its basic design—an enclosed harbor—is more appropriate for the Hellenistic

era than for any later period. If so, its date of construction was most likely late in the second century B.C. as well.

It also is likely that this installation was incorporated into Herod's grand plan for the harbor facilities of Caesarea and may have served some specialized role at that time. As part of Herod's port, it may have been a royal or ceremonial harbor or perhaps the home of his navy. In addition, its very existence, although probably in a ruinous state, may have been one of the major reasons the king selected this particular coastal site for his new city.

By the Byzantine era at the latest (probably after Anastasius), the inner basin had fallen out of commercial use but still served in some way as a freshwater collection basin. (A gradual sea level increase since the time of Herod had caused the freshwater table to rise.) Still later, it was completely filled in and used for other purposes.

Fig. 15. Pavers were placed in the inner harbor during the Byzantine era to form a basin to collect fresh water. A rising sea level had caused the freshwater table to rise. (Photograph by Mark Little)

Clearing operations above and adjacent to the mooring stone uncovered the pantry or dump area of a dwelling of the Crusader era (ca. 12th century A.D.). The inhabitants of this house probably were quite oblivious to the existence of an ancient harbor beneath them.

The second major land excavation was undertaken within one of the great *horrea* or warehouses that Herod built adjacent to the eastern quay of the inner harbor (Area I: 3). CAHEP received permission from the National Parks Authority of Israel and the Department of Antiquities to reopen and slightly extend two trenches that Negev had originally opened in the early 1960s within one of these magazines (fig. 16). Negev's excavations have not been published in final form and his preliminary accounts do not definitively date this structure (Negev 1963). CAHEP hoped to find evidence in its two probes to date the original fortification wall of Straton's Tower (the south and east walls of the *horreum*) against which the warehouses in this section of the

city were built. Negev had dated the vault itself to the Herodian building program. Presumably it was one of six or seven vaults that formed the podium on which the great temple to Augustus and Rome was constructed. If Negev was correct, the fortification wall, incorporated into this later construction, was Hellenistic. But when was it built?

CAHEP's two probes within the vault produced diagnostic sherds that date the fortification wall to the late second century B.C. (fig. 17); and as Negev had proposed, it was later incorporated into Herod's building program. The defensive system, of which this wall was a component, was probably erected at the same time as the round guard tower and the inner basin. These coordinated construction efforts suggest that at this time, the coastal settlement of Straton's Tower was transformed into a fortified city with an enclosed harbor. It may have been enlarged as well. The author of the metamorphosis of Straton's Tower from unfortified village to walled city was probably Zoilus, a

Fig. 16. The *horreum* first excavated by Negev, looking east. (Photograph by Mark Little)

Fig. 17. Interior of the *horreum* looking west. Negev's trenches are still visible. The Hellenistic fortification wall is to the left (south); the later wall to the right (north) and the vaulting clearly are from a different period of construction. This vault formed part of the podium for the temple of Augustus and Rome that stood above and dominated the harbor front. (Photograph by Mark Little)

shadowy local tyrant who is known to have controlled this section of the Palestinian coast during this period.

The 1984 season ended the first phase of CAHEP's explorations. During the summer of 1985, a study session was held at the site and in Haifa, where finds are now housed at the Center for Maritime Studies, to prepare final reports on the excavations to date. Four volumes are planned to present our findings to the scholarly community.

NOTES

[1]During May and June, 1984, more than 100 volunteers and a staff of 15 from Israel, the United States, Canada, England, Australia, and Japan participated in the fifth season of archaeological field work at Caesarea, conducted by the Caesarea Ancient Harbour Excavation Project (CAHEP). This international consortium of universities operates under the aegis of the Center for Maritime Studies of the University of Haifa with the endorsement of the American Schools of Oriental Research and the Israeli Department of Antiquities. Other institutional members of CAHEP are the University of Colorado, Boulder; the University of Victoria; and the University of Maryland, College Park. The University of Haifa was represented by Avner Raban (Project Director), Steven Breitstein (Operations Director) and Yossi Tur-Kaspa (Assistant Director). Codirectors were Robert L. Hohlfelder (Colorado), John P. Oleson (Victoria), and R. Lindley Vann (Maryland).

CAHEP's excavations were generously supported by the four participating universities, the Caesarea

ROBERT L. HOHLFELDER
SUPPLEMENT 25

Development Corporation, the National Endowment for the Humanities, the National Geographic Society, the Social Sciences and Humanities Research Council of Canada, and numerous private donors.

This report was prepared during a fellowship at Dumbarton Oaks in the spring of 1986. I wish to thank that institution for its generous support of my research on various problems relating to the harbors of Caesarea Maritima.
BIBLIOGRAPHY

Bull, R. J.
1982   Caesarea Maritima—The Search for Herod's City. *Biblical Archaeology Review* 8,3: 24–40.
Casson, L.
1971   *Ships and Seamanship in the Ancient World.* Princeton, NJ: Princeton University.
Hohlfelder, R. L.
1981   Coin Finds: A Conspectus. Pp. 46–51 in The Joint Expedition to Caesarea Maritima: Eighth Season, 1979. *Bulletin of The American Schools of Oriental Research* 244: 27–52.
1982   Caesarea Beneath the Sea. *Biblical Archaeology Review* 8,3: 42–47.
1983a   The Caesarea Coastline Before Herod: Some Preliminary Observations. *Bulletin of The American Schools of Oriental Research* 252: 67–68.
1983b   Caesarea Maritima. Pp. 191–92 in News Letter from the Levant, 1981 (Southern Sector). *American Journal of Archaeology* 87,2: 183–95.
1984a   Caesarea Maritima in Late Antiquity: An Introduction to the Numismatic Evidence. Pp. 261–85 in *Ancient Coins of the Graeco-Roman World: The Nickle Numismatic Papers.* Waterloo: Wilfrid Laurier Press.
1984b   Caesarea Maritima. Pp. 225–26 in News Letter from the Levant (Southern Section), 1982. *American Journal of Archaeology* 88,2: 217–28.
1985   Byzantine Coin Finds from the Sea: A Glimpse of Caesarea Maritima's Later History. Pp. 179–84 in *Harbour Archaeology. B.A.R. International Series 257.* Oxford: B.A.R.
Hohlfelder, R. L., and Oleson, J. P.
1980   Sebastos, the Harbor Complex of Caesarea Maritima, Israel: The Preliminary Report of

the 1978 Underwater Explorations. Pp. 765–79 in *Oceanography: The Past.* New York: Verlag.
Hohlfelder, R. L. *et al.*
1983   Sebastos: Herod's Harbor at Caesarea Maritima. *Biblical Archaeologist* 46,3: 133–43.
Levine, L.
1975   *Caesarea Under Roman Rule.* Leiden: E. J. Brill.
Negev, A.
1963   The Palimpsest of Caesarea Maritima. *London Illustrated News.* 2 November, 728–31.
Oleson, J. P.
1984   The Caesarea Ancient Harbor Excavation Project (CAHEP)—May 21–June 30, 1984. *Old World Archaeology Newsletter* 13:2: 9–11.
1985   Herod and Vitruvius: Preliminary Thoughts on Harbour Engineering at Sebastos, the Harbour of Caesarea Maritima. Pp. 165–72 in *Harbour Archaeology. B.A.R. International Series 257.* Oxford: B.A.R.
Oleson, J. P. *et al.*
1984   The Caesarea Ancient Harbor Excavation Project (C.A.H.E.P.): Preliminary Report on the 1980–1983 Seasons. *Journal of Field Archaeology* 11: 281–305.
Raban, A.
1984a   Caesarea Maritima, 1984. *Revue Biblique* 91,2: 246–52.
1984b   Caesarea Harbor Excavation Project, 1984. *Israel Exploration Journal* 34: 274–76.
Raban, A., and Hohlfelder, R. L.
1981   The Ancient Harbors of Caesarea Maritima. *Archaeology* 34,2: 56–60.
Ringel, J.
1975   *Césarée de Palestine.* Paris: Editions Ophrys.

The Sardis Campaign of 1984

CRAWFORD H. GREENEWALT, JR.
University of California
Berkeley, CA 94720

NICHOLAS D. CAHILL
University of California
Berkeley, CA 94720

MARCUS L. RAUTMAN
Miami University
Oxford, OH 45056

Excavation focused on monumental Lydian buildings and their surroundings in two regions of the city site. In one region near the Late Roman Synagogue there are two buildings; the better preserved is Colossal Lydian Structure (CLS) whose design and construction were clarified. More of a curious pile of clay and gravel heaped against one of the long sides was exposed, and dumped brick from its superstructure was analyzed. From the floor of a nearby Lydian residential unit that had been buried under the dumped brick were recovered more than 75 well-preserved artifacts, including two datable Attic cups. The other region is a spur of the Acropolis in the eastern part of the city state (ByzFort), where more of a Lydian terrace wall that enveloped the spur was traced and exposed. In both regions excavation uncovered more Roman material: near the Synagogue more of a colonnaded street; on the Acropolis spur, terrace rooms of residential units or small public facilities, some with opus sectile and mosaic floors. In the Necropolis west of the Artemis Temple, reexcavation of a Lydian chamber tomb (originally excavated in 1912) produced new information about the design and masonry features of the tomb and uncovered a well-preserved human skeleton. Chance discoveries included a Hellenistic grave stone inscribed in Greek and Lydian, for two separate burials, and an honorific monument for a priestess of Demeter Karpophoros and her father.

INTRODUCTION

Excavation and research at Sardis in 1984 (fig. 1) were conducted by the Archaeological Exploration of Sardis, or Sardis Expedition, jointly sponsored by the Fogg Art Museum of Harvard University, Cornell University, the American Schools of Oriental Research, and the Corning Museum of Glass and took place during two and a half months in the summer.[1] The primary aim of excavation was to clarify aspects of urban organization and layout in pre-Roman, especially Lydian, times; and excavation continued to focus on two regions of the site where monumental architecture of the seventh and sixth centuries B.C. indicates the location of important centers of urban activity in the Lydian city.[2] These excavations continued to uncover Roman residential units and public facilities, and in some places were designed to clarify the form and function of Roman features. To resolve uncertainties about the stratigraphy of Iron Age occupation levels at Sector HoB (House of Bronzes, being studied for publication by A. Ramage), a sondage was made in that sector. An unscheduled project was the reexcavation of a Lydian chamber tomb in the Necropolis region. Study of material recovered in earlier seasons included Iron Age artifacts from Sector HoB (by A. and N. H. Ramage), Attic pottery (by N. H. Ramage), molded bowls (by S. I. Rotroff), Byzantine glazed wares (by J. A. Scott), inscriptions on stone

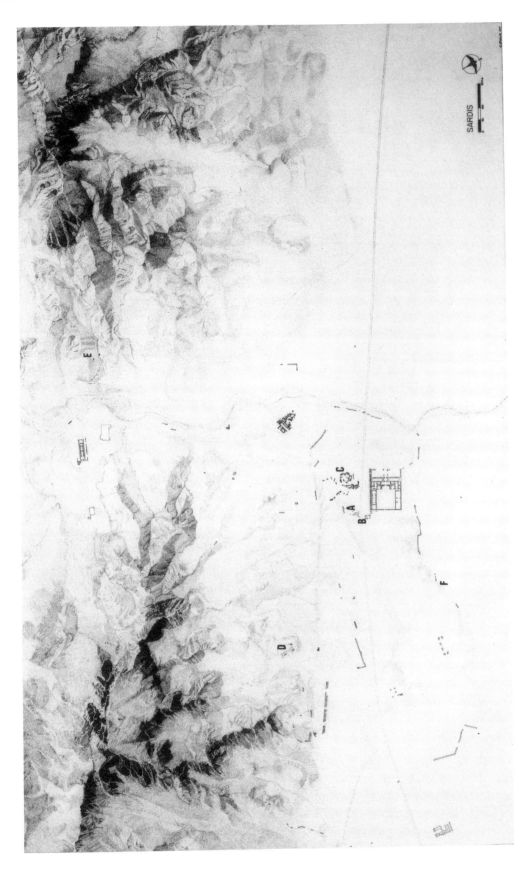

Fig. 1. Sardis, visual relief map of site and immediate environs (by C. H. Smith). A = Sectors MMS and MMS-S; B = Sector MMS-N; C = Sector HoB; D = Sector ByzFort; E = Tomb 813; F = Mound 2 (discussed in Greenewalt, Rautman, and Cahill, "The Sardis Campaign of 1985," this issue). Note: north is at the bottom in this map.

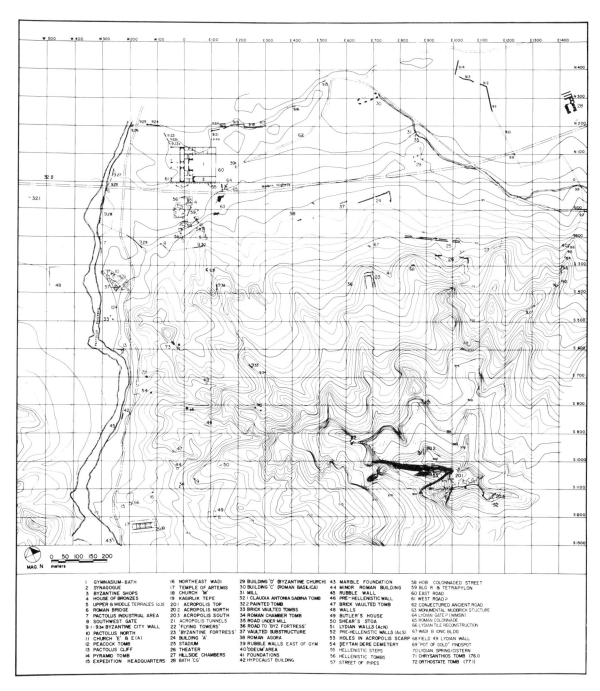

I GYMNASIUM-BATH	16 NORTHEAST WADI	29 BUILDING 'D' (BYZANTINE CHURCH)
2 SYNAGOGUE	17 TEMPLE OF ARTEMIS	30 BUILDING 'C' (ROMAN BASILICA)
3 BYZANTINE SHOPS	18 CHURCH 'M'	31 MILL
4 HOUSE OF BRONZES	19 KAGIRLIK TEPE	32 1 CLAUDIA ANTONIA SABINA TOMB
5 UPPER & MIDDLE TERRACES (a,b)	20 1 ACROPOLIS TOP	32 2 PAINTED TOMB
6 ROMAN BRIDGE	20 2 ACROPOLIS NORTH	33 BRICK VAULTED TOMBS
7 PACTOLUS INDUSTRIAL AREA	20 3 ACROPOLIS SOUTH	34 ROMAN CHAMBER TOMB
8 SOUTHWEST GATE	21 ACROPOLIS TUNNELS	35 ROAD UNDER MILL
9 1-9 34 BYZANTINE CITY WALL	22 'FLYING TOWERS'	36 ROAD TO 'BYZ FORTRESS'
IO PACTOLUS NORTH	23 'BYZANTINE FORTRESS'	37 VAULTED SUBSTRUCTURE
II CHURCH 'E' & E(A)	24 BUILDING 'A'	38 ROMAN AGORA
12 PEACOCK TOMB	25 STADIUM	39 RUBBLE WALLS EAST OF GYM
13 PACTOLUS CLIFF	26 THEATER	40 'ODEUM' AREA
I4 PYRAMID TOMB	27 HILLSIDE CHAMBERS	41 FOUNDATIONS
15 EXPEDITION HEADQUARTERS	28 BATH 'CG'	42 HYPOCAUST BUILDING

43 MARBLE FOUNDATION	58 HOB COLONNADED STREET
44 MINOR ROMAN BUILDING	59 BLG R & TETRAPYLON
45 RUBBLE WALL	60 EAST ROAD
46 PRE-HELLENISTIC WALL	61 WEST ROAD?
47 BRICK VAULTED TOMB	62 CONJECTURED ANCIENT ROAD
48 WALLS	63 MONUMENTAL MUDBRICK STUCTURE
49 BUTLER'S HOUSE	64 LYDIAN GATE? (MMSN)
50 SHEAR'S STOA	65 ROMAN COLONNADE
51 LYDIAN WALLS (AcN)	66 LYDIAN TILE RECONSTRUCTION
52 PRE-HELLENISTIC WALLS (AcS)	67 WADI B IONIC BLDG
53 HOLES IN ACROPOLIS SCARP	68 FIELD 49 LYDIAN WALL
54 ŞEYTAN DERE CEMETERY	69 "POT OF GOLD" FINDSPOT
55 HELLENISTIC STEPS	70 LYDIAN SPRING/CISTERN
56 HELLENISTIC TOMBS	71 CHRYSANTHIOS TOMB (76 I)
57 STREET OF PIPES	72 ORTHOSTATE TOMB (77 I)

Fig. 2. Sardis, general site plan.

(especially IN82.1, the boundary marker of the Artemis Sanctuary, which records the boundary established by Julius Caesar in the last month of his life, cf. Greenewalt *et al.* 1985: 53–92, by P. Herrmann), and Bronze Age pottery from the settlement site near Kılcanlar, north of the Gygaean Lake (by A. Gunter).[3] A regional survey project that is the joint effort of the Expedition and Doç. Dr. Recep Meriç, of Ninth of September University in Bornova-Izmir, was conducted under the direction of Meriç for a continuous fortnight and several weekends.

Fig. 3. Sector MMS-S, portal in Late Roman wall: threshold and iron pivot reinforcements.

In the following account, completed projects and isolated discoveries are more fully reported than ongoing projects and discoveries related to them.[4]

EXCAVATION

Sectors MMS, MMS-S, and MMS-N

Sector MMS is the low hill, the core of which is created by remains of Colossal Lydian Structure (CLS), located south of the Late Roman Synagogue, and Sectors MMS-S and MMS-N are adjunct sectors located respectively south and north of Sector MMS (fig. 2, nos. 63 [Sectors MMS and MMS-S], 64, 65 [both Sector MMS-N]). Between Sectors MMS and MMS-N the modern Ankara-Izmir highway creates a permanent line of demarcation. Sectors MMS and MMS-S were once differentiated by an intermediate saddle-like depression, traversed by a village road, in the landscape; excavation in this

saddle in 1983 and 1984 has made the distinction arbitrary.

Sectors MMS-S and MMS, Roman Features

Sector MMS-S, Arched Portal. The arched opening in the Late Roman wall (Greenewalt *et al.* 1983: 8) that forms the south limit of the colonnaded street (discussed below) was emptied of debris[5] to allow the excavators to determine the thickness of the wall and to clarify the nature of the opening. The wall proved to be 1.55 m thick. The opening is a passageway through the wall; it has a barrel-vaulted ceiling and a floor paved with marble slabs. A threshold block at the north end contains a pair of sockets for a bivalve door with leaves each 0.60 m wide (fig. 3). One of the sockets contained iron reinforcements for the door pivot: cylindrical ring, with wood pseudomorphs[6] on the inside surface; nail with broad, convex head. Another set of iron reinforcements—identical iron ring and broad-headed nail—presumably for

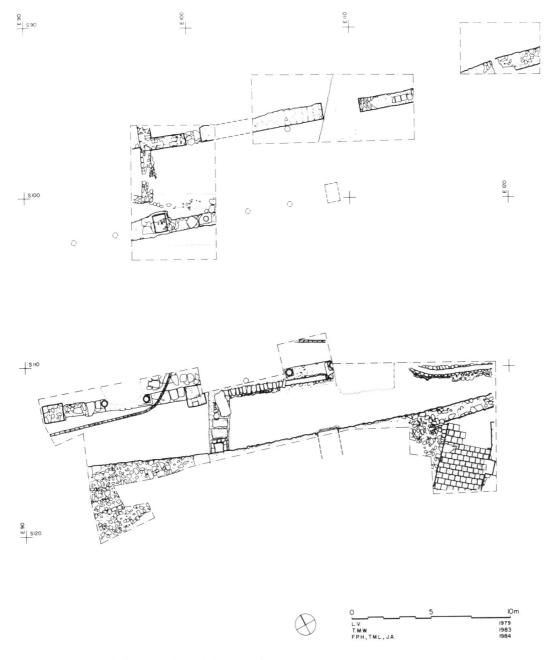

Fig. 4. Sector MMS, Roman colonnaded street, plan.

the other leaf, and other iron items suitable for door fittings (nails, and perhaps a hasp) were recovered in the debris that filled the opening (fig. 3 shows both sets of reinforcements next to the sockets).[7] Sockets and fittings support the implication of the size and form of the passage that this feature was a doorway rather than a niche or window. Since the top of the threshold is ca. 1.70 m above the door level of the colonnade ambulatory, however, there would have to have been an intermediate staircase; and the rough, irregular masonry of the wall face directly below the doorway threshold is likely to be the scar of that staircase.

C.H.G.

MMS Street. Previous excavation of the MMS sector has revealed a complex of late antique rooms built atop and into the remains of Colossal Lydian Structure. Two trenches located in the southwest part of the sector in 1984 revealed sections of a continuous wall running through the south part of the area, slightly askew of the B-grid. This long wall forms the north edge of a broad colonnaded street of the late Roman period, other parts of which were partially excavated in previous seasons as Sector MMS-S (Greenewalt *et al.*, 1983: 8–10; Greenewalt *et al.* 1985: 76; Greenewalt, Rautman, and Meriç 1986: 8–11). During the period of its use this street formed an important component of the city's urban framework. Its orientation suggests the street plan of eastern Sardis (as suggested by the standing building remains; Hanfmann 1983: fig. 167), and links the center of the late Roman city with the peripheral HoB quarter. Together with other known roads in the area, the street flanks the MMS building complex on a third side, defining an irregularly shaped *insula* that encloses the low mound of Colossal Lydian Structure.

Excavation in 1984 produced a detailed picture of the broad colonnaded thoroughfare that originally ran through the area (fig. 4). The street slopes gently upward toward the east and is defined by two tall parallel walls set ca. 18.0 m apart, which retain the pre-Roman topography to north and south. The 10.0 m broad central passage is flanked on either side by a colonnade and a ca. 4.0 m wide sidewalk or ambulatory. Both colonnades present an irregular alternation of piers and columns set at ca. 2.5 m intervals. Like other *emboloi* of late antiquity, various buildings opened directly off the colonnaded street, which played an important role in fifth-century urban life.[8]

The form of the late Roman street is closely linked with the Lydian features of Sector MMS. The remains of the truncated Lydian wall dominated the local topography prior to the street's construction. At this time a broad trough was cut through the archaic stone wall and mudbrick debris to a depth of the street surface, which rises at a ca. 7° slope from ca. *101.3 at E 100 to *103.5 at E 114. The close interrelation between Lydian and Roman features noted elsewhere in the sector (Greenewalt et al. 1985: 73; Greenewalt, Rautman, and Meriç, 1986: 1, 5) is seen in the Romans' incorporation of the Lydian stone wall into the fabric of the street's north wall, and in the reuse of the dense mudbrick detritus for artificial packing.

The north wall of the street stands ca. 18.0 m away from its south counterpart and reaches an excavated length of ca. 25.0 m. Both walls are built in the "banded rubble" technique characteristic of late Roman Sardis: roughly dressed fieldstones are laid in thick mortar beds, with occasional brick leveling courses running through the wall's thickness. Put-log holes in the masonry presumably supported scaffolding during construction. Toward the east this wall retains the lower parts of the Lydian wall as well as dumped Roman refuse. A 2.25 m wide opening in the north Roman street wall may originally have given access to a steep, stepped passage that led upward from street level to the crown of the MMS hillock. Further to the west the wall is freestanding and separates the north sidewalk from a small adjacent space, accessible from the street through a 0.95 m wide doorway that was originally arched. At the west edge of the trench the street wall turns to the north, enclosing this secondary space on the west and suggesting a change in the street beyond the limit of excavation. The original function of this space remains uncertain, but its street-side location would be appropriate for a small shop or office, similar to the long row of Byzantine shops to the north (Hanfmann 1983: 161–67).

The street's north colonnade lies parallel to the north wall at a distance of ca. 4.0 m. Within the small area exposed this colonnade presents a rectangular pier and a short column shaft. The pier is built of reused architectural fragments, sandstone blocks, and semifinished fieldstone, and is located immediately opposite a similar pier in the south colonnade. Both pier and column stand on a continuous mortared rubble foundation that steps gently upward toward the east at the level of the street surface. Fragments of fallen brickwork suggest that the north colonnade may originally have carried a brick arcade. The arrangement of parts is similar to the previously excavated section of the colonnade that faces south (Greenewalt, Rautman, and Meriç 1986: fig. 12).

Despite the street's ambitious planning, both roadway and flanking sidewalks shared a common sloping surface of packed earth. Fragmentary traces of plastered or mortared floors suggest that occasional attempts were made to level the trafficked surface as it rose with time, a characteristic

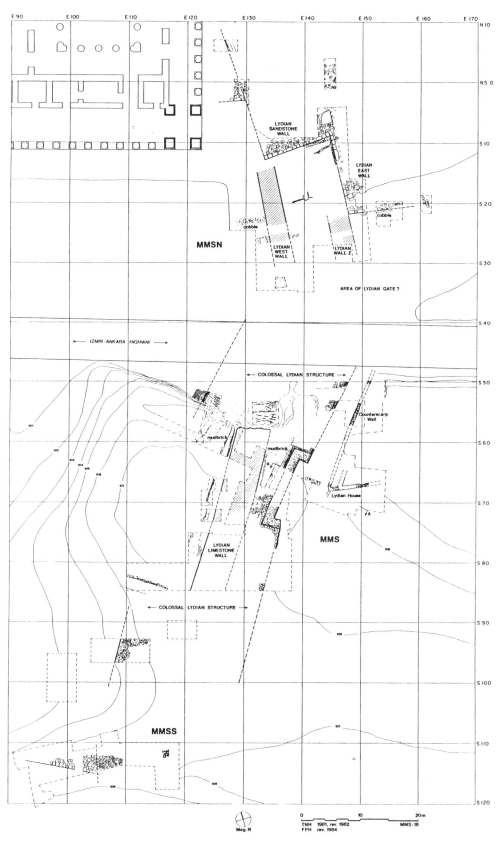

Fig. 5. Sectors MMS, MMS-S, MMS-N, pre-Roman features, plan.

of the south sidewalk noted in previous seasons (Greenewalt, Rautman, and Meriç, 1986: 10). No trace of the drains and water pipes found in the south part of the street were identified in the two 1984 trenches.

The stratigraphic evidence indicates that the street's primary period of use was during the fifth century A.D. A coin of Arcadius (395–408; 1984.138) from the initial sidewalk packing suggests that the street was laid out shortly after 400. An issue of Zeno (A.D. 476–491; 1984.135) found in a secondary stratum points to a possible reconstruction of the street arcade and resurfacing of the roadway toward the end of the century. Other numismatic finds indicate that the sixth century saw the gradual rise of the street's occupation level, which was compounded by the collapse of the north wall into the street around the middle of the sixth century. By this time the city apparently lacked the resources to repair the damage. Irregular makeshift walls of dry-laid masonry were installed in the north sidewalk passage, and the whole area became a common dumping ground during the late sixth and early seventh centuries.

In an effort to clarify related problems concerning the street system of western Sardis, a previously excavated trench nearby in sector HoB was cleaned and studied. This trench (at ca. E 44–63/S 99–109) lies on axis with the MMS Street ca. 30.0 m distant. The architectural remains located in this area include a large late Roman structure (Building R) and part of the HoB Colonnaded Street, which was first identified in 1964 and further explored in 1968 and 1970 (Hanfmann 1965: 11, 14–17, fig. 10; Hanfmann and Waldbaum 1970: 29; Hanfmann and Thomas 1971: 11). At the time of its initial excavation, parts of a north–south colonnade were identified, together with superimposed street surfaces covering drains and water pipes, and a building inscription that mentions a tetrapylon and two important streets (IN.68.19). Reexamination of the area suggests that the MMS Street may meet the HoB Colonnaded Street in a broad intersection near this point.

Stratigraphic study of the two streets confirms that both thoroughfares were laid out early in the fifth century as part of a major program renewing the Sardian urban fabric (Hanfmann 1983: 193). This apparent prosperity may have been short-lived, however, for the sequence of superimposed

packed earthen surfaces suggests that regular maintenance of the city's streets had ended by the late fifth or mid-sixth century, after which time scattered ramshackle structures, domestic in function, encroached upon parts of the sidewalks. The last phase of habitation along the streets documented by coin finds dates to the early seventh century, although the colonnades and flanking buildings may have remained standing until the middle of the seventh century.[9]

M.L.R.

Sector MMS, Roman Level. Roman levels were only excavated here within the apsidal room previously dug in 1980 and 1982 (fig. 9; Greenewalt *et al.* 1983: 1; Greenewalt *et al.* 1985: 68–73). The layer of fallen stucco encountered previously was excavated further; this produced a number of large fragments of ceiling (?) plaster with reed impressions on the back lying broken in place. Among the most notable fragments is a small section of a four- or five-line Greek inscription in gold leaf on a dark blue ground, reading [--] M [--] / [--] IΓΓ [--] / [--] ON [--] / [--] . [--]. A deposit of black glass chips and tesserae probably represents debris from mosaic construction. Little datable material was recovered from the layer; two coins found in 1982 suggested a date in the middle of the fourth century A.D.

Sector MMS, Lydian Levels

Exploration of the Lydian levels in sector MMS continued with three goals: to expose more of the west face of Colossal Lydian Structure; to record and study the layer of fallen brick debris on the east side of the structure; and to expose Lydian levels east of the structure and of the enigmatic "counterscarp" wall, which roughly parallels the structure.

West Face. Two trenches were begun from surface to expose part of the west face of Colossal Lydian Structure: at E110–120.75/S80.5–85 and E106–114/S93–97 (fig. 5, see above, "MMS Street"). The southern trench exposed a massive vertical wall face, almost certainly the west face of the structure, approximately parallel to the forward stone east face uncovered in 1982 and 1983 and about 23 m from the line of that face (fig. 5).

Fig. 6. Sector MMS, trench MMS-II: layers of sand, gravel, clay, etc. against the west face of Colossal Lydian Structure.

The face here is built of well fitted polygonal blocks, mostly sandstone and schist; it retains a packing of large rubble. East of the stone packing is a core or superstructure of mudbrick, probed in 1983. The masonry is differently worked from that of the east face: the blocks are generally smaller, squarer, more closely fitted in polygonal style, and a higher proportion of them are of sandstone, while most of the east face is of schist with some limestone and little sandstone, and the blocks are more oblong and less closely fitted. The reasons for this difference in technique are unclear.

The discovery of this stone west face suggests (1) that the west face changes in construction from sloped mudbrick on a low stone socle in the north to vertical stone construction in the south, just as the east face does (Greenewalt *et al.* 1983: 1–5; Greenewalt *et al.* 1985: 73–77; Greenewalt, Rautman, and Meriç 1986: 6); (2) that the west face changes orientation, following the east face; and (3) that the stone section of the structure is

at least 30 m long (from the northernmost point of the east face to the southernmost point of the west), too long for a tower or bastion (as already suggested, Greenewalt, Rautman and Meriç 1986: 6).

In front of the west stone face is a layer of fallen brick debris, similar to that found previously in front of the east face (below). This is the first time such brick debris has been discovered west of Colossal Lydian Structure; further north, layers of sand and gravel lie against the west face. The stone east face, however, is covered by similar brick debris, suggesting that the stone segment of the structure was topped by a brick superstructure.

A second trench just 8 m to the north, however, produced no clear trace of the west face of the structure (fig. 6). The stratigraphy here consisted of a series of layers of sand, gravel, clay and mudbrick, all sloping away from the structure at about 25–30°. These seem to overlie mudbrick construction of the structure, although no clear face of the structure was located. The layers were

clearly artificially deposited: according to the excavator, M. C. Miller, they were deposited from
below, not dumped from above; and they seem to
have been retained or stabilized by rough stone
and brick constructions. Pottery from the sand
and gravel layers was exclusively Lydian or earlier,
the latest material dating to about the mid-sixth
century B.C., although a number of phases are
represented. Some of these layers are probably
related to the sloping gravel and clay layers excavated just to the northwest in 1983, which produced Lydian and earlier (Early Bronze) material,
and to similar layers further north near the highway, excavated in 1977 and 1980, which covered
the mudbrick west face of Colossal Lydian Structure (Greenewalt 1979: 21, fig. 26; Greenewalt
et al. 1983: 1–6, fig. 3, "riverine fill;" Greenewalt,
Rautman, and Meriç 1986: 7–8). The interpretation of these strata, and the reasons for the apparent disappearance of the face of the structure
here, remain problematic.

Brick Fall Layer. Previous excavation has
shown that much of Colossal Lydian Structure
was encased by a thick layer of fallen brick and
brick debris, apparently the remains of its superstructure. This "brick fall layer" has been found
all along the east side of the structure, on the west
side in this year's southern trench, in sector
MMS-S to the south of the sandstone wall there;
and in sector MMS-N to the west of "Lydian
West Wall."[10] Another project of the 1984 season
was to record and study this layer, to learn more
about both the superstructure and the process of
its destruction. A section through the layer from
Colossal Lydian Structure to the tail end of the
layer was drawn, and samples of brick from the
layer analyzed in Berkeley (fig. 5 Section A-A;
fig. 7; cf. Greenewalt *et al.* 1983: 5–6, fig. 3).

The brick fall layer is composed of a mass of
brown, red and blue-green bricks and brick
debris, up to 3.5–4 m thick. The layer trails off to
the east and seems to end about 17 m from the
face of the Colossal Structure. It rests on a loose
layer of fallen stone 1–1.5 m thick, which rests in
turn on a sloping clay surface covering the socle
and "platform" of Colossal Lydian Structure.
The brick layer is stratified in lenses ca. 0.3–0.6 m
thick, which slope down from the face of the
structure at about 35°. These lenses vary in consistency from solid whole bricks with little or no
soil between them, to lenses of brown soil or
decayed mudbrick mixed with crumbled fragments

of green and red brick, to lenses entirely composed of crumbled red brick. All the material
seems to be brick from the structure superstructure, in varying states of decay.

A number of factors suggest that the brick fall
does not represent a natural collapse or erosion of
Colossal Lydian Structure, but a deliberate destruction of its superstructure. The composition of the
layer changes in different Lydian spaces, for instance west and east of the "counterscarp" wall,
with varying proportions of whole and crumbled,
and red, green, and brown brick filling different
areas. This could suggest a deliberate filling of
these spaces, using debris from slightly different
sources for different spaces. The stratification into
discrete lenses, together with the high proportion
of whole bricks and the often excellent preservation of unbaked mudbricks in the debris also
suggest a quick and deliberate destruction, rather
than a slower process of natural erosion or a
single, massive collapse. Finally, the brick fall is
restricted in extent, covering the entire east face
but apparently only parts of the west. Natural
erosion or collapse would probably have left more
traces of brick debris on the west face as well as
on the east.

A large proportion of the bricks in the debris
layer are baked and reddened by fire (up to half
the preserved complete bricks). Such red bricks
are found only in the tumbled debris from the
structure, not in the part still standing, which
shows no trace of burning. The nature of these
red bricks was investigated this year, to try to
determine the circumstances of their firing, particularly whether they were accidentally burned in
the destruction of Colossal Lydian Structure or
were deliberately fired before being built into the
structure (as M. L. Rautman was the first to suggest). In either case, the presence of the red bricks
only in the debris layer suggests a substantial
difference in construction between the superstructure and the standing remains of the structure:
either the superstructure was built with sufficient
timber to have burned this massive quantity of
mudbrick (the bricks themselves do not contain
straw or chaff that might burn) or it was built
with previously fired bricks. A number of factors
point to the latter conclusion.

The red bricks are for the most part uniformly
reddened throughout in an oxidizing atmosphere.

Fig. 7. Sector MMS, section through brick fall layer, on east side of Colossal Lydian Structure (A-A on fig. 5).

When differentially reddened, the less burnt part is almost without exception in the center of the brick, not at one edge, showing that the bricks were heated uniformly from all sides. This in itself strongly suggests that they were not baked while *in situ* in Colossal Lydian Structure, since such circumstances would not expose all edges of the bricks to uniform heat. The surfaces and edges of the bricks are often very crisp and clear, occasionally preserving finger marks and other irregularities from the original surface (fig. 8). A very few show signs of overfiring or vitrification but the surfaces of the vast majority are clean and unblemished.

To investigate the circumstances of firing, samples of different kinds of bricks were shipped to Berkeley for analysis. The original firing temperature was determined by refiring fragments of red baked bricks and unbaked mudbricks at temperatures between 400°C and 1000°C. Previously fired red bricks should show little change when refired below the original firing temperature, but should change in color, texture, and crystalline and mineral structure when heated above that temperature; while if the material used for making mudbricks for Colossal Lydian Structure was similar to that used for making the red bricks, it should be possible to duplicate the color and texture of the red bricks by firing mudbrick under the original firing conditions. Visual inspection of the refired samples suggested that the red bricks were originally fired at ca. 600°C–700°C. To try to refine these results, thin sections were made of samples of red bricks to explore changes in the crystalline and mineral structure; the sections proved uninformative however, since the bricks contain too much iron to allow the use of a petrographic microscope.

Samples of green mudbrick from the debris layer were formed into cubes 8 cm on a side (the minimum dimension of a brick) and fired at 700°C in a conventional electric kiln for varying lengths of time to determine the minimum time required to completely fire a single brick fragment to the core. The actual firing time would of course be considerably longer since the mass of brick would be so much greater. At least six hours were required to fully fire an 8 cm cube. Thus if the red bricks had been burned accidentally in the destruction of Colossal Lydian Structure, we must presume a fire that burned at at least 700°C for at least six hours and probably more, and timber construction in Colossal Lydian Structure sufficient to feed such a fire, and dispersed enough to provide even heat to all the

Fig. 8. Sector MMS, brick fall: red brick showing finger marks.

surfaces of most if not all the burned bricks. Such circumstances seem irreconcilable with the construction of comparable fortifications and with the relative lack of wood or charcoal in the destruction debris.[11]

The more economical hypothesis is that the bricks were deliberately fired before being built into the structure. Courses of such fired bricks could have served as a hard and weatherproof upper layer or surface on top of the structure, or perhaps formed subsidiary structures (buildings, crenellations, or the like). Vitruvius recommends using fired brick for the upper courses of house walls (*De Architectura* 2.8.18); and the method is still used in Iran (Wulff 1966: 109).

If fired brick was used for the upper courses of the structure, it would be among the earliest instances known of the use of fired brick on a large scale in the Aegean, and would further attest architectural interchanges between Lydia and the Near East, where such construction in fired brick had been common for millenia (Salonen 1972). Nonetheless it is notable that the fired bricks in the structure were not used for the socle or the face of the structure, common uses in Mesopotamia, but rather for the superstructure. Such use of fired brick also testifies to the great sophistication of brickworking in Archaic Lydia, already attested by, for instance, the selective use of "greasy" blue-green bricks for the face and coarser, less weather-resistant brown bricks for the core of the structure (Greenewalt, Sterud, and Belknap 1982: 18).

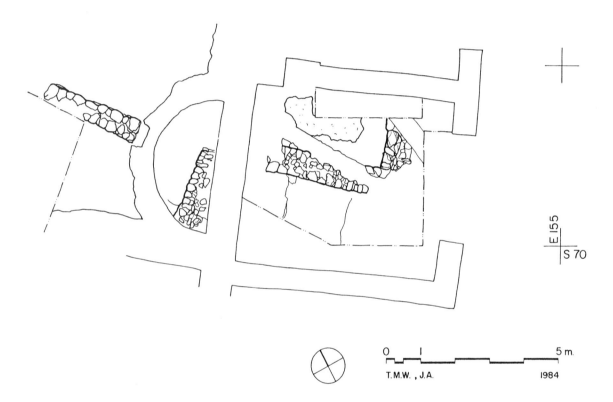

Fig. 9. Sector MMS, trench MMS-I, fourth century B.C. phase (within Late Roman apsidal room), plan.

East Side of Colossal Lydian Structure. Excavation on the east side of the Structure continued within the Roman apsidal room dug to the Roman floor in 1980 and 1982 (cf. Greenewalt, Rautman, and Meriç 1986: fig. 2, and fig. 9 here). The sequence here was more complete than in other trenches in the MMS sector, with two intermediate phases between the Lydian and Roman.

A portion of a possibly domestic structure, with stone wall foundations and a thin plaster floor, lay directly beneath the Roman levels; two other walls to the west may belong to this phase as well, although the association is not certain (fig. 9).

Dating evidence was limited but suggested a date in the fourth century B.C.

The fifth and later sixth centuries B.C. were represented only by water-washed strata and by a refuse pit containing decayed organic material, ash, pottery, and animal bones, mostly sheep and goats.

Diagnostic pottery from the pit included many jar fragments; "Achaemenid bowls" or phialai, including one with a two-letter incised Lydian inscription; a fragment of core-formed glass, and circular open lamps of Greek type (Howland

Fig. 10. Sector MMS, trench MMS-I, diagnostic material from refuse pit of early fifth century B.C.

1958, Type 21). Datable pottery, such as a fragment of a late Attic black figure/white ground lekythos with Dionysiac scene, an Attic black glaze lekythos foot, late banded lydions and the lamps, suggest a date in the first or second quarter of the fifth century (fig. 10). Seven bronze trilobate arrowheads were found in this and the following fourth-century phases; none came from strata dating to before the fifth century.

Levels of the Lydian period had been buried beneath a thick layer of brick debris, and were thus remarkably well preserved. The only disturbances to the final destruction level were created by a deeply-founded Roman wall, which crossed the apse of the Roman room, removing part of the Lydian floor below, and by some erosion at the far east end of the excavated space where the brick debris thinned out. Remains of the Lydian stratum consisted of part of a domestic structure, destroyed with most of its contents intact when Colossal Lydian Structure was demolished and the brick fall deposited. This structure is located east of the narrow "counterscarp" wall, which roughly parallels the structure; it incorporates the "counterscarp" as its west wall (figs. 5, 11). A second wall joins the "counterscarp," and continues east for at least 6.7 m.[12] Like the "counterscarp," this is built of mudbrick on a stone socle. Its north face is plastered with a smooth mud plaster, which has been baked to a red color. Hints of a blocked door or other feature in this

wall were not clarified by the end of the season. A third mudbrick wall abuts the north face of this wall, forming a space 1.2 m wide between it and the "counterscarp" wall. The east face of this wall was also treated with red burned mud plaster. To the south of the long east–west wall, a stone disc, probably a post support, suggests a roof or veranda, although there were no signs of roof fall. Seven iron "brackets" found in a line just west of this disc may belong to this covering. An open hearth lay between the post support and the wall.

The area south of the long east–west wall was excavated to the floor, which lay directly beneath the brick fall layer. Lying on this earth floor were about 50 pottery vessels, 13 loomweights, a spindle whorl, a number of metal artifacts and a variety of carbonized foodstuffs (figs. 11, 12). Most objects bore signs of burning, often intense. Four pottery vessels rested *in situ* on the floor: two cooking pots or *chytrai*, a cooking pot stand, and an amphora. The other vessels were found broken and scattered over these four pots, apparently fallen from a shelf or other fixture. Sealed and protected by the brick fall layer, this material provides a unique Lydian domestic assemblage, as well as a secure date for the deposition of the brick fall and hence for the destruction of Colossal Lydian Structure.

Pottery included a wide variety of shapes, mostly storage, cooking, serving, and eating vessels. Large storage vessels included an amphora decorated with streaky-glaze bands on the lower body and

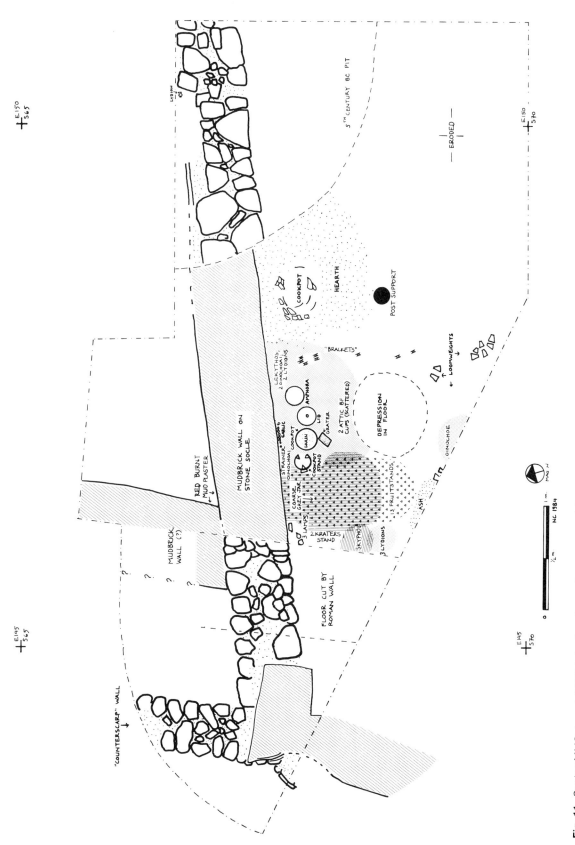

Fig. 11. Sector MMS, trench MMS-I, Lydian domestic area east of Colossal Lydian Structure, plan.

Fig. 12. Sector MMS, trench MMS-I, partial assemblage of material from Lydian domestic structure.

wavy lines on the shoulder and neck, found shat-
tered but with its base resting on the floor, and a
large coarse gray jar found scattered in the western
part of the space. The base and many sherds of
the gray jar had carbonized chickpeas clinging to
their interior surfaces, and it seems this jar was
used to store chickpeas. A cooking pot was also
being used for storage: this was found *in situ* next
to the amphora, filled with 1.5–2 liters of carbonized barley, its lid lying next to it.[13]

Cooking utensils included two more cooking
pots, one broken on the hearth, the other scattered; the pottery cooking stand, cylindrical in
shape, with three triangular "teeth" to support the
pot, and a single handle; a "bread tray"; a large
strainer with a wide, flat rim and dish-shaped
perforated center; a coarse bowl and an iron
grater, possibly a cheese grater.[14]

Eating and drinking vessels included thirteen
stemmed dishes or "fruitstands"; one plate; six to
nine skyphoi; two column kraters; a fragmentary
orientalizing stand; six trefoil oinochoai; and two
Attic black-figure cups.

The stemmed dishes and oinochoai came in various sizes, shapes, and decorations: eight large
stemmed dishes were decorated with bands of
black concentric circles on a red slip; two medium

stemmed dishes were similarly decorated; and
three small ones were decorated with a burnished
yellow slip. Four oinochoai were relatively large,
decorated with a streaky-glaze band on the lower
body and pendant tongues on the shoulder; one
was small, with lustrous red slip on shoulder and
neck; and one small oinochoe was decorated in
orientalizing fashion with a thick matte white slip
and brown bands and rosettes.[15]

Two Attic black-figure cups, a Little Master
band skyphos with two panthers in the field and a
Komast cup, were found broken and scattered
over a wide area, but could be almost completely
restored (fig. 13). The Komast cup has been
attributed to the Vienna Komast Painter, one of
the later Attic Komast Painters; Brijder dates a
similar cup to ca. 560–555 B.C. Haldenstein attributes the band skyphos to the Group of Louvre
CP10252.[16] N. H. Ramage, G. Bakır, J. Boardman, D. C. Kurtz, M. Robertson, and others
suggest a relatively early date, in the second quarter of the sixth century.[17]

Other vessels included three black marbled
lekythoi, a globular lekythos decorated with bands
of red slip, an imported (East Greek, Samian?)
globular lekythos, four lydions, and three lamps.[18]

Thirteen unbaked clay loomweights were found
clustered near the south balk of the trench, and

Fig. 13. Sector MMS, trench MMS-I, Attic Black Figure cups from Lydian domestic structure.

more probably remain in the unexcavated area to the south. Two sizes were distinguishable: eleven larger weights ca. 9 cm high, made of purplish clay, and two small weights ca. 6 cm high, of green clay. A single spindle whorl was found nearby. It seems possible that the weights fell from a loom, although no certain traces of the structure were uncovered, and the pattern of distribution does not yet reveal what sort of loom it might have been.

Except for the grater, metal objects were restricted to a few iron fittings, two bronze pins with bulb heads, and many small unidentifiable fragments. Other metal vessels could have been removed by the inhabitants or looted, however.

Foodstuffs included the barley and chickpeas mentioned above, stored in the *chytra* and gray jar respectively; lentils; and hexaploid wheat. In addition, about two heads of carbonized garlic were found adhering to the face of the east-west wall. Bones were notably scarce.[19]

> Continued excavation of this area in 1985, before this article went to press, revealed a further 100–150 artifacts, mentioned here for completeness' sake; fuller publication will follow in the accompanying preliminary report for that season (this issue, pp. 55–92). The additional pottery included a pithos, a hydria, another cooking pot stand, another coarse bowl, another column krater, two more skyphoi, another local globular lekythos, two more oinochoai, an orientalizing lid; five lydions, two Middle Corinthian quatrefoil aryballoi, a miniature plate or saucer, and three lamps, making a total of about 80 vessels. Weaving utensils included 33 more loomweights and 14

spindle whorls. Miscellaneous objects included a set of ten iron spits, a bronze bridle ornament, a trilobate bronze arrowhead, a small faience hawk, a bone or ivory disk (earring?) engraved with a rosette pattern, three silver fabric ornaments(?), three glass beads, a bone needle and needle case(?), 78 sheep knucklebones, a large seashell, a cover tile, a number of iron nails and other pieces of hardware, and a small rectangular bar of black chert or lydite, probably a touchstone for testing the purity of precious metals. About four liters of burned barley lying on the floor increased the number of foodstuffs from the space. The pattern of distribution of these artifacts suggests that many more have been lost to the Roman wall that cut into the floor.

The date of the assemblage can be fixed securely in the mid-sixth century. A carbon-14 date on organic material gave 2520 ± 50 B.P., or 570 ± 50 radiocarbon years B.C.[20] The local pottery is consistent with a mid-sixth century date, and the Attic cups and East Greek lekythos strongly suggest a date near the middle of the century. No material need be later than mid-century, and this dating seems assured for the destruction of the house, the deposition of the brick fall, and hence for the demolition of Colossal Lydian Structure. Such a date supports the hypothesis, proposed earlier on the basis of slimmer evidence, that the structure was destroyed by Cyrus of Persia between 547 and 542 B.C.[21] Earlier levels were not reached in this area, and the date of the construction of the house is uncertain.

This house is the first domestic unit discovered east of Colossal Lydian Structure, and proves that

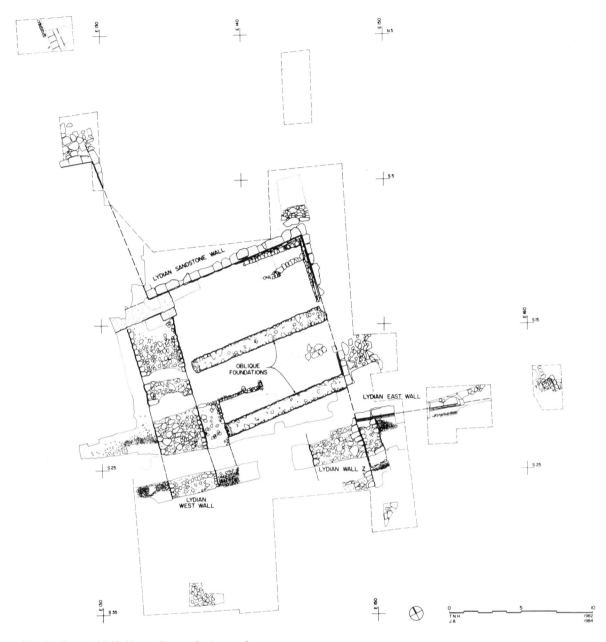

Fig. 14. Sector MMS-N, pre-Roman features, plan.

the structure, whatever its function, did not form the limit of occupation of Lydian Sardis. Its discovery also suggests that the "counterscarp" wall served at least in its later phases to keep housing from encroaching too close to the structure.

Fundamental questions remain about the function and purpose of Colossal Lydian Structure, and about the topography of Lydian Sardis in general. Did the structure form a defense work

at the limit of the formal city, e.g., a section of the city curtain and/or a tower and gate complex, as tentatively hypothesized in previous seasons (Greenewalt 1979: 25–26; Greenewalt, Sterud, and Belknap 1982: 21–24; Greenewalt *et al.* 1983: 6–8; Greenewalt *et al.* 1985: fig. 23), or did it serve some other functions? And if it did define the limit of the formal city, was the city core west or east of the structure? Previous research has concentrated on the area around the Pactolus as the city center, as implied by Herodotos (5.99–103);

Fig. 15. Sector MMS-N, Lydian building LEW–LSW: east–west segment inscribed with "masons' marks" (reentrant corner at far right).

recent excavation in the eastern part of the site has demonstrated the importance of this area as well in the Lydian period (see Hanfmann and Waldbaum 1975: 28–29, fig. 7; Hanfmann 1983: 44, 69–75, Plan 1 for hypothetical reconstructions of the city layout; Greenewalt *et al.* 1985: 64–67, Greenewalt, Rautman, and Meriç 1986: 13–17 and below, "Byzantine Fortress," for recently discovered monumental building in the far eastern part of the site).

The evidence of the "counterscarp" wall is yet ambiguous in this regard. Assuming Colossal Lydian Structure lay at the limit of the formal city, the "counterscarp" might have served as a *proteichisma* or other sort of defensive outwork, suggesting that the house excavated this season lay outside the defended area. Alternatively, the wall might have served to keep a clear space between the structure and the houses of the city, as recommended by Philo of Byzantium (*Belopoeica* 1.10; see, e.g., Lawrence 1979: 274–301 [*proteichisma*]; 76–77 [Philo, with commentary]). Until earlier levels are exposed in this area, we

cannot determine whether the "counterscarp" wall was originally built as a freestanding wall, perhaps an outwork, with housing added later, or if this area was densely occupied before the construction of Colossal Lydian Structure and the "counterscarp" wall built to control its extent.

Sector MMS-N

At Sector MMS-N (fig. 14) excavation aimed to clarify aspects of the monumental Lydian building LEW-LSW (terrace platform/gate ?); this building has a zigzag facade of ashlar masonry in limestone and sandstone and a solid core of rubble stone and coursed mudbrick (Greenewalt, Rautman, and Meriç 1986: 11–13). Specific aims in 1984 were to explain the ragged masonry joint in the reentrant corner where limestone and sandstone segments meet, to expose a segment of the sandstone facade that is extensively inscribed with "masons' marks," and to determine whether the building extended beyond the northernmost point to which the

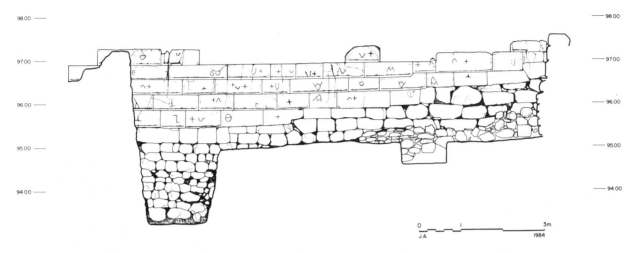

Fig. 16. Sector MMS-N, Lydian building LEW–LSW: east–west segment inscribed with "masons' marks," elevation.

facade had previously been traced, a point where it is disturbed by Roman intrusion.

At the reentrant corner neither the packing (of stone, earth, possibly disintegrated mudbrick) directly behind the masonry facade nor the evidence for an older building phase or phases below the facade (cf. fig. 15, far right) appeared to explain the loose, untidy joint of the limestone and sandstone masonry segments.

To expose the "masons' marks" on the more northerly east–west segment, earthy debris in front of the facade was removed from the level of the preserved top of the facade to that of the masonry foundations. The ashlar masonry thereby exposed "steps down" from east to west (with two courses at the east end, five at the west; figs. 15, 16). The faces of the blocks are finished with chisel-trimmed borders and hammer-dressed centers. All proper ashlars are inscribed, and exhibit a total number of some 30 marks, six of which are different and 18 of which occur in pairs. The most common marks are a pair, a cross and a U, which occur together nine times, and a bent-bar *alpha*, which occurs six times; a straight-bar *theta* may occur twice (figs. 15, 16).

The facade of LEW-LSW had been traced to the north ca. 11 m beyond the northeast salient corner (to ca. N. 2 / S. 130 on the 'B' grid), where the masonry of the facade is disturbed by Roman intrusions. For the next 2 or 3 m substantial

Fig. 17. Sector MMS-N, coursed mudbrick and fieldstones on the west facade line of Lydian building LEW–LSW, looking east. (The sondage in which these features are exposed appears at the upper left of the plan in Fig. 14.)

Fig. 18. Sector MMS-N, pottery fragments recovered below an occupation surface as old or older than Lydian building LEW–LSW.

that surface were recovered fragments of two Wild Goat-style oinochoai (P84.19: 8849 and P84.53: 8903), vessels with orientalizing decoration (griffin head(?), large rosette; the latter P84.68: 8932), and a Protocorinthian or Proto-corinthianizing aryballos (P84.7: 8936: fig. 18) which support, but do not refine, the *terminus* of ca. 575 B.C. suggested by a deposit with Middle Corinthian pottery excavated west of LEW in 1979.[25] For the chronology of the Roman surface (avenue or *plateia*) above the Lydian features, the recovery of a coin of the first century A.D. restruck with a countermark probably of the third century A.D. (C84.1: coin of Domitian restruck under Aurelian ?) beneath mortared metalling at the top of the fill in front of the inscribed segment of LEW-LSW indicates activity on this Roman surface in Late Roman times.

Sector HoB

The aim of excavation at Sector HoB was to clarify the chronology of Iron Age occupation strata, particularly the stratum that has been associated with a Cimmerian destruction of the mid-seventh century B.C. These strata were probed in a trench measuring 5 m on a side, dug within the large "Lydian Trench" (excavated in the 1960s; cf. A. Ramage on the stratification in this trench, in Hanfmann 1983: 26–33) from the level of a late seventh or sixth century occupation stratum. This trench, dug to a depth of ca. 3 m, exposed four occupation strata, which may be assigned to the seventh and eighth centuries; the uppermost of the four is the one associated in earlier excavations at HoB with the Cimmerian destruction.

The chronological evidence, which includes two Protocorinthian skyphos fragments with linear decoration (P84.63: 8897) from the stratum in question, and an early Bird Skyphos (P84.63: 8926; with nicked rim, evidently a local product) from half a meter below, requires further study before it can be interpreted. The "Cimmerian destruction" stratum produced evidence for industrial activity involving iron: a block of iron weighing 1 kg. 150 gr. (M84.11: 8930) and "blotched red-orange remains of iron detritus, scattered lumps of iron slag, and quantities of ash/charcoal."[26]

Roman features[22] rest on the line of the facade. To determine whether the facade continued beyond the Roman intrusions a sondage[23] was dug on the facade line ca. 11–12 m to the north; and exposed part of a substantial pre-Roman building that terminates to the west on the facade line (cf. plan in fig. 14, upper left). This building has a core of coursed mudbricks (some 0.35 m × 0.50 m, others 0.50 m on a side; ca. 0.10–0.12 m thick) arranged with their short ends parallel to the facade line, and a row of fieldstones on the facade line (fig. 17). For want of time excavation in front of the fieldstones did not penetrate below their resting level. Although ashlar masonry was not exposed, the orientation of mudbricks and field-stones and the thickness and nature of construction suggest that this building is LEW-LSW; the northward extent of which would therefore exceed 20 m from the northwest salient corner (cf. plan in fig. 14).

Excavation at the reentrant corner and in front of the inscribed segment of LEW-LSW produced fresh evidence for the chronology of the Lydian building and of the Roman avenue or *plateia* above (cf. Greenewalt, Rautman, and Meriç 1986: 13 and n. 16). An imported Wild Goat-style oinochoe fragment (P84.118:8994) recovered from the packing behind the reentrant corner should provide a *terminus ante quem* in the last quarter of the seventh century B.C. for the construction of LEW-LSW. In front of the corner,[24] at approximately the level of the lowest ashlar courses, were patches of an occupation surface of tamped earth that should be no later than LEW-LSW; below

In the three lower occupation strata, architectural features were rudimentary and few: simple field-stone and mudbrick walls, impressions of thatch or wattle construction, hearths and pits. These

Fig. 19. Sector HoB, bronze "finial" (M84.10: 8913).

strata produced high proportions of plain and cooking wares together with local painted wares of simple Geometric style, and quantities of small pottery-cut disks, some bored with a central hole and perhaps intended to be spindle whorls or stoppers.

Individual artifacts of intrinsic interest from the HoB trench included: fragments of a large skyphos with marbled decoration inside and out (P84.49: 8899; recovered from mixed debris well above the "Cimmerian destruction" stratum); a small bronze finial (?) with stylized crescent "horns" (M84.10: 8913; fig. 19);[27] a leech-type bronze fibula (M84.9: 8905); a glass bead (G84.5: 8923); and fragments of exceptionally fine black-burnished jugs (P84.64: 8927; P84.69: 8933).

Occupation strata were separated by thick lenses of sand and gravel that had evidently been deposited by water action of considerable force, presumably through the agency of the Pactolus stream (as excavator G. F. Swift, Jr. proposed two decades ago; cf. Hanfmann 1967a: 32); some of the gravel and sand layers resembled eddy deposit at the periphery of a water course.

Byzantine Fort (Sector Byzfort)

On the flat-topped spur of the Acropolis nicknamed Byzantine Fort, or ByzFort, in the eastern part of the city site (at ca. E. 630–730 / S. 310–410 on the 'B' grid), the aim of excavation was to

trace the extent and clarify the setting of the Lydian terrace discovered in 1983 (Greenewalt, Rautman, and Meriç 1986: 13–17).

The Lydian terrace construction, which had been exposed at the north end of the spur in the previous season, was traced for another 40 m to the south on the east side of the spur: a 7 m long segment of masonry facade was exposed 35 m beyond the segment at the northeast corner located in 1983 (figs. 20, 21); and the newly exposed segment continues south (i.e., disappears into the south scarp of the trench). This segment of facade is two or three blocks thick. Two courses and only the tops of the blocks were exposed; Late Roman construction that abuts the terrace on the outside conceals the masonry face and the original rubble and boulder packing behind the masonry masks the inner sides of the blocks. As in the case of terrace segments exposed in 1983, the packing of the newly exposed segment (illustrated in the view taken before excavation, Greenwalt, Rautman, and Meriç 1986: fig. 20) survives in better condition than the masonry facade (which had been robbed in post-Lydian times; see below) and indicates that the facade originally rose, as the packing still does, another 7 m above the two exposed courses. All the material removed in excavation to expose this segment was post-Lydian, and so yielded no new evidence for the date of the Lydian terrace.

The existence of the Lydian terrace is now confirmed for those north and east sides of the spur where the slope is steep (fig. 20), where rubble packing is exposed, and where there is a trough marking the trench dug to quarry terrace masonry in post-Lydian times—the very features that gave promise of the terrace and inspired the search for it in 1983 and 1984. On the west side of the spur and further south on the east side the slopes are less steep, show no rubble packing, and contain no trough; suggesting that the terrace did not continue or was continued in a different form, or that the masonry was not quarried on those sides.

At the northeast corner of the spur, further excavation in front of the east stretch of terrace facade exposed in 1983 showed that the masonry of that stretch stands six courses (and 3.3 m) high instead of only two courses, as supposed in 1983 (fig. 21).

Roman occupation material at sector ByzFort has been exposed in trenches essentially designed

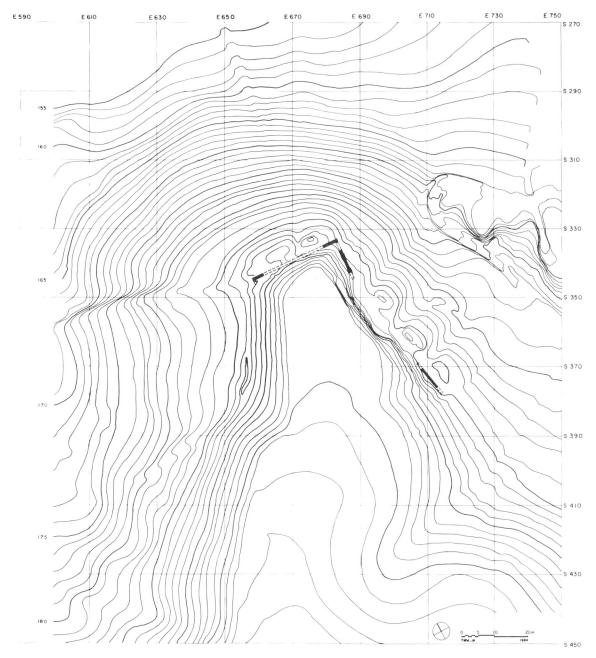

Fig. 20. Sector ByzFort, topographic plan. Heavy black lines indicate exposed masonry facade of Lydian terrace.

to reveal the Lydian terrace and its adjacent features.[28]

In the more southerly of the two excavation trenches dug in 1984 (at ca. E. 705–715 / S. 370–382 on the 'B' grid; not shown in fig. 20) parts of two rooms with marble opus sectile floor paving (geometric designs in white and gray) and base-

board revetment were exposed on the highest part of the east slope. Adjacent to these and lower down on the slope is a barrel-vaulted chamber (ca. 3 × 5 m), possibly a cistern. Filling most of the interior of this chamber is a later kiln (diameter 2.5–3 m; standing to a maximum height of 3.5 m); powdered lime on the kiln floor and the absence of a separate firing chamber suggest that the kiln was used to burn lime.[29] Lower down on the slope are walls that abut the Lydian terrace facade.

At the north end of the spur is a massive terrace built of mortared rubble with some marble *spolia*; under, through, and over these Roman terrace remains are several water conduits.

> Vertical seams and horizontal surfaces within the Roman terrace mass attest for it several building phases, the latest of which are evidently Late Roman. The water conduits include both covered channels and pipe lines; at least three of the latter have settling basins. The earliest conduits may be Hellenistic; the latest postdates the Roman terrace and the rooms reported below.

Built against the Roman terrace on the northeast side of the spur are rooms that evidently belonged to one or more residential units or small public facilities, perhaps including a bath.[30] Coins recovered under the floor surface of one room and the style of a geometric mosaic in another suggest for these rooms a final phase of occupation in the fifth or sixth century A.D.[31] The room with the mosaic floor is the best preserved and most coherent of the three (figs. 22, 23). Features are best preserved at the uphill end, entirely lost on the downhill end. The mosaic design and preserved architectural setting suggest that the room may have been square, 4.7 m on a side. The geometric motifs and patterns and the colors of the mosaic are attested elsewhere in mosaics at Sardis.[32] The walls had a baseboard of marble revetment and an upper surface of molded and painted plaster.

> "The wall decoration probably belongs to the same phase as the installation of the mosaic. The band of marble revetment at the base of the wall (held in place by iron pins, of which two remain) was 0.40 m high. Although only a few scraps of white marble remain *in situ*, impressions in the mortar that bore the revetment (including horizontal as well as vertical seams) suggest a complex geometric scheme. None of the wall plaster remained *in situ*, but fragments fallen on the floor suggest the following reconstruction: a plaster molding 0.2 m high crowned the marble revetment. Above this molding there was a band of painted plaster 0.13 m high. The colors used in this band are blue-green and red-violet, in varying degrees of intensity, here lighter, there darker. The design, perhaps simple "marbling," is uncertain. There was a taller panel above this band; its height is unknown. The colors used are more

Fig. 21. Sector ByzFort, Lydian terrace: masonry facade and boulder packing at the northeast corner (east side).

muted: a ground of light brownish-red with patterns in a slightly darker hue and possibly also white. Again, the design (flowers with stems and tendrils in the darker hue and leaves in white?) is uncertain" (C. Ratté, 1984 *ByzFort* Final Report manuscript, pp. 11–12).

The most recent feature encountered in excavation is the trench created to remove the limestone ashlar blocks of the Lydian terrace facade (cf. Greenewalt, Rautman, and Meriç 1986: 15–17 and n. 21). An iron chisel (M84.8: 8898) recovered resting on the surface of terrace facade masonry some 45 m south of the southeast corner provided dramatic testimony to this operation. The date of demolition remains uncertain, but is unlikely to be earlier than the fifth century A.D.[33]

Lydian Chamber Tomb (no. 813)

In the necropolis of the Pactolus valley one of the chamber tombs of the Lydian and Lydo-Persian periods, i.e., sixth–fifth centuries B.C.,

Fig. 22. Sector ByzFort: Roman mosaic floor, looking north.

which H. C. Butler's expedition excavated before World War I, was reexcavated to examine and record unusual features of the tomb: an entrance staircase and two stelai that flank the entrance. The tomb is located on the north side of Butler's "Nekropolis Hill," the ridge west of the Pactolus stream opposite the Artemis Temple (at ca. W. 606–610 / S. 1170–1175 on the 'B' grid, figs. 24, 25).[34] This tomb is called the "Stele Tomb" in Butler 1922, and was designated no. 813 in the Butler expedition tomb numbering system.[35]

Tomb 813 is noteworthy for its built features, the only tomb of the sixth–fifth centuries B.C. at Sardis known to have built steps and two stelai, and only one of two such tombs at which stelai survived *in situ*; and for the variety and quality of grave offerings, several of which still survive and all of which are documented in surviving records.

Eighteen objects are recorded as recovered from the tomb by the Butler expedition: eight pottery vessels (one Attic black-figure oinochoe, two

Lydian skyphoi, three unglazed jugs, one black-glaze "alabastron"), five terracottas (two small protomai, three figurines in the forms of dove-on-fruit, goose, dog), the bronze end of a pole, two jewelry items (cylinder seal, group of three gold appliques), an eye-shaped amulet of glass or faience, and a stone alabastron. Four of the pottery vessels (three jugs, one ceramic alabastron) and one of the jewelry items (cylinder seal) were recovered from a sarcophagus in the tomb; the rest evidently were "lying broken just inside the entrance, and some jewelry upon the floor" (Butler 1922: 116). Only the terracottas and the jewelry are known to exist today, the former in New York (Metropolitan Museum of Art), the latter in Istanbul (Archaeological Museums).[36] The pottery and the glass/faience amulet all are illustrated, together with the terracottas, in Butler 1922: 118 Ill. 124; and the jewelry is published in Curtis 1925: 14, 39–40, nos. 12, 104.

Chronologically diagnostic items suggest that the tomb was closed in the first quarter of the fifth century B.C.[37]

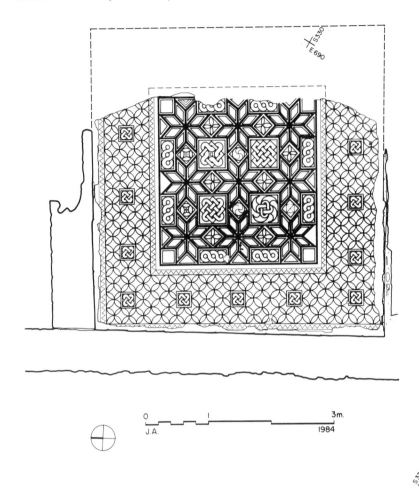

Fig. 23. Sector ByzFort: Roman mosaic floor (drawing by J. Aker).

Of the 1,100-odd chamber tombs excavated by the Butler expedition, Tomb 813 is the only one for which it is now possible to correlate a specific location with a tomb number and contents. Sometime after excavation, the tomb facade became buried in eroded earth and the location of the tomb forgotten. In 1980 illicit excavation exposed the better-preserved stele and part of the staircase. Probably on that occasion the stele was pulled down and dislodged from its socket, evidently for the first time since its erection in the fifth century B.C. Otherwise no damage was done; and at the time of excavation in 1984 the condition of these built features remained virtually unchanged since 1912.[38]

Disturbance to the stele had a positive result, since it led to clarification of the original support system of the stele. The lower end of the shaft had been socketed in a rectilinear U-shaped base, the open end of which was closed by the staircase (the back arm of the base abutting the staircase side, the front arm resting against the face of the lowest riser, at which point the riser face is point-stippled). The socket of the base is 0.065–0.92 m broader than the stele is thick; the excess space was plugged behind the shaft by stones and, above the stones, by a narrow capping of lead (M84.19: 8992), which was poured in place. The U-shaped base supported a crowning L-shaped collar, which wraps snugly around the back and outer (west) sides of the stele, terminating on the latter side flush with the stele face (fig. 24, lower left). The same arrangement presumably served for the east stele, the lower end of which is still secure in its mounting.

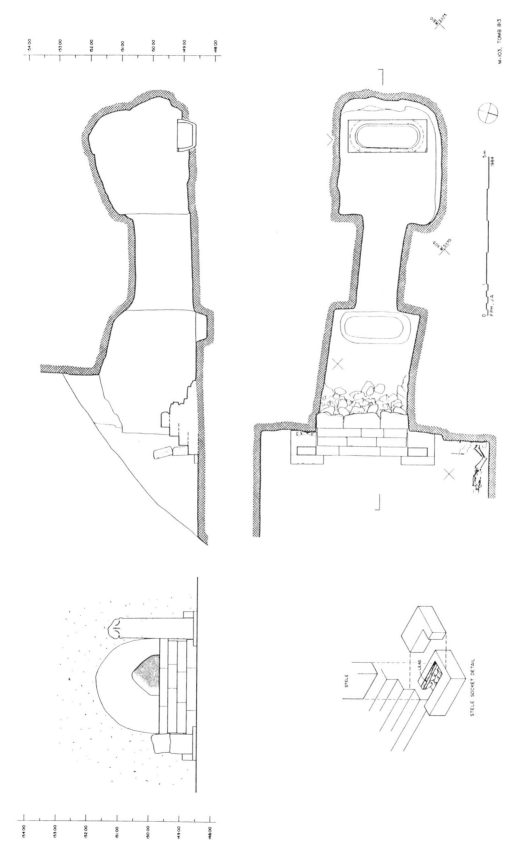

Fig. 24. Lydian Tomb 813: plan, elevation, section, isometric detail of stele support.

Fig. 25. Lydian Tomb 813: facade.

The width and position of these support stones are inaccurately represented in the Butler expedition plans and elevations (figs. 26, 27). Far more serious, however, are the discrepancies in design, proportion, and dimensions between the Butler expedition drawings and the features exposed in 1984. Unlike the tomb shown in the Butler expedition drawings, the tomb excavated in 1984 (1) has an antechamber with (2) a sunken pit of the size and shape appropriate for a sarcophagus; (3) has a "floor" (i.e., the artificially-created conglomerate surface in antechamber, corridor, and main chamber) level with the bottom of the staircase, not with the staircase top (as figs. 26 and 27 suggest); (4) has a main chamber too small to accommodate four sarcophagi comparable in size to the one sarcophagus it contains; and (5) lacks a depression for a "sunken" sarcophagus in the front of the main chamber.

Either the tomb was inadequately recorded at the time of excavation or accurate records were unavailable when publication accounts were prepared. Well-intentioned improvisation and guesswork plausibly account for the errors. The person responsible for the plans in figs. 26 and 27 might have made the staircase fill rather than frame the antechamber through misunderstanding or memory lapse and disbelief in the plausibility of the actual arrangement (further discussion below), and guessed at dimensions and proportions. The contour of the antechamber ceiling, which has no rationale in the plans in figs. 26 and 27, appears in both of the Butler expedition elevation drawings, as if uncomprehendingly retained from accurate drawings made on the spot. The existence of the antechamber would explain the restoration of a masonry facade, an unprecedented feature in Lydian chamber tombs and one that a tomb with the plan of figs. 26 and 27 would not have required. Butler's written account is far more consistent with the actual tomb design than are the graphic records. The photograph published as an interior view of the "Stele Tomb" (i.e., Tomb 813) in Butler 1922: 160 Ill. 177, on the other hand, may actually be that of another tomb.[39]

Should the "sunken sarcophagus" that "contained the bones of a large man, his gold ring and seal"[40] and that fig. 27 shows at the front of the

Fig. 26. Lydian Tomb 813: Butler expedition plan and elevation, reproduced from Littmann 1916: 25; with the permission of E. J. Brill.

chamber (although the bedrock "floor" at the front of the chamber contains no depression) be understood to have been located in the depression in the antechamber floor? Removal of that sarcophagus by the excavators or by subsequent plunderers could explain the absence of a sarcophagus in that depression in 1984; and the sarcophagus fragment recovered in front of the tomb in 1984 (below) might be part of that sunken sarcophagus.

The Butler expedition's recording errors might have been generated by anomalies in the design of Tomb 813: the staircase that rises *from* the level of the tomb "floor" and the wide opening of the tomb entrance at the top of the staircase. The staircase must have been symbolic (like Anatolian symbolic tomb doors; see "Unexcavated Antiquities," below). Had a floor existed at the level of the top step[41] it would have created an abnormally low antechamber and would have been rather shallow. A downward incline would have been required at least 2.5 m behind the staircase if the corridor between antechamber and chamber were

to have functioned as more than a crawlway. So abrupt and unnecessary an ascent and descent is illogical. The steps, furthermore, 0.28–0.30 m high, are rather high for functional steps.

The implication that no floor existed at the level of the top step makes even more puzzling the wide opening above, an unusual feature for chamber tombs at Sardis, which typically have narrow entrances (doorways leading to dromoi). Symbolic stairs that close the lower facade suggest that the upper facade would also have been closed; and the upper facade could only have been closed by a built structure. That rationale presumably underlies the Butler expedition restored facade in fig. 27 (cf. Butler 1922: 166–67; this would be evidence that the errors in the published plan resulted from inadequate records rather than from conflation of two tombs). No trace of such a structure, however, has been recovered or is cited in Butler's account, and the top step of the staircase shows no cuttings or setting lines for a superstructure. No other chamber tomb at Sardis has a constructed facade.[42]

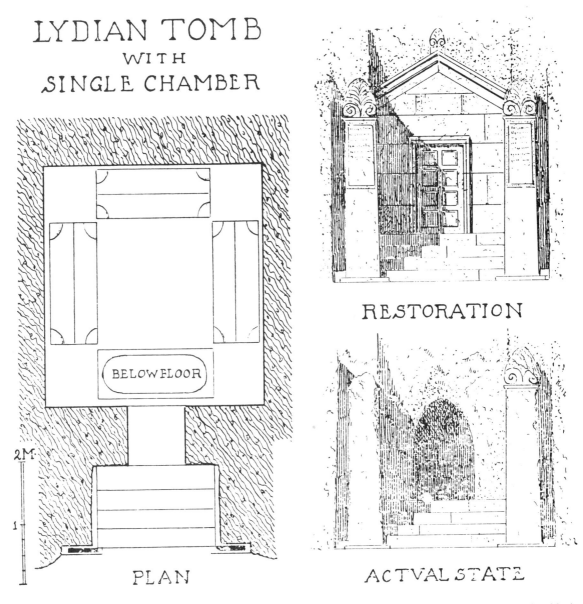

Fig. 27. Lydian Tomb 813: Butler expedition plan and elevations, reproduced from Butler 1922: 161 III. 178; with the permission of E. J. Brill.

The ashlar risers of the staircase are backed and supported on large unworked stones of schist and sandstone, and on limestone chips, the latter presumably created when the staircase blocks and stelai received their final trim. The oval depression at the inner end of the antechamber has the size and shape appropriate for a "bathtub"-type sarcophagus. The main chamber contains a limestone sarcophagus of "bathtub" type, which rests lengthwise across the back of the chamber and slightly below the bedrock "floor" level of the rest of the chamber.[43]

Parts of the lip are missing, otherwise the sarcophagus is in good condition and intact. It has the characteristic thick rectilinear lip, rectangular in plan, and rounded, trough-like body of the "bathtub" type. The long sides of the body are articulated with shallow horizontal flutes, six on each side (probably no more, although the underside of the sarcophagus was not exposed). The

Fig. 28. Lydian Tomb 813: male skeleton outside and west of tomb entrance.

Fig. 29. Lydian Tomb 813: male skeleton (feet) outside and west of tomb entrance.

bottom has no "drain" hole, as in some "bathtub"-type sarcophagi.

No remains of a lid or of other sarcophagi were recovered in the chamber; but a "bathtub" sarcophagus chest fragment was recovered in front of the chamber. A few small fragments of Lydian pottery were recovered in front of the tomb, including a fragment with orientalizing decoration and curious form, possibly to be explained as part of a large strainer-spouted vessel.[44]

Outside the tomb, just to the west of the entrance, excavation in 1984 exposed two large items that the Butler expedition evidently had missed: a terracotta sarcophagus and a human skeleton (figs. 28, 29). Both rested on fill a few centimeters higher than the bottom of the staircase and against the vertical scarps of the cliff from which the tomb had been dug. The sarcophagus has the characteristic fabric and form of Lydian terracotta sarcophagi at Sardis. Oriented east–west, it was preserved to a length of ca. 1.2 m; both ends were broken and partly missing. The skeleton (figs. 28, 29) is oriented perpendicular to the sarcophagus, i.e., approximately north–south, with head to the north; it rested against the cliff scarp to the west, partly, it seemed, under an overhang of the scarp. The feet rested under dislocated

Fig. 30. Early Hellenistic grave stele, with texts in Greek and Lydian (IN84.2 / NoEx84.3).

Fig. 31. Roman monument with honorific texts, from Sanctuary of Demeter *Karpophoros*? (IN84.1 / NoEx84.2).

sarcophagus fragments and several fieldstones, the pelvis over a sarcophagus fragment. The skeleton, evidently of a mature male, rested on one side, turned to the west; with right arm bent, right hand over heart (finger bones among rib bones), left arm extended, left hand over groin, legs bent.[45] The fill on which the sarcophagus rested indicates that it was deposited after the construction of the tomb, and the skeleton clearly was deposited after the sarcophagus; but neither need significantly postdate the tomb.

UNEXCAVATED ANTIQUITIES

Of the several antiquities that became exposed through natural causes or illicit excavations and were recovered by the expedition in 1984, the following are particularly noteworthy:

Small grave stele with pedimental crown, inscribed with texts in Greek and Lydian (IN84.2 / NoEx84.3), recovered by a site guard from the

east bank of the Pactolus stream just south of sector PC (at ca. W. 200 / S. 700 on the 'B' grid; fig. 30). The two texts were inscribed consecutively and attest separate uses of the stele to mark two different graves. The original text is the Greek: in three lines and as many words it commemorates a Mysian (Dromōn, the son of Ephesos; *Dromōn Ephesou Mysios*). The letter forms suggest to Gusmani a date in the end of the fourth or first decade of the third century B.C. The second text, in Lydian (no. 108 in the Lydian *corpus*) is inscribed on the smooth vacant space below the Greek; five lines survive. It commemorates one Baki[vas]; named his father, apparently also his grandfather, and possibly the person who set up the memorial; and closes with a conventional Lydian imprecation against defilers of the grave. (For texts and commentary, Gusmani 1985).

Inscribed marble block in the form of a "horned" altar (IN84.1; NoEx84.2; fig. 31), recovered from a torrent bed ca. 700–1,000 m west of the Pactolus stream ca. 50 m south of the Ankara–Izmir highway.[46] Two opposite sides carry relief decoration: (a) snake rising from woven basket between two upright torches; (b) two crossed torches fastened in the middle with fillet. The other two sides carry texts in Greek, each recording honors to an individual by the *dēmos*: in one (17 lines) the honored is Tiberios Klaudios Theogenes Lachanas, *agoranomos*, *grammateus tou demou*, and *ergepistatēs*; in the other (11 lines) Klaudia, "daughter of Theogenes, *kaueis*, wife of Klaudios Diodoros Lachanas, mother of the Klaudioi Theogenes, Menogenes, and Diodoros, priestess (*hiereia*) of Demeter *Karpophoros*." L. Robert identifies the two as father and daughter, and sees as significant that the offices of *agoranomos* and priestess of Demeter *Karpophoros* were held by family members with the surname Lachanas, i.e., lit. "greengrocer."[47] (For *kaueis*, a word derived from Lydian meaning priestess and in other contexts associated with Artemis, see Buckler and Robinson 1932: 66–69 nos. 51–54.)

Fig. 32. Symbolic doorstone, from necropolis (NoEx84.10).

Fig. 33. Statue of lion, from the Late Antique fortification wall of the Acropolis (NoEx84.6).

The text for Klaudia closes *hētis enthade kathierōtai* ("she who was consecrated there"), implying that the block had been set up in the Sanctuary of Demeter. The remote provenience of the block from the city (200–500 m beyond Roman graves outside the settlement) parallels the locations of Demeter sanctuaries at other city sites, including Priene, Knidos, Cyrene, Selinus; cf. Vitruvius 1.7; and there are mortar and stone walls in the bottom and sides of the torrent bed, where the block was recovered, which could be ancient. Nevertheless, more specific evidence is needed in addition to the block to establish its provenience as the locale of Demeter's Sanctuary; for such blocks were frequently reused in construction at Sardis in later antiquity and were sometimes transported considerable distances.[48]

Symbolic door stone (NoEx84.10; fig. 32), recovered from the necropolis region west of the Pactolus stream.[49] A block of limestone, the "door" is broader than it is high and relatively thick (H. 0.58 m; W. 0.655 m; Th. 0.32 m). On the front surface it is articulated in three planes with an outer flat frame on all four sides, an inner flat frame at top and sides with interconnecting crossbars, and four "panels" within inner frame and crossbars. In proportions and articulation it resembles another symbolic door of limestone, which was recovered not far away by the Butler expedition and is inscribed with two texts in Lydian (together no. 4 in the Lydian *corpus*; Buckler 1924: 8–11, no. 4).[50]

Marble statue of a lion, *couchant* (NoEx84.6; fig. 33),[51] recovered from the fortification wall at the southeast end of the Acropolis. One of many *spolia* built into the Acropolis wall, the statue had been immured right side up and facing out (south), with chest and front legs projecting slightly from the plane of the wall face.[52] Recent vandalism to that part of the wall surrounding the statue, apparently part of an attempt to extract the statue, prompted removal by the expedition. The modeling of the body has suggested to Ratté a date in the fifth century B.C.[53]

C.H.G.

NOTES

[1]The Archaeological Exploration of Sardis is financially supported by many private corporate and individual donors. Fieldwork is authorized by the General Directorate of Antiquities and Museums, a subdivision of the Ministry of Culture and Tourism of the Republic of Turkey. It is a pleasure to acknowledge the essential and sympathetic support of officers of the General Directorate, especially Director General Dr. Nurettin Yardımcı, Deputy Directors Tanju Özoral and Nadir Avcı, Director of Excavations Division Kudret Ata, and Excavations Division Assistant Meral Gözübüyük. The last was Government Representative to the Expedition in 1984; ever supportive of worthy causes and ready to help with active participation and with wise, perceptive suggestions, she made the season for all members a more fulfilling experience. The Expedition is similarly grateful to officers of the Archaeological and Ethnographical Museum in Manisa, particularly to Director Kubilây Nayır for his staunch and generous support and sympathetic interest in the Expedition's programs.

The following comprised the 1984 season staff: C. H. Greenewalt, Jr. (University of California at Berkeley; field director); A. Ramage (Cornell; associate director); T. Yalçınkaya (Betonsan, A. S., Manisa; administrative officer and agent); J. A. Scott (Harvard; executive director and head of publications for Phase 1); K. J. Severson (New York University, Institute of Fine Arts, Conservation Center; senior conservator); H. F. Beaubien (New York University, Institute of Fine Arts, Conservation Center; conservator); H. Kökten (Ege Üniversitesi; Orhan Ragip Gündüz Memorial Trainee in Conservation); K. E. Welch (Cornell; registrar, numismatist, archaeologist); R. E. Mooney (Harvard; registrar, archaeologist); C. H. Smith (draftsman); D. R. Nickel (Cornell; photographer); F. P. Hemans, III (Boston University; architect); T. M. Wilkinson (University of Maryland; architect); J. Aker (Cornell; trainee in architecture); R. Meriç (Dokuz Eylül Üniversitesi, Bornova-Izmir; regional survey director); S. Emir (Dokuz Eylül Üniversitesi, Bornova-Izmir; regional survey associate and architect); A. Meriç (Ankara Üniversitesi; regional survey associate); E. Demirbek (Dokuz Eylül Üniversitesi, Bornova-Izmir; regional survey associate); O. Ermişler (Archaeological Museum, Konya; government representative for regional survey); M. L. Rautman (Miami University, Ohio; senior archaeologist); D. M. O'Higgins (Cornell; archaeologist); M. C. Miller (Harvard; archaeologist); N. D. Cahill (University of California at Berkeley; archaeologist); C. J. Ratté (University of California at Berkeley; archaeologist); D. N. Smith (University of California at Berkeley; archaeologist); N. H. Ramage (Ithaca College; specialist for Attic pottery); S. I. Rotroff (Hunter

College; specialist for Hellenistic and Roman relief wares); A. C. Gunter (University of Minnesota; specialist for prehistoric pottery); P. Herrmann (Hamburg University; specialist for Greek and Latin inscriptions). To all these for hard and exemplary work, generous and lively spirit, and steady teamwork, warm and grateful thanks.

[2]One of these regions is located just south and southeast of the Late Roman Synagogue (part of the Roman Gymnasium–Bath Complex). The recognition of massive mudbrick construction—part of Colossal Lydian Structure—there in 1976 by A. and N. H. Ramage led to excavation of Sectors MMS, MMS-S, and MMS-N in 1977 and subsequent seasons; Greenewalt 1979: 21–26; Greenewalt, Sterud, and Belknap 1982: 18–24; Greenewalt et al. 1983: 1–8; Greenewalt et al. 1985: 68–80; Greenewalt, Rautman, and Meriç 1986: 1–13.

The other region is located in the eastern part of the city site, on the Acropolis spur called Byzantine Fort or ByzFort where excavation in 1983 exposed parts of a monumental Lydian terrace; Greenewalt, Rautman, and Meriç 1986: 13–17; for another Lydian terrace on an adjacent spur, Greenewalt et al. 1985: 64–67.

[3]These studies are scheduled to appear in the Sardis Reports and Sardis Monographs series, published by Harvard University Press.

[4]As in the case of previous Sardis reports in this journal, this account draws extensively on the information and ideas presented in the mid-season and final report manuscripts prepared in the field by excavators and support staff. These invaluable documents are on file in the Sardis Expedition Office, University Art Museums, Harvard University.

[5]The debris consisted of tumbled brick and stone; it continues beyond the terminal point of excavation, at the plane of the further wall face. The doorway opening is 2.2 m high and 1.25 m wide.

[6]For pseudomorphs, "Formation of Fossilized Fabrics . . ." etc., Chemical and Engineering News 1984: 28–30; cf. Jakes and Sibley 1985; Majewski in Greenewalt and Majewski 1980: 138–40.

[7]For ancient metal door fittings, Robinson and Graham 1938: 249–63 and references.

[8]Two other colonnaded streets are known at Sardis: the Main Avenue to the north (Hanfmann 1962: 40–45) and the HoB Colonnaded Street (below). The MMS Street may be one of the two emboloi mentioned in a building inscription (IN.68.18) found nearby in 1968 (Hanfmann and Waldbaum 1970: 28, fig. 16; Foss 1976: 115 no. 18). The term embolos appears in related contexts at Lydian Thyateira (Radet 1887: 473–74, with corrections in Secck 1901: 168–69), perhaps referring to a recently excavated but unpublished street (mentioned in Foss 1977: 485), and at Ephesus (Foss 1979: 65–66, n. 39). Concerning the role of the colonnaded embolos in late antiquity see Claude 1969: 60–69.

[9]The amount of accumulated debris between this final documented occupation level and the mass of fallen

masonry vaulting adjacent to Building R suggests that the destruction of the street did not occur at the time the street went out of use, but after a number of additional years had passed. These intervening years saw the dumping of large quantities of late Roman domestic debris in the MMS Street to the east (Greenewalt et al. 1985: 76; Greenewalt, Rautman, and Meriç 1986: 8–11). The subsequent violent destruction of the lower city is documented by the collapse of such major architectural features as the HoB Colonnaded Street vaulting (Hanfmann 1972: 162, fig. 121), the Synagogue north wall (Hanfmann 1966: 52, fig. 42), and the Marble Court (Hanfmann 1983: fig. 223).

[10]MMS: Greenewalt 1979: 25; Greenewalt, Sterud, and Belknap 1982: 18; Greenewalt et al. 1983: 5–6; Greenewalt et al. 1985: 73–76. MMS-S: Greenewalt et al. 1985: 78, disposed in fall lines from east to west; Greenewalt, Rautman, and Meriç 1986: 9. MMS-N: Greenewalt, Sterud, and Belknap 1982: 20. Notable absences so far include the west side of Colossal Lydian Structure between the highway and ca. S 85–90.

[11]Wooden construction in Colossal Lydian Structure: Greenewalt 1979: 23–24; Greenewalt et al. 1983: 8–10; Greenewalt, Rautman, and Meriç 1986: 7; charcoal in brick debris: Greenewalt et al. 1983: 6; however, the quantity of wood in the preserved structure and charcoal in the debris of the superstructure seems quite insufficient to have produced such a massive fire.

[12]Counterscarp wall: Greenewalt et al. 1985: 73–78, figs. 19, 20. Pottery recovered in 1982 suggested that this wall was built at about the same time as Colossal Lydian Structure, in the later seventh or early sixth century B.C. Weathering over the last two years has revealed further mudbrick joints in the superstructure of this wall, and the original proposal that it was built of both mudbrick and pisé must be modified: no sign of pisé is now visible. The exact relationship between the new east–west wall and the "counterscarp" was not clear at the end of the season. The socle of the east–west wall abuts, at a higher level, the socle and mudbrick superstructure of the "counterscarp" wall. The upper parts of the mudbrick superstructures of the two walls seem to bend, however; the brickwork may have been repaired or replaced at a later date. The southern continuation of the "counterscarp" may be another addition.

[13]Amphora: inv. P84.99/8971. Gray jar: inv. P84.109/8982. Chytra: P84.102/8974, see further chytrai below. That this vessel had been used for cooking as well as storage was suggested by heavy burning on its underside, as well as by its cookingware fabric. Lid: P84.77/8943. Full catalogue descriptions of the material from this assemblage will be published when the entire assemblage has been excavated and mended. Foodstuffs identified by G. Hillman (below).

[14]Chytrai: on hearth, P84.110/8983; the other, broken, not mended or inventoried in 1984. Cooking stand: P84.85/8953. Bread tray: not mended or inventoried in

1984. Strainer: P84.93/8965 (a very unusual shape). Bowl: P84.89/8957. Grater: M84.17/8981. Other Sardian *chytrai*: Greenewalt 1978. See also Amyx 1958: 211–13. Bread trays: Ramage 1978: fig. 18; Hanfmann 1962: 13. Cooking stands: most recently, Scheffer 1981. Strainers: Amyx 1958: 261–64. Cheese graters: Amyx 1958: 262, n. 45. Cooking assemblages in general: Sparkes 1962.

[15]Stemmed dishes: small P84.79/8947; P84.84/8952; P84.93/8965. Medium: P84.82/8950; P84.92/8961. Large: P84.83/8951; P84.86/8954; P84.87/8955; P84.88/8956; P84.90/8959; P84.91/8960; P84.96/8968; P84.103/8975. Three stemmed dishes had graffiti or monograms incised on their lower surfaces, possibly owner's marks. Plate or shallow dish: not inventoried 1984. Skyphoi: P84.75/8941; P84.76/8942; plus fragments of four to seven others not mended or inventoried in 1984. Kraters: P84.98/8970; P84.111/8985. Orientalizing stand: P84.106/8978; only the foot is preserved. The skyphoi and kraters and stand were all found in the western part of the excavated space, which had been cut by a Roman wall; this disturbance probably accounts for the relatively poor preservation of these vessels, and it is possible that the original assemblage would have included more of these and other shapes. Oinochoai: small red-dipped: P84.105/8977; streaky glaze with tongues P84.100/8972; P84.101/8973; P84.108/8980; one not mended or inventoried in 1984. Orientalizing oinochoe: P84.95/ 8967. On Sardian stemmed dishes and oinochoai: Greenewalt 1978.

[16]Letter to N. H. Ramage, 21 January 1985.

[17]Attic Komast cup: P84.56/8909, cf. Brijder 1983: 82–84, pl. 6d (no. K98). Band skyphos: P84.57/8910. The opinions of Bakır, Boardman, Kurtz, and Robertson were expressed verbally or in letters. For both cups, Ramage 1985; 1986.

[18]Marbled lekythoi: P84.73/8939; other two not inventoried in 1984. Globular lekythos: P84.97/8969. Imported lekythos: P84.78/8946, cf. Boardman and Hayes 1966: nos. 839–42, from Level 8 or 7, dated to pre-565 or pre-530 B.C. Lydions: P84.74/8940; P84.81/8949; P84.94/8966; and P84.80/8948, larger than the others. Lamps: L84.10/8937; L84.11/8962; L84.12/8964. They are very similar to the collection of ten lamps found in HoB (Hanfmann 1961: 12).

[19]Identified by G. Hillman, except for the garlic, which was identified by members of the expedition. Barley is six-row, hulled, a primitive form of the barley grown in the region today. Emmer (*Triticum dicoccum*) and hexaploid wheats are present. The chickpeas are remarkably small; similar tiny chickpeas were found in the palace quarters at Gordion. (Information kindly supplied by K. L. Gleason and M. Nesbitt.)

[20]Beta Analytic No. Beta-10749.

[21]Greenewalt *et al.* 1983: 6; Greenewalt *et al.* 1985: 73. On the problems of this historical date, Cargill 1977; Burstein 1984.

[22]The most conspicuous of these features today is a paving of marble slabs that rests at a level appreciably higher than the level of the Synagogue porch floor; it appears at the far right, curbed by a modern brick retaining wall, in Hanfmann 1983: fig. 240.

[23]The sondage measured 2 m × 4 m., and is located at E. 125–128 / N. 5–7 on the 'B' grid.

[24]Of intrinsic interest are ceramic items recovered from a gravel layer that may have been contaminated or deposited in late Hellenistic or Roman times: an orientalizing dish with cut-away lip (P84.27: 8858); a faience aryballos (P84.55: 8907); and an Attic band cup or skyphos (P84.35: 8868).

[25]"A layer of limestone chips from trimming the blocks (of LEW) lies over a lens of ashy earth containing fragments of Middle Corinthian skyphoi" (Greenewalt *et al.* 1983: 14). "Two (pottery fragments), at least, are from Middle Corinthian skyphoi, and it is not impossible that all three pieces belong to the same cup. This gives a *terminus post quem* of ca. 580 for the lense and other pottery from the same lense and below support a date for the lense in the second quarter of the sixth century. . . . This lense lies under the limestone working chip layer that runs up against the lower two courses of the LEW" (V. J. Harward, 1979 *MMS-N* Final Report manuscript, p. 7).

[26]Excavator C. N. Sandberg, 1984 *HoB* Final Report manuscript, p. 2. For iron and iron working at Sardis in the Lydian period, Waldbaum 1983: 5, 8–9, 23–26, and catalogue references.

[27]The tip of one "horn" (right hand tip, fig. 19) was broken after excavation. Solid cast; lower end of shaft pierced with horizontal hole. H. 0.045 m. Th. 0.008 m.

[28]Roman features and trenches appear on the state plan (BF 11; not reproduced in this report), not on the topographic plan in fig. 20. In 1984 Roman material was exposed in an area of ca. 115 m² some 40 m to the south on the east side of the spur.

[29]The kiln was largely "self-buried" in collapsed material from its upper walls. A coin of Tiberius II (A.D. 578–582; C84.5, a half follis) recovered at the bottom of that material shows that the collapse took place after A.D. 578/579.

[30]A hypocaust pillar tile that had been built into one wall of the mosaic room and fragments of several terracotta wall-flue studs that were recovered in loose fill at the northeast end of the spur are, especially when considered with the several water conduits with settling basins that criss-cross the north end of the spur, the evidence of a bath unit. Many wall-flue studs ("screwdrivers," *Ton-nägeln*; for an alternative system to *tegulae mammatae*) were recovered in surveys in the northeast part of the city site in 1977–1979 ("large Roman ceramic industrial objects, cylindrical with a flare at one end," [Freedman in Greenewalt 1979: 4]). W. Radt and F. K. Yegül kindly provided the func-

tional identification and the following references: Radt
1980: 411–12; Cagnat and Chapot 1916: 219–21, fig. 115;
Thouvenot and Luquet 1951: 18–19; Lezine 1964: fig. 12.

[31] The many coins included one of Zeno (A.D. 476–91;
inventoried 1984.60) and "eight obscure fifth–sixth century monogram types" (C. Ratté, 1984, *ByzFort* Final
Report manuscript, p. 9).

[32] J. Aker, who prepared a graphic rendering of the
mosaic, noted the following "materials and colors . . . :
terracotta (red and yellow), schist (dark blue), glass
(light blue), limestone (white), a black volcanic stone,
and marble (rose). The tesserae are . . . less than 0.01 m
square" (C. Ratté, 1984, *ByzFort* Final Report manuscript, p. 11).

For similar mosaics at Sardis, Hanfmann 1962: 16–
20; Majewski in Hanfmann 1967: 26–37, figs. 50–56;
32–46. To the patterns and motifs illustrated in Blanchard *et al.* 1973, only a few in the 1984 Sardis mosaic
are closely similar; e.g., nos. 54 (Solomon's knot), 84
(circlet of peltae around a Solomon's knot), 109 (quatrefoil), 437 (diaper of intersecting circles).

[33] The latest diagnostic item recovered from the trough
in 1984 is a fragment of a Byzantine sgraffito bowl; that
fragment might be intrusive, however, and need not be
contemporary with the trough.

[34] For the Nekropolis Hill (or first Nekropolis, first
Nekropolis hill), Butler 1922: 78, 115–16; and for the
South and Southwest Nekropoleis, Butler 1922: 140–41,
163–64.

The reexcavation of Tomb 813 grew from an inten-
tion to locate the tomb site on the site grid ('B' grid).
After illicit excavation had exposed tomb features in
1980 (text, below, and n. 38) the Expedition reburied
those features to protect them. Because subsequent
erosion obscured the site, the features had to be partly
exposed again to confirm the location of the tomb; and
partial exposure prompted full exposure.

At the end of the 1984 season the more complete stele
(reerected in fig. 25) was placed face downward, and it
and other stone features again were covered with earth
for protection.

[35] Tombs on the Nekropolis Hill were designated by T
(for Tomb) followed by a number, e.g., T813; tombs in
the South and Southwest Nekropolis (above, n. 34)
respectively by TS and TSW. More than 1,100 tombs
on Nekropolis Hill were opened by the Butler expedition (the highest number in surviving records being T1,
107). The only Butler expedition Sardis series volumes
in which tomb numbers are recorded are those on
coins, jewelry, and Greek and Latin inscriptions (respectively Bell 1916, Curtis 1925, and Buckler and Robinson
1932).

[36] Descriptions of the pottery, inventoried P1373,
1375, 1377–1380, by G. H. Chase survive (on file cards;
Sardis Expedition Office, Harvard University). The five
terracottas are MMA 26.126.5, 8, 9, 20, 21. The bronze

end of a pole, inventoried Br. 1975, was interpreted as
the end of a bier pole; for which kind of funerary
equipment Butler's team recovered evidence from other
graves (six iron rings, inventoried M5, 9, 13, interpreted
as rings for bier poles, from three tombs, T142, T231,
T329a; and "bits of rotted wood" from the poles themselves, Butler 1922: 159). The glass/faience eye was
inventoried Gl. 191. Nine other eyes of the same material were recovered from other tombs (T363, T817,
T824; three eyes from each tomb). No descriptions or
detailed photographs of any of them survive. Princeton
University Sardis archives negative number 60, from
which Butler 1922: 118 Ill. 124 is derived, preserves a
clearer image than the published version. C. G. Simon,
who has recognized that the eye is upside-down in this
picture, kindly provided references to general parallels
in Boardman 1967: 241 no. 580—to which add Jacopi
1931: 107 no. 14 (from Kameiros, Grave 26)—and
Egyptian parallels in Petrie 1906: 17–18; and has
observed that the parallel in Gjerstad *et al.* 1935: 322
(M50.16a, from Marion Tomb 50, a single interment
assigned "to the very end of Cypro-Archaic II," i.e., the
first quarter of the fifth century B.C.) is reasonably
close. The stone alabastron from Tomb 813 was inventoried Sv. 58; no description or photograph survives.

[37] The most important items for chronology are the
Attic black-figure oinochoe and the cylinder seal. The
oinochoe was attributed by Beazley to the Class of
Vatican G49 (Beazley 1956: 533 no. 10); that Class is
near the Athena Painter, whose "prime" Haspels placed
ca. 490–480 (Haspels 1936: 163). N. H. Ramage kindly
provided these references.

For the cylinder seal (Istanbul Archaeological Museums no. 4581; Butler 1922: 121 Ill. 131; Curtis 1925:
39–40 no. 104, and pls. 10, 11) E. Porada has suggested
a date late in the reign of Darius I (d. 486 B.C.) because
of the following features (information provided and
quoted from letters of February 22, March 8, and May
17, 1985: (1) The triangular crenelations of the crown of
the royal hero (cf. sealings of the 32nd year of Darius I,
Schmidt 1957: 18–19 nos. 2, 3, pl. 3; "later cylinders
have smaller and more numerous crenelations on the
crown of the royal hero"). (2) The flat or only slightly
dentate tops of the sphinxes' headdresses (cf. a sealing
of Darius I, Schmidt 1957: 18, sealing no. PT4 673, pl.
3). (3) The use of "pedestal" figures (cf. Schmidt 1957:
7, 9, 18, 19; in contrast to the "later impressions [which]
show a simpler composition with only one register of
figures").

The rest of the grave offerings are compatible with
the date of the oinochoe and cylinder seal. One of the
terracotta protomes (MMA 26.164.8; Butler 1922: 118
Ill. 124, left) and the dove-on-fruit terracotta (MMA
26.164.20) closely resemble terracottas that Higgins has
dated to the early fifth century (Higgins 1954: 68–69
nos. 139, 141; 78 nos. 183–84, 185.

[38]The very top of the better-preserved stele anthemion has the gray color characteristic of limestone that has had long exposure to the air in recent times, and suggests that the stele had remained upright with its topmost part exposed on the hillside, probably about flush with the surrounding earth. Unrecognized by Harvard-Cornell expedition members (including the writer, who wandered over this hillside intermittently during the course of 25 seasons), the stele top may have been spotted by the illicit excavator, who appreciated its anomaly in the landscape and therefore was prompted to dig.

The upper part of the more poorly preserved (east) stele disappeared at sometime after excavation, as comparison of remains existing in 1984 (fig. 25) with a 1912 photograph of the tomb facade (Princeton Sardis Archive no. 60) shows. The small stele fragment that appears on the tomb steps in Butler 1922: 116 Ill. 122 was recovered in front of the tomb, together with another anthemion fragment; both fragments are now inventoried S84.2: 8991. For conditions in the tomb interior, see below.

[39]Even if the middle sarcophagus in Butler 1922: 160 Ill. 177 rested on a pile of earth (so that the three sarcophagi could be interpreted as resting close together, rather than separated by short horizontal distances), it was difficult in 1984 to envisage how a view of the main chamber of Tomb 813 taken from above could show the corridor ceiling and walls in the way that they appear in Ill. 177. The sloping conglomerate strata in the back wall of the chamber in Ill. 177 resemble those in Tomb 813, but are not sufficiently distinctive to be significant.

Substitution of a photograph of a different tomb by the Butler expedition might have been as inadvertent and is hardly more reprehensible than the degree of improvisation attested in the graphic records of the tomb.

[40]Butler 1922: 117. The seal is Curtis 1925: 39–40, no. 104 (further, above, n. 37). The "ring" is cited only in this passage; whether it refers to the small ring at one end of the seal (Curtis 1925: pl. 10) or to a separate item (of which there are no other records) is unclear.

[41]No trace of a floor at the level of the staircase top was detected.

[42]Repairs to an existing two-chamber tomb, the original conglomerate facade of which had been damaged or destroyed (perhaps from erosion or inept digging of the outer chamber), could explain the built facade.

[43]The conglomerate "floor" surface of the main chamber was carefully cleaned to ensure detection of any depression that might exist. In places the cleaning removed a few centimeters of the conglomerate (which is of uneven consistency and compactness).

[44]P84.54: 8906, recovered just east of the east stele. If from a strainer-spouted vessel, the vessel would have

had a spout covered at the inner end, like examples from Gordion (e.g., Chase 1921: 116, fig. 3) and unlike the Lydianized version from Sardis (Chase 1921: 114–17; Butler 1922: 119 Ill. 126; from Tomb 720, now Metropolitan Museum of Art 14.30.9); and it would be appreciably larger than other strainer-spouted vessels, with a thick spout not less than 0.06 m wide.

[45]In the 1985 season S. C. Bisel examined the skeleton bones and reported as follows. "Male skeleton in excellent condition. . . . He was aged at 29 years from the pubic symphysis. However, skull sutures were largely closed, presumably prematurely. The general appearance of the post-cranial skeleton also suggests about 29 years: lack of bony outgrowths, heavy cortical bone. His stature is calculated to be 170.0 cm. (Trotter and Gleser formulae). He is of a rather linear and slight build, not at all muscular in either arms or legs. There was some flattening of the pelvis (PBI=73.6) and the femora (PMI=71.9). The tibae were not flattened (PCI=71.88). The flattening could indicate less than optimum nutrition. On the other hand, he is somewhat tall (although his period is unknown), and the bone cortex is heavy. These latter two facts point to good nutrition. His teeth are without lesion: no caries nor antemortem loss. However, he had lost bone in the gingival spaces, indicating periodontal disease. The parietals are very slightly thickened, suggesting a very slight healed anemia. There are no signs of other disease or trauma." (1985, *Human Skeletal Material at Sardis* manuscript, p. 1).

[46]For the location, Butler 1922: pl. 1; near the juncture of the torrent bed, indicated by a single broken line, and a village road (extant in 1984), indicated by a double dashed line, at "MAIN HIGHWAY" west of the Pactolus stream.

[47]L. Robert kindly provided the following references. For the surname Lachanas, Masson 1973: 7–9, 19; Robert and Robert 1973: 77 no. 91; cf. Robert and Robert 1961: 130 no. 71 (*lachanopōlēs*). For the use of analogous surnames in Asia Minor, Robert and Robert 1983: 252–55; and in general Robert 1963. For Demeter at Sardis, Apollonius of Tyana, *Epistulae* 75; Robert 1973: 485–87 (inscription of the third century A.D., recording statues of the children of Kore; cf. Greenewalt 1973: 26–27).

For the cult of Demeter Karpophoros in eastern Lydia, at the Persian colony *hē Dareioukomētōn* in the Hyrkanian Plain, and in Ionia (Ephesos) and Phrygia (Pessinus, Ankara, Ikonion), Kern 1901: 2745–48; Anabolu 1984: 5, no. 4, fig. 14 (garland altar dedicated to Demeter Karpophoros, from Ephesus, Selçuk Museum no. 1728).

[48]For example, two blocks from elevated pedestals of columns of the Artemis Temple, which were exposed in excavation some 1,200 m north of the Temple, by the side of the Roman east–west avenue (at ca. E. 128 / S. 14 on the 'B' grid); Greenewalt 1982: 101; Greenewalt

et al. 1983: 12 fig. 13, "recut column drum."

[49]According to a responsible site guard the stone was turned up during spring plowing on the top of the hill immediately north of Butler's "Nekropolis Hill" (see n. 34; also north of Tomb 813) and separated from that Hill by an east–west ravine. For symbolic doorstones, Waelkens 1985.

[50]Ca. 100–300 m away?; on the other side of the same ravine (cf. n. 49), further to the east. " . . . found on April, 1910, in the loosely built wall closing the dromos of a single-chamber tomb in the northeast face of the Nekropolis Hill, fronting on the deep ravine which opens into the west side of the Pactolus almost opposite to the temple" (Buckler 1924: 9). On the Lydian inscriptions (together no. 4 in the Corpus) that appear on this stone Gusmani has commented as follows (letter of February 20, 1984). "We have two Lydian texts on the same stone, concerning apparently the same person (Manes, son of Alus), but mentioning different parts of the tombs and also different gods who have to punish anyone who will damage the funeral monument. Letters of both texts have the "rounded" form like in the inscriptions of the fourth century B.C., although text B offers one of the rare attestations of Ɋ (with the value of ʋ̓) and also once a ╪ (line 2) instead of ╥ (which is also attested in this inscription). Thus one could think of the second half of the fifth century, but real evidence for a higher chronology seems to me lacking."

[51]Head, neck, left shoulder and foreleg, right paw missing; in top of hindquarters, dowel hole. Under the hindquarters, between the underside of the body and the top of the plinth, an open space. Pr. L. 0.80 m; W. of plinth 0.29 m; Pr. H. 0.39 m.

[52]The incorporation of other *spolia*, with important decorated sides facing out, sometimes right side up, often seems to have been done partly with a view toward display. The *spolia* in the Acropolis fortifications include more than 20 inscriptions (with testimonial, honorific, dedicatory, and funerary texts): Buckler and Robinson 1932: nos. 9, 10, 13, 15, 19, 31 (?), 34, 43, 44, 45, 67, 74, 77, 78, 81, 83, 99, 137, 148, 196, 197, 226, 227.

[53]For other stone statues of lions *couchant* from Sardis, Greenewalt, Rautman, and Meriç 1986: 22–23 and n. 31; Hanfmann and Ramage 1978: 20–23.

BIBLIOGRAPHY

Amyx, D. A.
  1958   The Attic Stelai Part III: Vessels and Other Containers. *Hesperia* 28: 164–310.

Anabolu, M. (U.)
  1984   Bati Anadoldu'da bulunan Hellenistik Çağ ve Roma Imparatorluk Çağı Girland (Askı)lı Sunakları. *Arkeoloji-Sanat Tarihi Dergisi* (Ege Üniversitesi Edebiyat Fakültesi Yayınları) 3: 1–17.

Beazley, J. D.
  1956   *Attic Black-Figure Vase-Painters.* Oxford: Clarendon.

Bell, H. W.
  1916   *Coins Part I, 1910–1914; Sardis* XI. Leiden: Brill.

Blake, M. E.
  1947   *Ancient Roman Construction in Italy from the Prehistoric Period to Augustus.* Carnegie Institution of Washington Publications, 570. Washington: Carnegie Institution.

Blanchard, M. *et al.*
  1973   Répertoire graphique du décor géométrique dans la mosaïque antique. *Bulletin de l'Association Internationale pour l'Étude de la Mosaïque Antique*, 4.

Blinkenberg, C.
  1931   *Lindos, Fouilles de l'Acropole 1902–1914, I. Les Petits Objets.* Lindos, Fouilles et Recherches 1902–1914. Berlin: Walter de Gruyter.

Boardman, J.
  1967   *Excavations in Chios 1952–1955; Greek Emporio.* The British School of Archaeology at Athens, suppl. 6. London: Thames and Hudson.

Boardman, J., and Hayes, J.
  1966   *Excavations at Tocra I: The Archaic Deposits I. British School at Athens* suppl. 4 Oxford: Thames and Hudson.

Brijder, H. A. G.
  1983   *Siana Cups I and Komast Cups.* Allard Pierson Series vol. 4. Amsterdam: Allard Piersen Museum.

Buckler, W. H.
  1924   *Lydian Inscriptions Part II; Sardis* VI.2. Leiden: Brill.

Buckler, W. H., and Robinson, D. M.
  1932   *Greek and Latin Inscriptions.* Sardis VII. Leiden: Brill.

Burstein, S. M.
  1984   A New *Tabula Iliaca*: The Vasek Polak Chronicle. *J. P. Getty Museum Journal* 12: 153–62.

Butler, H. C.
  1922   *Sardis* I, *the Excavations Part I, 1910–1914.* Leiden: Brill.

Cagnat, R., and Chapot, V.
   1916   *Manuel d'Archéologie Romaine*, I. Paris: Picard.
Cargill, J.
   1977   The Nabonidus Chronicle and the Fall of Lydia. *American Journal of Ancient History* 2: 97–116.
Chase, G. H.
   1921   Two Vases from Sardis. *American Journal of Archaeology* 25: 111–17.
Chemical and Engineering News
   1984   Formation of Fossilized Fabrics Focus of Textiles Research Project. September 10, 1984: 28–30.
Claude, D.
   1969   *Die Byzantinische Stadt in 6. Jahrhundert.* Munich: Beck.
Curtis, C. D.
   1925   *Jewelry and Gold Work Part I 1910–1914*; *Sardis* XIII. Rome: Sindacato Italiano Arti Grafiche.
Foss, C.
   1976   *Byzantine and Turkish Sardis.* Sardis Monograph, 4. Cambridge, MA: Harvard.
   1977   Archaeology and the "Twenty Cities" of Byzantine Asia. *American Journal of Archaeology* 81: 469–86.
   1979   *Ephesus after Antiquity: A Late Antique, Byzantine, and Turkish City.* Cambridge: Cambridge University.
Gjerstad, E., *et al.*
   1935   *The Swedish Cyprus Expedition; Finds and Results of the Excavations in Cyprus 1927–1931*, II. Stockholm: Swedish Cyprus Expedition.
Greenewalt, C. H., Jr.
   1973   The Fifteenth Campaign at Sardis (1972). *Bulletin of the American Schools of Oriental Research* 211: 14–36.
   1972   Two Lydian Graves at Sardis. *California Studies in Classical Antiquity* 5: 113–45.
   1978   *Ritual Dinners in Early Historic Sardis.* University of California Publications: Classical Studies 17. Berkeley: University of California.
   1979   The Sardis Campaign of 1977. *Bulletin of the American Schools of Oriental Research* 233: 1–32.
   1982   Sardis, 1979. *Türk Arkeoloji Dergisi* 26: 95–109.
Greenewalt, C. H., Jr., and Majewski, L. J.
   1980   Lydian Textiles. Pp. 133–47 in *From Athens to Gordion; The Papers of a Memorial Symposium for Rodney S. Young.* University Museum Papers, 1, ed. K. DeVries. Philadelphia: The University Museum.

Greenewalt, C. H., Jr.; Ramage, A.; Sullivan, D. G.; Nayır, K.; and Tulga, A.
   1983   The Sardis Campaigns of 1979 and 1980. *Bulletin of the American Schools of Oriental Research* 249: 1–44.
Greenewalt, C. H., Jr.; Rautman, M.; and Meriç, R.
   1986   The Sardis Campaign of 1983. *Bulletin of the American Schools of Oriental Research Supplement* 24: 1–30.
Greenewalt, C. H., Jr.; Sterud, E. L.; and Belknap, D. F.
   1982   The Sardis Campaign of 1978. *Bulletin of the American Schools of Oriental Research* 245: 1–34.
Greenewalt, C. H., Jr.; Sullivan, D. G.; Ratté, C.; and Howe, T. N.
   1985   The Sardis Campaigns of 1981 and 1982. *Bulletin of the American Schools of Oriental Research Supplement* 23: 53–92.
Gusmani, R.
   1985   Lydische Neufunde aus Sardis. *Kadmos* 24: 74–83.
Hanfmann, G. M. A.
   1961   The Third Campaign at Sardis (1960). *Bulletin of the American Schools of Oriental Research* 162: 8–49.
   1962   The Fourth Campaign at Sardis (1961). *Bulletin of the American Schools of Oriental Research* 166: 1–57.
   1965   The Seventh Campaign at Sardis (1964). *Bulletin of the American Schools of Oriental Research* 177: 2–37.
   1966   The Eighth Campaign at Sardis (1965). *Bulletin of the American Schools of Oriental Research* 182: 2–54.
   1967a The Ninth Campaign at Sardis (1966). *Bulletin of the American Schools of Oriental Research* 186: 17–52.
   1967b The Ninth Campaign at Sardis (1966). *Bulletin of the American Schools of Oriental Research* 187: 9–62.
   1972   *Letters from Sardis.* Cambridge, MA: Harvard.
   1983   *Sardis from Prehistoric to Roman Times; Results of the Archaeological Exploration of Sardis 1958–1975.* Cambridge, MA: Harvard.
Hanfmann, G. M. A., and Ramage, N. H.
   1978   *Sculpture from Sardis: The Finds through 1975.* Sardis Report 2. Cambridge, MA: Harvard.
Hanfmann, G. M. A., and Thomas, R. S.
   1971   The Thirteenth Campaign at Sardis (1970). *Bulletin of the American Schools of Oriental Research* 203: 5–22.

Hanfmann, G. M. A., and Waldbaum, J. C.
1970 The Eleventh and Twelfth Campaigns at Sardis (1968, 1969). *Bulletin of the American Schools of Oriental Research* 199: 7–58.

Hanfmann, G. M. A., and Waldbaum, J. C.
1975 *A Survey of Sardis and the Major Monuments Outside the City Walls.* Sardis Report 1. Cambridge, MA: Harvard.

Haspels, C. H. E.
1936 *Attic Black-Figured Lekythoi.* École Française d'Athènes; Travaux et Mémoires publiés par les professeurs de l'Institut Supérieur d'Études Françaises et les Membres Étrangers de l'École, IV. Paris: de Boccard.

Higgins, R. A.
1954 *Catalogue of the Terracottas in the Department of Greek and Roman Antiquities, British Museum I.* London: British Museum.

Howland, R. A.
1958 *Greek Lamps and Survivals.* The Athenian Agora 4. Princeton: American School of Classical Studies at Athens.

Jacopi, G.
1931 Esplorazione Archeologica di Camiro I. Scavi nelle Necropoli Camiresi 1929–1930. *Clara Rhodos* 4. Rhodes: Istituto Storico-Archeologico.

Jakes, K. A., and Sibley, L. R.
1985 Textile Fabric Pseudomorphs: What They Are, Where They Are Found, and What They Tell Us. *American Journal of Archaeology* 89: 335.

Kern, O.
1901 Demeter. Cols. 2713–64 in *Paulys Real-Encyclopadie der Classischen Altertumswissenschaft, Neue Bearbeitung,* ed. G. Wissowa; IV. Stuttgart: Metzler.

Lawrence, A. W.
1979 *Greek Aims in Fortification.* Oxford: Clarendon.

Lezine, A.
1964 *Architecture Romaine d'Afrique; recherches et mises au point.* Publications de l'Université de Tunis, Faculté des lettres et des sciences humaine, 1; archéologie, histoire, 9. Paris: Presses Universitaires de France.

Littmann, E.
1916 *Sardis VI, Lydian Inscriptions Part I.* Leiden: Brill.

Masson, O.
1973 Quelques noms de métier grecs en -as et les noms propres correspondants. *Zeitschrift für Papyrologie und Epigraphik* 11: 1–19.

Petrie, W. M. F.
1906 *Hyksos and Israelite Cities.* British School of Archaeology in Egypt and Egyptian Research Account, 12. London: School of Archaeology, University College.

Petrie, W. M. F.; Mackay, E.; and Wainwright, G.
1910 *Meydum and Memphis (III).* British School of Archaeology in Egypt and Egyptian Research Account, 16.

Radet, G.
1887 Inscriptions de Lydie. *Bulletin de Correspondence Hellénique* 11: 445–84.

Radt, W.
1980 Pergamon. Vorbericht über die Kampagne 1979. *Archäologischer Anzeiger*: 400–22.

Ramage, A.
1978 *Lydian Houses and Architectural Terracottas.* Sardis Monograph, 5. Cambridge, MA: Harvard.

Ramage, N. H.
1985 Two New Attic Cups and the Siege of Sardis. *American Journal of Archaeology* 89: 347.
1986 Two New Attic Cups and the Siege of Sardis. *American Journal of Archaeology* 90: 419–24.

Robert, J., and Robert, L.
1961 Bulletin Épigraphique. *Revue des Études Grecques* 74: 119–268.
1973 Bulletin Épigraphique. *Revue des Études Grecques* 86: 48–211.
1983 *Fouilles de l'Amyzon en Carie, I; Exploration, Histoire, Monnaies et Inscriptions.* Paris: de Boccard.

Robert, L.
1963 *Noms Indigenes de l'Asie Mineure Gréco-Romaine.* Bibliothèque archéologique et historique de l'Institut français d'archéologie d'Istanbul, 13. Paris: Maisonneuve.
1973 Epigraphie et antiquités grecques. *Annuaire du Collège de France* 73: 473–92.

Robinson, D. M., and Graham, J. W.
1938 *The Hellenic House; A Study of the Houses Found at Olynthus with a Detailed Account of Those Excavated in 1931 and 1934.* Excavations at Olynthus, VIII. Baltimore: Johns Hopkins.

Salonen, A.
1972 *Die Ziegeleien im alten Mesopotanien.* Suomalainen Tiedeakatemian Helsinki Toimituksia 171. Helsinki.

Schede, M.
1964 *Die Ruinen von Priene; kurze Beschreibung.* 2nd ed. Berlin: de Gruyter.

Scheffer, C.
1981 *Acquarossa 2.1 Cooking and Cooking Stands in Italy,* 1400–400 B.C. Skrifter Utgivna av Svenska Institutet i Rom 4°, 38.2.1. Stockholm: Paul Åströms Förlag.

Schmidt, E. F.
1957 *Persepolis II: Contents of the Treasury and Other Discoveries.* The University of Chicago Oriental Institute Publications, 69. Chicago: University of Chicago.

Secck, O.
1901 Decemprimat und Dekaprotie. *Klio* 1: 97–187.

Sparkes, B. A.
1962 The Greek Kitchen. *Journal of Hellenic Studies* 82: 121–37.

Thouvenot, R., and Luquet, A.
1951 Les Thermes de Banasa. *Publications du Service des Antiquités du Maroc* 9: 33–40.

Waelkens, M.
1985 *Die kleinasiatischen Türsteine. Typologische und epigraphische Untersuchungen zu den kleinasiatischen Grabreliefs mit Scheintür.* Mainz: von Zabern.

Waldbaum, J. C.
1983 *Metalwork from Sardis.* Sardis Monograph, 8. Cambridge, MA: Harvard.

White, D.
1975 Excavations in the Sanctuary of Demeter and Persephone at Cyrene 1973: Third Preliminary Report. *American Journal of Archaeology* 79: 33–48.

Wulff, H. E.
1966 *The Traditional Crafts of Persia.* Cambridge, MA: Massachusetts Institute of Technology.

Young, R. S.
1981 *Three Great Early Tumuli.* University Museum Monograph 43. The Gordion Excavations Final Reports I. Philadelphia: University Museum, University of Pennsylvania.

The Sardis Campaign of 1985

CRAWFORD H. GREENEWALT, JR.
University of California
Berkeley, CA 94720

MARCUS L. RAUTMAN
Miami University
Oxford, OH 45056

NICHOLAS D. CAHILL
University of California
Berkeley, CA 94720

Excavation took place in four regions of the city site. At sector MMS, in one of the Late Roman residential units two rooms and a well were excavated. In the Lydian stratum, a domestic building that had been destroyed ca. 550 B.C. yielded much carbonized grain and 100–150 artifacts, primarily of clay and metal and primarily associated with food, drink, textile production, and personal adornment; nearby Colossal Lydian Structure was shown to have had a large reentrant corner in the vertical stone facade of its west side.

At sector ByzFort (a spur of the lower north slope of the Acropolis) one corner of the Archaic terrace that envelopes the outer end of the spur was exposed to its preserved height of 5 m; context pottery suggests for terrace construction a date of ca. 560–500 B.C. Archaic deposits on both the slope and the summit of the spur yielded many architectural terracottas and fragments of multicolored chalcedony (presumably from a stoneworking atelier).

In a long chain of mounds at the north side of the city site, excavation revealed a huge building of Lydian or Lydo-Persian date, which evidently forms the core of one or more of the mounds.

At sector HoB a test trench exposed a simple child burial of the early first millennium B.C. and below, a 6 m-thick deposit of water-laid gravel, sand, and silt.

Excavation and research at Sardis in 1985 were conducted by the Archaeological Exploration of Sardis, or Sardis Expedition, jointly sponsored by the University Art Museums of Harvard University, Cornell University, the American Schools of Oriental Research, and the Corning Museum of Glass; they took place during two and a half months in the summer.[1] The primary aims of excavation were to clarify the form and function of monumental buildings and building complexes of the Archaic period[2] in two regions of the city site (sectors MMS and ByzFort; Greenewalt, Cahill, and Rautman this issue, fig. 1; fig. 2, nos. 63, 23); to uncover more of a well-preserved Lydian domestic deposit and of a Late Roman residential unit

in one of those regions (sector MMS); to test the implications of surface debris that a substantial occupation stratum of the Archaic period rested close below the modern surface in a hitherto unexcavated region of the city site (Mound 2; Greenewalt, Cahill, and Rautman this issue, fig. 1; fig. 2, near no. 9.16); and to check the stratigraphy of early Iron Age occupation deposits in an excavation sector of the 1960s (the large "Lydian Trench" in sector HoB; Greenewalt, Cahill, and Rautman this issue, fig. 1; fig. 2 between nos. 4, 56, 59). Study of materials and context data from earlier seasons included Bronze Age deposits and stratigraphy at sector HoB (by D. G. Mitten); Iron Age deposits and stratigraphy at sector HoB (by A. Ramage); deposits and stratigraphy at

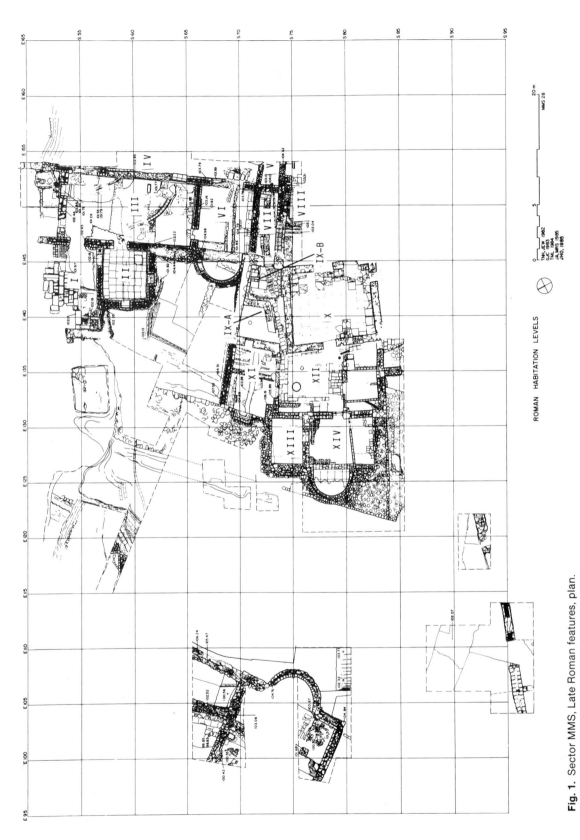

Fig. 1. Sector MMS, Late Roman features, plan.

sector PC (by N. H. Ramage; Greenewalt, Cahill, and Rautman this issue, fig. 2, no. 13; for this sector, Hanfmann 1960: 12–19; 1961: 17–24); Lydian and other Archaic Gray Wares (by C. G. Simon); molded and appliqué relief wares (by S. I. Rotroff); Byzantine glazed wares (by J. A. Scott); plant remains (by M. Nesbitt); and human skeletal remains (by S. C. Bisel).

SECTOR MMS

At this sector, located southeast of the Roman Gymnasium–Bath Complex (Greenewalt, Cahill, and Rautman this issue, fig. 1; fig. 2, no. 63) and marked in the landscape by a low artificial hill (substantially created by the ruins of a huge building of the Lydian period, Colossal Lydian Structure), excavation has been conducted in annual seasons since 1977 and has revealed major occupation strata of the Lydian and Late Roman periods; for work in 1984 and earlier seasons, see Greenewalt, Cahill, and Rautmann, this issue.

C.H.G.

Sector MMS, Roman features

Excavation at sector MMS continued to explore the Late Roman residential complex discovered in 1978 (Greenewalt, Sterud, and Belknap 1982: 15). Work in 1985 helped refine earlier findings, which had identified few traces of post-Lydian habitation prior to the area's systematic urban development in the fourth and fifth centuries A.D. Changing patterns of use suggest that the neighborhood entered a period of marked decline, hastened by natural trauma, in the mid or late sixth century. In its present, partially excavated state, the sector presents three clusters of domestic spaces that apparently belonged to three contemporary and interrelated, but functionally independent, residences of the Late Roman period (fig. 1). During 1985 attention was directed to the study of features partially cleared in previous seasons, excavation of three new rooms of one residence, and a limited magnetometer survey of the sector's environs.

Room III is an elongated trapezoidal space located in the northeast part of the sector. The room had been cleared to its latest occupation phase in earlier seasons (Greenewalt, Rautman, and Meriç 1986: 4–5; = "Room B"). Renewed

excavation beneath this large Late Roman space revealed a densely packed sequence of occupation levels, walls, and hydraulic features. Above the debris of Colossal Lydian Structure (postponed for excavation in a future season; below) were identified isolated traces of habitation that may date as early as the fourth century B.C. The primary architectural development of the area was undertaken in the third or fourth century A.D. when the room's east and west walls were first laid out, roughly oriented to the 'B' grid. Three internal partition walls were removed at different points during the fifth century and the enlarged room was progressively embellished with various waterworks, marble paving, and wall painting. Contextual finds suggest that the space attained its final form as the result of a major reconstruction campaign during the late fifth or early sixth century.

In the central part of the Late Roman complex three additional spaces were excavated opening to the east off the open Court XII. The large Room X was one of the most prominent and public parts of this Late Roman residence. The smaller Rooms IX-A and IX-B stand further removed from Court XII and probably functioned as utilitarian facilities for the household. Throughout their occupation Rooms IX-A, IX-B, and X were accessible through a continuously changing series of openings in their walls, which stand to a preserved height of 1.5 to 2.5 m. Excavation in 1985 identified only the latest phases of their use, leaving the earlier occupation of these rooms to be explored in a future season.

Room X was completely exposed in its final occupied state to present a large interior space, trapezoidal in plan. The oblique orientation of the room's walls with respect to neighboring spaces may reflect the proximity of the colonnaded street that lies approximately 5.0 m to the south (below). The room was restored later in the fifth century, at which time a broad doorway was opened near the middle of the west wall, connecting Room X with the southeast corner of the adjacent Court XII. Other earlier openings in the east and south walls joined this space with neighboring, still unexcavated parts of the residence. As a result of this reconstruction, the room's floor level was raised and paved with large terracotta tiles, while its walls were replastered and frescoed.

The most striking of Room X's furnishings from this phase is a fountain or large basin set against the east wall. Mounted on a marble platform, this

Fig. 2. Sector MMS, Late Roman features, Room X: reassembled basin; view to northeast.

feature was constructed of five marble blocks, which were recovered either *in situ* or fallen in place (fig. 2, reassembled). Four of the slabs were originally mortared and clamped together to form a tank measuring 0.62 m × 0.63 m × 0.78 m, with a capacity of 305 liters. A fifth slab found nearby probably served as a lid. The front block carries on its face a large cross carved in low relief. Details of the floor's paving and the basin's clamping suggest that the tank was assembled expressly for its use here. A continuous flow of water was supplied through two small terracotta pipes located at opposite ends of the tank, and was available either by dipping or through a side tap. The basin's intended function, while uncertain, need not have been specifically ceremonial or sacral. Its prominent Christian imagery would have been appropriate to fifth-century Sardis generally and likely reflects the special importance of a dependable water supply to the life of any Anatolian city.[3]

Other furnishings recovered from Room X's final occupation phase include three architectural capitals, one of which was installed against the west wall to support a small tile-lined bin. A small marble basin was recessed into the floor near the west doorway. Twenty-two fragments were also found of a marble sigma-table with raised rim that may have stood in this or another nearby room.

The precise date and reasons why Room X's habitation ceased remain uncertain. As was the case with other parts of the same complex (Greenewalt, Rautman, and Meriç 1986: 1–6), shortly after the time of its abandonment the room began to be quarried for reusable building materials, in particular its marble furnishings and large floor tiles. The collapse of its roof interrupted the room's dismantling *in medias res*. Two marble thresholds had already been removed and numerous floor tiles, freshly pried from their mud mortar bedding, stood propped against the walls when the space was abruptly covered with a thick

Fig. 3. Sector MMS, Late Roman features, Room X: state at the time of dismantling.

blanket of roof tiles (fig. 3). After the mid-sixth century the space remained unroofed and unoccupied, with an uneven surface covering its undisturbed contents and collapsed superstructure.

Several small, irregular spaces adjoined Room X to the north (fig. 4). The north and west walls of these rooms were built of mortared rubble masonry with brick bands, were faced with a mud plaster, and stood directly atop of and retaining the mudbrick debris of Colossal Lydian Structure. An L-shaped partition wall originally subdivided this area into two small trapezoidal spaces and a

short corridor that led eastward from the open Court XII. Doorways connected Room IX-A with both this corridor and Room IX-B to the east. A low, broad niche in the south wall of Room IX-A contained a terracotta basin and a small drain. The room's tile floor was removed together with all other furnishings in the sixth century, leaving only a short column shaft standing at the room's center. A covered drain extends the length of the corridor and Room IX-B, originally carrying waste water from Court XII toward the east. The floor of Room IX-B is paved with large tiles and schist slabs. Built into the northeast corner of the room

Fig. 4. Sector MMS, Late Roman features, Rooms IX-A and IX-B.

is a deep, tile-lined basin with a maximum capacity of 290 liters. A continuous floor of water was provided by intake, drainage, and overflow conduits.

Both Rooms IX-A and IX-B remained in use until the mid-sixth century. About this time the area apparently was stricken by the same event that collapsed the roof of Room X. In contrast to the latter, the smaller spaces were reconstructed as a single Unit IX and reoccupied. The interior partition wall was removed and the north wall was partially rebuilt using large ashlar blocks. A new opening was cut through the south wall communicating with Room X. The floor level was raised ca. 1.0 m and was partially paved with large marble slabs set in a mud mortar. A massive bench built of architectural spoils was set against the west wall (fig. 5). Contextual finds indicate that this rebuilt space remained in use during the later years of the sixth century.

Recovered from the packed fill of Room IX were two nonjoining fragments of a broad shallow plate with a grooved rim and a recessed base (fig. 6, right and left fragments).

P85.27A and B: 9091. The plate is formed of "Asia Minor 'Light-Coloured Ware'" decorated with fish and other aquatic motives in a scraped champlevé technique described by Hayes 1972: 409–10; 1980: 534. Both fragments belong to the same vessel of which a third piece was found in a nearby room in 1983 (P83.62: 8829; Rautman in Greenewalt, Rautman, and Meriç 1986: 4, fig. 4; here fig. 8, middle fragment).

Earlier work at Sector MMS identified and partially excavated a well located near the northwest corner of the open court XII (Greenewalt, *et al.* 1985: 73; 72: fig. 18). In 1985 excavation of this well was continued to a depth of 22.5 m below the court's surface, where sterile soil was reached. The well comprises a single vertical shaft, ca. 0.88 m in diameter at its mouth, which cuts through the

Fig. 5. Sector MMS, Late Roman features, Room IX: bench; view to northwest.

5.0 m tall mass of Colossal Lydian Structure's stone platform (cf. Greenewalt, *et al.* 1985: 76, fig. 21). The upper 11.0 m of the well is lined with mortared schist blocks reinforced by bands of paired brick courses with footholds set at ca. 0.80 m intervals. The lower shaft is less regularly constructed of mortared fieldstone with broken brick fragments. Coin and pottery finds from the lower strata indicate that the well was installed in the early part of the sixth century (half-follis of Justinian I, 527–38; C85.16). The absence of whole vessels among the light quantities of recovered pottery suggests that the well may not have been used much after the time of its installation. After passing from its intended use, the well shaft was deliberately filled with dumped architectural debris during the late sixth or early seventh century.[4]

Related excavations were conducted in the area of the colonnaded street that bounds the Late Roman residential complex on the south. Previous work in the sector had identified the form and

scale of this feature, together with several flanking buildings and an irregular passageway leading north from the north colonnade (Greenewalt, Cahill, and Rautman, this issue). Further excavation of this area did not locate any standing walls or surfaces related to this passage, but revealed a deep, irregular hollow carved into the stone platform of Colossal Lydian Structure during the Late Roman period. This pit was evidently used primarily for the systematic dumping of Late Roman habitational debris, which eventually filled the colonnaded street itself.

Study of the dumped material suggests that the area's infilling occurred in three major phases, beginning as early as the late fifth and continuing through the late sixth or early seventh century. Finds consisted primarily of large storage vessels and cooking wares (75–80 percent of the total). Especially common among the table wares was a class of shallow bowl that imitates the Phocaean Red Slip ware vessels of the late fifth and early

Fig. 6. Sector MMS, fragments of plate in "Asia Minor 'Light-Colored Ware'" (P83.62: 8829; and P85.27A and B: 9091).

Fig. 7. Sector MMS, terracotta lamp with Jewish symbols, from dump near colonnaded street (L85.29: 9056).

sixth centuries (Hayes 1972: 329–38, form 3; 1980: 525 for the provenience). Sparse numismatic finds confirm that dumped material may have begun to accumulate as early as the late fifth century while the passage and colonnaded street became choked with debris during the sixth century.

Among the most interesting objects recovered from the dump were a number of molded terracotta lamps, one of which presents Jewish symbols on its face (fig. 7).

> L85.29: 9056. The lamp is nearly complete, missing only part of its nozzle. The body is round and flat, with an unpierced lug handle. The underside has parallel ridges extending from handle to base and under its nozzle, with a double-ring base enclosing a *planta pedis*. The upper rim presents two radial bands with inscribed circles. The disc contains four Jewish symbols grouped around an elaborate menorah. The menorah stands on a tripod base with circular medallions on its upper shaft and arms, which support seven lights. Flanking the menorah are the *lulav*, or palm branch, and *ethrog*, or fruit, on the left, and the curved *shofar*, or ram's horn, and four-part *matzo*, or unleavened bread (or *manna*, the bread from heaven), on the right. Two filling holes flank the menorah stand.[5]

Toward the close of the 1985 season a preliminary magnetometer survey was conducted in a 250 m^2 area in the south part of sector MMS. The area was surveyed with a McPhar model proton magnetometer at 1.0 m intervals from a sensor height of ca. 1.5 m. The data were graphically analyzed on an Epson HX20 computer.[6] The results of this limited investigation suggest the presence of major architectural features in the area surveyed. A diagonal feature located at E 135–45/S 85–95 on the 'B' grid corresponds to the anticipated line of the colonnaded street's north wall, located further to the west in 1984 (Greenewalt, Cahill, and Rautman this issue). The area surveyed stands at the probable entrance from the street to the adjacent residence. The second sample revealed a dense but inarticulate concentration of remains along the eastward line of the street's south wall at E 120–35 / S 105–115 on the 'B' grid. The dense matrix may reflect either the street's collapsed south colonnade or a nearby unidentified feature, perhaps an intersecting thoroughfare from the south.

M.L.R.

Sector MMS, Lydian Features

Domestic Building East of Colossal Lydian Structure. Excavation continued on the east side of Colossal Lydian Structure, where in 1984 part of a well-preserved domestic building was uncovered (Greenewalt, Cahill, and Rautman this issue; Ramage 1986). This building had been burned and buried under a deep layer of brick

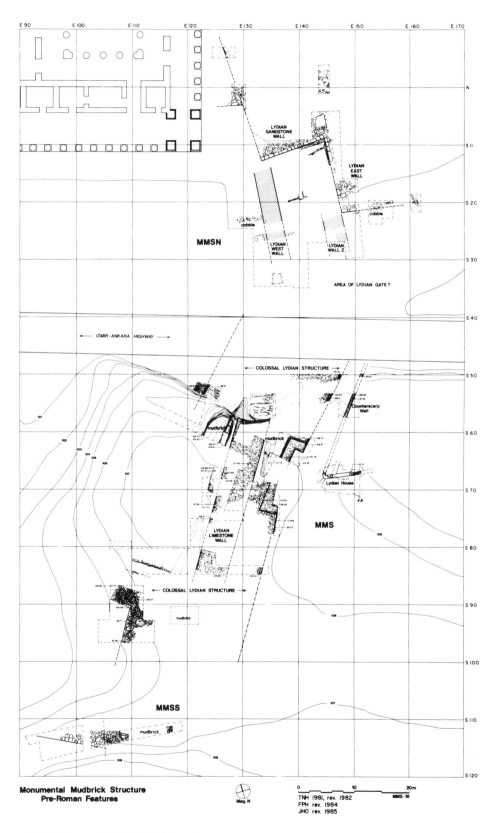

Fig. 8. Sectors MMS, MMS-S, MMS-N, pre-Roman features, plan.

debris when the neighboring structure was destroyed, so that its architecture and contents
remain remarkably well preserved. Local and
imported (Attic black figure, Eastern Greek) pottery recovered in 1984 and a carbon-14 date suggest that the domestic structure was destroyed in
the mid-sixth century B.C., probably in the capture
of the city by Cyrus of Persia between 547 and
542 B.C. This material thus represents a sealed,
well-dated, and remarkably complete Lydian domestic assemblage, and provides a secure date for
the destruction of Colossal Lydian Structure.

Work continued in two areas, both of which
have been explored in past seasons. The area
exposed in 1984, within the limits of Roman
apsidal room VI, was expanded southwards to the
south wall of the Roman room, and the entire
area within the limits of Roman room III, to the
north, was excavated to the top of the "brick fall
layer" (hereafter: Brick Fall), which covers the
Lydian remains (figs. 1, 8, 9; for excavated features
above the Brick Fall, above). Exposure of the
Lydian remains immediately below Brick Fall is
planned for 1986.

Further excavation of the space within the limits
of Roman room VI uncovered a significant quantity of new material and answered a number of
questions about the architecture of the building.
The building seems to have undergone a number
of architectural phases, some of which remain
unclear.

> The earliest feature here is probably the "counter-
> scarp" wall, probably built about the same time
> as Colossal Lydian Structure. The east–west
> house wall (Lot 14/16) uncovered in 1984 abuts
> the "counterscarp" wall, and might be a later
> addition. The "counterscarp" wall proper, how-
> ever, ends at this corner; its southward continua-
> tion (Lot 36) is a separate structure whose
> construction is quite different. Finally, the wall
> parallel to the "counterscarp" wall (Lot 31 wall)
> abuts and is probably later than the east–west Lot
> 14/16 wall.
>
> In its original construction, a drain was built into
> the Lot 36 wall: a channel passes through the
> socle of the wall, and two stones from the lining
> of the drain lead up to this channel. The drain
> was blocked and out of use by the final phase of
> the building, however.[7]

Areas of the main floor and the narrow space
between the "counterscarp" wall and Lot 31 wall

were covered with burned reeds or thatch, further
evidence that these spaces were roofed.

In general, pottery and other finds were most
densely concentrated along the walls, where they
seem to have fallen from shelves or other furniture
(figs. 10, 11). Other than iron hardware, little
remains that can help reconstruct the furniture:
the fire that destroyed the building consumed the
wood so thoroughly that only its presence and the
direction of the grain can be distinguished, and in
some cases no trace at all may be left. At the foot
of the east wall (Lot 36), iron nails and other
hardware, and a layer of wood charcoal are probably the remains of a shelf or other furnishing,
which seem to be anchored to the wall by setting a
framework of wooden beams into the mudbrick.
Channels for these beams still remain in the brick
wall. This stands in contrast to the situation at the
foot of the north wall, where last year the distribution of finds also suggested that much of the
pottery fell from a shelf, but very little charcoal
and no nails or other hardware belonging to
furniture were found.[8]

A diverse assemblage of artifacts lay at the foot
of the east wall, including cooking implements,
vessels for drinking, foodstuffs, cosmetic and other
small containers, and a variety of jewelry and
trinkets. Cooking utensils here included a second
cooking stand, a coarse bowl, and a set of about
ten iron spits.[9]

> The spits are all different: seven are circular in
> section and three rectangular; and one ends in a
> point, two in blunt ends, one in a chisel-like end,
> one in a leaf end, and one in a loop. The longest
> preserved spit is about 0.60 m long, but all have
> been cut off by the Roman wall that intruded the
> Lydian stratum. They seem to have been tied in a
> bundle with iron wire.

Vessels used for drinking included an almost
complete column krater, a fragmentary hydria,
and two squat oinochoai.[10] Other scattered objects in this area included a very fragmentary
Corinthian-type cover tile, a bronze arrowhead,
and a bone needle and tube (needle case ?).[11] In
addition, about 4 liters of carbonized barley lay
on the floor; the barley had probably been stored
in some perishable container, a basket or bag.[12]
All this material seems to have fallen from a shelf,
although the spits may have been leaning against
the wall.

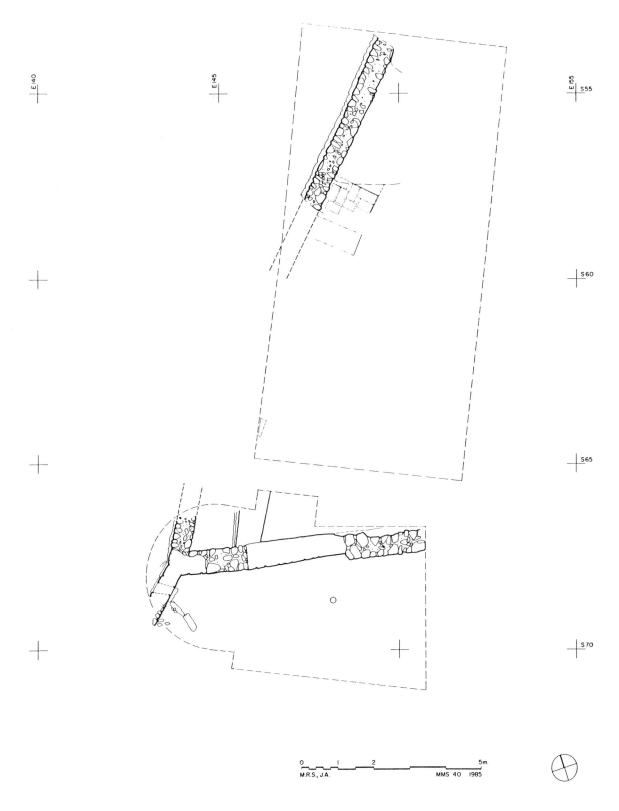

Fig. 9. Sector MMS, Lydian domestic structures: architecture, plan.

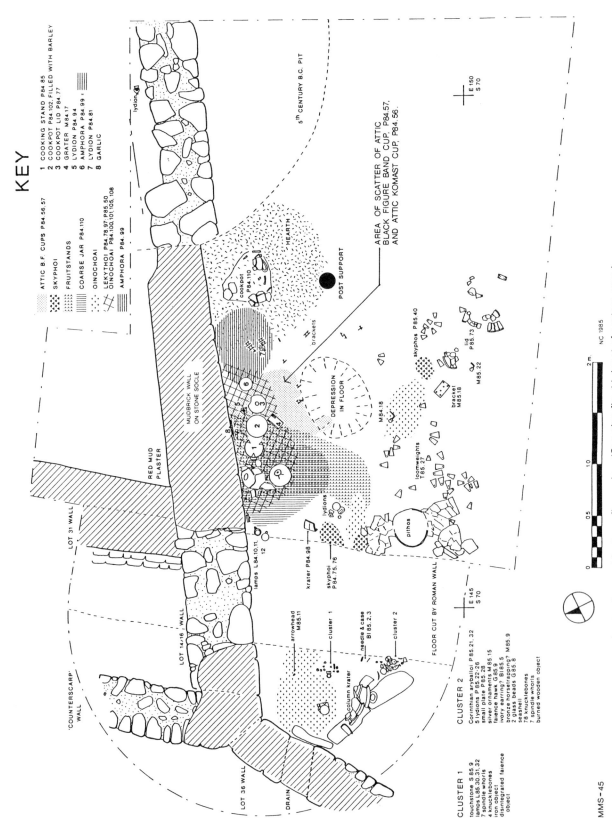

KEY

		1	COOKING STAND P84.85
		2	COOKPOT P84.102, FILLED WITH BARLEY
		3	COOKPOT LID P84.77
		4	GRATER M84.17
		5	LYDION P84.94
		6	AMPHORA P84.99
		7	LYDION P84.81
		8	GARLIC

	ATTIC B.F. CUPS P84.56,57
	SKYPHOI
	FRUITSTANDS
	COARSE JAR P84.110
	OINOCHOAI
	LEKYTHOI P84.78,97,P85.50
	OINOCHOAI P84.100,101,105,108
	AMPHORA P84.99

CLUSTER 1
touchstone S 85.9
lamps L85.30,31,32
7 spindle whorls
4 knucklebones
iron object
disintegrated faience
object

CLUSTER 2
Corinthian aryballoi P85.21,32
5 lydions P85.22-26
small plate P85.28
silver ornaments M85.15
faience hawk G85.9
ivory earring? B185.5
bronze horsetrapping? M85.9
2 glass beads G85.8
seashell
78 knucklebones
7 spindle whorls
burned wooden object

MMS-45

Fig. 10. Sector MMS, Lydian domestic structures: objects on floor, plan. (See also fig. 11, inset of eastern area.)

INSET: UPPER LAYER
IN EAST

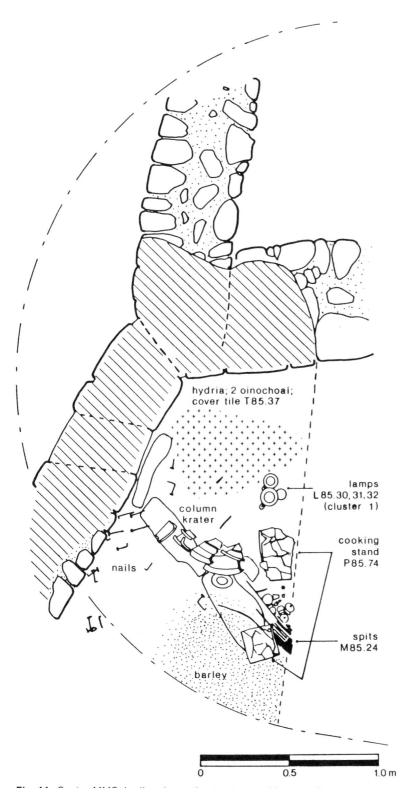

hydria; 2 oinochoai;
cover tile T85.37

lamps
L85.30, 31, 32
(cluster 1)

column
krater

cooking
stand
P85.74

nails

spits
M85.24

barley

0			0.5			1.0 m

Fig. 11. Sector MMS, Lydian domestic structures: objects on floor, plan; inset
of eastern area in fig. 10.

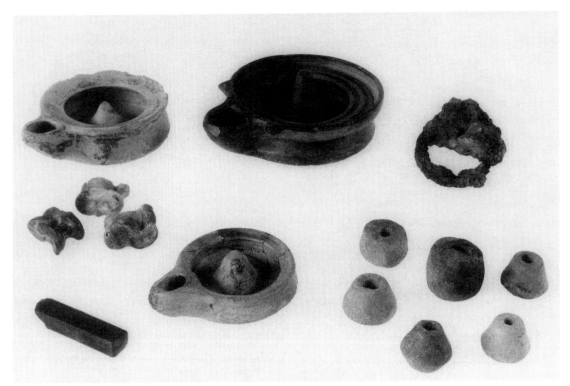

Fig. 12. Sector MMS, Lydian domestic structures: select artifacts from Cluster 1.

Two separate and discrete clusters of objects were found in this area (Clusters 1 and 2 in figs. 10 and 11). Their tight packing and the nature and small size of the individual objects suggest that these objects were stored in boxes or other containers that have disappeared without leaving a trace. The smaller cluster of objects, Cluster 1, contained three lamps, seven clay spindle whorls, a very decayed faience or glass object, an unidentified iron object, four sheep knucklebones, and a small bar of black chert, 1.2 cm × 1 cm in width–height and 5.2 cm long, broken at one end (fig. 12).[13] Greenewalt (after Moore and Oddy 1985) suggested that this bar was a touchstone for assaying the purity of gold, and Doç. Dr. Yılmaz Savaşçin and Doç. Dr. Orhan Kaya, of the Geology Division, Aegean University (Bornova-Izmir) confirmed that identification.

> The stone was tested at the Aegean University by x-ray fluorescence to detect traces of gold that might remain on its surface, but none were found. This does not necessarily affect its identification as a touchstone, however: gold might have been cleaned or burned off. This type of stone is too soft to be a whetstone (according to Savaşçin and Kaya), but is still used by jewelers to test precious metals.

The discovery of one of the earliest known touchstones in this context at Sardis is especially appropriate since the mineral was known in antiquity, as it is today, as Lydian stone (Lydite). The Greek term for touchstone, βάσανος, while Egyptian in origin, may have come into Greek via the Lydian language (Sethe 1933). Theophrastus and Pliny claim the "River Tmolus" (presumably meaning the River Pactolus, which rises in Mt. Tmolus) as the source of Lydian stone, and describe its properties and use (Theophrastus, *De Lapidibus* 4. 45–47; Pliny, *Historia Naturalis* 33. 43. 126. See also Moore and Oddy 1985). Until more of the building is excavated, one can only speculate about the uses of a touchstone in this domestic context.

The larger cluster, Cluster 2, contained seven small vessels for oil and unguents: two Corinthian quatrefoil aryballoi (Middle Corinthian, according to Amyx and Mansfield), and five local lydions (figs. 13, 14, 15).[14] A small plate or saucer might also have been associated with the cosmetics.[15] This cluster also contained a variety of small trinkets, ornaments, and personal objects: a pierced ivory or bone disk decorated with an incised rosette (an earring?); a faience hawk pendant; a small, pierced silver crescent (fabric ornament?); a

Fig. 13. Sector MMS, Lydian domestic structures: Cluster 2 *in situ*.

silver strip twisted into a ring at one end, perhaps an earring or ornament; a fragment of a silver bead; two glass beads; a bronze object, perhaps a horse trapping; a small iron buckle; seven more spindle whorls; a bivalve shell; 78 more sheep knucklebones; two lumps of clay-like substance; fragments of carbonized string; and other unidentified small objects.[16] Other perishable objects left few traces: a wooden object about 8 cm long could be discerned.

In the central part of the space were scattered 33 pyramidal loomweights (fig. 16). Together with the 13 loomweights found in 1984, the total count is 46, scattered over an area 2.3 m east–west × 1.3 m north–south. Forty-two of these are of the larger size (9 cm high) and 4 smaller (6 cm). The thread holes of all these weights are worn from use. Although they were not found laid out in parallel lines, the scatter of the weights and the presence of larger fragments of wood charcoal only in this part of the floor, apparently from beams or poles about 5 cm wide, would support the suggestion made in 1984, that the loomweights fell from a loom when the building burned. The number of weights is appropriate for a single loom.[17] No obvious traces of cloth or other weaving paraphernalia remained, but two peculiar, almost identical pieces of hardware may belong to

Fig. 14. Sector MMS, Lydian domestic structures: select artifacts from Cluster 2.

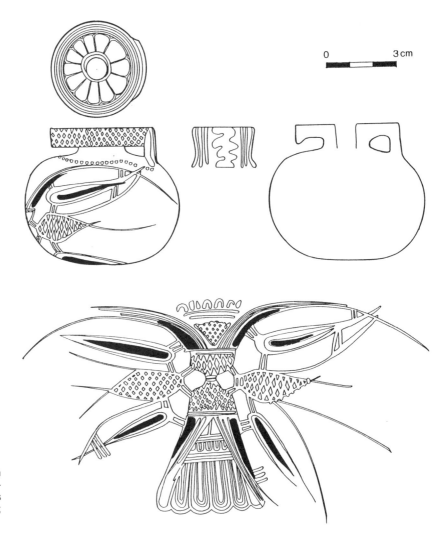

Fig. 15. Sector MMS, Lydian domestic structures: Corinthian quatrefoil aryballos from Cluster 2 (P85.21: 9070; drawing by H. Kökten).

some implement used with the loom. Each of these has an L-shaped iron shaft, like a large nail, and a semicircular, disk-shaped bronze head (mounted on edge; fig. 17). Traces of the wooden pole or beam to which one shaft was attached remained. They might have served as handles of some sort.[18]

Other objects found in this area include a pithos; two skyphoi; a lid with orientalizing decoration (red and white bands and concentric circles); two oinochoai; and a lekythos.[19] Some of these seem to have fallen and rolled from the shelf against the east wall, suggesting that a great deal of material has been removed by the Roman wall that intruded into the Lydian floor.

N.D.C.

Lydian or Lydo-Persian Vase Fragment with Horse's Head. A sondage below the floor of Room IX-A in the Late Roman residential complex that overlies Colossal Lydian Structure produced a noteworthy vase fragment showing a bridled horse's head (fig. 18).[20]

The fine quality of incision and the combination of incision with outline-and-reserve are unusual on local pottery; but clay and glazes look local. Style, iconography, and context suggest outside chronological limits of ca. 625–450 B.C.[21]

M. A. Littauer, who identified the bridle parts labeled in fig. 20, has commented, "the down-turned cheek pieces of the bit are typically Ionian, but the diagonal noseband I know of only in late Assyrian reliefs" (for the cheek piece, Åkerström

1966: 43–44, pl. 16.2, a terracotta revetment plaque of unknown provenience now in Paris; for the diagonal noseband, Albenda 1977: 41, fig. 41 [Assyrian relief of Sennacherib]); and, on the possibility of the dart form as a spear head (considered unlikely by A. E. Furtwängler because of the thickness and size), "if the horse is a chariot horse, a spear in this position would not be properly balanced" (Littauer and Crouwel 1983).

Colossal Lydian Structure. Excavation on the west side of sector MMS (at E. 106–112/S. 87–93 on the 'B' grid, which exposed the Roman dumped material, reported above) aimed to expose more of the west face of the Structure (Greenewalt, Rautman, and Cahill 1986: 7–8) and to determine the relationship of the face to the layers of sand, gravel, clay, and mudbrick that had been exposed 8–12 m to the north in previous seasons. Excavation in 1985 exposed a further segment of stone face, which includes an abrupt angle jog to the west (figs. 8, 19) and indicates that the layers are likely to be part of the earth core of the Structure.

Ca. 6 m of the structure west face oriented NNE/SSW and nearly 4 m of the face oriented NNW/SSE are exposed. These two segments meet in a reentrant corner with an angle of slightly more than 90°. Exposed parts of the face show a construction of rough blocks of sandstone, limestone, and schist laid in uneven courses. The higher proportion of flatter stones in the NNW/SSE segment suggests that the two segments might belong to different construction phases (since the face at the reentrant corner is concealed [by Brick Fall; below], the nature of the joint—butt or bond—was not identified).

In front of the face, and along the west side of the 1985 trench is Brick Fall (i.e., mudbrick and semibaked brick from the superstructure of Colossal Lydian Structure; Greenewalt, Cahill, and Rautman this issue; above, this article); which was not excavated in 1985.

That the jog to the west terminates in a jog to the northeast is implied by the segment of west face located some 37 m north (just south of the modern highway); that a jog to the northeast is located

Fig. 16. Sector MMS, Lydian domestic structures: scatter of loomweights and other objects *in situ*.

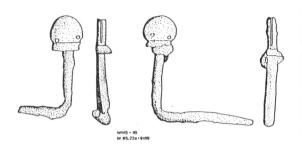

Fig. 17. Sector MMS, Lydian domestic structures: hardware with L-shaped iron shafts and bronze heads (M84.18: 8984 and M85.22: 9189; drawing by H. Kökten).

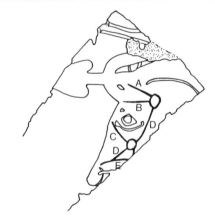

Fig. 18. Sector MMS, Lydian or Lydo-Persian vase fragment (P85.67: 9178. Drawing by J. Becker shows bridle parts as identified by M. Littauer: [A] poll piece; [B] brow band; [C] diagonal noseband; [D] cheekstrap; [E] cheekpiece).

just beyond the 1985 west trench scarp (fig. 19) is suggested by the appreciable north–south bias in the orientation of the Brick Fall. (If the jog to the northeast were located significantly further west, the orientation of the Brick Fall ought to be more nearly east–west. Note: the "ragged" west termination of stone construction shown in the plan, fig. 8, is not a true edge, but the exposed limit of stone construction, beyond which the stone is covered by Brick Fall).

Behind the stone masonry of the face is a substantial rubble stone packing, ranging in thickness from 2 to 3.5 m. Although well preserved behind the straight segments, the packing is substantially intruded behind the reentrant corner, as a result of scavanging in Late Roman times; above.

Behind the rubble stone packing is an earthy deposit of layered construction, which consists (to the extent investigated) of an upper layer of sandy soil, 2 m thick, and a lower layer of earth and disintegrated mudbrick. Similarity to the layers of sand, gravel, clay, and mudbrick exposed 8–12 m to the north in 1984 (Greenewalt, Cahill, and Rautman this issue) and earlier seasons suggests that both layered deposits belong to the same feature. The relationship of the 1985 deposit to the stone packing and face suggests that the layered deposits are not a separate feature, as had been supposed,[22] but an integral part of the structure.[23]

SECTOR BYZFORT (BYZANTINE FORT)

Sector ByzFort (located at ca. E. 630–730/ S. 310–410 on the 'B' grid; Greenewalt, Cahill, and Rautman this issue, figs. 1, 2, no. 23) is one of three natural flat-topped spurs that project from the north flank of the Acropolis,[24] and one of two

that were amplified with terrace construction in the Archaic period. (For the spur with a terrace facing of irregular large stone masonry, Greenewalt, *et al.* 1985: 64–68 ["Field 49" Wall].) The aim of excavation at ByzFort in 1985 was to expose for recording and display a substantial segment of terrace face at the northeast corner of the spur, from the foundations to the top preserved masonry course (for previous work, Greenewalt, Rautman, and Meriç 1986: 13–17; Greenewalt, Cahill, and Rautman this issue and fig. 20), and to determine the nature of Lydian occupation on the summit of the spur at its outer (north) end.

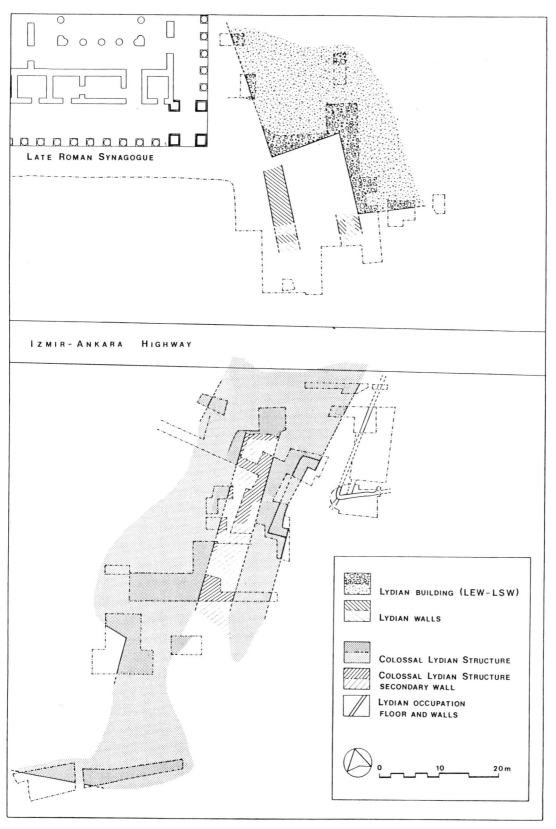

Fig. 19. Sectors MMS, MMS-S, MMS-N, pre-Roman features, interpretive plan (prepared by J. Becker).

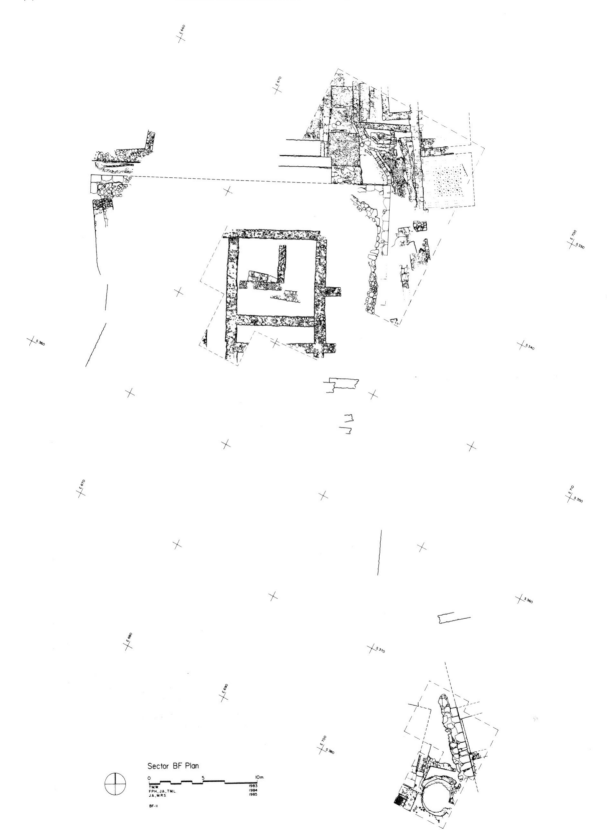

Fig. 20. Sector ByzFort, state plan.

ByzFort, Northeast Corner

Post-Archaic Features. Above the Archaic terrace are post-Archaic floors, walls, drains, and other features attesting ten or more building periods and phases between the fourth century B.C. and the sixth century A.D. (fig. 20). Of these features, those exposed just outside the face of the Archaic terrace at the northeast corner of the spur (in an L-shaped area of ca. 25–30 m²) were removed in 1985. The dismantling of these features clarified the sequence and chronology of them and of related post-Archaic features that were not removed.

The most monumental of these features is a massive Roman terrace wall (not removed), located on the north side of the spur, just outside the face of the Archaic terrace. The Roman terrace may have been an addition or repair to the Archaic one; it was built in several phases of

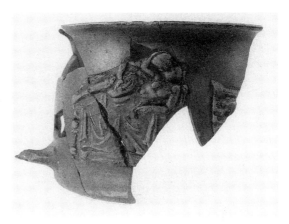

Fig. 21. Sector ByzFort, Pergamene ware kantharos with appliqué decoration (P85.47: 9152).

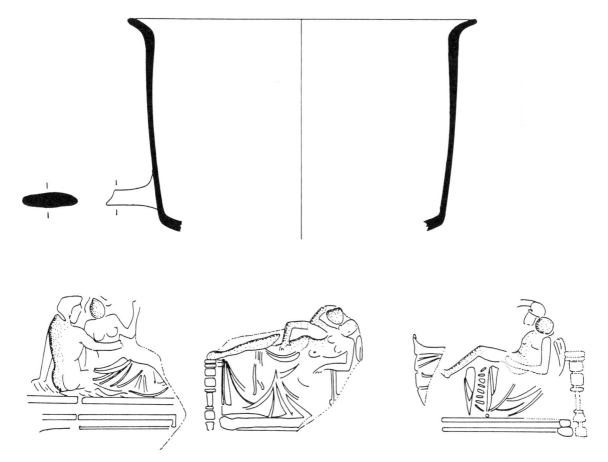

Fig. 22. Sector ByzFort, Pergamene ware kantharos with appliqué decoration (P85.47: 9152; profile and appliqué renderings by H. Kökten).

construction, and of concrete and mortared rubble with liberal use of marble *spolia*. An initial date of construction early in the first century A.D. is indicated by the chronologically homogeneous artifacts recovered from the foundation trench; included in this assemblage is the Pergamene-ware kantharos with relief appliqués showing erotic scenes (figs. 21, 22).[25]

The Roman terrace is older than the Roman multiroom unit(s) at the northeast corner of the spur, including the room with the mosaic paving discovered in 1984 (Greenewalt, Cahill, and Rautman this issue, figs. 22, 23).

From a Roman occupation surface (at *185.3) later than the initial construction phase of the terrace were recovered fragments of painted plaster, which included "a fine molded and cut plaster wall molding. . . . at least two fragments of a plastered column or pilaster, much of it colorfully painted in red, yellow, and various shades of green or blue. The designs include geometric panels, simple ornamental patterns, and floral motifs such as garlands with light green stems, dark bluish leaves, and red berries on a yellow ground" (excavator C. Ratté, *ByzFort* 1985 final report manuscript, p. 5; the molding is WP85.1: 9182).

A late Hellenistic deposit (fill adjacent to a wall "at least two building phases earlier" than initial construction of the Roman terrace) yielded a curious item that might belong to *opus sectile* architectural ornament: three narrow rectilinear bars of cut stone, two of "porphyry," one of green slate, cemented together at their sides in an L-shaped arrangement.[26]

The Hellenistic cobble pavement north of the Archaic terrace (cf. Greenewalt, Rautman, and Meriç 1986: 17 and fig. 25) was removed. Diagnostic pottery recovered beneath the pavement included a fragmentary fish plate (P85.30: 9107; with an *alpha* incised on the inside surface) and nothing that to S. I. Rotroff "need be later than 200 B.C." (C. Ratté, *ByzFort* 1985 midseason report manuscript, p. 5). Beneath the cobble pavement were a series of "pebble and sherd" surfaces; diagnostic pottery beneath them suggested to Rotroff a date in the mid-third century B.C. (and included an echinus bowl in gray ware, which illustrates the survival of an early Lydian ceramic tradition in the Hellenistic Age; P85.46: 9151; cf. Schäfer 1968: 29–30).

Fig. 23. Sector ByzFort, Archaic terrace, northeast corner; view to south-southwest.

Archaic Features. The Archaic terrace face at the northeast corner stands 5 m and 11 courses high. The bottom three courses are a three-stepped "foundation," narrower and more roughly trimmed than the rest, and mostly built of schist; the courses above are built (like all those exposed in previous seasons) of neatly cut blocks of white limestone (cf. Greenewalt, Rautman, and Meriç 1986: 15–16 and figs. 20–22; Greenewalt, Cahill, and Rautman this issue, fig. 21; figs. 23, 24 here).

The terrace rests on Acropolis conglomerate; the level of the lowest courses is adjusted to the terrain and steps down from south to north. The three-stepped "foundation" is "built mostly of schist but includes an occasional rough block of sandstone or limestone. Each of these courses steps in about 0.15 m from bottom to top. They are 0.2–0.3 m high. The length of the stones varies from 0.4 to 1.2 m. They are either roughly hewn or carefully selected for a naturally appropriate shape." Above the "foundation" are eight

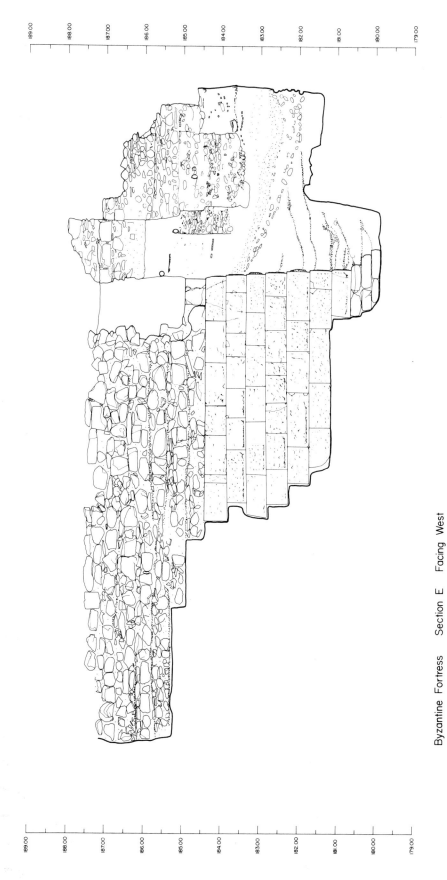

Fig. 24. Sector ByzFort, Archaic terrace, northeast corner; elevation of east face.

courses of limestone. "The height of these courses ranges from 0.50–0.58 m. Each course steps in 0.03–0.04 m from the course below." At the corner the width of the quoins varies from 0.42 m to 0.65 m, the length from 0.85 m to 1.60 m. "Elsewhere on the north face the length of the blocks ranges from 0.70 m to 1.13 m. The width of the drafted margins is also irregular: as much as 0.05 m, as little as 0.01 m; sometimes it 'fades away' altogether. The projection of the centers varies as well. It can be as great as 0.07 m; it is usually closer to 0.02 m or 0.03 m. On a few blocks the distinction between edge and center is indistinct."

At least four exposed blocks in three courses contain small rectilinear cuttings (visible in figs. 23, 24). "These cuttings are present only at seams between courses, always in the lower course of a seam. On average, they measure 0.1 m in width, 0.05 m in height, and 0.28 m in depth." The purpose of these cuttings is unclear to us; might they be sockets for scaffolding (Ratté), or for leveling rods (M. J. Mellink)? Quoted passages are adapted, with permission, from C. Ratté, *ByzFort* 1985 final report manuscript, pp. 9, 10.

The earth in which these courses were buried contained layers of limestone chips that can only be detritus from the final trimming of blocks of the terrace face, deposited when the terrace was built (fig. 25).[27] These layers provide evidence for two significant aspects of the terrace: the original concealment of most or all of the surviving face;[28] and the date of construction.

The lower face may have been buried to stabilize terrace construction, which originally rose another 8 m to the top of the spur (as layers of limestone chips in the fieldstone and boulder packing behind the face attest; Greenewalt, Rautman, and Meriç 1986: 16, and below); and which must rest on a relatively narrow shelf above a steep drop-off (cf. the contours in Greenewalt, Cahill, and Rautman this issue, fig. 20; a retaining wall of some kind presumably supported the earth fill that rested against the lower terrace face).[29]

Diagnostic artifacts sealed by these layers provide evidence for the date of terrace construction. The artifacts are all of sixth century B.C. shape or decorative types, and suggest that the terrace was built no later than ca. 500 B.C., probably at least a decade or two before ca. 500 (Greenewalt, Rautman, and Meriç 1986: 16 and fig. 23; for architectural terracottas recovered in this context, below).

Fig. 25. Sector ByzFort, Archaic terrace: east face near northeast corner at end of 1984 season, with layers of limestone chips (at lower right).

The most diagnostic item is a small fragment of an Attic black-figure amphora (fig. 26), the decoration of which has suggested to G. Bakır a date no earlier than ca. 560 B.C., and to D. von Bothmer "a work by" the Painter of Louvre F6;[30] in which case the fragment should provide a *terminus ante quem* of ca. 560 for the construction of the terrace. The evidence of context artifacts, therefore, indicates that the terrace was built either during the reign of Croesus (ca. 560–547 B.C.)[31] or in the first decades of Persian rule.

The implicit arrogance in the environmental design of the ByzFort and other Archaic Acropolis terraces (at "Field 49" and on the summit), which impose topiary design on natural landscape features, is consistent with the ostentation of Croesus reported in historical sources. The pre-Persian precedent of the "Field 49" terrace, and the absence of a precedent in Iran before the time of Cyrus the Great are factors that favor for the ByzFort and Acropolis summit terraces a date in the reign of Croesus.[32]

Fig. 26. Sector ByzFort, Attic black-figure amphora fragment (P85.29: 9107).

Fig. 27. Sector ByzFort, marble slab with volute ornament (S85.14: 9150).

ByzFort, Summit

Excavation on the summit of the ByzFort spur (in a trench ultimately 13.7 × 12 m, against the north and east edges) exposed a Roman multi-room unit, late Hellenistic features, and two Archaic strata (fig. 20).

Post-Archaic Features. The Roman multiroom unit rested just below modern ground surface; some of its walls have long been exposed at the east edge of the spur (Greenewalt, Rautman, and Meriç 1986: fig. 20). Of this unit parts of three rooms or corridors and all of one large, nearly square "room" (ca. 6.5 × 7 m) were excavated (fig. 20). The large "room" appears to have been subdivided into narrower west and broader east segments by a north–south partition, which had the form of a low balustrade supporting at least two columns, the whole made of brick with a plastered and at least partly painted surface. The larger segment of the room east of the balustrade may have been an open court. Associated pottery suggests for these rooms a date in the first century A.D.

The walls of all rooms are of homogeneous construction (mortared fieldstone with occasional bricks); and although some walls do not bond, they do not appear to reflect different building phases. The floor of the large "room" was best preserved in the northeast quadrant, where it was a substantial construction of hard pink mortar over cobble metalling. A segment of balustrade (eight brick courses high) and a column (with a preserved height of 1.5 m) rested face down in the west half of the "room"; this structure appears to have fallen from west to east. The column shafts were made of wedge-shaped bricks with curved exterior surfaces; the shaft diameter, 0.35 m, corresponds to the thickness of the balustrade bricks. The west face of the balustrade had two consecutive plaster surfaces: the older was painted with bands in light blue, red-orange, yellow, and black; the outer is a coarser-grain plaster, and showed no trace of paint. For the east face there is evidence for a plain white plaster surface.

Below the floor level of the large "room," foundations of an L-shaped wall and two north–south water conduits (a rectilinear channel and a line of terracotta pipes) that were cut by the "room" walls attest occupation in late Hellenistic-early Roman times.

The date of diagnostic artifacts recovered from debris above architectural features of the unit and from intrusive fill that had penetrated below the floor level of some rooms ranged from Hellenistic (coins) to early Roman (pottery, terracottas). Noteworthy items included a bone handle with lion-head terminal, two skyphos fragments with appliqué molded-relief decoration, and a fragmentary terracotta figurine, perhaps representing Cybele.[33]

Archaic Features. Archaic deposits were exposed only below the west side of the large "room" of the Roman unit, in a space ca. 3.8 m on a side. Two phases were tentatively identified: one represented by features to be associated with Archaic terrace construction; the other, evidently earlier, represented by building foundations of stone and brick,[34] the lower part of a pithos containing carbonized grain, and a marble slab carved in relief with a double volute motif (which rested against the stone foundation; fig. 27).[35]

Features to be associated with the Archaic terrace are a layer of limestone chips, presumably part of an internal working surface and analogous to the chip layers outside the masonry face; and, ca. 1.5 m below, a dense stratum of fieldstones and

boulders, presumably terrace packing. The chip
layer was present throughout the space except at
the south end. The fieldstone-boulder stratum
occurs only at the north end of the excavated
area and rests against bedrock, which inclines
steeply to the north; the upper portion of this
stratum was excavated.

The building foundations are located at the south
side of the excavated space, and project from the
south scarp. They are not sealed by the limestone
chip layer (which terminates just to the north of
them), but they rest in a distinctive earthy matrix
that extends beneath the chip layer (to the north);
and therefore seem to belong to a building phase
that antedates the chip layer (and the Archaic
terrace). Diagnostic pottery from this stratum is
consistent with a date before ca. 560 B.C., the
terminus ante quem for terrace construction
(above).[36]

ByzFort, Chalcedony and Architectural Terracottas from Archaic Contexts

Deposits associated with Archaic terrace construction both at the northeast corner of the
ByzFort spur (i.e., limestone chip layers and intermediate strata) and on the summit (i.e., limestone
chip layer and fieldstone boulder stratum) yielded
two kinds of artifacts in quantity: fragments of
multicolored chalcedony and roof and revetment
tiles.

Chalcedony. The chalcedony fragments range
from chip to fist-size hunks; their bright colors
and contrasting color combinations (e.g., red and
black, yellow and red; gray with purplish veins)
and high gloss of broken surfaces are visually
striking. Only two shaped pieces were recognized:
a fragmentary red-and-yellow stand or unfinished
bowl, and a fragmentary purple-veined gray bowl.
The latter, shallow with simple profile, resembles
chalcedony bowls from Lydo-Persian and Persian
contexts in western Asia Minor (the İkiztepe
tumulus near Güre, in the province of Uşak) and
Iran (Persepolis). The unshaped flakes and hunks
presumably are wasters from a stoneworking
atelier.[37]

Architectural Terracottas. Roof and revetment
tiles were particularly plentiful in the fieldstone-
boulder stratum on the spur summit; but they also
appeared in the chip layer on the summit and in

Fig. 28. Sector ByzFort, selection of architectural terracottas from Archaic deposits.

and between chip layers outside the Archaic terrace face (at the northeast corner). Several of the
molded and painted sima and revetment tiles
belong to types not before recovered at Sardis by
the Harvard-Cornell Expedition, and two clarify
the design and painting of previously attested
types (fig. 28).

T85.23: 9114, a corner sima tile with "Theseus
and Minotaur" motif, shows that "Minotaur's"
legs (on this piece attested for the first time) were
bent—not straight, as restored in the Sardis Expedition Terracotta Reconstruction display; T85.35:
9157 may preserve the lower body and thighs of
"Theseus" in the same tile type, and shows the
same stance.[38] T85.3: 9031 is the second example
of the partridge-file type recovered at Sardis (for
the first, Ramage 1978: 18, no. 11); and confirms
the use of two glazes and the general painting
scheme adapted for the Lydian Terracotta Reconstruction display.[39] T85.33: 9142 and T85.38:
9164 are examples of pattern types that were
recovered at Sardis by the H. C. Butler Expedition (Shear 1926: pls. 6, 12–14, figs. 9, 22); and
T85.25: 9116 is evidently an unattested figural
type (panel showing rampant hoofed animal with
head turned back). Unusual also are T85.28: 9129
(border with relief maeander pattern, repeated by
incised line), T85.32: 9141 (sima tile with scroll/
lyre motif adjacent to spout), T85.34: 9143 (with
painted bud chain border ornament), T85.31: 9140
(with scroll; scroll and background black). T85.30:
9139 has an egg and dart border pattern with
exceptionally well-preserved paint.

"MOUND 2"

At the north limits of Roman Sardis, between
the Roman Gymnasium–Bath Complex and Build-

Fig. 29. Mound 2, selection of Archaic artifacts recovered on the south side of the Mound.

ing CG (Greenewalt, Cahill, and Rautman this issue, fig. 2, nos. 1 and 28) is a chain of mounds with an east–west orientation. The north sides of the mounds are abutted by the Late Roman city wall (Hanfmann and Waldbaum 1975: 37, fig. 11; stretches 15–21, including Towers 1 and 2). During Urban Survey Project efforts in 1977 four mounds were recognized (Freedman in Greenewalt 1979: 4), and, although the long double-humped form of one, "Mound 2," might perhaps as logically be interpreted as two mounds, the 1977 designations have been retained: from west to east, Mounds 1–4.

That these anomalous humps in the landscape are artificial has long been recognized. Their surfaces are thick with artifacts: Roman material dominates (especially on Mound 1, highest and widest of the four, on which hunks of mortared rubble are visible); but Archaic material is also present (Freedman in Greenewalt 1979: 4, and fig. 2); and already in 1977 A. Ramage speculated

that a single Archaic building, such as a city wall (predecessor to that of Late Roman times), or a chain of buildings formed the core of the more westerly mounds if not of the entire chain.

During another surface reconnaissance in the beginning of the 1985 season, a substantial concentration of Archaic artifacts was located on the south side of Mound 2 (fig. 29); this concentration was the first evidence for a specific place on the mounds where Archaic strata might be anticipated close below modern ground surface.[40] Two small sondages (together ca. 25.5 m^2; at E. 455–465/ N. 225–240 on the 'B' grid; fig. 2) exposed parts of a monumental Archaic building, more than 10 m long and more than 5 m thick, with an east face oriented diagonally to the line of the mounds (figs. 30, 31). Exposed parts of the building face show ashlar masonry in white limestone, with chisel-drafted borders and hammer-dressed centers. Seven courses of this masonry are attested; the lowest of these courses may rest as much as 3

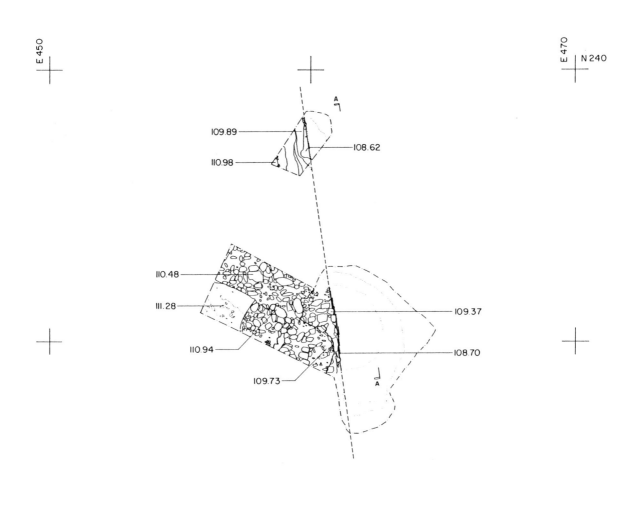

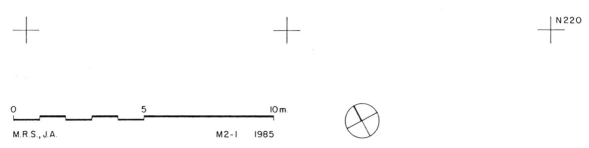

Fig. 30. Mound 2, plan of trenches.

Fig. 31. Mound 2, monumental Archaic building exposed in the larger trench; view to north.

to 4 m above the building foundations, if modern ground surface at the foot of Mound 2 is a reliable indicator of ancient ground level.

The limestone blocks vary in height, 0.36–0.47 m, and in length: the average length is ca. 0.70 m; one block is 2 m long. One block carries a chiseled "mason's mark," in the form of an *O*. Above the top limestone course on part of one exposed segment rise six courses of masonry in smaller, brick-sized blocks of schist or gneiss. These blocks are loosely aligned and jointed, as if their construction had been disturbed; too little of the building was exposed to permit identification of these small blocks as an original or secondary feature of construction. The exposed core of the building consisted largely of fieldstones and boulders, and included a carbonized timber (0.16 m wide), resting at right angles to the face (and identified as oak, by J. Aker, on the basis of cellular structure). Over and in front of core and face (and accounting for most of the debris in which these features were buried) was a very loose accumulation of fieldstones, boulders, and

much disintegrated, fire-reddened brick (ranging from near-complete bricks to powder), and charcoal lumps; all of which material is presumably fallen superstructure of the building.[41]

For the date of this building, features of the masonry face provide the best evidence. Ashlar masonry in white limestone with chisel-drafted borders and hammer-dressed or point-stippled centers is a distinctive feature of several buildings at Sardis that can be dated on the basis of historical or contextual evidence between the latter part of the seventh and the early fifth century B.C.[42] A date between ca. 625 and 475 B.C., which masonry evidence suggests would be supported by the minimally diagnostic pottery fragments recovered in the building debris (streaky glaze and banded pottery—one banded fragment embedded in a hunk of semi-baked brick), and by the pottery and terracotta fragments recovered on ground surface directly above the building (fig. 29; above, and n. 40).

Too little of the building was exposed to justify assumptions about its form, size, and function (and the marked difference in orientation between building face and mound chain frustrates simple assumptions). Exposed parts show, however, that the building was large; and logic suggests that it is no anomaly in the mound chain. Building and context indicate that an important part of Archaic Sardis, unrelated to Acropolis construction,[43] was located far to the east of the Pactolus valley (as G. M. A. Hanfmann long ago postulated). The extensive and uncontaminated fallen superstructure, furthermore, suggests that the lower part of the building and nearby features may be as well preserved as at Colossal Lydian Structure in sector MMS (under the comparable Brick Fall).

SECTOR HoB

Excavation at sector HoB (Greenewalt, Cahill, and Rautman this issue, figs. 1, 2) aimed to clarify early Iron Age and Late Bronze Age occupation sequences (in connection with studies in preparation by A. Ramage and D. G. Mitten).[44]

The test trench begun in 1984 (4 m × 5 m; at W. 1-E. 4/S. 111–116 on the 'B' grid) was continued with a vertical extension of another 7.5 m and a modest lateral extension (2 × 5 m; at E. 4-6/S. 103–108 on the 'B' grid; to serve as a ramp for the removal of earth from deep levels of the original trench).

Exposed were characteristic HoB sequences of water-laid sand and gravel layers, thin lenses of occupation debris, and occupation strata containing modest architectural features. Strata below levels reached in 1984 contained Lydian Geometric and Gray Ware pottery and two bronze fibulae of Blinkenberg types IV and XII.[45] Below these strata was a child burial: the articulated skeleton of a child in a roughly fetal position (fig. 32) rested in a clay-lined pit with a diameter of ca. 0.50 m; the only grave gift detected was a plain bronze

Fig. 32. Sector HoB, child burial (10th or 11th century B.C.?).

"(ear) ring" (excavator P. E. Mooney), recovered under the right side of the skull. Stratigraphic considerations point to a date in the 10th or 11th century B.C. The burial pit had been dug into "the uppermost stratum of a series of gravel, sand, and water-deposited silt layers that continue vertically for more than 6 m to the lowest excavated point in the trench, at *89.00."[46] Whether this massive deposit was created by the Pactolus stream (cf. G. F. Swift, Jr., in Hanfmann 1967: 32) or by erosion from the Acropolis was not determined.

C.H.G.

NOTES

[1]The Archaeological Exploration of Sardis is financially supported by a number of private corporate and individual donors. Fieldwork is authorized by the General Directorate of Antiquities and Museums, a division of the Ministry of Culture and Tourism of the Republic of Turkey. It is a pleasure to acknowledge the support and efforts of officers of the General Directorate, especially Director General Dr. Nurettin Yardımcı, Deputy Director Tanju Özoral, Director of Excavations Division Nimet Berkok, Excavations Division

Assistant Meral Gözübüyük, and Government Representative to the Sardis Expedition in 1986 Rafet Dinç. The conscientious and honorable efforts of Miss Gözübüyük were particularly effective. Manisa Museum Director Kubilây Nayır was, as always, a staunch friend, whose perceptive and sympathetic ideas, wise advice, and generous help significantly contributed to the achievement and positive experiences of the 1985 season.

The following made up the 1985 season staff: C. H. Greenewalt, Jr. (University of California at Berkeley; field director); A. Ramage (Cornell; associate director); D. G. Mitten (Harvard; associate director); T. Yalçınkaya (Betonsan, A. S., Manisa; administrative officer and agent); J. A. Scott (Harvard; executive director and head of publications for Phase I); H. F. Beaubien (New York University, Institute of Fine Arts, Conservation Center; senior conservator); L. A. Goldberg (New York University, Institute of Fine Arts, Conservation Center; conservator); İ. Kazmirci (Ege Üniversitesi; assistant in conservation and draftsman); H. Kökten (Ege Üniversitesi; Orhan Ragip Gündüz Memorial Trainee in Conservation); S. H. Langdon (University of Wisconsin; registrar); B. A. Baxter (Harvard; assistant registrar and numismatist); D. R. Nickel (Cornell; photographer); F. P. Hemans, III (Boston University; senior architect); J. Aker (Cornell; architect); M. R. Stankard (Cornell; architect); M. L. Rautman (University of Wisconsin; University of Missouri-Columbia; senior archaeologist); K. E. Welch (Cornell; archaeologist); H. S. Wiesner (Harvard; archaeologist); R. E. Mooney (Harvard; archaeologist); N. D. Cahill (University of California at Berkeley; archaeologist); C. J. Ratté (University of California at Berkeley; archaeologist); N. H. Ramage (Ithaca College; specialist for Attic pottery and for sector PC); S. I. Rotroff (Hunter College; specialist for Hellenistic and Roman relief wares); C. G. Simon (University of California at Berkeley; Fitzwilliam Museum; specialist for Lydian and regional gray wares). To all these for hard work, supportive attitudes, and cheer, heartfelt thanks. The substance of this report reflects staff achievements, and depends fundamentally on midseason and final report manuscripts, which are stored in the Sardis Expedition Office in Cambridge, MA, and in the Expedition compound at Sartmustafa.

[2] Archaic in this report is a time designation that refers to the seventh and sixth centuries and the beginning of the fifth century B.C. The term is not always appropriate for Sardis, where earlier Lydian material that is associated with artifacts in the Archaic style of Greece is scarcely distinguishable from later Lydian material produced during Persian hegemony and contemporary with Greek Classical styles.

[3] Similar Late Roman basins are found locally in the adjacent Room IX-B (fig. 4), at the House of Bronzes (Hanfmann 1959: 23, figs. 8, 27), and in the Byzantine shops (Hanfmann 1960: 32–33, fig. 18), all of which probably served domestic functions. A similar cross-adorned basin covered by a pedimented roof on columns is known at Ephesus (baptistry narthex adjoining church of St. John; Hörmann et al. 1951: 56–57, fig. 6, pl. 12:2). Both basins in the MMS residence should be distinguished from those large public reservoirs or nymphaea that often were added to peristyle courts in Late Roman Asia Minor (e.g., Ephesus [Jobst 1977: e.g., figs. 78, 103, 201], Side [Mansel 1978: 249–50, fig. 279], and Apamea [Balty 1984: 496]). For the cross type, cf. the carved keystone of a nearby monumental building at Sardis (Hanfmann and Thomas 1971: 11, 13, fig. 7).

[4] The lower 20.0 m of the well in Court XII were excavated in 54 units, with regular changes of baskets to maintain stratigraphic control. The relatively late date of the well's construction suggests that sixth-century Sardis was experiencing serious problems with its traditional gravity-fed water supply. Excavation in other parts of the site supports this interpretation. Few pipes are known to have been installed locally after A.D. 500, and other late wells are known at sector PN (Hanfmann 1962: 18; 1963: 20). Similar factors may have prompted the abandonment by the sixth century of residences built on the slopes of the Sardian Acropolis, such as those identified at sector ByzFort (Greenewalt, Rautman, and Meriç 1986: 17).

[5] Although the lamp's Jewish iconography is unusual at Sardis, its general type is well represented both locally and throughout the eastern Mediterranean. A provisional typology of menorah lamps is found in Reifenberg 1936 (cf. especially the example from Ephesus, pl. 9, fig. 13; reference courtesy of G. M. A. Hanfmann and research assistant Joanne Bloom); see also Goodenough 1953: 3, 101–18. Concerning other evidence from the Jewish community at Sardis in Late Roman times see most recently Hanfmann 1983: 168–90 (Chapter 9, "The Synagogue and the Jewish Community").

[6] The magnetometer survey was supervised by H. Williams of the University of British Columbia. Initial analysis of the data was done by R. Jones of the British School of Archaeology in Athens, with a program supplied by Bradford University. Thanks for these glimpses into unexcavated parts of Sardis are due to the helpfulness of these and other colleagues.

[7] Recent years have seen some changes in the Sardis recording system, including the use of "lot numbers" to identify architectural features and soil strata. These correspond to, for instance, "locus numbers" in the Gezer system, and will be referred to here when necessary to clarify the description.

[8] The "brackets" found in 1984, together with two more found in 1985, probably belonged to the roof rather than to furniture, since they were found in a line stretching 2.8 m from the north wall, far beyond the reasonable width of the shelf, and at the edge of the scatter of pottery, and thus probably at the edge of the shelf.

[9]Cooking stand P85.74: 9193; bowl P85.62: 9172. At the end of the 1985 season much material remained to be mended and inventoried. Spits M85.24: 9191. On spits in general, see Furtwängler 1980.

[10]Not mended or catalogued at the end of the 1985 season.

[11]Cover tile T85.37: 9124; arrowhead M85.11: 9111; needle B85.2: 9080; tube/needle case B85.3: 9082. The arrowhead is the first such to be found in a secure Lydian context in this area.

[12]Identified by M. Nesbitt, London University, Institute of Archaeology.

[13]Lamps L85.30: 9074, L85.31: 9077, L85.32: 9087. Spindle whorls T85.11: 9095, T85.12: 9096, T85.13: 9097, T85.19: 9103, T85.20: 9104, T85.21: 9105, T85.22: 9106, all made of unbaked clay in various forms, conical, biconical, and cylindrical. Touchstone S85.9: 9083.

[14]Corinthian aryballoi P85.21: 9070 (intact) and P85.32: 9112 (only the lower portion preserved). Both are similar to Payne 1931: 147, fig. 54D; 287 beneath no. 485A. Lydions P85.22: 9075, P85.23: 9076, P85.24: 9078 (a miniature lydion), P85.25: 9089, P85.26: 9090.

[15]Plate or saucer P85.28: 9092.

[16]Ivory disk BI85.5: 9134. Cf., for example, Hogarth 1908: pl. 35, no. 16; Dunbabin et al. 1962: 437–39, pl. 186; none are identical, however. Faience hawk pendant G85.9: 9136, a common type: Webb 1978: nos. 485–550. Silver crescent, strip, bead M85.15: 9135. Glass bead G85.8: 9081.

Bronze object (horse trapping?) M85.9: 9086. This consists of a bronze disk, 1.8 cm in diameter, with four notches cut from its rim so that it resembles a cloverleaf, to the back of which is attached a short cylinder. The cylinder is pierced laterally by four holes at right angles to each other. Objects with a similar pierced cylinder ("junction box") have been found at Sardis and other sites, and are usually interpreted as horse trappings (riemenkreuzungen), used to fasten bridle straps where they cross (Waldbaum 1983a: 40–41, nos. 85–86; cf. 41–42, nos. 87–88, which seem to be the same sort of object, for which see Waldbaum 1983b. On horse trappings in general and these objects in particular, see Anderson 1961: 50–63, esp. 59, n. 16–17). Two were found in situ in a horse burial at Norşun Tepe (Hauptmann 1972: 105–7; 1983: esp. 264–66). Many horses depicted on the Apadana reliefs at Persepolis are shown equipped with horn-shaped ornaments where their bridle straps cross, and thirty-three horn-shaped objects resembling the ornaments on the reliefs, some ending in a "junction box," were found in the Treasury there, suggesting further that the "junction box" is characteristic of this type of horse trapping (Schmidt 1957: 100, pl. 79, nos. 4–5). However, relatively few of these objects have been found in contexts that elucidate their use, and other interpretations of individual objects might be possible. No other artifacts associated with horses were found in this cluster or in the room.

Spindle whorls T85.9: 9093, T85.10: 9094, T85.14: 9098, T85.15: 9099, T85.16: 9100, T85.17: 9101, T85.18: 9102. Huge numbers of astragaloi have been found in occupation contexts at Gordion, where groups of up to 494 were found stored in single vessels (deVries 1980: 37). Astragaloi are also found in very large numbers in graves, 128 or more in one grave at Sardis (Greenewalt 1972: 138–39). Another tomb, excavated by the Butler expedition, yielded an amphora "filled with astragaloi" (Tomb 720; description in field card P1279 by G. H. Chase; I owe this information to C. H. Greenewalt). "According to Herodotus (1.94) the Lydians invented the game of knucklebones."

[17]Hoffmann 1964; Carington Smith 1975; McLauchlin 1981. The number of loomweights on an ancient loom was estimated by G. R. Davidson at about 60–70 (Davidson and Thompson 1943: 65–73). At Gordion, 21 loomweights were found in a row 1.59 m long, in TB 7, giving the size of one of the looms in use there. Huge numbers of loomweights were stored in some of the buildings (up to 800 in TB 1), with comparable quantities of spindle whorls (about 175 in CC 3), but these attest the production of textiles on a massive palatial scale, rather than typical household production (DeVries 1980, esp. 39–40). Groups of loomweights from houses at Olynthus typically range in number from about 20 to 60 or more, although it is often unclear whether these had fallen from a loom or were being stored. One loom, however, had 43 weights of three different types, found in a line 1.10 m long. Larger numbers were occasionally found, for instance a cluster of 247 loomweights in one house, again attesting mass production (Robinson 1946: 207; 34 n. 105). There may well be more loomweights in the unexcavated area south of this year's trench. For the products of Lydian looms, see Greenewalt and Majewski 1980.

[18]Hardware with L-shaped shafts M84.18: 8984 and M85.22: 9189; for locations, fig. 10.

[19]Skyphos P85.40: 9127; lid P85.73: 9192. The other vessels were not mended or inventoried at the end of the 1985 season.

[20]P85.67: 9178. Recovered from "hard packed earth underneath marble slab paving" at E 137.5-140.5/S 70-72.5 on the 'B' grid. From the shoulder of lebes or crater. Clay fine, micaceous, reddish-brown (Munsell 2.5 YR 5/6). Inside, streaky glaze. Outside, white slip over which figural decoration in brown glaze (dark where concentrated, pale where thin) and incision.

[21]To A. E. Furtwängler on brief examination and to the writer, several aspects of the fragment (for the writer the naturalism of the eye, implied narrative character of the vase picture [from the bridle and adjunct features], implied model of Attic black-figure painting [from the incision]) suggested a date in the later sixth or first half of the fifth century. An Eastern Greek-style pottery fragment with chariot horses from Old Smyrna, for which E. Akurgal proposed a date of

640–630 B.C. (Akurgal 1983: 142, pls. Ea, 109a) and the unique Late Assyrian parallels to the nose band remarked by M. A. Littauer, however, may support an earlier date. (For bridled cavalry horse[s] of Achaemenid style on a bowl from Cappadocia [Maşat Höyük], Özgüç 1982: 51, 123, pls. 1, 64.)

To date, pre-Hellenistic pottery recovered from the Brick Fall layer of Colossal Lydian Structure (presumably the context of P85.67: 9178) and from the surface of the hillock largely created by the structure has seemed no earlier than ca. 575 B.C. Diagnostic pottery items include fragments of Little Master cup and Fikellura amphora from Brick Fall (Greenewalt *et al.* 1983: 6; Greenewalt *et al.* 1985: 73, 76, fig. 22) and a black-figure fragment that G. Bakır has suggested may be by the Polos Painter, and which would therefore be Attic, not "Eastern Greek or Anatolian," as published (Greenewalt, Sterud, and Belknap 1982: 20, 24, figs. 20, 21).

[22]The writer even had considered that the layers might be part of a siege mound (Greenewalt 1985: 210), even though evidence that this side of the structure was extramural is slight; cf. Cahill in Greenewalt, Cahill, and Rautman (this issue; for substantial construction of the Archaic period to the east, however, above, preceding section in text).

[23]A layer of "hard-packed, clay like" soil that "contained exclusively Lydian pottery" rested on Brick Fall at the northwest corner of the trench. Excavator K. E. Welch hypothesized that this "somewhat problematic layer" is debris from the structure core, which originally rested at a relatively high level, behind the brick superstructure, and, after the collapse of the superstructure (which resulted in Brick Fall) "slumped into its present position . . . when there was nothing left to retain it" (K. E. Welch, *MMS* III 1985, final report manuscript, pp. 7–8).

[24]According to D. F. Belknap, these three spurs together with three narrower ones also on the north side of the Acropolis belong to a fluvial terrace formed by the Hermus River and dissected by erosion in the late Pleistocene or Holocene age; Belknap in Greenewalt, Sterud, and Belknap 1982: 8–10, with figs. 5, 6 (the latter showing the most easterly of the flat-topped spurs, investigated by N. D. Cahill in 1983; Greenewalt, Rautman, and Meriç 1986: 17–18). For the prominence in the landscape of the three flat-topped spurs, Greenewalt, Rautman, and Meriç 1986: 14, fig. 18.

[25]Kantharos P85.47: 9152; cf. Schäfer 1968: 64–100, esp. 68–69, 79–80. Other diagnostic items included a fragment of another vessel decorated with relief appliqué, P85.71: 9187; a fragmentary piriform jar of Pergamene ware, P85.41: 9128; fragments of a green-glaze open vessel and of late Hellenistic-early Roman lamps.

[26]Quotes are from C. Ratté, *ByzFort* 1985 final report manuscript, p. 5. The colored bars, S85.10: 9110, are approximately the same size; for each, max. pr.

L. 0.0252 m; W. 0.014–0.017 m; Th. 0.017 m. The ensemble has a smooth exterior surface and a rough interior, with traces of mortar. The earliest evidence for colored *opus sectile* in wall decoration of Greek, or Hellenizing, architecture is the third-hand report, published in 1581, of the interior of the Mausoleum of Halicarnassus, with "listeaux ou plattes bandes de marbre de diuerses couleurs ornées do moulures et sculptures, . . ." (Jeppesen and Luttrell 1986: 186); for C. T. Newton's translation of this account, Newton and Pullan 1862: 76–79; Jeppesen 1958: 12; for the credibility of the account, Jeppesen and Luttrell 1986: 170–74. The oldest surviving examples are from Pompeii and Herculaneum (e.g., the House of the Colored Capitals, VII.4.31–51, at Pompeii; the House of the Telephos Relief at Herculaneum). For the First Pompeian or Masonry style, Bruno 1969; Laidlaw 1985.

[27]The disposition of these layers shows that their deposit was not contemporaneous with the setting of individual courses and suggests that in some places burial of the face followed construction of several courses, that in others the original chip deposits had been disturbed and the chips redeposited during construction of the terrace. The disposition of chip layers is recorded in C. Ratté, *ByzFort* 1985 final report manuscript, pp. 12–13, and in Ratté's fieldbooks.

[28]For concealment the limestone chip layers by themselves are conclusive evidence. The absence in the terrace masonry of systematic, crisply-defined borders on block faces (the purpose of which is presumably to enhance appearances, either as a feature in its own right or as an aid to final trim), in contrast to the presence of such borders in other masonry construction at Sardis (e.g., revetment walls on the Acropolis summit; tomb chamber of Alyattes; crepis wall in Karnıyarık Tepe, the "Tomb of Gyges") is consistent with intent to conceal the masonry.

[29]Like the lower revetment wall on the Acropolis summit, Ramage 1972: 15–19.

[30]The amphora fragment, P85.29: 9107, measures only 0.026 × 0.026 m, and is 0.003 m thick. Bakır opined that the incised lines are too thin to be earlier than the time of Lydos and Tyrrhenian amphorae. Von Bothmer's opinion was based on a color photograph. In a letter of 23 September 1985 he wrote, "the red rim of the shield and the careless incisions on the thighs suggest a work by the Painter of Louvre F6. . . , one of two or three warriors standing side by side, rather than a single warrior as on *ABV* 125, 39." (As an example of such a work, von Bothmer sent pictures of an amphora by the painter of Louvre F6 in the Paris market.)

[31]For evidence that the fall of Croesus occurred in the later 540s, see Cargill 1977 and Burstein 1984.

[32]The case for Lydian and Ionian inspiration and workmanship on the closely similar Tall-i Takht at Pasargadae, royal city of Cyrus the Great in Iran, has been argued by C. Nylander; Nylander 1970: 75–91;

Stronach 1978: 20–23.

[33]The red-orange pigment on the painted plaster of the Roman balustrade was identified by conservator L. A. Goldberg was vermillion, possibly with some haematite and red ochre particles, on the basis of analysis of small samples that were exported to the U.S. with the permission of Turkish authorities. One sample was mounted in Aroclor 5442 and examined under a polarizing light microscope at magnifications of 100X and 400X. "Another sample was subjected to a wet chemical test to verify the presence of mercury" (manuscript report by Goldberg).

The bone handle, BI85.1: 9010, is 0.050 m long and contains a segment of iron bar. The skyphos or kantharos fragments are P85.3: 8997 and P85.4: 9020. The terracotta figurine, T85.1: 9024, is generally similar to Cybele figurines from Troy and Pergamon, Thompson 1963: 77–84; Töpperwein 1976: 49–53.

[34]The brick was partly burnt; whether deliberately semibaked (like that of Colossal Lydian Structure at sector MMS [for which Cahill in Greenewalt, Cahill, and Rautman this issue] and presumably of the Archaic building in Mound 2 [see n. 40]) or as a consequence of destruction was unclear.

[35]This fragment, S85.14: 9150, is evidently the top projecting part of a thicker member, which functioned as a support: the back surface is an irregular break; the ragged edge at the back of the volute underside indicates that the original member extended below the volute, behind its plane; and the top surface, flat and scored with striations, resembles a bearing surface. L. 0.32 m; H. 0.128 m; Th. 0.043 m.

[36]Diagnostic pottery included a black burnished ("bucchero") rim of a jug type common at Gordion, P85.54: 9162; a trefoil-mouth oinochoe with simple orientalizing decoration, P85.49: 9155; a large closed vessel with geometric bichrome decoration, P85.49: 9155; and a Corinthian vessel (with profile like that of an olpe shoulder; with glazed inside) decorated outside with black ground and incised scale pattern, P85.48: 9153. None of the Anatolian pottery can be precisely dated. The assemblage may indicate for the stratum a date between ca. 630 and 575 B.C.

[37]The shaped pieces are respectively S85.13: 9147 and S85.12: 9144. The parallel from the İkiztepe tumulus near Güre (cited in Tezcan 1979: 394) is in Ankara, Museum of Anatolian Civilizations 75.10.66. For stone bowls from Persepolis (the Treasury of the Palace), Schmidt 1957: pls. 57, nos. 5–7; 62, nos. 5, 9, 11. Doç. Dr. Yılmaz Savaşçın, of the Geology Division, Aegean University (Bornova-Izmir), who examined the fragments, said that the same kind of chalcedony occurs in natural deposits in the region between Salihli and Uşak.

[38]For the tile type and its theme, Shear 1923; 1926: 9–12; Hanfmann 1958: 65–72. For the recreated tiles, Greenewalt, Sterud, and Belknap 1982: 29, fig. 29; Greenewalt et al. 1983: 27, fig. 34; Ramage and Ramage

1983: 24, fig. 27. Once the recreated "Theseus and Minotaur" tiles had been installed, the lifeless imbalance of form and space created by the restored straight-leg stance—of the several stance options that at the time of recreation had seemed possible for the unattested lower part of the tile, the one endorsed by the writer as being the least controversial—was recognized to be implausible for Archaic Greek (and Lydian hellenizing) design.

[39]For partridge file-type tiles, Greenewalt et al. 1983: 28 and references. The use of two glazes/slips and the color scheme used for the partridges of the reconstructed tiles at Sardis (for which Greenewalt et al. 1983: 28); Ramage and Ramage 1983: 24, fig. 27) were proposed by M. D. Morris.

[40]Concentrated in an area of ca. 100 m^2 were some 20–25 diagnostic Archaic pottery items (bowls, skyphoi, dishes, crater painted in streaky glaze with superposed bands in dark or white, or in black-on-red; local "Ionian cup" with concentric rings or spirals in the tondo; wavy-line closed vessel), a terracotta sima plaque fragment with molded griffin in relief; and countless fragments of semibaked brick (similar to that of the Brick Fall from Colossal Lydian Structure).

Until 1985 the considerable surface area of the mounds, their thorough surface cultivation, and the apparent thickness of Roman overburden had discouraged plans to excavate for Archaic deposits below the mound surfaces.

[41]The situation resembles that of Colossal Lydian Structure with its Brick Fall (above). One of the bricks carried an incised mark that resembles neither an alphabetic letter nor an alphabetic monogram; T85.7: 9056.

The looseness of the debris created treacherous digging conditions and precluded maintenance of vertical trench scarps (hence the irregular trench contour shown in figs. 30, 31).

[42]The earliest building with such masonry should be the crepis wall of Karnıyarık Tepe, the "Tomb of Gyges" tumulus at Bin Tepe (Hanfmann 1983: 57–58 and figs. 105–110). If not Gyges' tumulus (v. Smith 1986, for philological evidence that gugu should not be Gyges in Lydian), Karnıyarık Tepe nevertheless should date no later than ca. 610 B.C. (the accession of Alyattes): a tumulus so large and ostentatious is unlikely to have been raised for less than a king; and the last Lydian kings, who ruled in the sixth century, either had no tumulus (presumably; Croesus) or had one elsewhere (Alyattes; cf. von Olfers 1858; Hanfmann 1963: 52–57). Charcoal grains from a lens of dumped debris (which also contained pottery of somewhat diagnostic shapes and decoration; Hanfmann 1966: 27, and fig. 23) deep within Karnıyarık Tepe yielded a C^{14} date of 2560 ± 90 B.P., or 610 B.C. ± 90 years (Beta Analytic, Inc., Coral Gables, FL; job no. Beta-13711, reported 22.X.1985). For the dates of other graves that contain similar masonry, Hanfmann 1963: 57–59; 1964: 55–56. For the date of masonry on the Acropolis summit and at sector

ByzFort, Ramage 1972: 15–19 and above). This kind of masonry is not attested in Hellenistic or Roman construction.

[43] As T. N. Howe has postulated, the Archaic terraces at ByzFort and "Field 49" (above, and n. 32) could belong to a program of Acropolis building independent of the lower city.

[44] Ramage and Mitten's studies concern the results of excavation at HoB between 1958 and 1970; for a preliminary summary, see Ramage in Hanfmann 1983: 26–33.

[45] These fibulae are M85.20: 9185, type IV (similar to another from sector HoB recovered in 1984, M84.9: 8905), and M85.21: 9186. For fibulae from Sardis, Waldbaum 1983a: 112–16; Caner 1983: 23.

[46] R. E. Mooney, *HoB* 1986 final report manuscript, p. 7. Pottery in these water-laid layers included a few diagnostic fragments of Protogeometric, sub-Mycenaean, and Late Bronze Age shapes and decorative conventions; but out of context they provide at best only general clues to the locale and level of Bronze Age occupation in this part of the sector.

REFERENCES

Åkerström, A.
1966   *Die Architektonischen Terrakotten Klein-asiens.* Skrifter Utgivna av Svenska Institutet i Athen, 4°, XI. Lund: Gleerup.

Akurgal, E.
1983   Alt-Smyrna I, Wohnschichten und Athena-tempel. Türk Tarih Kurumu Yayınları, V. 40. Ankara: Türk Tarih Kurumu.

Albenda, P.
1977   Landscape Bas-Reliefs in the *Bīt-Ḥilāni* of Ashurbanipal. *Bulletin of the American Schools of Oriental Research* 225: 29–48.

Anderson, J. K.
1961   *Ancient Greek Horsemanship.* Berkeley, CA: University of California.

Balty, J. C.
1984   Notes sur l'habitat romain, byzantin et arabe d'Apamée: rapport de synthèse. Pp. 471–501 in *Apamée de Syrie. Bilan des recherches archéologiques 1973-1979, Aspects de l'architecture domestique d'Apamée*, ed. J. Balty. Fouilles d'Apamée de Syrie, Miscellanea 13. Brussels: Centre Belge de Recherches Archéologiques à Apamée de Syrie.

Bruno, V.
1969   Antecedents of the Pompeian First Style. *American Journal of Archaeology* 73: 305–17.

Burstein, S. M.
1984   A New Tabula Iliaca: The Vasek Polak Chronicle. *J. Paul Getty Museum Journal* 12: 153–62.

Caner, E.
1983   *Fibeln in Anatolien I.* Prähistorische Bronzefunde XIV. 8. Munich: C. H. Beck.

Cargill, J.
1977   The Nabonidus Chronicle and the Fall of Lydia. *American Journal of Ancient History* 2: 97–116.

Carington Smith, J.
1975   *Spinning, Weaving and Textile Manufacture in Prehistoric Greece.* Ph.D. Dissertation, University of Tasmania, Hobart.

Davidson, G. R., and Thompson, D. B.
1943   *Small Objects from the Pnyx*, I. *Hesperia* Supplement 7. Princeton: American School of Classical Studies.

DeVries, K.
1980   Greeks and Phrygians in the Early Iron Age. Pp. 33–49 in *From Athens to Gordion. The Papers of a Memorial Symposium for Rodney S. Young*, ed. K. DeVries. University Museum Papers 1. Philadelphia, PA: The University Museum, University of Pennsylvania.

Dunbabin, T. J. *et al.*
1962   *Perachora, the Sanctuaries of Hera Akraia and Limenia, II: Pottery, Ivories, Scarabs and Other Objects from the Votive Deposit of Hera Limenia excavated by Humphry Payne.* Oxford: Clarendon.

Furtwängler, A. E.
1980   Zur Deutung der Obeloi im Lichte samischer Neufunde. Pp. 81–98 in *Tainia. Festschrift für Roland Hampe*, eds. H. A. Cahn and E. Simon. Mainz: Philipp von Zabern.

Goodenough, E. R.
1953   *Jewish Symbols in the Greco-Roman Period.* New York: Pantheon.

Greenewalt, C. H., Jr.
1972   Two Lydian Graves at Sardis. *California Studies in Classical Antiquity* 5: 113–45.
1979   The Sardis Campaign of 1977. *Bulletin of the American Schools of Oriental Research* 233: 1–32.
1985   Sardis, 1984. Pp. 209–11 in Recent Archaeological Research in Turkey. *Anatolian Studies* 35.

Greenewalt, C. H., Jr.; Cahill, N. D.; and Rautman, M. L.
1987   The Sardis Campaign of 1984. *Bulletin of the American Schools of Oriental Research Supplement* 25: 13–54.

Greenewalt, C. H., Jr., and Majewski, L. J.
1980   Lydian Textiles. Pp. 133–47 in *From Athens to Gordion. The Papers of a Memorial Symposium for Rodney S. Young*, ed. K. DeVries. University Museum Papers 1. Philadelphia, PA: The University Museum, University of Pennsylvania.

Greenewalt, C. H., Jr.; Ramage, A.; Sullivan, D. G.; Nayır, K.; and Tulga, A.
1983   The Sardis Campaigns of 1979 and 1980. *Bulletin of the American Schools of Oriental Research* 249: 1–44.

Greenewalt, C. H., Jr.; Rautman, M. L.; and Meriç, R.
1986   The Sardis Campaign of 1983. *Bulletin of the American Schools of Oriental Research Supplement* 24: 1–30.

Greenewalt, C. H., Jr.; Sterud, E. L.; and Belknap, D. F.
1982   The Sardis Campaign of 1978. *Bulletin of the American Schools of Oriental Research* 245: 1–34.

Greenewalt, C. H., Jr.; Sullivan, D. G.; Ratté, C., and Howe, T. N.
1985   The Sardis Campaigns of 1981 and 1982. *Bulletin of the American Schools of Oriental Research Supplement* 23: 53–92.

Hanfmann, G. M. A.
1958   Lydiaka. *Harvard Studies in Classical Philology* 63: 65–79.
1959   Excavations at Sardis, 1958. *Bulletin of the American Schools of Oriental Research* 154: 5–32.
1960   Excavations at Sardis, 1959. *Bulletin of the American Schools of Oriental Research* 157: 8–43.
1961   The Third Campaign at Sardis (1960). *Bulletin of the American Schools of Oriental Research* 162: 8–49.
1962   The Fourth Campaign at Sardis (1961). *Bulletin of the American Schools of Oriental Research* 166: 1–57.
1963   The Fifth Campaign at Sardis (1962). *Bulletin of the American Schools of Oriental Research* 170: 1–65.
1964   The Sixth Campaign at Sardis (1963). *Bulletin of the American Schools of Oriental Research* 174: 3–58.
1966   The Eighth Campaign at Sardis (1965). *Bulletin of the American Schools of Oriental Research* 182: 2–54.
1967   The Ninth Campaign at Sardis (1966). *Bulletin of the American Schools of Oriental Research* 186: 17–52.
1983   *Sardis from Prehistoric to Roman Times; Results of the Archaeological Exploration of Sardis 1958–1975*. Cambridge, MA: Harvard.

Hanfmann, G. M. A., and Thomas, R. S.
1971   The Thirteenth Campaign at Sardis (1970). *Bulletin of the American Schools of Oriental Research* 203: 5–22.

Hanfmann, G. M. A., and Waldbaum, J. C.
1975   *Sardis Report 1. A Survey of Sardis and the Major Monuments Outside the City Walls*. Cambridge, MA: Harvard.

Hauptmann, H.
1972   Die Grabungen auf dem Norşun-Tepe, 1970. *Middle East Technical University Keban Project Publications* 1.3. Ankara: Middle East Technical University.
1983   Neue Funde eurasischer Steppennomaden in Kleinasien. Pp. 251–70 in *Beiträge zur Altertumskunde Kleinasiens; Festschrift für Kurt Bittel*, eds. R. M. Boehmer, H. Hauptmann. Mainz: Philipp von Zabern.

Hayes, J. W.
1972   *Late Roman Pottery*. London: British School at Rome.
1980   *Supplement to Late Roman Pottery*. London: British School at Rome.

Hoffmann, M.
1964   *The Warp-Weighted Loom; Studies in the History and Technology of an Ancient Implement*. Studia Norvegica 14. Oslo: Universitetsforlag.

Hogarth, D. G.
1908   *Excavations at Ephesus, the Archaic Artemisia*. London: British Museum.

Hörmann, H. *et al.*
1951   *Die Johanneskirche*. Forschungen in Ephesos 4.3. Vienna: Österreichisches Archäologisches Institut.

Jeppesen, K.
1958   *Paradeigmata; Three Mid-Fourth Century Main Works of Hellenic Architecture Reconsidered*. Jutland Archaeological Society Publications IV. Aarhus: Aarhus University.

Jeppesen, K., and Luttrell, A.
1986   *The Maussolleion at Halikarnassos, Reports of the Danish Archaeological Expedition to Bodrum, 2. The Written Sources and their Archaeological Background*. Jutland Archaeological Society Publications 15. 2. Aarhus: Aarhus University.

Jobst, W.
1977   *Römische Mosaiken aus Ephesos I. Die*

Hanghäuser des Embolos. Forschungen in Ephesos 8. 2. Vienna: Österreichische Akademie der Wissenschaften.

Laidlaw, A.
1985 *The First Style in Pompeii; Architecture and Painting*. Archaeologica 57. Rome: Georgio Bretschneider.

Littauer, M. A., and Crouwel, J. H.
1983 Chariots in Late Bronze Age Greece. *Antiquity* 57: 187–92.

Mansel, A. M.
1978 *Side. 1947–1966 Yılları Kazıları ve Araştırmalarının Sonuçları*. Ankara: Türk Tarih Kurumu.

McLauchlin, B. K.
1981 New Evidence on the Mechanics of Loom Weights. *American Journal of Archaeology* 85: 79–81.

Moore, D. T., and Oddy, W. A.
1985 Touchstones: Some Aspects of their Nomenclature, Petrography and Provenance. *Journal of Archaeological Science* 12: 59–80.

Newton, C. T., and Pullan, R. P.
1862 *A History of Discoveries at Halicarnassus, Cnidus, and Branchidae*. London: Day and Son.

Nylander, C.
1970 *Ionians in Pasargadae; Studies in Old Persian Architecture*. Boreas; Uppsala Studies in Ancient Mediterranean and Near Eastern Civilizations 1. Uppsala: Uppsala University.

von Olfers, J. F. M.
1858 Über die lydischen Königsgräber bei Sardes und den Grabhügel des Alyattes, nach dem Bericht des K. General-Consuls Spiegelthal zu Smyrna. *Abhandlungen der Königlichen Akademie der Wissenschaften zu Berlin* 539–56.

Özgüç, T.
1982 *Maşat Höyük II. Boğazköy'un Kuzeydoğusunda bir Hitit merkezi / a Hittite center northeast of Boğazköy*. Türk Tarih Kurumu Yayınları V. 38. Ankara: Türk Tarih Kurumu.

Payne, H.
1931 *Necrocorinthia; A Study of Corinthian Art in the Archaic Period*. Oxford: Clarendon.

Petrie, W. M. F.
1906 *Hyksos and Israelite Cities*. British School of Archaeology in Egypt and Egyptian Research Account 12. London: School of Archaeology, University College.

Ramage, A.
1972 The Fourteenth Campaign at Sardis (1971). *Bulletin of the American Schools of Oriental Research* 206: 9–39.

1978 *Lydian Houses and Architectural Terracottas*. Sardis Monograph 5. Cambridge, MA: Harvard.

Ramage, A., and Ramage, N. H.
1983 *Twenty-Five Years of Discovery at Sardis, 1958–1983*. Cambridge, MA: Archaeological Exploration of Sardis.

Ramage, N. H.
1986 Two New Attic Cups and the Siege of Sardis. *American Journal of Archaeology* 90: 419–24.

Reifenberg, A.
1936 Jüdische Lampen. *Journal of the Palestine Oriental Society* 16: 166–79.

Robinson, D. M.
1946 *Excavations at Olynthus 12; Domestic and Public Architecture*. Johns Hopkins Studies in Archaeology 36. Baltimore, MD: Johns Hopkins University.

Schäfer, G.
1968 *Hellenistische Keramik aus Pergamon*. Pergamenische Forschungen 2. Berlin: Walter de Gruyter.

Schmidt, E. F.
1957 *Persepolis II. Contents of the Treasury and Other Discoveries*. The University of Chicago Oriental Institute Publications 69. Chicago: University of Chicago.

Sethe, K.
1933 Die Bau- und Denkmalstein der alten Ägypter und ihre Namen. *Sitzungsberichte der Deutschen Akademie der Wissenschaft zu Berlin* 894–905.

Shear, T. L.
1923 A Terra-Cotta Relief from Sardis. *American Journal of Archaeology* 27: 131–50.

1926 *Terra-Cottas, Part One; Architectural Terra-Cottas, Sardis X*. Cambridge: Cambridge University.

Smith, D. N.
1986 *Herodotos' Use of Material Evidence*. Ph.D. dissertation, University of California, Berkeley.

Stronach, D. B.
1978 *Pasargadae; A Report on the Excavations Conducted by the British Institute of Persian Studies from 1961 to 1963*. Oxford: Clarendon.

Tezcan, B.
1979 İkiztepe Kazısı. Pp. 391–97 in *VIII Türk Tarih Kongresi, Ankara, 11–15 Ekim 1976; Kongreye Sunulan Bildiriler* I. Türk Tarih Kurumu Yayınları IX. 8. Ankara: Türk Tarih Kurumu.

Thompson, D. B.
1963 *The Terracotta Figurines of the Hellenistic*

Period. Troy, Supplementary Monograph 3. Princeton, NJ: Princeton.

Töpperwein, E.
1976   *Terrakotten von Pergamon.* Pergamenische Forschungen 3. Berlin: Walter de Gruyter.

Waldbaum, J. C.
1983a   *Metalwork from Sardis.* Sardis Monograph 8. Cambridge, MA: Harvard.

1983b   An Unfinished Bronze Ibex from Sardis. *Antike Kunst* 26: 67–72.

Webb, V.
1978   *Archaic Greek Faience; Miniature Scent Bottles and Related Objects from East Greece, 650–500 B.C.* Warminster: Aris and Phillips.

The Neolithic Village of ᶜAin Ghåzāl, Jordan: Preliminary Report on the 1985 Season

GARY O. ROLLEFSON
Department of Anthropology
San Diego State University
San Diego, CA 92182

ALAN H. SIMMONS
Desert Research Institute
P.O. Box 60220
University of Nevada
Reno, NV 89506

The 1985 emergency excavation season at ᶜAin Ghåzāl recovered two new groups of PPNB plaster human statuary. One group consisted of a single statue head while the other group contained a minimum of 11 statues and busts. A series of radiocarbon dates chronicles the PPNB development of the site from 7250–6200 B.C., and additional information was obtained from later PPNC and Yarmoukian occupations.

INTRODUCTION

It was originally planned that the third season of excavations in 1984 would mark the end of the first phase of the ᶜAin Ghåzāl Archaeological Project, a phase oriented principally to the rescue of many archaeological features exposed and damaged by commercial and highway construction over the past 20 years. Subsequent field campaigns were to focus on undisturbed areas of the large Neolithic town. However, two pits containing molded plaster fragments similar to the human statuary recovered in 1983 (Rollefson et al. 1985) were discovered in the final week of the 1984 season, and this led to an emergency rescue season for the summer of 1985 (Rollefson and Simmons 1986).[1]

The work in 1985 focused on two very different problems. The first pit in Square 3081 (fig. 1) was small, and preparation for removal of the plaster fragments entailed only the partial excavation of sterile fill, the consolidation of the artifacts, and the isolation of the cache on a pedestal of basal clay for crating, packing, and extraction from the trench (cf. Rollefson 1983). Because the sediments in and around the pit were sterile, the plaster

fragments were the only cultural information this trench produced in 1985.

The second pit was more formidable in both dimensions and demands. While work was under way by the conservator on the small pit in Square 3081, a trench measuring approximately 3.0 × 1.5 m was opened in Square 3282, just to the northwest (fig. 1), to expose the larger statuary cache. Eventually this trench yielded more than 3.2 m of deposits down to sterile basal clay, exposing approximately 1.2 to 1.4 m of Yarmoukian occupations in the upper part of the sequence and nearly 2.0 m of Pre-Pottery Neolithic (PPN) habitations in the lower part (fig. 2). As work progressed on the statuary cache in Square 3282, the trench was expanded another 2.0 m toward the west to increase the exposure of the Yarmoukian levels. Altogether, the Yarmoukian material recovered in 1985 came from a maximum area of about 3.5 × 3 m to an average depth of approximately 1.3 m. The PPN excavations sampled a maximum of about 3.0 × 2.0 m (at the bottom of the bulldozer section) with an average thickness of about 2.0 m. The volume of sediment is thus nearly 13.7 m^3 for the Yarmoukian period and 12 m^3 for the PPN layers.

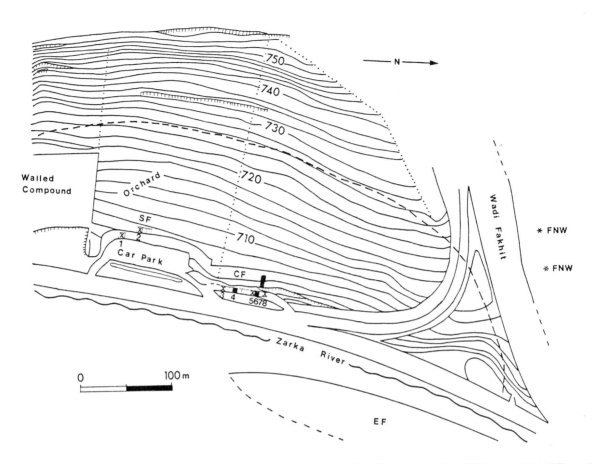

Fig. 1. ʿAin Ghazāl site maps, showing the location of the South Field (SF), Central Field (CF), East Field (EF), and Far Northwest (FNW) sections of the site. Numbered excavation squares show the location of radiocarbon samples referred to in Table 6: 1:Square 4048; 2:Square 4452; 3:Square 3273; 4:Square 3076; 5:Square 3080; 6:Square 3081; 7:Square 3282; 8:Square 3083. (Drawing by Deborah Fridell)

Although the excavation team gave principal attention to excavating during the six-week season in 1985, the return to ʿAin Ghazāl also provided the opportunity to complete the photography and stratigraphic drawing of the more than 600 m of bulldozer sections, a task we began in 1984. During this work, small stratified samples of PPNB artifacts were excavated from two severely damaged houses in the Central Field (from Square 3285, 15 m north of Square 3282, and from Square 3288, an additional 15 m north of Square 3285). In addition to the collections of chipped stone tools, faunal remains, and sparse small finds, an important exposure of painted designs on a house floor was also recorded (below).

THE STATUARY REMAINS

When the pits were discovered in 1984, the team strongly suspected that both pits contained important new evidence of PPNB plaster human statuary. Fieldwork in 1985 confirmed the theory, but the methods used to remove the statuary allowed for little detailed examination in the field.

The Statue Head (Square 3081)

The excavators uncovered a small depression, ca. 40 × 30 × 20 cm that had been dug into sterile basal clay; in the center of this pit they found a single plaster human statue head, placed face down and covered with a fill of fine clay with inclusions of small fragments of chalk and yellowish floor plaster. This interment was later covered by redeposited clay that eventually became compacted, characterized as a stable surface for an unknown period of time. Several stages of domestic building construction occurred subsequently. From the contents of a stone-lined pit stratigraphically later than the statuary deposit,

1987 THE EARLY NEOLITHIC VILLAGE OF ᶜAIN GHAZĀL, JORDAN 95

an abundant charcoal sample yielded a date of 7100 ± 80 B.C. (below), which indicated that the statue head was even older. To our knowledge, this makes the ᶜAin Ghazāl specimen the oldest known statuary in the Near East, almost 1,000 years earlier than the date suggested for the material from Jericho (Kenyon 1957: 74).[2]

Due to the weight of successive deposits above the pit, the hollow statue head collapsed into itself. Several *in situ* fragments suggest that the original ear-to-ear diameter was approximately 15–20 cm, which would be within the range for the dimensions for heads in the statuary cache from 1983. Other similarities with the 1983 material are revealed by corded impressions on the interior surface, indicating a similar method of construction (Rollefson 1983: 30); the molded ear fragment (left side?) is similar (Tubb 1985). Bitumen eyeliner surrounded one eye, which retained a thin circular disc of bitumen representing the iris, features also noted among the 1983 statuary cache. But there were also some distinctive features: the nose of the head from Square 3081 appears to be less stylized and more detailed, and the entire exterior surface of the head appears to have been "washed" with a dilute suspension of a red pigment, giving the whole sculpture a characteristic pinkish hue not seen in the 1983 objects.

The Large Cache of Statuary (Square 3282)

The second statuary cache was located beneath approximately 2.5 m of cultural deposits (fig. 2). Because it lay deep in the section, a great deal of time was necessary to expose and prepare the objects for removal; this also afforded the opportunity to obtain a complete stratigraphic sequence of occupations for this part of ᶜAin Ghazāl.

Like its counterpart in 1983, this collection of plaster statues and busts was found carefully placed in two tiers in a large pit (ca. 1.5 × 1.0 m) that had been cut through the floor of an abandoned house. The upper layer had evidently been exposed some time later in view of its relatively poorer condition: the statuary was badly cracked and the surfaces had developed a deep gray color as the result of the presence of an overlying and even intermingling ashy deposit. The southeastern corner of the cache had been badly damaged in antiquity by an intrusive pit, and the disturbance to this part of the statuary group was further aggravated by bulldozers that cut through the outer edge of the pit.

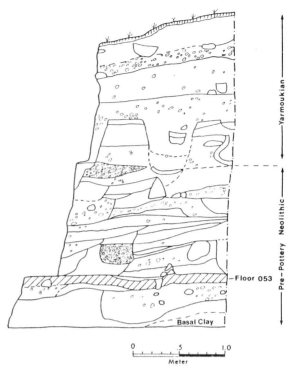

Fig. 2. Stratigraphic sequence in south balk of Square 3282. The statuary pit cut through Floor 053 near the bottom of the section. (Drawing by Deborah Fridell)

In-field conservation efforts concentrated on the recovery of loose statuary fragments, the removal of unstable rubbly components in the pit that may have caused additional damage during the transportation of the cache to the laboratory, and on the consolidation of exposed but relatively intact figures. Less of the pit contents was exposed than with the 1983 cache, and thus less information about the more recent finds is available at this time. Nevertheless, several points can be made that show both shared and distinctive features between the two major statuary collections.

The 1985 group was rigidly aligned along a northeast–southwest axis, with heads oriented to the southwest end of the pit (Rollefson 1983: 30; fig. 1 here). Busts and statues were mingled together in the cache from Square 3282, not in separate groups as was the case with the 1983 collection. Because of the damage incurred to the upper layer, it was not always possible to distinguish busts and statues, but at least seven figures were detected; how many more may have occupied the southeast part of the pit could not be estimated in the field (fig. 3). The lower layer of statuary, which was in an excellent state of preservation, required less preparatory work, so little is known of the composition of this tier beyond the unmistakable outlines of at least four more busts or statues (fig. 4).

The method of statue and bust manufacture appears to be congruent with the figures of the 1983 group (Rollefson 1983: 30–32), but details concerning cosmetic treatment of the faces and other areas of the bodies are very scanty. Bitumen eyeliner was found on several faces in the upper tier, but there did not seem to be green dioptase powder on the lower eyeliner segment in the 1985 statuary (Tubb 1985) as there was on pieces found in 1983. One iris was visible, and initial impressions suggest it may be more angular than the circular irises of the 1983 cache; on the other hand, this may simply represent a post-depositional distortion. A small bust face from near the northeast end of the cache appears to share the distinctive "pink wash" visible on the single head from Square 3081.

Although it is clear that the larger cache from 1985 is from a later stratigraphic context than the single head from Square 3081, the temporal relationship of both to the 1983 group of statues and busts is as yet difficult to determine. Charcoal samples from Squares 3282 and 3076 should provide absolute dates in the near future, but for now it appears probable that both large groups come from the early to middle part of the seventh millennium. In any event, it is evident now that a highly sophisticated system of ritual and religion was developed at a very early point in ᶜAin Ghazāl's history, and that this tradition long continued to play a major role in the daily and seasonal lives of the community.

OTHER ARTIFACT SAMPLES

The 1985 fieldwork produced another formidable collection of artifacts and other archaeological information despite the small scale of labor invested during the season. At the present time preliminary analysis of the data is still under way, so only a small amount of interpretation can be relayed.

Chipped Stone Artifacts

More than 20,000 chipped stone artifacts were retrieved from *in situ* deposits in 1985; all of them

Fig. 3. Upper layer of the statuary cache in Square 3282, still surrounded by part of Floor 053. Note the heavy damage to the southeast corner of the pit at upper left. (Photograph by Curt Blair)

have been sorted into major artifact classes (Table 1)[3] and classified according to major tool types (Table 2). The amount of debitage in the PPNB layers is very high considering the relatively small volume of excavated sediment, and this is primarily due to the presence of an extraordinarily dense "chipping floor" just beneath the statuary cache in Square 3282.

The chipping floor (Locus 122) was distinct from other PPN loci in more ways than simply the extreme density of artifacts. The locus represented the entire sequence of lithic reduction of cores to produce suitable blanks for tool manufacture, and the retouch of what must have been a very large number of tools is represented by the dominance of tiny microflakes (note 3). Comparing the artifact class counts in Table 1 for Locus 122 and other PPN loci, every category is significantly different at the .001 or higher level in chi-square tests except for flakes ("other flakes" and "palaeolithic" categories are not taken into account here). Why the flake counts are so similar is not known at this time, although there seems to be an unexplained inverse correlation between flakes and bladelets. It is also curious to note that cores are so poorly represented on the chipping floor, although the small number recovered from Locus 122 may simply reflect sampling bias because of the small area excavated. On the other hand, this particular spot may have been the location of normal core testing and cortex removal prior to taking prepared cores elsewhere for subsequent blank production.

TABLE 1. Absolute and Relative Frequencies of Chipped Stone Artifact Classes from the 1985 Excavations at ᶜAin Gĥazāl

	PPN– Locus 122		Locus 122		PPN Total			Yarmoukian		
	n	%	n	%	n	%	%'	n	%	%'
Bladelets	262	6.0	601	16.7	863	10.8		90	4.9	
Blades	1979	45.3	1317	36.6	3296	41.4	50.3	556	30.3	34.3
Flakes	1805	41.3	1457	40.5	3262	40.9	49.7	1067	58.1	65.7
C.T.E.[a]	143	3.3	183	5.1	326	4.1		24	1.3	
Burin spalls	113	2.6	18	0.5	131	1.6		18	1.0	
Other flakes	15	0.3	12	0.3	27	0.3		9	0.5	
Cores	51	1.2	11	0.3	62	0.8		73	4.0	
(Tools)					(708)	(8.9)		(216)	(11.8)	
Subtotals	4368	100.0	3599	100.0	7967	99.9		1837	100.4	
Microflakes	598	(10.3)	5716[b]	(49.4)	6314	(36.4)		380	(12.3)	
Debris	814	(14.1)	2264[b]	(19.5)	3078	(17.7)		860	(27.9)	
Palaeolithic	8	(0.1)	2	(0.0)	10	(0.1)		8	(0.3)	
Totals	5788		11,581		17,369			3085		Total = 20,454

[a]C.T.E. refers to core trimming elements.
[b]These are estimates based on weights of counted samples.

Fig. 4. Lower tier of statuary in Square 3282. (Photograph by Curt Blair)

Although the flake:flake comparisons for Locus 122 vs. other PPN loci are not statistically significant, differences in blade:flake ratios are meaningful. For Locus 122 the ratio is 47.5:52.5, while for all the other PPN loci the ratio is just reversed at 52.3:47.7. The predominance of flakes in Locus 122 is attributable to the effects of core preparation (especially in terms of the relatively high numbers of cortical flakes). If the artifacts from Locus 122 are excluded from comparisons with the collections from earlier excavation seasons at ʿAin Gh̊azāl, the blade:flake ratios of all PPN loci are very close (cf. Rollefson and Simmons 1986: Table 2). Even when the Locus 122 sample is included with the other PPN loci sampled in 1985, the blade:flake ratio is still slightly in favor of blades, a distinct technological variation from the Yarmoukian collections recovered in 1985 (Table 1).

For the Central Field Yarmoukian layers, the blade:flake ratio is very low, a phenomenon noted in the 1984 season. The ratio is also significantly lower than the Yarmoukian samples excavated from the South Field (cf. Rollefson and Simmons 1986: Tables 1–3). Since the 1985 Central Field exposures represent less than one-fourth those of the South Field, sampling bias may account for some of the significance. In part, at least, this is reflected by the circumstances of the cultural deposits. The South Field produced little or no evidence of domestic architecture, while the artifacts from the Central Field appear to be closely associated with work carried out near the dwellings of the Yarmoukian residents (below).

The chipped stone tools from the PPN and Yarmoukian levels are tabulated in Table 2 (figs. 5–7). For the aceramic Neolithic, the correspondence with the tools from the 1984 Central Field samples is remarkably similar, especially in terms of projectile points, sickle blades, and burins, which together account for more than one-half the 1985 inventory. Values for other tool classes oscillate above and below the mean for the 1982–1984 samples, but this may be due to the relatively small volume of sediments excavated in 1985.

A comparison of tool counts of the 1984 South Field and 1985 Central Field Yarmoukian samples (cf. Rollefson and Simmons 1986: Table 4) indicates major variations, particularly in terms of sickle blades (but note the small absolute numbers in both cases), burins, scrapers, and bifacial tools. Once again, both sampling bias and domestic/

TABLE 2. Absolute and Relative Frequencies of Tool Types from the 1985 Excavations at ʿAin Gh̊azāl (*in situ* Samples Only)

	PPN		Yarmoukian	
Tool type	*n*	*%*	*n*	*%*
Spear points	30	5.5	6	3.4
Arrowheads	—	0.0	7	4.0
Sickles	48	8.9	5	2.8
Burins (all types)	228	42.1	39	22.2
Truncations	17	3.1	7	4.0
Scrapers (all types)	37	6.8	22	12.5
Denticulates	33	6.1	14	8.0
Notches	36	6.6	18	10.2
Perforators/awls/drills	32	5.9	21	11.9
Bifacial tools	35	6.5	22	12.5
Knives	19	3.5	5	2.8
Backed blades	13	2.4	8	4.5
Tanged blades	5	0.9	—	0.0
Other	9	1.7	2	1.1
Subtotals	542	100.0	176	99.9
Retouched blades	28	(4.9)	2	(1.1)
Retouched flakes	4	(0.7)	—	(0.0)
Subtotals	574		178	
Utilized blades	70	(9.9)	8	(3.7)
Utilized flakes	20	(2.8)	9	(5.1)
Indeterminate	44	(6.2)	21	(11.9)
Totals	708		216	

nondomestic contexts probably contribute to the differences.

It was remarked at the end of the 1984 season at ʿAin Gh̊azāl that the Yarmoukian burins represented distinctly different configurations in contrast to this class of tools in the PPNB period (Rollefson and Simmons 1986: Table 5), and Table 3 provides support from the 1985 samples for this observation.

In 1984 a series of aceramic Neolithic cultural deposits (South Phase III) underlay the Yarmoukian levels in the South Field. Among the finds that distinguished the South Phase III assemblages from both the Yarmoukian and PPNB cultural materials, burins also played a major role (Rollefson and Simmons 1986: Table 5). Unfortunately, we have not been able to conclude positively that a "Final PPN" or "PPNC" series also

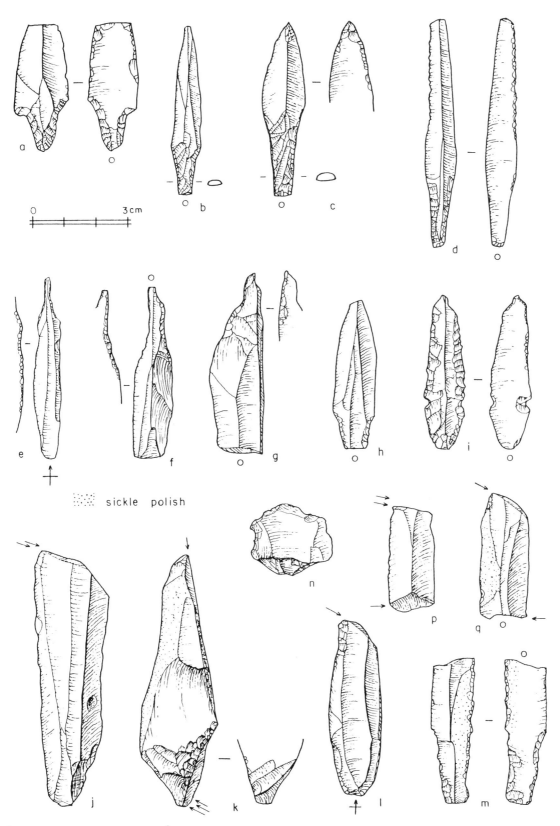

3 cm

sickle polish

Fig. 5. PPN artifacts from ᶜAin Għazāl, 1985. a–c, h–i) projectile points; d) tanged microdenticulate "saw"; e–f) drills; g) borer; j,l, p–q) transverse burins; k) opposed burin; m) tanged sickle blade; n) wedge. (Drawing by Brian Byrd)

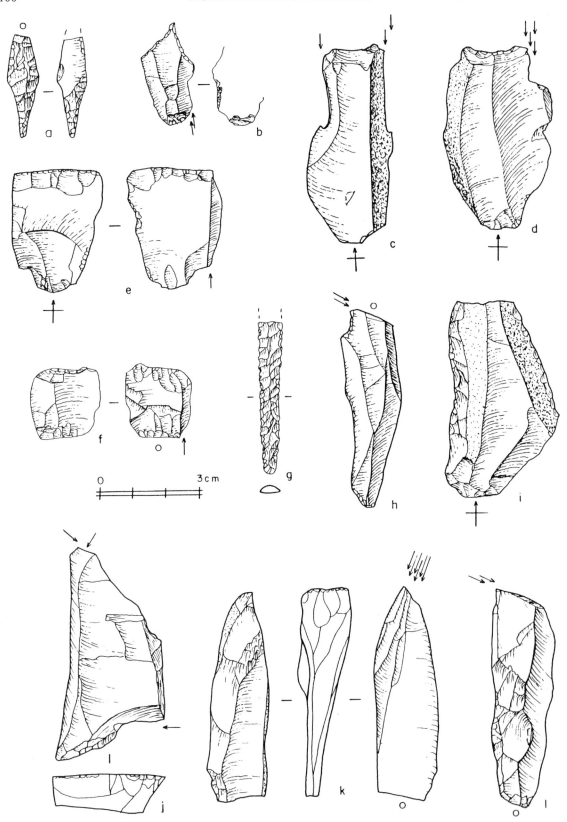

Fig. 6. Flint artifacts from ʿAin Ghazāl 1985. a) arrowhead; b) borer; c–d) burins on truncations; e–f) wedges; g) microdenticulated "saw" with slight sheen; h,l) transverse burins; i) sidescraper; j) opposed burin; k) "other" burin. g–l are PPN; a–f are Yarmoukian. (Drawing by Brian Byrd)

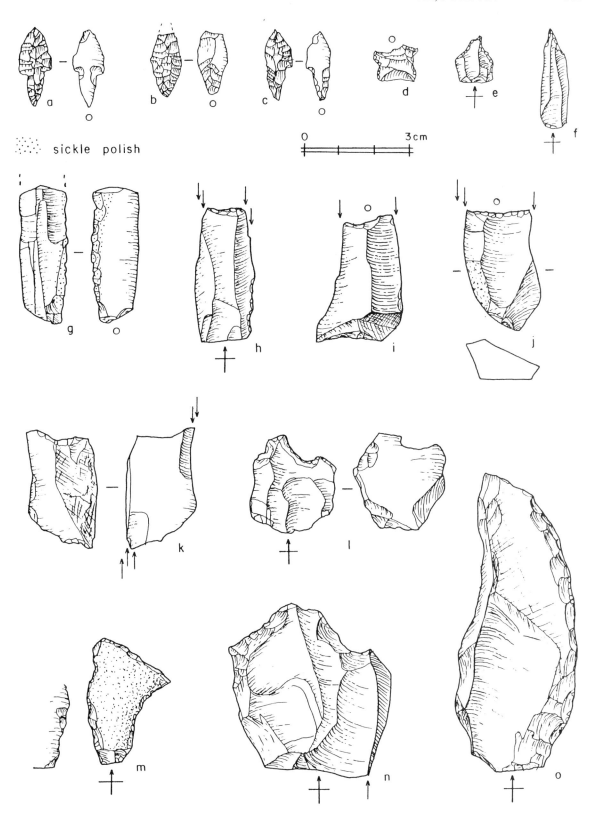

Fig. 7. Yarmoukian artifacts from ʿAin Gȟazāl 1985. a–c) arrowheads; d–f) borers; g) truncated sickle blade; h–k) truncation burins; l) wedge; m) cortical scraper; n) "other" (sidescraper + notch + burin); o) sidescraper. (Drawing by Brian Byrd)

TABLE 3. Absolute and Relative Frequencies of Burin Types (above) and Classes (below) from the 1985 Samples from ʿAin Ghazāl

Burin type	PPN		Yarmoukian	
	n	%	n	%
Simple	5	2.2	2	5.1
Angle	5	2.2	1	2.6
Transverse	133	58.3	6	15.4
On break	13	5.7	1	2.6
Core	1	0.4	—	0.0
Straight dihedral	8	3.6	2	5.1
Canted dihedral	9	3.9	8	20.5
Double	8	3.6	4	10.3
Opposed	23	10.1	4	10.3
Concave truncation	3	1.3	4	10.3
Convex truncation	3	1.3	2	5.1
Oblique truncation	3	1.3	—	0.0
Combination	5	2.2	2	5.1
Indeterminate	9	3.9	3	7.7
Totals	228	100.0	39	100.1

			x^2		
Simple	158	72.1	.001	11	30.6
Complex	52	23.7	.001	19	52.8
Truncation	9	4.1	.01	6	16.7
Totals	219	99.9		36	100.1

TABLE 4. Groundstone Artifacts from the 1985 Excavations at ʿAin Ghazāl

Artifact class	PPN	Yarmoukian
Muller, basalt	1	—
Muller, other stone	—	2
Quern	2	—
"Stone bowl" mortar	—	2
Pestle, miniature	—	1
Burnishing stone	1	1
Stone weight	1	1
Perforated stone	1	1[a]
Grooved stone	1[b]	—
Incised stone	—	1
"Worked stone"	—	1

[a]Basalt
[b]"Shaft straightener"

TABLE 5. Small Finds from the 1985 Excavations at ʿAin Ghazāl

	PPN	Yarmoukian
Bone Tools		
Spatulas	3	1
Awls	8	1
Needle/pin	2	—
Worked fragment	2	1
Clay objects		
Human figurine	5	—
Equid (?) figurine	—	1
Unidentified animal	1	—
Sphere	3	1
Spindle whorl	—	1
Potsherd (sundried)	1	—
Molded fragment	3	1
Reed-impressed fragment	1	—
Jewelry		
"Bracelet"/circular pendant	1	2
Greenstone bead	1	—
"Blackstone" bead	1[a]	—
Fossil bead	1[b]	—
Carnelian fragment	—	1[c]
Other		
White ware fragment	—	1
Sweetclam shell	1	—
Cockle shell	—	1
Unidentified shell	1	—
Fine-grained greenstone	1	—

[a]Burned, identification difficult
[b]Blastoid-like
[c]Unworked chunk

exists in the Central Field, primarily (we suspect) because the area sampled in 1985 was so small. For example, the upper strata of the PPN sequence excavated in 1985 produced no architecture or human burials that were taken to be independently significant indications of cultural differentiation in the South Field, nor were the 1985 faunal samples large enough to distinguish parallels with the important developments seen in the South Phase III collections from 1984.

Despite the sampling problems entailed by so small an exposure in 1985, six principal phases of PPN occupation could be identified in the Square 3282 section. The latest of these phases had two components (Phase VI-A and B), and the burins from the latter component suggest the possibility of a PPNC occupation. Compared to the burin classes from the lower phases in Square 3282, the following ratios were obtained for simple:complex:truncation configuration for the Phases I–

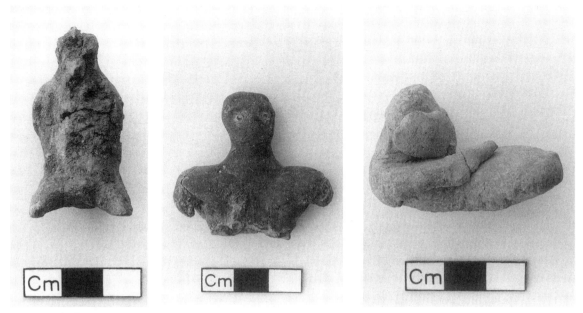

Fig. 8. (Left) Frontal view of a standing human figurine of clay. (Photograph by Curt Blair)

Fig. 9. (Center) Upper torso and head of "muscular" male figurine. Note the eyes. (Photograph by Curt Blair)

Fig. 10. (Right) Side view of the tragic "Pieta" clay figurine from ᶜAin Gȟazāl. The right arm crosses the abdomen while the left hand is wrapped around the face. (Photograph by Curt Blair)

VI-A (n = 165) vs. VI-B (n = 54) samples—75.8: 23.0:1.2 vs. 61.1:25.9:13.0. The simple burin class is different at the .05 level of significance, but the complex counts are not; the same situations were noted in the 1984 PPNB and PPNC samples (Rollefson and Simmons 1986: Table 5). The number of truncation burins in the Phases I–VI-A sample is too small (n = 3) to make valid statistical comparisons with Phase VI-B, but it is tempting to suggest that a "real" distinction does exist. It must be emphasized, however, that the data are too weak to make anything but the most tenuous case for a PPNC presence in this excavation trench.

Groundstone Artifacts

Table 4 shows the distribution of groundstone artifacts and little additional comment is required here other than to note the absolute rarity of such artifacts in the PPN and Yarmoukian layers.

Small Finds

Table 5 lists small finds and other artifacts recovered during the 1985 season. As with the

Central and South Field samples in 1984, a variety of bone tools was present in the PPN layers although such implements were decidedly rare in Yarmoukian contexts.

Although there were few small clay animal figurines in the sediments excavated in 1985, human figurines were well represented in the PPN deposits. One of these is a small standing figure from the fill surrounding the statuary cache in Square 3283 (fig. 8). The face is badly damaged, as are the chest and abdomen, and its sex cannot be determined; but it appears to be a person in a slightly stooped posture with both arms placed behind the back either in a relaxed attitude or to support some ill-defined load. Another figurine, broken across the chest, appears to be a robust male (fig. 9) with well-developed shoulder and pectoral muscles. The delicately modeled head shows details of the brow, nose, and jawline, and the eyes at one time may have been inset with some nonplastic material.

Finally, another figurine is pervaded with pathos (fig. 10): lying on its back with the right arm and hand placed over the abdomen, this individual appears to reflect a moment of extreme grief in the attitude of its raised head comforted by the

TABLE 6. Radiocarbon Dates from Samples Excavated in 1984 at ʿAin Ghazal[a]

Sample	Square	Local phase[b]	Years B.C.			Comments
GrN-12959	3076	I/II	7050	±	90	Older than the 1983 statuary cache
GrN-12960	3080	III	7080	±	80	
GrN-12961	3080	II	6980	±	60	
GrN-12962	3080	I	6730	±	190	Inverted, too young, note large ± range
GrN-12963	3081	IV	7020	±	80	
GrN-12964	3081	IV	7020	±	80	
GrN-12965	3081	III	7100	±	80	Inverted, but ± overlaps with other samples
GrN-12966	3083	VI	7250	±	110	Large ± overlaps with other samples from this square
GrN-12967	3083	IV	6980	±	80	Later than the skull cache
GrN-12968	3083	III	7020	±	110	Overlaps with ± range of other samples in this square
GrN-12969	3273	VII	6860	±	80	
GrN-12970	3273	V	6700	±	200	Inverted, but ± overlaps with other sample in this square
GrN-12971	4048	—	6510	±	90	Earliest evidence of occupation in the South Field
GrN-12972	4452	—	6215	±	50	Base of 15-meter building

[a]Cf. fig. 1.

[b]"Local phase" refers to the phase within each of the excavation squares and is not necessarily equivalent to the phases recorded in other excavation units.

left hand wrapped across the face. The painful inspiration captured in this remarkable object will never be known, but the statue is powerful testimony to the emotional range of early Neolithic artists.

For the other small finds listed in Table 5, little is noteworthy in comparison to earlier seasons at ʿAin Ghazal except that small geometric objects of clay were rare as were jewelry pieces and marine shells.

ARCHITECTURE

Except for occasional fragments of plaster flooring in the upper parts of the PPN sequence, the only substantial architecture in Square 3282 was the house through which the statuary pit had been dug. The excavation trench located the north, west, and south walls of the western portion of the structure, but how much had been destroyed to the east by bulldozers cannot be determined. The area preserved within the remaining section was approximately 5 m (north–south) × 1.9 m (east–west). The construction techniques appeared to be standard PPNB in character, with walls of stone and a floor of polished lime plaster bearing sketchy evidence of red ochre paint. Two—possibly three—large posts (each larger than 40 cm in

diameter) evidently supported roof beams, while at least five smaller postholes may have contained secondary structural posts. No evidence of an interior hearth was found in this room, but if one had existed, it was probably destroyed by the statuary pit. The poor condition of the plaster floor reflects a relatively long period of exposure to weathering, indicating that the building had been abandoned long before the statuary was placed beneath the floor.

In nearby Square 3285 (10 m north of Square 3282), remnants of a house severely damaged by bulldozers were exposed and the fill in this structure was cleared down to the floor. Constructed immediately on top of sterile basal clay (and thus probably dated somewhat earlier than the house in Square 3282), the north, west, and south walls enclosed a space 3.5 m (north–south) × 1.5 m (maximum, east–west), in which a replastered floor remained. In the northwest corner of the room a small Late Acheulian biface leaned against the wall. Typical of PPNB architecture, the floor surface reflected a singular type of decoration. The central stretch of the floor was covered with repeated red "commas" applied using a finger-painting method; the northernmost reaches of the floor were too badly eroded for us to detect any designs, but near the southwest corner of the room was a small red ellipse (ca. 60 × 30 cm) of solid red surrounded by an area of smudges and irregular patches of red paint.

The Yarmoukian layers in Square 3282 contained abundant evidence of architecture, all of which indicates that the later inhabitants stayed at ʿAin Ghazāl in relatively flimsy, temporary structures. Several examples of semisubterranean pit dwellings were uncovered, some with interior storage features (one of which had "beehive" contours) and possible interior partitions associated with puddled mud floors. One structure included a poorly preserved plaster-lined pit that may have been an interior hearth. No structure was completely exposed, so it is not possible to estimate the size of these shelters with any accuracy; one appeared to extend at least 3 m in maximum dimension. Although more detailed analysis is necessary to allow us to understand the Yarmoukian situation more clearly, the general picture appears to be consistent with periodic, perhaps seasonal, visits to ʿAin Ghazāl, perhaps in conjunction with the annual rounds associated with nomadic pastoralism (Köhler-Rollefson, Gillespie, and Metzger n.d.).

RADIOCARBON DATES

We have recently received a series of 14 radiocarbon dates for samples from the Central and South Field excavations in 1984, which provide a firm basis for interpreting the earlier history of the occupation of ʿAin Ghazāl (Table 6).

The dates from the Central Field (Squares 3273–3083) reveal that the village was established about 7250 B.C. and had a long period of development. By about 6500 B.C. the village suddenly increased in size, based on the sample from just above sterile basal clay in Square 4048 in the southwest corner of what today is a car park (fig. 1). Population continued to increase during the latter part of the seventh millennium; by 6200 B.C. the construction of the 15-meter building had begun in the South Field, as shown by the date from a log at the base of the structure (Square 4452). This date also provides a *terminus post quem* for the emergence of the final PPN development (the "PPNC") at ʿAin Ghazāl contained in the occupational series above the floor of the 15-meter complex (Rollefson and Simmons 1986).

Several other radiocarbon samples being processed at the University of Arizona NSF Linear Accelerator Facility include two samples from PPNC contexts and one sample from the East Field test trenches. When the results are finally available, the chronological framework for this important cultural development at ʿAin Ghazāl will be established.

CONCLUSIONS

Four excavation seasons at ʿAin Ghazāl (1982–1985) have produced a staggering wealth of archaeological information. The impact of this material on the interpretation of crucial Neolithic socioeconomic and sociocultural developments has already been dramatic, but so far only a minute amount of information has been analyzed in depth. To understand the critical evolution in more detail and to make more meaningful comparisons with contemporary trends in the region, it is time to call a temporary halt to the acquisition of additional raw data and to begin the intensive analysis of what has already been painstakingly accumulated. Members of the ʿAin Ghazāl Archaeological Project now intend to devote the next two years or more to laboratory research on the archaeological samples, in preparation for the first volume of the ʿAin Ghazāl site report. We intend to resume full-scale field operations as early as 1988.

NOTES

[1] The ʿAin Ghazāl Archaeological Project, cosponsored by the Institute of Archaeology and Anthropology of Yarmouk University, received funding from the National Geographic Society (USA); the Department of Antiquities of Jordan; Alia, the Royal Jordanian Airlines; and the Cobb Institute of Archaeology at Mississippi State University (USA). The staff consisted of the authors, who were codirectors; St. John Simpson and Marcia Donaldson (senior field staff); Emusaytif Suleiman (Department of Antiquities inspector); Ilse Köhler-Rollefson and Ellen McAdam (senior laboratory staff); Lynn Grant (conservator); and Curt Blair (photographer and archaeological assistant).

[2] Kenyon (1957: 74) gave a date of 6250 B.C. for the end of the PPNB sequence at Jericho, and her notes suggest that Garstang's statuary must have dated to this

part of the sequence (Kenyon 1981: 268; Garstang 1935; 1936). However, subsequent radiocarbon dates for Jericho have tended to confuse the absolute chronology to some degree (Kenyon 1971: 332; 1981: 502–4), although it still appears that the Jericho statuary probably dates to the second half of the seventh millennium.

[3]The amount of minute microflakes and debris from Locus 122 associated with core reduction and tool retouching was much too large to count individually. Instead, several sizable samples for each category were counted and weighed to calculate an approximation based on the total weights for each class of artifacts.

BIBLIOGRAPHY

Garstang, J.
1935   Jericho: City and Necropolis. Fifth Report. *Annals of Archaeology and Anthropology* (Liverpool) 23 (3–4): 143–84.
1936   Jericho: City and Necropolis. Report for the 6th and Concluding Season. *Annals of Archaeology and Anthropology* (Liverpool) 24: 67–90.
Kenyon, K.
1957   *Digging Up Jericho*. New York: Praeger.
1971   *Archaeology in the Holy Land* (3rd ed.). London: Ernest Benn.
1981   *Excavations at Jericho: Volume III*. London: British School of Archaeology in Jerusalem.
Köhler-Rollefson, I.; Gillespie, W.; and Metzger, M.
n.d.   Hunting and Herding at Neolithic ʿAin Ghazāl: Preliminary Report on the Animal Remains from the First Three Seasons (1982–1984).

Rollefson, G.
1983   Ritual and Ceremony at Neolithic ʿAin Ghazāl (Jordan). *Paléorient* 9(2): 29–38.
Rollefson, G., and Simmons, A.
1986   The Neolithic Village of ʿAin Ghazāl, Jordan: Preliminary Report on the 1984 Season. *Bulletin of the American Schools of Oriental Research Supplement 24*: 145–64.
Rollefson, G. *et al.*
1985   Excavations at PPNB ʿAin Ghazāl (Jordan) 1983. *Mitteilungen der Deutschen Orient Gesellschaft* 117: 69–116.
Tubb, K.
1985   Preliminary Report on the ʿAin Ghazāl Statues. *Mitteilungen der Deutschen Orient Gesellschaft* 117: 117–34.

The Early Bronze IV Fortified Site of Khirbet Iskander, Jordan: Third Preliminary Report, 1984 Season

Suzanne Richard
Drew University
Madison, NJ 07940

Roger Boraas
Upsala College
East Orange, NJ 07019

This report briefly summarizes the results of the 1981 and 1982 seasons at Khirbet Iskander and reevaluates those results in light of the 1984 campaign. The report also summarizes the work carried out in two EB IV cemeteries (D and E), provides a tentative stratigraphic outline of the site, and gives a cursory analysis of the pottery. Finally, the significance of Khirbet Iskander for EB IV studies generally is discussed. After three seasons of excavations and the recovery of five occupational phases, it is possible to conclude that Khirbet Iskander was a permanently settled EB IV site, probably occupied throughout the period, ca. 2350– 2000. With its fortifications, monumental architecture, broad- and long-room houses, storeroom of pottery, bench-lined rooms, etc., Khirbet Iskander demonstrates a cultural continuity with the preceding EB III period and illuminates sedentary adaptation in EB IV.

INTRODUCTION

The Khirbet Iskander Expedition is designed to study sedentary adaptive strategies in EB IV (2350–2000 B.C.), a so-called "nomadic interlude" between the urban eras of the EB II–III (3100–2350 B.C.) and the Middle Bronze Age (2000–1550 B.C.). Although Kathleen Kenyon disassociated EB IV culture from the Early Bronze Age proper (Kenyon, Bottero, and Posener 1971), a growing body of evidence from Transjordan and, in particular, Khirbet Iskander, demonstrates strong continuities with EB III traditions, including urban traditions. Thus, the expedition provides an excellent opportunity to examine sedentary adaptations in Palestine–Transjordan in a way that should offer suggestions about the nature of this enigmatic culture and its relationship to the preceding urban city-state system.

Excavations in Jordan over the past 15 years have made it increasingly clear that EB IV was a period of urban regression, not a nomadic interlude (Richard 1980; 1987). We now know that our perspective of the EB IV culture was in the past distorted by the very nature of the excavated remains, namely, vast isolated cemeteries and ephemeral settlements. The evidence led to postulations that Amorite nomads invaded the country from Syria. Today, however, excavations in Jordan at such sites as Bâb edh-Dhrâᶜ (Schaub and Rast 1984), Iktanu (Prag 1974), Ader (Cleveland 1960), Tell Um Hammad (Helms 1986), Arôᶜer (Olávarri 1969), Tell el-ᶜUmeiri (Geraty, *et al.* 1986), Tell Abu en-Niᶜaj (Steven Falconer, personal communication), as well as at Khirbet Iskander have illuminated a significant level of sedentarism and a continuation of Early Bronze Age traditions.

Khirbet Iskander illustrates that extensive EB IV sedentary occupation, including fortified towns, existed in a period during which pastoral nomadism is thought to have characterized the level of economic subsistence and social organization. The site appears to have been the home of a permanent agricultural community where continuity with Early Bronze urban traditions, particularly

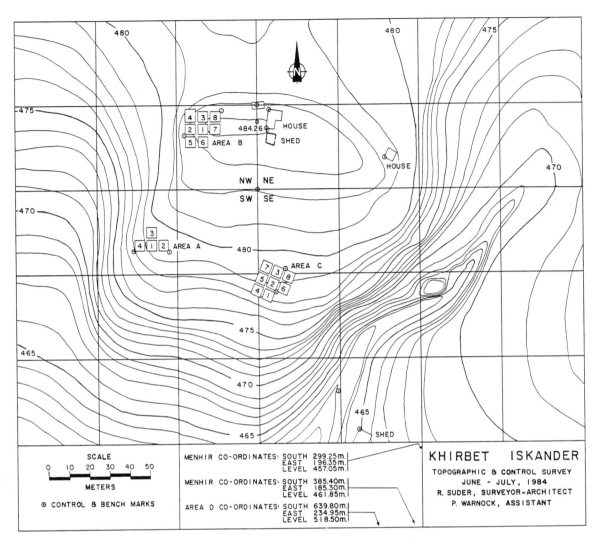

Fig. 1. Contour map of the mound showing the three excavated areas, A, B, and C.

town planning, is manifest. The results from Khirbet Iskander call for revision and reevaluation of our conceptualizations of the EB IV culture and its relationship to the urban Early Bronze Age. Sociocultural change at ca. 2350 B.C. now appears to have been far less dramatic than hitherto believed, and the adaptive strategies of the EB IV peoples were not everywhere as simple as the current pastoral-nomadic model would suggest (Dever 1980).

SUMMARY OF EARLIER WORK

The third season of excavations at Khirbet Iskander was carried out between July 2 and

August 6, 1984, under the auspices of the American Schools of Oriental Research in cooperation with the Department of Antiquities of Jordan.[1] In the past three seasons, work has focused on the excavation of EB IV levels. However, Parr (1960) found earlier occupation at the site and this occupation was also demonstrated by a sherd survey conducted in our pilot season, 1981 (Richard 1982). Surface survey and test excavation at that time affirmed both Glueck's (1939) and Parr's (1960) earlier conclusions that there was important EB IV domestic occupation at Khirbet Iskander. Multiphased architecture in the form of rectangular houses, domestic appurtenances such as tabûns and food preparation equipment (querns and

grinding stones), as well as large quantities of
pottery, encountered in test Areas A and B,
demonstrated that the inhabitants of Khirbet
Iskander were permanent settlers.

In 1982 work continued in Areas A and B and a
new field, Area C, was opened (see fig. 1). Major
discoveries of habitational traditions at the southwest corner of the mound (Area A) included a
well-built east–west wall (1.25 m deep × 0.75 m
wide) bonded with or adjoined to a series of
similarly constructed north–south walls. At the
time, these substantial walls were thought to represent terracing of the mound where it begins to
slope sharply to the south. Multiphased rectangular houses came to light on the interior and
exterior of the east–west line. Tabûns, hearths,
pits, and a great deal of pottery—including a
whole cooking pot—and food preparation equipment evidenced continuous domestic settlement.
A short five-week season in 1984 precluded further work in Area A.

Concerning the "terrace" walls, the 1984 excavation of Area C has now shed some light on the
Area A situation. Walls of similar dimension,
construction, and orientation function in the latest
phase in Area C as an element in a monumental
building complex. Greater depth of excavation is
necessary, however, to illuminate the depth and
original purpose of these walls. If an architectural
link between the two areas is correct, and if the
western wall (1.50 m × 0.75 m) boundary of a
cobbled courtyard that Parr (1960: 130) uncovered
on the eastern crest is, as it seems, comparable, we
may in the future be able to correlate the stratification across the mound by a series of probes to
check the line of this wall. In Area A, surface
demarcations indicate that the "terrace" wall
extends to the north along the western crest. One
should thus expect to find a similar architectural
phenomenon along the northern crest of the site.

Although a massive fortification (Richard and
Boraas 1984; below) encloses the site along the
north, walls similar to the "terrace" wall appear to
be a structural design in Area B also. It is a major
goal of the forthcoming season to determine both
the nature of these unusual walls—whether defense
or terrace—and their stratigraphic and functional
(if any) relationship to the massive outer perimeter
fortification. Clearly to be differentiated from these
two structural traditions are the typical domestic
house walls at Khirbet Iskander, which consistently are of the two-row, two-three course type.

In 1982 major discoveries were also made at the
northwest corner of the mound in Area B (Richard
1983; Richard and Boraas 1984). There, Glueck
(1939) earlier observed that well-preserved domestic structures lay immediately within a massive
perimeter wall that included a corner bastion. The
1984 season has considerably clarified the phasing
of the domestic complex, definitively affirmed an
EB IV date for the fortifications, and provided
some insight into the stratigraphic relationship
between the two. (For a reevaluation of the Area
B remains, see below.)

Finally in 1982, exploration at the southeast
corner of the mound in Area C uncovered what
appears to be the subsidiary fortification bisecting
the mound approximately in the middle, as Glueck
reported. Although of only two rows and two
courses, this wall is ca. 1.50 m wide and is composed of boulders that give it a monumental look.
Surface traces indicate that the Glueck wall continues both to the west and to the east of Area C.
Also discovered just north of the Glueck wall was
a structure flanking a bench-lined passageway. All
the evidence led us to believe that we had uncovered the eastern "guardroom" of a gate complex (Richard and Boraas 1984). In 1984 extensive
exposure of the building complex in Area C
resolved some problems but raised many more.

This report will concentrate on the results of
the 1984 campaign in preliminary form. It includes
a summary and reevaluation of the two areas
excavated in 1984, Areas B and C, as well as a
tentative stratigraphic outline and cursory analysis
of the pottery. It will also include a summary of
the work carried out in two cemeteries, D and E.
Finally, the significance of Khirbet Iskander for
EB IV studies generally will be discussed.

THE 1984 FIELD SEASON

Area B

Of the four squares worked in 1982 (B1–4),
excavation continued only in a 1.0 m extension of
B4 to the north. The focus of work in Area B was
in new squares B5–8 (fig. 1). The goals in this area
were 1) to find the foundation trench for the
perimeter wall/tower by means of the section in
B4 against Wall 4020, 2) to achieve greater horizontal exposure of the domestic complex discovered in 1982, and 3) to investigate earlier phases
of this complex. Having reached these goals by

the end of the season, we now can date the outer fortifications and outline the EB IV phasing on the mound for the first time.

Broadly speaking, there are three stages to the Area B settlement: prefortified, fortified, and post-fortified (Richard 1986). Specifically, it appears that there are at least four and perhaps five EB IV phases at Iskander, based on discoveries in the Area B domestic complex thus far. From the top, Phase A designates the latest domestic complex. Phase B represents an earlier domestic complex with "bench-lined upper storeroom." Phase C is a still earlier phase of the Area B complex as discerned almost solely from the discovery of a "lower storeroom." Phase D constitutes the erection of the fortifications and the founding of the domestic complex/settlement, the latter as yet not reached. Phase E, the earliest occupation level reached so far, signifies a prefortification habitation layer.

Fortifications (Phases C–D)

Prior to the 1984 season, it was not possible to date the fortifications and the corner "tower." In 1984 definitive evidence for an EB IV date appeared in two squares, B4 and B8 (fig. 3). In B4 the foundation trench of the massive perimeter wall (4020) was found. Pottery from the trench included an EB IV holemouth and a rim of an imported caliciform cup from Syria of the white-on-black variety. The gray metallic sherd has a white band of paint just below the lip. Although this trade ware is fairly popular in northern Palestine, the Iskander and Beᶜer Resisim examples (Cohen and Dever 1981: 63) now extend the network to Transjordan and the Negev. Once fully excavated, the 1.0 m probe against the north face of Wall 4020 revealed that the perimeter wall was of massive construction and well coursed (fig. 2). Eleven surviving courses reached a height of almost 3.0 m. The wall was founded on a leveling layer of small rock and rubble set in a clear but shallow foundation trench. The exterior face of the wall showed a long history of gradual spills of soil tilting away from the wall toward the north.

In B8, additional evidence in support of EB IV use of the wall came to light. The 2.5 m wide perimeter wall uncovered in B3 in 1982 continued to the east through square B8 and beyond (figs. 3, 4). This segment of the perimeter wall has not yet been fully articulated; however, excavation revealed a bond with a north–south transverse sec-

Fig. 2. North face of Perimeter Wall/Tower 4020; note the line of the foundation trench near the bottom of the section (photo by Edyth Skinner).

tion (Wall 8059), which also functioned as an EB IV house wall. Wall 8059 runs under Phase A domestic house Wall 8003 and continues into square B7 to the south where a bench-lined wall (7013–7017) adjoins it on the west. Within the bench-lined room a storeroom of whole and restorable EB IV pottery was recovered in Phase B. This transverse wall was also utilized as a house wall for the "lower storeroom" in B8 (Phase C).

Transverse Wall 8059 raises questions concerning the construction of Outer Perimeter Wall 4020–3017–8024 and Inner Perimeter Wall 3011–8063. It was reported earlier that Inner Wall 3011 with Rubble Core 3016 was a later addition whose purpose was to reinforce the town wall at some point (Richard and Boraas 1984: 77–78, figs. 13, 14). The fact that inner and outer walls, 8024–8063, are both related to Transverse Wall 8059, however, suggests that the entire wall may have

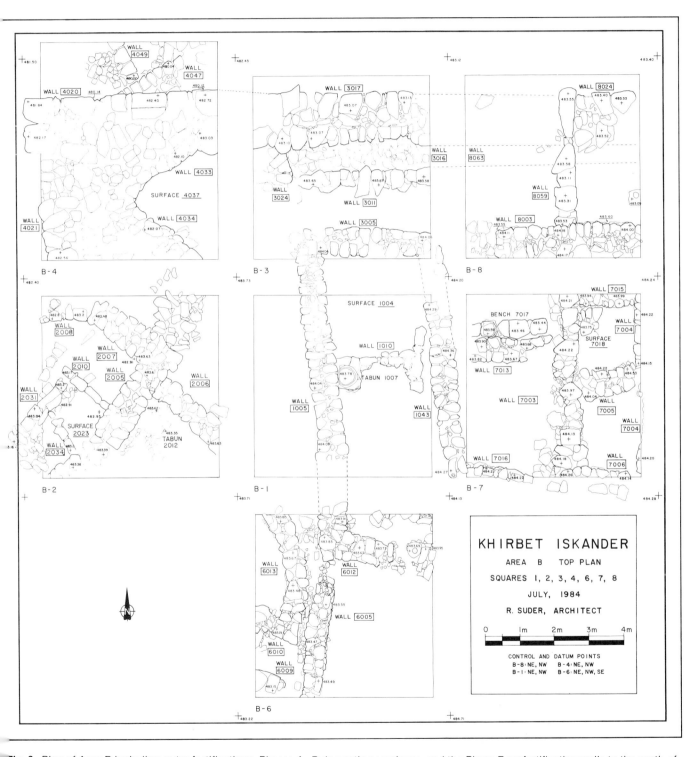

Fig. 3. Plan of Area B including outer fortifications, Phases A–B domestic complexes, and the Phase E prefortification walls to the north of Wall 4020.

Fig. 4. Square B8 looking south at Phase A house, Wall 3003; note also the bond between Transverse Wall 8059 and the outer perimeter wall; the depth reached in the "lower storeroom," Phase C (photo by Edyth Skinner).

been erected contemporaneously. In light of this new information from B8 on the construction techniques employed in the perimeter wall, we can now interpret the crosswall fragment encountered in 1982 in B3 (Richard and Boraas 1984: fig. 13). At that time it was reported that the cornering of Crosswall 3024 and the Outer Perimeter Wall 3017 proved that the inner section of the wall must have been added later. Closer inspection of Crosswall 3024, however, suggests it was a vertical section through the entire perimeter wall. This construction question needs to be resolved, since a later date for the inner wall would affect the phasing and plan of the domestic complex.

Similar construction techniques in the fortifications have been observed at Bâb edh-Dhrâᶜ and Numeira (Rast and Schaub 1978: 10, fig. 7; 1980: 40–42, fig. 15). At both sites, a perimeter wall of interior/exterior sections with rubble core includes transverse sections ca. 7.0 m apart. The two transverse sections at Iskander are ca. 8.0 m apart. Only at Iskander, however, does a section extend beyond the limit of the fortifications for use as a house wall. A goal for the next season will be to resolve the uncertainty over the construction of the outer and inner segments of the perimeter wall.

What is certain about the fortifications at Iskander is that their founding in Phase D dates to EB IV. Likewise, it is now almost certain that

Fig. 5. Square B4 domestic walls below Fortification Tower 4020 to the east; Phase E (photo by Edyth Skinner).

Fig. 6. Square B7 looking west, at the "bench-lined room" upon which the EB IV vessels rested; Phase B (photo by Edyth Skinner).

the fortifications had gone out of use by Phase A. In fact, there is evidence that already by Phase B the fortifications were no longer in use, although only more extensive excavation of this level in relation to the fortifications will determine this. The "lower storeroom" Phase C is clearly within the fortifications; the founding settlement, Phase D, has not yet been reached, except for the fortifications.

Of great interest to the expedition are the results of Parr's soundings on the eastern crest, where a wall 2.30 m wide was found to rest on bedrock, ca. 3.00 m below the surface (Parr 1960: 129). The dimensions of this wall and its depth from the surface parallel almost exactly our perimeter defensive wall in Area B, although since B is the highest point on the mound, we have not yet reached bedrock. A major goal for next season is to excavate several strategically placed probes around the mound to determine the line of the

perimeter fortification and the presence of earlier fortifications, if any.

Prefortified Settlement (Phase E)

Beneath the massive northern defense perimeter wall and extending north from its line were partial remnants of two earlier wall foundations (4049 and 4047), set to form a corner (see figs. 3, 5). Both are at angles indicating a different orientation than that established by the defense construction. This domestic structure of an earlier settlement (which may or may not have been fortified by a wall on a different line) shows that at one time occupation continued beyond the northern crest of the present mound north into the plain, which extends for some distance. Glueck had observed EB IV pottery and occupation in this area.

This domestic structure has been dated to EB IV on the basis of the ceramics found with the debris above and around the walls, although neither founding levels nor a surface has yet been reached. Thus, it is possible that this structure predates the EB IV period. Further excavation next season will resolve this issue.

The Domestic Complex (Phases A-B-C)

As mentioned, the fortifications including two transverse sections were erected in Phase D. The earliest evidence thus far for domestic usage within the fortifications is the Phase C "lower storeroom" in B8 and possibly several wall lines in B1. A large quantity of pottery was discovered in B8 on both sides of Transverse Wall 8059, which appears to have been used as a house wall (fig. 4). Perimeter Wall 8024/8063 served as the northern boundary of the room. Excavation in connection with these lower levels has not yet reached a surface. The pottery, EB IV whole and restorable vessels along with extraordinary quantities of sherds, was found in a matrix of mudbrick debris and rubble, clear evidence of the destruction to Phase C. A layer of rock tumble separates this pottery from Phase B above. The pottery is discussed below. Excavation next season will concentrate on exposing complete architectural plans for this phase.

The Phase B remains illuminate the architectural plan of a portion of a domestic complex at Khirbet Iskander (see fig. 3 and compare fig. 10). It includes a reuse of Transverse Wall 8059, which again appears to act as a house wall between two

Fig. 7. Square B7, large EB IV store-jar resting on paver inside the bench-lined room; looking west (photo by Edyth Skinner).

rooms in B8 and B7. At the northwest corner of B7 a row of benches against Wall 7013 formed the southern boundary of a room. EB IV storejars lay on the bench (fig. 6). A paver below and alongside the bench, upon which rested an unusually large storejar with rope molding, marked the surface level of the room (fig. 7). Quantities of whole and restorable pottery were found in this room and at the same level in B8. Pottery continued into the balk at either end. The bench-lined room extends westward into B1, where in 1981 the enigmatic Structure 1010 with fragmentary wall and pavers was discovered. In B7, to the east of Transverse Wall 8059 another Phase B room was cleared. Pavers in one corner suggest a base for the placement of storejars, as was the case in the bench-lined room. Just as Transverse Wall 8059 defines the eastern terminus of the bench-lined room, Transverse Section 3024 may define the western boundary.

Although Transverse Wall 8059 was in use in Phase B, it does not appear that the perimeter wall was in use, at least not the inner section. Otherwise, there is no way to explain the fact that some of the pottery in this phase lay at the edge and partially over the inner perimeter wall (figs. 8, 9). The west balk of B8 likewise shows pottery tipping over the very edge of the inner perimeter wall. A probe to the east of B8 next season should clarify the relation of the Phase B settlement to the fortifications.

Phase A represents the latest EB IV occupation on the mound (figs. 3, 10). Extensive domestic habitation in the form of broad- and longroom houses with common walls is located about 4.0 m south of the outer fortifications, which were almost certainly not in use in this phase. Exterior surfaces to the north of Walls 3005 and 8003, though destroyed by erosion toward the northern edge of the mound, appear to have originally overlain the outer fortifications. A number of the house walls of Phase B are reused, particularly in Squares B7–B8. Good interior surfaces correlate with domestic features such as Tabûn 1007 in B1, Tabûn 2012 in B2, and work areas or pens adjoining the western face of the B2 structure.

The best preserved building is the B1 house with dimensions of 8.5 m × 3.5 m within the walls. A door socket and door opening in the south wall show it to be a longroom house. Built up against the inner wall of the room was a two-phased tabûn. Several large firepits or hearths nearby evidence the use of this large building as a kitchen. On the evidence of Wall 6005 to the south in B6, it appears that yet another house lies beyond the B1 house, unless this proves to be a courtyard wall. Adjoining the B1 house to the east is a slightly smaller room with an auxiliary partitioned room beyond it.

Due to its different orientation, the B2 house with its pens and work areas and its tabûn has always posed a problem. In 1984 the discovery of

Fig. 8. Square B8 looking southwest as pottery of Phase B is emerging. Note the relationship of the pottery to Outer Perimeter Wall 8063 (photo by Edyth Skinner).

Fig. 9. Square B8, pottery of the Phase B storeroom (photo by Edyth Skinner).

Curvilinear Wall 6013 in B6 finally linked the B2 house with the rest of the domestic complex and showed that the B2 tabûn is within the corner of a courtyard, unlike the interior B1 tabûn. Since the curvilinear courtyard wall effectively blocks an opening in a B6 wall, it could reflect a late alteration within Phase A (for a full description of the B2 structures, see Richard and Boraas 1984). These structures seem to represent outdoor features like courtyards and pens that have been built along the western crest of the mound beyond the housing area.

On the basis of the plan we now have for the Phase A settlement, we may observe that town planning at Khirbet Iskander is not inconsistent with the settlement plans for Early Bronze Age sites such as Arad, Bâb edh-Dhrâᶜ, and Numeira. Series of interconnected broad- and longroom houses of various shapes and sizes are arranged around courtyard areas. It is, however, too early to say whether or not "blocks" of houses separated by streets are the norm as attested especially at Arad and Tell el-Farᶜah (N). Glueck simply noted that extensive domestic architecture was present

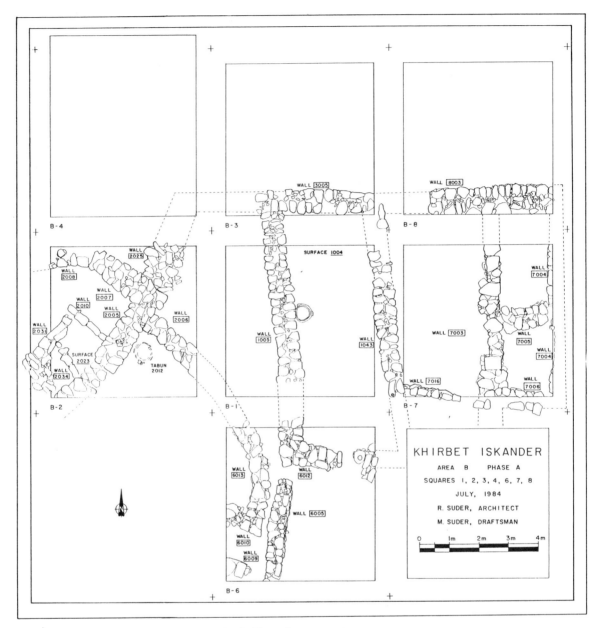

Fig. 10. Area B: drawing of domestic complex in Phase A.

along the northern perimeter wall. Throughout the area, huge saddle querns and many grinding stones and flints provide additional evidence for the intense domestic use of this area.

It is difficult yet to draw any definitive comparisons between the plans of the Phases A and B domestic complexes, as presently exposed. In general, however, it does appear that 1) the orientation of the rooms remains more or less the same; 2) there was no break in occupation between the two, given the immediate superimposition of Phase A surfaces and buildings, and in some cases the reuse of earlier walls; 3) the Phase B (and Phase C) utilization of the northern rooms as pottery storerooms was superseded by a domestic phase as denoted by tabûns, pens, domestic equipment, etc. Numerous questions remain to be resolved: When and how did the fortifications go out of use? Do the successive complexes show significant change in plan and material culture? Is

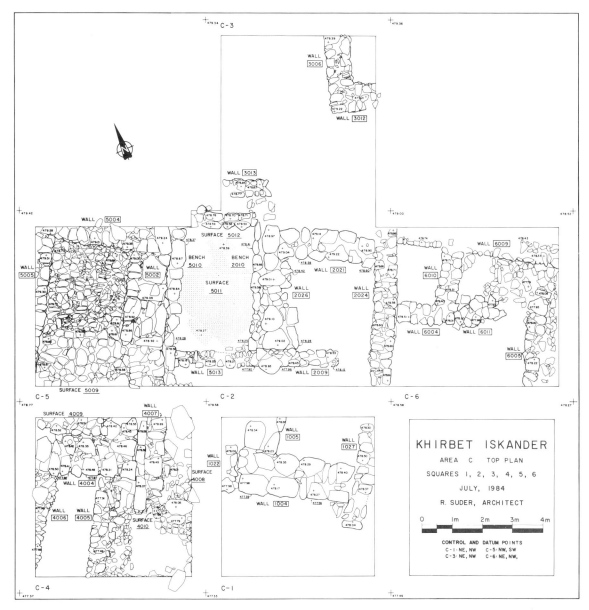

Fig. 11. Plan of Area C: the "tripartite" complex and associated features to the east and north. From left: a) room with cobbled pavement; b) bench-lined "passageway" with "threshold" and steps; c) partitioned room. Note the "Nelson Glueck" wall, 4004–1004 running east–west.

there a transitional EB III/EB IV phase beneath the outer fortifications?

Area C

Area C is located at the southeastern corner of the mound just at the point where the mound begins to slope sharply to the south (fig. 3). The goal of the 1984 season was to investigate the area west of the purported passageway in search

of the anticipated symmetrical western flank of the bench-lined "guardroom." Thus we laid out squares C4 and C5 to the west. To achieve a greater exposure of the entire complex, we also opened C6 to the east and C3 to the north.

The internal phasing of Area C structures is highly complex and a definitive interpretation must await further excavation. As presently visible in the plan (fig. 11), the tripartite complex appears to comprise two chambers ("guardrooms") that

Fig. 12. Area C looking north; C2 monumental wall abuts C6 wall of small-scale construction; also note the C6 rectangular structure and apparent counterpart in C3 at the top of the photo (photo by Edyth Skinner).

flank a passageway lined with benches on either side. Although reported earlier that the Glueck wall (1004) was stratigraphically later than the C2 structure, it is now clear that it is an integral part; both the Glueck wall (1004) and Wall 2021 abut Wall 2024/1027. The enigmatic break between the western boundary wall of the C2 room (Walls 2026 and 1005) may be a doorway or it may simply reflect later disturbance. In C5, the western chamber, a beautifully paved surface within the room extends into C4 right up to the Glueck wall (4004). Likewise the eastern wall of the room, Wall 5002–4007, adjoins the Glueck wall. Thus, it is certain that all of these structures at one time existed as a single entity.

At least two major phases have thus far been recognized in Area C. The Glueck Wall Segment 4004 overlies Wall 4006, tentatively construed to be a domestic wall, whose extreme northeast–southwest alignment at the western edge of Square C4 may well connect it with a currently unexcavated structure to the west. No certain super-imposition can be cited for contiguous Wall 4005. Since Wall 4005 is on the same alignment as Walls 4007/5002, it is possible that it served as the founding structure supporting part of the mass of Wall 4007.

Similarly, the discovery of small-scale walls, i.e., 0.75 m wide, constructed of small stones, in Squares C6 and C3 shows them to be deeply founded. Founding levels for these small-scale walls have not yet been reached, but on the basis of similarly constructed walls in Area A, it is expected that they will measure ca. 1.25 m in depth. The northern wall of C5 (5004), in the small-scale construction mode, is comparable to the C6 walls. It is clear that the more massively constructed walls of the C2 chamber (2026/2021), founded much higher, were set in against Wall 2024 (fig. 12). Earlier occupation in association with Wall 2024, but below the surface of the C2 chamber, moreover, came to light in the form of a surface on which smashed, flat-lying pottery and roof collapse with charred timbers were found.

Fig. 13. Area C looking roughly east, with Monumental Wall 5002 (the western sector) in foreground; across the "passageway" are the bench-line and eastern sector. Note the discrepancy in height of Wall 5013/2009, at the right (photo by Edyth Skinner).

Regarding an earlier phase in Area C, Wall 2009 in Square C2 originally belonged to a domestic structure from a phase antedating the "passage" complex; and it was later incorporated into the greater whole, becoming the southern wall of this gate structure (Richard and Boraas 1984). Massive Stone Wall 2026 runs up to and over Wall 2009, thus incorporating the latter into the overall structure (fig. 13). Due to destruction between seasons, the overlying boulders were mostly no longer visible in 1984. The western continuation of Walls 2009 as 5013, some 0.30 m lower, has the appearance of having been "trimmed down" on its western half to provide a threshold or "sill" (figs. 13, 14). To the west it is clear from the superimposition of massive Wall 5002 that "Threshold" 5013 is an earlier wall. This discrepancy and others to be noted below between the eastern and western flanking rooms raise important questions concerning the construction history of the Area C complex. At any rate, all the data suggest that a significant alteration in architectural plan and therefore function occurred late in EB IV at this edge of the mound.

With regard to the "tripartite" architectural complex as a whole, although in the plan the complex seems to consist of two parallel walled chambers flanking a specially prepared bench-lined passageway, closer inspection shows the chambers to be not entirely symmetrical. The western structure is better preserved and better constructed; it bonds with adjacent walls, and

does not show the discontinuity south of Threshold Wall 5013 as does the eastern structure (figs. 14, 15). Likewise, the flanking Bench-row 5010 shows the same continuity, and extends past the southern limit of the eastern bench installation. Furthermore, the western bench-row is composed of flat boulders that are noticeably wider, and in most cases longer, than those employed in its eastern counterpart.

An added factor pertaining to this issue is the presence of a fully intact stone pavement (5009–4009) enclosed within the western compartment (fig. 14). No corresponding pavement was uncovered in the eastern chamber, which is further differentiated by a partition wall. The paved surface itself appears to reflect two clear construction phases. The northern half of the room is composed of small stones while approximately on the east–west line of Wall 5013–2009 a clear change is discernible to large pavers that continue southward up to Wall 4004. That the western chamber was roofed is indicated by two sockets in the northern pavement and one in the southern pavement.

The area south of the "threshold" is largely unexcavated. However, such work as that carried out does not suggest an opening in the Glueck east–west wall (1004–4004). An uninterrupted east–west line would support the notion that the area delimited by massive walls is an internal, bench-lined chamber whose access is by way of the steps on the north (below). On the other hand, Wall

Fig. 14. Squares C5 and C4 looking roughly south, at pavement of the western sector (photo by Edyth Skinner).

1022 may be a blockage, and perhaps only at that time was the passageway remodeled into an interior chamber.

Some discussion is in order regarding the gypsum coating or plasterlike surfacing that lapped over the stones of "Threshold" 5013 and continued beyond the southern edge. A very similar surfacing material on line with that located within the benched area and equal to the founding level of massive flanking Wall 4007 came to light in 1984. This could indicate the continuation of a solitary plastered passage between the major walls at some point before the "blockage" of the Glueck wall. It is becoming increasingly clear that "Threshold" 5013 may be distorting our view of this entire complex (fig. 15). With evidence from a balk section illuminating a plaster surface at the level of the top of Wall 5013, it is no longer certain that the latter wall was in use contemporaneously with the bench-lined area. It cannot be ruled out, however, that this area was reconstituted from a

passageway with threshold to an interior room with plasterlike surfacing.

Excavation of the balk between C2/C5 and C3 has provided information pertinent to the interpretation of the bench-lined area. The stepped-platform discovered beneath the northern balk is composed of stones arranged in two levels. The upper level leads to a packed surface of soil and stone fragments equivalent in height to the two bench rows, spanning the entire 2.10 m width of the "passage" on its northern end (fig. 16). The stones comprising the steps of the platform are comparable to those that flank Wall 2005/2026. The stone portion of the "platform" consists of the top stones of a wall; its position and character suggest that it may be a northern counterpart to the so-called "threshold." Although the stepped platform extends beyond the northern terminus of the flanking chambers, it is clearly associated with flanking bench lines 5012 and 2010. The very presence of the stepped platform at the north-

Fig. 15. View to the south, roughly, of the Area C bench-lined "passageway" and "threshold" (photo by Edyth Skinner).

Fig. 16. Squares C2–C5 bench-lined "passageway" looking roughly north, at steps and platform (photo by Edyth Skinner).

ern end of the passage complicates the interpretation of the entire "tripartite" complex as finally constituted.

Beyond this wall and to the north exists a rather extensive space devoid of structures, at a level roughly equivalent to the walking surface of the passage. This open area continues to the northeast corner of Square C3 where a rectangular structure of a construction comparable to the C6 features was encountered (fig. 12). It is reasonable to suppose that the C3 feature connects with the northern extension of Wall 2024 and thus there is a structural and functional linkage between these small rectangular chambers in both areas. The consideration of these chambers as storage areas is inconsistent with the absence of storage vessels and the general scarcity of even fragmentary ceramic material. Neither their original function nor their functional relationship to the complex further west is evident as yet.

By way of interpretation, one is safe in concluding that due to the monumental construction, unlike any domestic architecture found elsewhere on the site, the Area C structures represent a

Fig. 17. Tomb E3, to the north, with EB IV pottery at the entrance of the chamber; behind the vessels lay a skull on either side of a bone pile (photo by Edyth Skinner).

public complex of some sort. Whether the "tri-partite" complex is a gateway or merely a series of longrooms (one of which is a bench-lined assembly room) within the subsidiary fortification wall will remain unclear until further excavation clarifies this situation.

Any interpretation of these structures, however, must take into account the discoveries of Parr (1960: 130). His excavations uncovered similar structures on the eastern edge of the mound (1960: 130), although he does not mention any monumental walls as in Area C. In his Trench 1 (apparently just east of our Area C), he noted that earlier walls (his Period 3[1]) had been incorporated into a new structure consisting of a cobbled courtyard (2.50 m × 4.00 m) bounded on the west by a substantial stone wall 1.50 m high and 0.75 m wide. The cobbled surface in Area C is 6.0 m × 2.50 m, bounded on the north by a "small-scale" wall (0.75 m × 1.25? m). In all probability, the eastern wall of Parr's courtyard (which had disappeared downslope) is equivalent to our Glueck wall. His excavations, by the way, give us our only clue as to the relationship of the "terrace" walls (1.25 , × 0.75 m) and the Glueck wall to the massive fortifications that surround the site: in his Trench 1, these structures overlay the massive 2.3 m wide fortification.

CEMETERIES

A survey of the region in the immediate vicinity of the site located two cemeteries, Area D on the ridge south of the site across the wadi, and Area E immediately east of the site. To the west, some evidences appeared in a cultivated area that suggested the possibility of tombs, although further investigation is necessary to confirm this. When Nelson Glueck visited Khirbet Iskander, he observed that it consisted of two sectors: the western was the tell proper and the eastern, between two subsidiary north–south wadis, was, he surmised, a vast cemetery. In this area he noted numerous standing and fallen menhirs of various sizes, circles of stones, platforms, etc. It is no longer possible to see most of these features or to understand the context in which they were situated. However, having found the vast cemetery surmised by Glueck, as well as five menhirs, we may hypothesize that at least for Iskander, menhirs are somehow connected with burial traditions. The cemetery materials will be published separately, so there will be no attempt here to provide an exhaustive description of the tombs and their contents.

The Area E cemetery site consists of numerous apparent natural concavities in outcroppings of bedrock that had been further carved out by the EB IV peoples. These outcrops are of a type of conglomerate, actually a mixture of limestone and chert that became cemented together through a natural process. One does not cut through this material easily, as the excavators discovered. Small apertures just above ground level gave a clue as to the location of a tomb. Excavation of nine of these apertures showed five sterile chambers, one double-chambered feature whose silt

Fig. 18. Disarticulated burials and assorted grave goods in the shaft tomb, Chamber E9, looking to the west; note fragments of large restorable platter-bowl and four-spouted lamps (photo by Edyth Skinner).

and ash layers and total lack of cultural evidence suggest its use as an oven (probably modern), and three chambers with skeletal and artifactual remains.

Tomb E3 proved to be a very small chamber tomb containing a double disarticulated burial (fig. 17). Two skulls, one of a child, were found disposed on either side of a central bonepile, although some bones had been placed over the skulls as well. Set along the width of the entrance to the tomb were four whole vessels, all dating to EB IV; these were two bowls (one inside the other), a one-handled juglet, and a teapot. They sat upright on a prepared surface of small stones. The skulls both faced east. There is no evidence to suggest that this very small, irregular chamber ever included a shaft.

A second small cavity, E2, revealed a few long bone fragments only. Tomb E9 differed significantly from E3 and E2 in terms of size, construc-

tion, and inclusions (fig. 18). The aperture of this tomb proved to be a break through the chamber roof, for once inside, further excavation uncovered both a blocking stone and a lintel which, along with a crude stone wall, had originally blocked the chamber at the base of a shaft. The destruction of the shaft, and the fallen position of the blocking stone and the lintel indicate considerable disturbance to this tomb. That shaft tombs are a burial tradition in Cemetery E is now confirmed by a number of shafts, as exposed by a recent road cut through the area.

The E9 burial itself was a disarticulated interment of three adults. Bones and broken pottery were widely scattered over the chamber floor. There was no evidence that this was originally an articulated burial, although the interments seemed to be mostly complete skeletons. The grave goods included a large platter bowl, three lamps, a teapot, and several small bowls, as well as a fragment of a copper pin or awl and a broken basalt grinding stone.

Salvage excavations in Cemetery D on the southern ridge took place after the close of the season in 1984.[2] About midway up the slope, some 10 m west of a school used as a dig-house in 1982, a bulldozer cut had inadvertently broken through the shafts of one row of tombs. During this post-dig expedition, three tombs were excavated along the row of the bulldozer cut, along with one tomb from the row above. A rough count of the rows of tombs cut into the side of the hill indicates the presence of possibly hundreds of tombs.

The shafts of the Cemetery D tombs, in general, are spaced about 4–5 m apart; from the tomb excavated in the row above, it appears that the rows are similarly spaced. All of the tombs are of the round shaft, single chamber variety. Likewise they share some common characteristics such as disarticulated multiple burials and typical EB IV grave goods. All contained fill reaching virtually to the ceiling of the chambers and each tomb had suffered substantial roof collapse. As a result of this collapse, all of the pottery lay not only broken, but scattered all across the chamber. The chamber floors were consistently below the level of the shaft surface, usually ca. 0.75 m. All the tomb chambers had domed roofs. One noteworthy discrepancy among these tombs was their chamber shape, which ranged from square to oblong to semiround. This lack of symmetry no doubt relates to the rock formation in these different areas. One should also note that a type of plaster was used in each of the tombs to seal more tightly the blocking stone and entrance to the chamber.

Several of the tombs included steps at the base of the shaft. The architectural features of D2 are of particular interest, for included among them are an alcove with bench and an entrance with two steps plus jamb-like projections carved out of the rock. Two capstones at the base of the shaft, one *in situ*, the other not, alerted us to the fact that a reuse of this tomb had taken place. The nature of the disturbance to this tomb, unfortunately, made it almost impossible to separate any layers. Reconstructed bowls come from pieces scattered throughout the fill of the tomb. Skeletal remains were scanty and in bad condition. What is noteworthy is the vast amount of pottery recovered. Close to 100 vessels have been restored.

The usual EB IV forms, mostly red-slipped and burnished, a copper dagger, an awl plus pin fragments and two beads round out the corpus of materials.

Tombs D3 and D4, on the other hand, yielded discernibly discrete burial groupings, really piles of broken pottery and skeletal remains. The blocking stones for these two tombs lay inside the chambers, whether pushed in by looters or fallen in because of the bulldozer cut. Surprisingly, several whole vessels had survived the effects of roof collapse in D3: three jars and six lamps. Finally a tomb with complete shaft, D5 was excavated upslope. Expecting to find an undisturbed tomb, we were surprised to find again that the entire chamber was filled with roof collapse. Only one whole vessel at the entrance to the chamber and several sherds and bones within the tomb gave any suggestion of use.

POTTERY

A detailed analysis of the ceramics from the five phases at Iskander is presently underway and will be published separately. The following report is intended only to introduce the Iskander corpus of whole and restorable pottery recovered in the B8–B7 storerooms. One of the more surprising discoveries is the mixture of types, ware, and decoration in this context. Red-slipped and burnished pottery occurs alongside pottery normally considered to be the latest and characteristic of Dever's Family S (Amiran's Family A). Dever's Family S (southern) consists of a repertory of unslipped vessels in gray ware—the hallmarks are cups, ovoid storejars, platter bowls and teapots, whose decoration is distinguished by a great variety of incising, rilling, combing, and punctures (Dever 1980: fig. 4; Amiran 1969: pl. 22).

Besides an overlap on ware and decoration, types thought to be a hallmark of Family S—that is, large ovoid storejars in gray ware with band-combing—are now attested in Transjordan. Although the Iskander storejars (not all are ovoid) are not illustrated here, they are numerous and parallel Family S closely. They have everted necks, luted on secondarily; and they show the typical variety of decoration below the neck: band-combing, single wavy incision ("scrabbled" ware), slash marks, molding, punctures. Moreover, this storeroom area yielded handleless jars, as well as

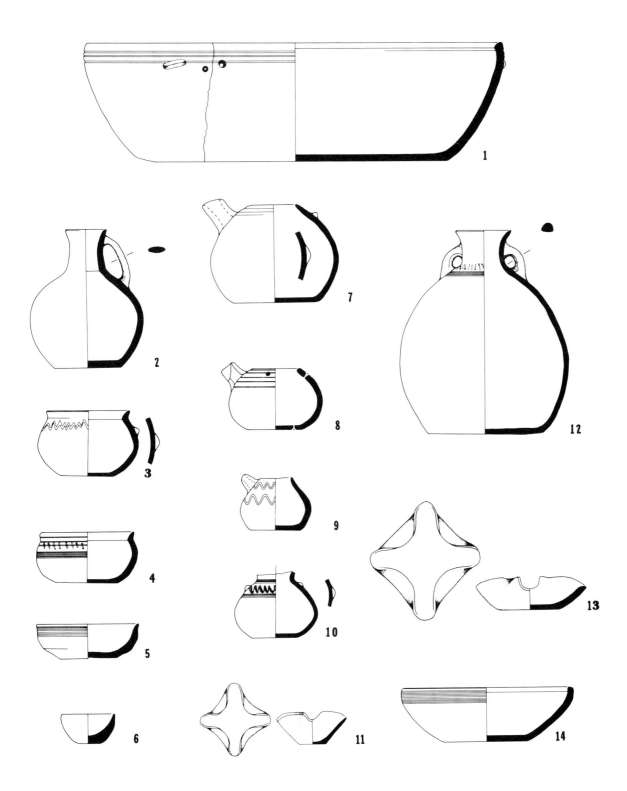

Fig. 19. Selection of EB IV pottery discovered in Phases B–C storerooms; red-slipped and burnished vessels include nos. 1, 3–5, 7, 9–10, 14.

jars with knobs and jars with envelope ledge-handles—all contemporaneous (figs. 9, 20). The data suggest, at this stage, that some of the typological attributes thought to be diagnostic in terms of chronology (Richard 1980; Dever 1980) may actually be a reflection of regional differences. Recently, Helms (1986) noted that the pottery at Tell Um Hammad exhibits types characteristic of all the families. He has tentatively suggested that all the regional families may be contemporaneous since similar forms are found irrespective of ware, slip, paint, or incisions.

Once the Iskander corpus is fully studied in relation to the architectural phasing, we will have a firmer idea of whether the current EB IVA–B–C terminology as it presently stands can be maintained or if revisions are in order (see Richard 1980). There is definitely more overlapping of families and styles than previously seemed the case. Nonetheless, typological development is evident in the Iskander pottery as well as at other sites. The diagnostics distinguishing EB IVA–B–C may have to be revised in terms of regional sequences.

Without a doubt, the red-slipped and burnished rilled-rim platter bowl is the most popular vessel at Iskander and in Transjordan generally, south of the Wadi Zerqa. At Tell Um Hammad in the Jordan Valley, for example, red slip and the platter bowl tradition are virtually unknown. At 0.60 m in diameter, fig. 19:1 is one of the largest such vessels to be published, another from Jebel Qaᶜaqir is ca. 0.50 m in diameter (Dever 1981: fig. 3:1). Knobs, or in this case a small plain handle, are frequently-attested attributes on storejars, small bowls and jars (fig. 19:3, 10), teapots, and cups. This platter bowl illustrates one variety of incision found at Iskander, widely separated deep incised lines. Also common to the bowl tradition generally are fine combing (as fig. 19:14), and deep indentations that give the shoulder the appearance of a rilled exterior. Examples of platter bowls in tombs at Iskander show that the type was not confined to domestic contexts.

Although found in a matrix of rubble collapse, fig. 19:2 is complete except for a nick at the rim. This unslipped vessel demonstrates close affinities with the typical EB III high-necked, high-shouldered jug. Indicative of the EB IV, though, is the strap handle attached just below the lip. Cup-bowls (fig. 19:3–4) with flanged rims and graceful rounded shape are extremely common at

Fig. 20. One of the large storejars reconstructed shortly after excavation from Area B storeroom; note folded envelope ledge-handles, fine everted rim, and band-combing (photo by Edyth Skinner).

the site and again illuminate a form paralleling EB III types closely, e.g., at Tell el-Ḥesi (Fargo 1979: fig. 1:19–22) and Jericho (Kenyon and Holland 1982: fig. 82). Again, a range of incised decoration occurs on this type, here with red slip as well. Closely related are shallow bowls with offset rim (fig. 19:5). Interestingly, the cup tradition for which the EB IV period has always been generally known, is not excessively popular in Transjordan, on the basis of the Iskander evidence and other published sites. Simple cups like fig. 19:6, bead-rim cups, goblets, and some examples of early-looking "caliciform" cups (Olávarri 1969: fig. 2:9) are known, but there is no question that the popularity of the "caliciform" tradition is a phenomenon of Family S. Whether this is a chronological or a regional distinction remains to be seen.

A range of teapot forms, often with knobs or lug handles and almost all red-slipped and burnished, show rills, single incised lines, and single wavy lines. Numerous parallels can be cited for fig. 19:7–9 at ᶜArôᶜer, Bâb edh-Dhrâᶜ, Jericho, etc. Fig. 19:10 is an example of a vessel that shows an overlapping of two traditions once thought to be chronologically distinct, i.e., it is red slipped and burnished but decorated with band combing.

Perhaps a bit surprising, or at least unexpected, is the advanced form of the EB IV lamps found at Iskander. This form has in the past generally been connected with the fully developed "MB I" tradition of western Palestine (Dever 1973: 48; Richard 1980: 18). Although early lamps like the ones at Bâb edh-Dhrâᶜ (Schaub 1973: fig. 6:1) have been found, figs. 19:11 (although a miniature) and 13 are common at the site and in the tombs (see also examples in the cemetery at Tiwal esh-Sharqi, Helms 1983).

The completely intact bottle amphoriskos illustrated in fig. 19:12 comes as a surprise given the rubble context in which it was found. As far as I am aware this is the first attestation of such a band-comb bottle amphoriskos in Transjordan. Again, one may cite numerous parallels in Family S, as well as in the Jericho and the Central Hills families (e.g., Kenyon and Holland 1982: fig. 96; Cohen and Dever 1981: fig. 10:18–21).

It is too early to draw definitive conclusions about the Khirbet Iskander pottery, since the earliest EB IV levels are not well known. Tentatively, though, one can advance the view that occupation at the site probably extends throughout the period, ca. 2350–2000 B.C., both from a consideration of the range of types and from their typological development and the extent of occupation. The corpus as it is now emerging links Iskander closely to the Jericho/Central Hills/ Southern families (see Dever 1980 for a discussion of these families). Dever, as early as 1973, posited a direct relationship between Transjordan and Family S. He saw the Transjordanian materials as the "missing link" between EB III and classic "MB I." The Khirbet Iskander ceramics more clearly than ever support a very close relationship between these areas. What remains to be determined is whether the Khirbet Iskander "mixed pottery" will ultimately prove to be transitional to or contemporary with Family S.

CONCLUSIONS

The results of three seasons of excavation at Khirbet Iskander demonstrate clearly that sedentary strategies, in this case a small town or regional center, are an important socioeconomic component of the EB IV culture. The growing list of EB IV settlement sites from Transjordan corroborates this view. One can only surmise from survey work in Palestine that a similar phenomenon occurs there, although those sites remain largely unexcavated. It is now clear that preconceived ideas concerning the period were largely responsible for the interpretation as nomadic of what actually was significant evidence for sedentary occupation, e.g., Jericho (Prag 1986), where EB IV occupation extends across the entire mound. Kenyon had dismissed the slight EB IV (her EB–MB) house walls as indicating a nonurban occupation during this period by "seminomadic pastoralists who had no interest in walled towns" (Kenyon, Bottero, and Posener 1971: 567). Extensive occupation may exist at other sites as well, e.g., Megiddo. It is evident that the model of pastoral-nomadism (Dever 1980), which has value for regional application, is obscuring our perspective on the EB IV peoples as a whole, and that newer models that seek to comprehend the EB IV archaeological record in its entirety are needed.

By way of extrapolation from the evidence at Iskander and other sites, it is possible to produce a long list of continuities with Early Bronze Age tradition, irrespective of an almost universal stratigraphic break throughout Palestine–Transjordan. Although originally I posited strong continuities with Early Bronze tradition almost principally upon a comparison of ceramics (1980), today the list may be greatly extended to include the following: 1) red-slipped and burnished pottery; 2) multiple burial in shaft tombs; 3) similar metal types; 4) substantial broad- and longroom houses, some with benches; 5) massive fortifications; 6) public complexes; 7) permanent storage facilities; 8) similar lithics; 9) significant pottery production; 10) multiphased sedentary occupation; 11) evidence for sociopolitical stratification; 12) sanctuaries; 13) significant amounts of food production equipment; 14) town planning.

Almost all the reasons Kenyon cited for designating the period a seminomadic one are no longer tenable. Her reasons were the following: 1) stratigraphic break; 2) no walled towns; 3) contrast in domestic architecture, no evidence for solidly built houses; 4) no large tombs with multiple burials; 5) material equipment in tombs different; 6) pottery forms so different from red-slipped Early Bronze Age types; 7) great weapons contrast (Kenyon, Bottero, and Posener 1971: 567–68).

In light of the strong continuities with Early Bronze tradition, it is difficult to support any view (including the terminology) of this period as "intermediate" in any sense (but cf. Amiran and Kochavi 1986; Prag 1984; 1985). The material culture manifests its Early Bronze heritage; it likewise exhibits contacts with recent innovations and new traditions within the Syrian assemblage. More in keeping with the nature of the evidence today is the conceptualization that the EB IV peoples are an indigenous culture and that the extent of Syrian influence on this culture has been grossly overemphasized. The most important obstruction to a view of the EB IV peoples as indigenous has been the misconception that the shift from EB III to EB IV was from sedentarism to nomadism, whereas in reality the shift was from urban to nonurban (i.e., village, town, and pastoral) adaptive strategies.

Indeed, the only conceivable means to understand the level of sedentarism in EB IV and the continuation of EB III urban traditions is to posit a model of cultural change, especially for Transjordan, which is less abrupt than hitherto believed (Richard 1980; 1987). Sociocultural change at the EB III/IV horizon (in this case greater pastoralism and village/town life as opposed to urban settlement) is better understood as a change in emphasis of production and organization in response to irreversible stresses on the urban system, rather than as an abrupt shift to a new sociocultural phenomenon (Salzman 1978). Newer views on sociocultural change, that is, greater fluidity in subsistence strategies (cultural adaptation) along the urban/nonurban continuum, provides the mechanism for change. Thus, depending on circumstances, e.g., political stability, there will be a greater or lesser stress on a range of adaptive strategies that are institutionalized within the culture (Salzman 1978; 1980).

In the absence of centralized political control, a less integrated, more politically autonomous society emerged following the collapse of the urban city-state system, as evidenced by the regional nature of the material culture. This loosely integrated society comprising a large pastoral population, small agricultural communities, and a few regional centers (small towns), reflects a readaptation to a level of political autonomy probably best explained by the chiefdom model (Service 1962; Richard 1987).

NOTES

[1] The expedition would also like to acknowledge its affiliation with Drew University and Upsala College. The expedition is indebted to Adnan Hadidi, Director-General of Antiquities in Jordan, and to his staff for their continued assistance and support. The Department once again enabled us to use houses at the Wadi Wala Government Station for our base camp and provided storage space and help in restoring pottery. We would also like to thank, once again, members of the Department of Archaeology, the University of Jordan for the loan of dig equipment. A special thanks likewise must go to David McCreery, director of the American Center of Oriental Research in Amman for his help at many points. Likewise, special thanks to Abdelmajid Bashabsheh, Department of Agriculture, Madaba, who as director of the Wadi Wala Agricultural Station was of great help to the expedition. The expedition would especially like to acknowledge the help and assistance in numerous ways over the years of Glen Peterman, administrative assistant of ACOR. Thanks to Glen almost all the pottery from Iskander has been drawn.

The expedition is grateful to the following for financial support: The Endowment for Biblical Research for funding the 1981 season; Seton Hall University for additional financial support in 1981; the National Endowment for the Humanities for its support of the second season (RO-20386-82); and a special thanks to all the private donors for making our 1984 season a possibility.

The 1984 staff consisted of Suzanne Richard (director); Roger S. Boraas (associate director); Andrew Dearman and Jonathan Elias (area supervisors); James D'Angelo (tombs supervisor); Edyth Skinner (photographer); Robert Suder (architect/surveyor); Marlin White (camp manager); Sarah White (artist); Nancy Broeder (pottery registrar); Jeannette Ohlson (object registrar and square supervisor); Peter Warnock (palaeobotanist/assistant architect); Mary Louise Mussell (assistant field supervisor); Louis Lanese (engineer who experimented with infrared thermography). Square supervisors were William Agee, Gary Grisdale, Mary Ann Kaub, Tom Reid, Rozanna Pfeiffer, J. Stirling Dorrance, William Hammond, and Steve Taylor. Volunteers were Suzanne Gallagher, Jack Livingston, Robert Broedere, and Ann Ross. Abu Arif was our cook and Hussein Qandil was the Department of Antiquities representative.

[2]This work was conducted under the auspices of The Department of Antiquities, whose director Adnan Hadidi suggested the project and generously provided the financial support needed to excavate in Cemetery D. The director would like also to express gratitude to the staff of the Department for assistance with photography and restoration, and for the use of field equipment and storage space. The author and Hussein Qandil, representative of the Department of Antiquities, along with three workmen excavated tombs D2-5.

BIBLIOGRAPHY

Amiran, R.
1969   *Ancient Pottery of the Holy Land.* Jerusalem: Massada Press.

Amiran, R., and Kochavi, M.
1985   Canaan at the Close of the Third Millennium B.C.E.—An Independent Culture or the Final Phase of the Early Bronze Age? Pp. 361–65 in *Eretz Israel* 18. Jerusalem: Israel Exploration Society (Hebrew; English summary 77–78*).

Cleveland, R.
1960   The Excavation of the Conway High Place (Petra) and Soundings at Khirbet Ader. *Annual of the American Schools of Oriental Research* 34–35. New Haven, CT: American Schools of Oriental Research.

Cohen, R., and Dever, W. G.
1981   Preliminary Report of the Third and Final Season of the "Central Negev Highlands Project." *Bulletin of the American Schools of Oriental Research* 243: 57–77.

Dever, W. G.
1973   The EB IV–MB I Horizon in Transjordan and Southern Palestine. *Bulletin of the American Schools of Oriental Research* 210: 37–63.
1980   New Vistas on the EB IV ("MB I") Horizon in Syria-Palestine. *Bulletin of the American Schools of Oriental Research* 237: 35–64.
1981   Cave G 26 at Jebel Qaᵓaqir: A Domestic Assemblage of Middle Bronze I. Pp. 22–32* in *Eretz Israel* 15. Jerusalem: Israel Exploration Society.

Fargo, V.
1979   Early Bronze Age Pottery at Tell el-Ḥesi. *Bulletin of the American Schools of Oriental Research* 236: 23–40.

Geraty, L. T., *et al.*
1986   Madaba Plains Project: A Preliminary Report of the 1984 Season at Tel el-ᶜUmeiri and Vicinity. Pp. 117–44 in *Bulletin of the American Schools of Oriental Research* Supplement No. 24, ed. W. E. Rast. Winona Lake, IN: Eisenbrauns for the American Schools of Oriental Research.

Glueck, N.
1939   Explorations in Eastern Palestine, pt. 3. *Annual of the American Schools of Oriental Research* 18–19. New Haven, CT: American Schools of Oriental Research.

Helms, S. W.
1983   The EB IV (EB–MB) Cemetery at Tiwal esh-Sharqi in the Jordan Valley, 1983. *Annual of the Department of Antiquities of Jordan* 27: 55–85.
1986   Excavations at Tell um-Hammad, 1984. *Levant* 18: 25–50.

Kenyon, K. M., and Holland, T. A.
1982   *Excavations at Jericho: The Pottery Type Series and Other Finds,* Vol. 4. London: British School of Archaeology in Jerusalem.

Kenyon, K. M.; Bottero, J.; and Posener, G.
1971   Syria and Palestine, c. 2160–1780 B.C. Pp. 532–94 in *Cambridge Ancient History,* 3rd revised ed., Vol. 1, Part 2. Cambridge, England: Cambridge University.

Olávarri, E.
1969   Fouilles à ᶜArôᶜer sur l'Arnon. *Revue Biblique* 76: 230–59.

Parr, P.
1960   Excavations at Khirbet Iskander. *Annual of the Department of Antiquities of Jordan* 4–6: 128–33.

Prag, K.
1974   The Intermediate Early Bronze–Middle Bronze Age: An Interpretation of the Evidence from Transjordan, Syria, and Lebanon. *Levant* 6: 69–116.
1984   Continuity and Migration in the South Levant in the Late Third Millennium: A Review of T. L. Thompson's and some other views. *Palestine Exploration Quarterly* 116: 58–68.
1985   Ancient and Modern Pastoral Migration in the Levant. *Levant* 17: 81–88.
1986   The Intermediate Early Bronze–Middle Bronze Age Sequences at Jericho and Tell Iktanu Reviewed. *Bulletin of the American Schools of Oriental Research* 264: 61–72.

Rast, W. E., and Schaub, R. T.
1978   A Preliminary Report of Excavations at Bâb

edh-Dhrā[c], 1975. Pp. 1–32 in Preliminary Excavation Reports: Bâb edh-Dhrā[c], Sardis, Meiron, Tell el-Hesi, Carthage (Punic), ed. D. N. Freedman. *Annual of the American Schools of Oriental Research* 43. Cambridge, MA: American Schools of Oriental Research.

1980   Preliminary Report of the 1979 Expedition of the Dead Sea Plain, Jordan. *Bulletin of the American Schools of Oriental Research* 240: 21–61.

Richard, S.

1980   Toward a Consensus of Opinion on the End of the Early Bronze Age in Palestine–Transjordan. *Bulletin of the American Schools of Oriental Research* 237: 5–34.

1982   Report on the 1981 Season of Survey and Soundings at Khirbet Iskander. *Annual of the Department of Antiquities of Jordan* 26: 289–99.

1983   Report on the Expedition to Khirbet Iskander and its Vicinity, 1982. *Annual of the Department of Antiquities of Jordan* 27: 45–53.

1986   Excavations at Khirbet Iskander, Jordan: A Glimpse at Settled Life during the "Dark Age" in Palestinian Archaeology. *Expedition* 28: 3–12.

1987   The Early Bronze Age in Palestine: The Rise and Collapse of Urbanism. *Biblical Archaeologist* 50, 1: 22–43.

Richard, S., and Boraas, R. S.

1984   Preliminary Report of the 1981–82 Seasons of the Expedition to Khirbet Iskander and its Vicinity. *Bulletin of the American Schools of Oriental Research* 254: 63–87.

Salzman, P. C.

1978   Ideology and Change in Middle Eastern Tribal Societies. *Man* 13: 618–37.

Salzman, P. C., ed.

1980   *When Nomads Settle: Processes of Sedentarization as Adaptation and Response.* New York: Praeger.

Schaub, R. T.

1973   An Early Bronze IV Tomb from Bâb edh-Dhrâ[c]. *Bulletin of the American Schools of Oriental Research* 210: 2–19.

Schaub, R. T., and Rast, W. E.

1984   Preliminary Report of the 1981 Expedition to the Dead Sea Plain, Jordan. *Bulletin of the American Schools of Oriental Research* 254: 35–60.

Service, E. R.

1962   *Primitive Social Organization.* New York: Random House.

Preliminary Report on the 1985 Season of the *Limes Arabicus* Project

S. Thomas Parker

North Carolina State University

Raleigh, NC 27695

The 1985 season was designed to shed further light on the evolution of the Roman fortified frontier east of the Dead Sea between the late third and early sixth centuries. Excavation of the legionary fortress of el-Lejjūn revealed new elements of the headquarters building, barracks, fortifications, and a church. Some evidence suggested that the legion was reduced in strength by 50 percent less than a century after its establishment at Lejjūn. Soundings at Qaṣr Bshīr, a castellum *15 km northeast of Lejjūn, confirmed it was designed for a cavalry unit. Extensive new areas of both the frontier zone itself and the desert fringe east of the frontier were surveyed, revealing not only the Roman frontier, but also its Moabite and Nabataean predecessors.*

INTRODUCTION

The following report is a summary of the results of the third season of the *Limes Arabicus* Project, in preliminary form. It follows the schema of previous reports (Parker 1982: 1–26; 1985: 1–34). It includes a brief historical background, a stratigraphic summary, results from excavated areas with the el-Lejjūn legionary fortress, soundings of the *castella* of Qaṣr Bshīr and Khirbet el-Fityān, survey of the frontier zone, and survey of the desert fringe just east of the frontier. Some tentative historical conclusions are offered, based on this evidence. Finally, a numismatic appendix of all coins recovered in 1985 is presented by John Wilson Betlyon.

BACKGROUND

The *Limes Arabicus* Project seeks to gain an understanding of the historical development of the sector of the Roman frontier east of the Dead Sea from the late third to the mid-sixth centuries. The beginning of this period witnessed a dramatic military buildup in this region, including the erection of new fortifications, systematic repair of the regional road network, and the arrival of new military units (fig. 1). For about two centuries the frontier (in Latin, a *limes*) remained well fortified, but by the early sixth century there appears to have been a widespread abandonment of most of these frontier forts.[1] Therefore, the project seeks to answer two principal historical questions: What can account for the massive military buildup in this sector about A.D. 300? Why were most of the fortifications abandoned about two centuries later?

A four-part program is being employed to answer these questions: 1) large-scale excavation of the legionary fortress of el-Lejjūn (the largest military site in this sector), 2) limited soundings of several smaller fortifications, 3) intensive archaeological survey of the frontier zone, 4) a parallel survey of the desert fringe east of the frontier to learn about the nomadic tribes. Three of five planned campaigns have been conducted thus far: in 1980, 1982, and 1985. Additional campaigns are scheduled for 1987 and 1989.

STRATIGRAPHIC SUMMARY

The first season of excavation in 1980 at Lejjūn, combined with the soundings at Khirbet el-Fityān and Rujm Beni Yasser, established a basic stratigraphic sequence based on associated numismatic

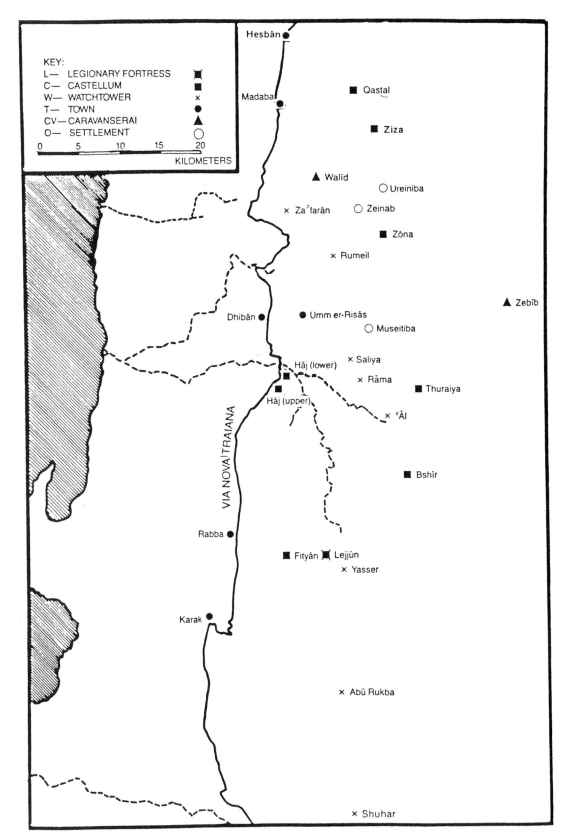

Fig. 1. Map of the central sector of the Arabian frontier east of the Dead Sea.

TABLE 1. Stratigraphic Designations

Stratum	Period	Approximate Dates
VII	Early Roman	ca. 63 B.C.–A.D. 135
	Post Stratum VII Gap	ca. A.D. 135–284
VI	Late Roman	ca. 284–324
VB	Early Byzantine I	ca. 324–363
VA	Early Byzantine II	ca. 363–400
IV	Early Byzantine III–IV	ca. 400–502
III	Late Byzantine I–II	ca. 502–551
	Post Stratum III Gap	ca. 551–1900
	(intermittent use as a camp site and cemetery)	
II	Late Ottoman	ca. 1900–1918
I	Modern	ca. 1918–

and ceramic evidence (Parker 1982: 3–5). Results from 1982, including further excavation of Lejjūn and soundings at Qaṣr Bshīr, permitted a slightly more refined stratigraphic sequence (Parker 1983: 216; 1985: 1–2). Results from 1985 have not altered the primary sequence of occupation at Lejjūn (ca. A.D. 284–551) but did produce the first evidence of Umayyad (ca. 661–750) occupation, albeit rather minor and confined to a single area, the northwest angle tower. This material is as yet insufficient to justify it as a new stratum. Otherwise, the stratigraphic framework is little changed (Table 1).

Stratified Early Roman (Nabataean) evidence has come only from Rujm Beni Yasser, ca. 1.5 km east of Lejjūn. The fortress itself has yielded very small amounts of Nabataean pottery, although never in a stratified context. This suggests that a small Nabataean site may have been obliterated completely by the subsequent massive legionary occupation.

The reign of Diocletian (284–305) remains the most likely date for the construction of the Lejjūn fortress. This date is supported by the plan of the fortress, the numismatic evidence, and pottery from the foundation levels of the enclosure wall and barracks. The erection of Qaṣr Bshīr is firmly dated to this period by an *in situ* Latin building inscription of 293–305 (*CIL* 3.14149). This era also witnessed the construction of Khirbet el-Fityān (perhaps on Iron Age foundations) and the reoccupation of Rujm Beni Yasser (Parker 1982: 11–18).

The earthquake of 363, known from literary evidence to have been severe locally (Russell 1980: 47–64; 1985: 42), seems to have had a profound impact at Lejjūn. The *mansio* in the *vicus* was destroyed and never rebuilt. The original Late Roman barracks within the fortress were demolished to their foundations; new barracks were erected along a slightly different alignment (Parker 1985: 9–10, 13–14). The church within the fortress appears to have been built in the late fifth century.

The smaller posts of Fityān, Yasser, and Qaṣr Bshīr appear to have been abandoned by the end of the fifth century, as evidenced by the absence of Late Byzantine (i.e., sixth and early seventh century) stratification at all three sites. Occupation at Lejjūn, however, continued into the early sixth century. The earthquake of 502 severely damaged the *principia* and barracks, but was followed by some modest attempts at reconstruction. This final period of occupation within the fortress was punctuated by the earthquake of 551, which led to the collapse of the many structures and the end of substantial occupation.

There is some evidence for intermittent use of the fortress during the Islamic era, no doubt due to the presence of a perennial water source, ᶜAin Lejjūn. This use included camping in the ruins of the northwest angle tower in the Umayyad period (661–750). There is also evidence for a limited reoccupation of Qaṣr Bshīr in this period. A few scattered sherds and coins of the Ayyubid/Mamlūk (1174–1516) and Ottoman (1516–1918)

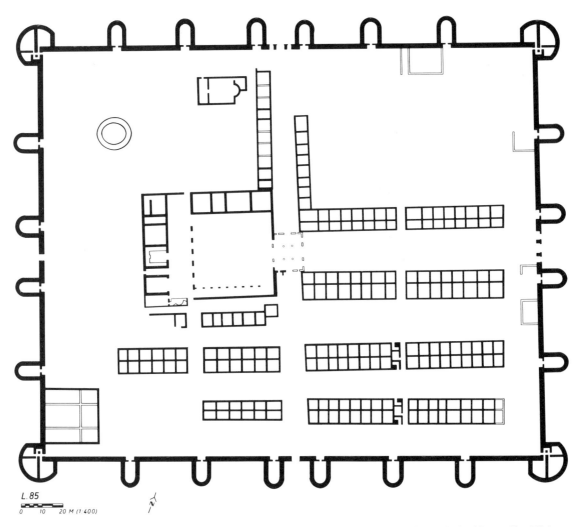

Fig. 2. Plan of the legionary fortress of el-Lejjūn in the Byzantine period (ca. 363–551). Architect: Jim Michener; surveyors: Bert de Vries, Dan Ritsema.

periods attest use of the ruins as a Bedouin cemetery and occasional campsite. Just prior to the
First World War Turkish military barracks were
constructed on a ridge west of the fortress. The
Turkish barracks were built with stones robbed
from the Roman fortress. The departure of the
Turkish garrison by 1918 again left the site unoccupied. After the Second World War the Maᶜaita
tribe began agricultural activities in the valley.

EXCAVATION OF THE LEJJŪN
LEGIONARY FORTRESS

Plan of the Fortress[2]

The Lejjūn fortress offers the rare opportunity
to study a late Roman legionary fortress built *de*

novo on a virgin site and not complicated by
significant later occupation. The site has long
been identified as Betthorus, base of *legio* IV
Martia, ca. A.D. 400 in the *Notitia Dignitatum*
(*Or.* 37.22). This identification is still unproven by
any epigraphic or other evidence but remains
probable. The fortress (fig. 2) measures 242 ×
190 m and covers an area of 4.6 ha (ca. 11 acres).
The fortress is protected by an enclosure wall
2.40 m thick and studded with projecting towers.
Each wall is pierced in the middle by a gate. Two
major streets intersect at a right angle at the
groma or middle of the fortress: the *via praetoria*
extends from the east gate to the *groma*, the *via
principalis* runs from the north gate to the south
gate. Near the intersection of the two streets at the
groma is the *principia* or headquarters building.

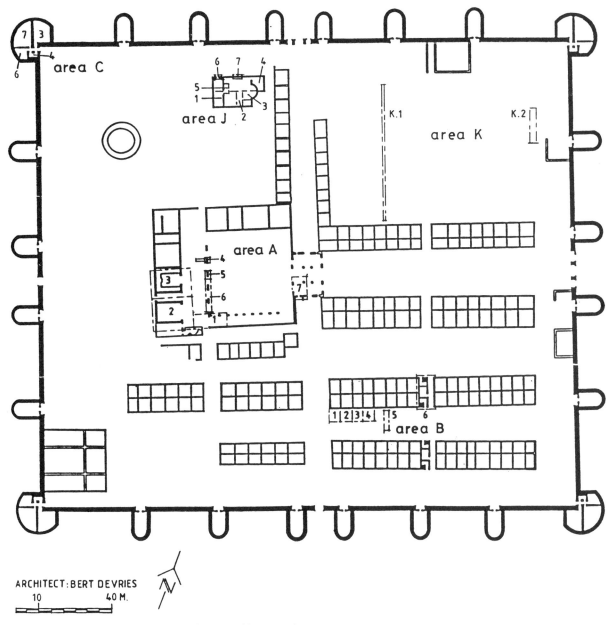

Fig. 3. Schematic plan of the Lejjūn fortress with excavation areas.

The entire eastern half of the fortress is devoted to blocks of barracks. The identity of several structures in the western half is less clear, although the apsidal building southwest of the north gate (*porta principalis sinistra*) is now known to be a church. The circular depression in the northwestern quadrant is probably a cistern.

The objectives in excavating Lejjūn are to learn its complete stratigraphic history, to shed light on the garrison and its role in the military frontier, and to recover data about the late Roman legion and *limitanei* (frontier forces) of the late Empire. The strategy has been to sample through excavation each principal component of the fortress: the headquarters building, barracks, fortifications, and the church (fig. 3). A major structure in the *vicus* has also been sounded. This proved to be a *mansio* or caravanserai (Parker 1985: 13–14, fig. 13).

A major achievement of the 1985 season was completion of a completely remeasured and detailed overall plan of the fortress drawn by the project architects under Bert De Vries (fig. 2),

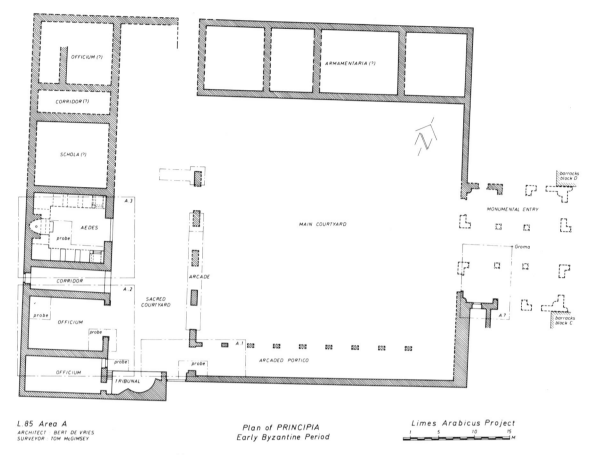

Fig. 4. Plan of the *principia* (Area A).

superseding that of Domaszewski (Brünnow and Domaszewski 1905: pl. 42). Their descriptions and photographs, however, made before establishment of the Late Ottoman resettlement ca. 1900, are still invaluable.

The Headquarters Building (Principia): Area A

The Lejjūn *principia* is truly unique among legionary headquarters buildings. Important Tetrarchic parallels are known in the east: at Luxor in Egypt and the so-called "Camp of Diocletian" at Palmyra. But the former was a conversion of a pharaonic temple while the latter was built within an existing domestic quarter. The Lejjūn *principia* remains the only legionary headquarters building constructed *de novo* yet excavated in the eastern Empire. It therefore offers an unparalleled opportunity to address key issues concerning the development of late Roman military architecture.

The headquarters building (63 × 52.50 m) is situated in its traditional location behind the *groma*

or the intersection of the *via praetoria* and *via principalis* in the middle of the fortress (fig. 4). The structure consists of four essential elements: 1) a monumental entrance at the *groma*, 2) an outer or public courtyard, 3) an inner transverse courtyard, and 4) a block of official rooms serving as administrative offices and containing the legionary shrine, or *aedes*.

Work in 1985 continued in the L-shaped area in the southwestern quadrant of the building, encompassing a portion of the outer courtyard, inner courtyard, and official range of rooms. This sector was also worked in both previous seasons. In addition, excavation was initiated in the *groma* fronting the *principia*.

The major elements of the building's plan were elucidated in 1980 and 1982 (Parker 1982: 5–8; 1985: 2–9). Some further details were revealed this season. In 1985 the complete stratigraphic profile of the *principia* was obtained. Although its major walls appear to date from the primary stratum (VI) of fortress construction, the building was

Fig. 5. The southwestern quadrant of the monumental gatehouse (*groma*) fronting the *principia*, from the northeast. Note the engaged columns.

thoroughly remodeled in the late fourth century, perhaps following the 363 earthquake.

Excavation of one quarter of the *groma* revealed a monumental gatehouse or entrance hall (ca. 18 × 17 m), reminiscent of the legionary head-quarters buildings at Lambaesis in Numidia and at Palmyra. The tentative reconstruction (fig. 4) consists of a *quadrifrons* hall with each facade pierced by three openings. Two smaller passage-ways flank a larger central opening, wide enough to accommodate wheeled traffic. The interior of the hall was built of ashlar limestone masonry and was decorated with engaged columns which once carried Nabataean-style capitals (fig. 5). The rough and rather unattractive chert walls of an adjoining guardroom were disguised by the application of fine white stucco molded to simulate ashlar lime-stone. The date of construction of this gatehouse is as yet undetermined.

Monumental gate halls fronting the *principia* appear to be a late development in Roman mili-tary architecture. Four parallels are known. The earliest (late second century) is from the legionary fortress at Lauriacum in Noricum on the Danube. The early third century Severan *principia* at Dura Europus in Syria includes a square, tower-like entrance hall. A two-storied gate hall at Lam-baesis was rebuilt under Gallienus (253–268) over a Hadrianic foundation. A fourth example may be cited from *Mauretania Caesariensis*: the fort at Rapidum which was rebuilt during the Tetrarchy with such a gate hall (Kolbe 1974: 291, 295; Rakob and Storz 1974: 266; Fellmann 1976: 180; A. Johnson 1983: 120). Not surprisingly, mid-third century military rosters preserved on papyri from Dura indicate that the *groma* was a routine post for guard duty (Fink 1971: 128, 136).

The *groma* gave access to the large public court-yard (ca. 38 m^2). Arcaded porticoes supported by square piers extended along the southern and (presumably) northern side of the courtyard. The *armamentaria* or weapons stores traditionally located against the perimeter of the outer court-yard in many *principia* of the Principate are

Fig. 6. Interior of the legionary shrine (*aedes*).

notable by their absence at Lejjūn. A series of rooms attached to the northern wall may have served this function, but this must be tested by excavation.

The outer public courtyard was separated from the inner sacred courtyard by a limestone arcade of piers and arches. The inner courtyard could be entered either from the outer courtyard via passages through the arcade or from outside the building via lateral doorways in the south and (presumably) north walls. At the southern end of the inner courtyard was the *tribunal* or elevated platform (8 × 4 m), decorated by a semicircular niche and reached by a staircase. From the *tribunal* officers could address small contingents of troops assembled in the inner courtyard.

West of the courtyard and south of the *aedes*, in the official range of rooms, further excavation was conducted in a large room (7 × 10 m) identified as an *officium*, perhaps the *tabularium legionis*. Recovery of several phases of hearths, numerous fragments of cooking pots, and charred animal bones suggested considerable domestic

activity in one corner of this room. Limited excavation of the narrow space between this room and the *aedes* to the north confirmed an earlier supposition that this was a corridor leading from the sacred courtyard to the west or rear of the building.

The interior of the *aedes* or legionary shrine (9 × 10 m) was rebuilt after the 363 earthquake with a U-shaped platform extending around three sides (fig. 6). Access to the platform, supported by the barrel-vaulted substructures discovered in 1982, was provided by staircases in the southeast and (presumably) northeast corners of the room. Another staircase led up to the platform on the west wall that supported the legionary standard base. The standard base was raised above the level of the platform and was framed by an apsidal niche. Bits of gold foil, recovered from the socle of the standard base in 1982, probably were scraped off the *aquila* or eagle standard of *legio IV Martia*. Just in front of the central staircase on the floor of the *aedes* were the remains of an oval, gypsum plaster installation. This may have once

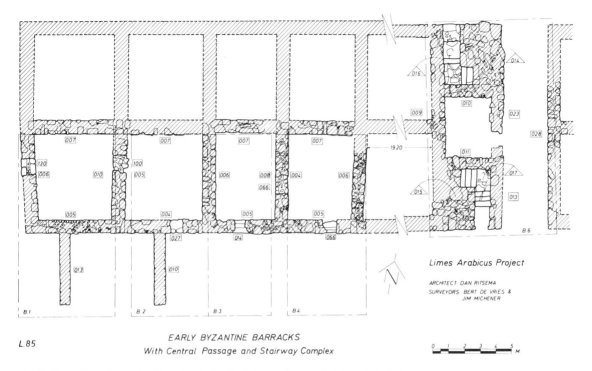

L.85

EARLY BYZANTINE BARRACKS
With Central Passage and Stairway Complex

Limes Arabicus Project

ARCHITECT DAN RITSEMA
SURVEYORS BERT DE VRIES &
JIM MICHENER

0 1 2 3 4 5 M

Fig. 7. Plan of the barracks (Area B) in the Early Byzantine period (ca. 363–502).

served as a base for an imperial statue. This installation, the central staircase, the standard base, and the *aedes* entrance are all on an east–west axis with the entrance to the *principia*, the *groma*, the *via praetoria*, and the *porta praetoria*, as is typical of the symmetry of Roman military architecture. There was no evidence of an underground vault that might have served as the legionary *aerarium* or treasury. But a handful of stray coins found at the entrances to the barrel vaults suggested that the vaults themselves may have served this purpose.

The earthquake of 502 resulted in some damage to the *principia*. The garrison clearly lacked the resources for a proper restoration, such as that of the late fourth century, as evidenced by the consolidation and packing of collapsed roof tiles and other debris to create new, higher floors in some rooms and both courtyards. Doorways were outfitted with higher secondary thresholds to accommodate the raised floor levels. The former arcade that separated the outer and inner courtyards was simply converted into a rough wall composed of reused blocks that filled in the gaps between the piers. This preserved the principal architectural divisions of the building, albeit in rather shoddy fashion.

The demobilization or transfer of the legion ca. 530 resulted in the cleaning out and essential abandonment of the *principia* for the final two decades of the fortress's history. The final earthquake of 551 appears to have largely demolished the standing walls of the structure.

The Barracks (Areas B and K)

The entire eastern half of the fortress was devoted to blocks of barracks. A major goal was to reconstruct the plan of these blocks to extrapolate the size and internal organization of the legion. A second major goal was to recover cultural material relating to the legionary garrison, including evidence on the supposed transformation of the late Roman *limitanei* from full-time soldiers to a peasant militia.

Four major barracks blocks are visible on the surface (fig. 2). Three of these are located south of the *via praetoria* and one to the north. Domaszewski's old plan shows each of these extant blocks as a continuous range of 18 double rooms along either side of the central spine wall. Previous excavations in 1980–1982 proved that the supposed double rooms were in fact only single rooms, fronted by courtyards of irregular size

Fig. 8. One of the two L-shaped staircases (B.6) that gave access to the roof of the Byzantine barracks; view is from the northeast.

(Parker 1982: 8–10; 1985: 9–10). Completion of the redrawn plan in 1985 revealed that the long blocks were in fact not continuous but bisected by a passageway.

Excavation continued in Area B, a set of rooms within the second block north of the southern wall (fig. 3). In 1980 and 1982 four rooms and associated courtyards (B.1–4) at the western end of block B, south of the central spine wall, were excavated (fig. 7). B.2 and B.3 were completely excavated in 1982. The other two (B.1 and B.4) were finished this season. In addition, two more trenches (B.5 and B.6) were laid out farther down the block to the east. B.5 (8 × 2 m) was laid out to recover more of the plan of the primary Late Roman (Stratum VI) barracks found in 1982 (fig. 7). A secondary goal was to section the alleyway between blocks A and B. B.6 (13 × 9 m) was laid out to investigate the passageway that bisected the block and connected the alleyway between blocks A and B with that between blocks B and C. A

small room of uncertain purpose opened onto the passageway. The small room was flanked on both north and south by L-shaped staircases entered from the two alleyways. These staircases gave access to the roof of the barracks, perhaps to facilitate roof maintenance (fig. 8).

The evidence obtained offered further support for the stratigraphic framework for this barracks specifically and the fortress generally as elucidated in the previous seasons (Parker 1982: 5, 8–10; 1985: 2, 9–10).

Strata VI–VB (ca. 284–363) witnessed the erection and initial occupation of the garrison, probably terminated by the earthquake of 363. A partial plan of this primary barracks was recovered in Area B (fig. 9). Important new evidence about this period was obtained from two long trenches (Area K; cf. fig. 3) in the northeastern quadrant. This sector is mostly devoid of surface ruins and appears largely empty on both Domaszewski's plan and more recent aerial photographs. How-

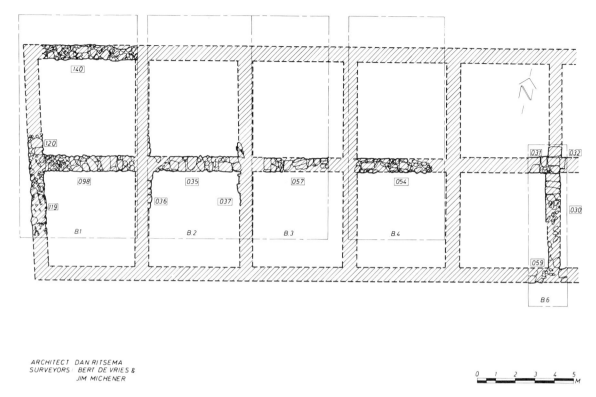

ARCHITECT DAN RITSEMA
SURVEYORS BERT DE VRIES &
          JIM MICHENER

0   1   2   3   4   5
▬▬▬▬▬▬▬▬▬▬M

Fig. 9. Plan of the barracks (Area B) in the Late Roman period (ca. 284–363).

ever, several fragments of walls appear on Domas-zewski's plan and traces of a few wall lines are still discernible on the surface. Further, surface sherd-ing of this quadrant produced a pottery sample that was over 70 percent Late Roman in date (i.e., late third and early fourth centuries). Thus two trenches were laid out to determine whether bar-racks existed here during Strata VI–VB.

One trench (K.1, 56 × 1.5 m) ran south from near the north enclosure wall to the northern face of block D. Another trench, K.2 (14.5 × 2.5 m), was extended parallel to and just west of the eastern enclosure wall in an effort to locate the eastern terminus of these early barracks. The foun-dations of four barracks blocks, each separated from others by intervening alleys, were found just below the surface. The walls were associated with late third–early fourth century pottery and with three coins, dated 335–350, 347–350, and 355–361.[3] The barrack rooms were identical in size to those of the same period in Area B. The plans appear to be essentially similar to the later Byzan-tine barracks of Strata VA–III (cf. figs. 7–9). The major difference is that there were apparently

eight barracks blocks in the eastern half of the fortress as originally built (fig. 10). But following the demolition of the eight old barracks to their foundations in the late fourth century (presumably after the earthquake of 363), only four new blocks were reconstructed. This implies a 50 percent reduc-tion in the size of the IV *Martia.*

The Fortifications (Area C)

The formidable fortifications of Lejjūn fall clearly into the late Roman tradition of military architecture, which emphasized a defensive strat-egy based upon heavily fortified strongpoints (Luttwak 1976: 159–70; S. Johnson 1983; Lander 1984: 168–262). The major components at Lejjūn are the enclosure wall, 20 U-shaped interval towers, four semicircular angle towers, and four gateways. The project is sampling each component of the fortifications of the fortress. In 1980 a section through a segment of the northern enclo-sure wall was completed (Parker 1982: 10–11). Representative angle and interval towers were excavated in 1982 (Parker 1985: 11–13, fig. 10).

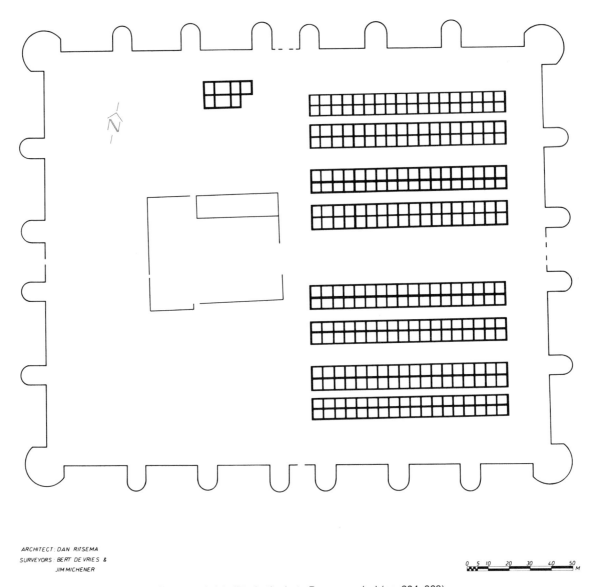

ARCHITECT: DAN RITSEMA
SURVEYORS: BERT DE VRIES &
        JIM MICHENER

Fig. 10. Plan of the legionary fortress of el-Lejjūn in the Late Roman period (ca. 284–363).

Work in 1985 continued in the northwest angle tower (number VI on Domaszewski's plan). The major goals were to check the accuracy of Domaszewski's plans and sections and to recover the occupational history of the tower. A gateway will be excavated in a future season.

The tower measures ca. 20 m in diameter (fig. 11). The tower walls project 6 m from the enclosure wall before curving to form a semicircle. The interior of the tower is divided into four rooms. The small southeast room, completely cleared in 1982, contains the entrance into the tower from the fortress, a corridor providing access to the

three other ground floor rooms, and a staircase reaching to the upper stories (fig. 12). This season the other three rooms of the first story were partially excavated. All were roofed by a series of parallel limestone arches that carried oblong roofing slabs (fig. 13). Several of the arches had fallen with their blocks still closely aligned. As in past seasons, Bedouin burials from the Islamic period were encountered in the rubble near the surface (fig. 14). Holes (for tethering animals?) were drilled in the springers of several arches in the larger northwest and northeast rooms, suggesting their use as stables. No mangers have yet

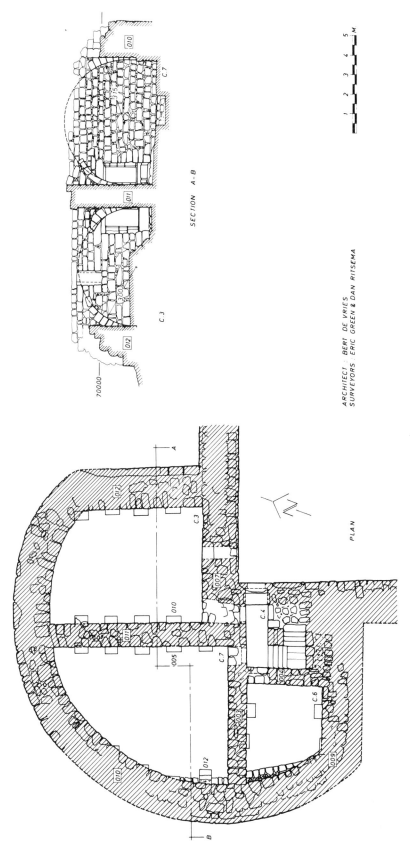

Fig. 11. Plan and elevation of the northwest angle tower (Area C).

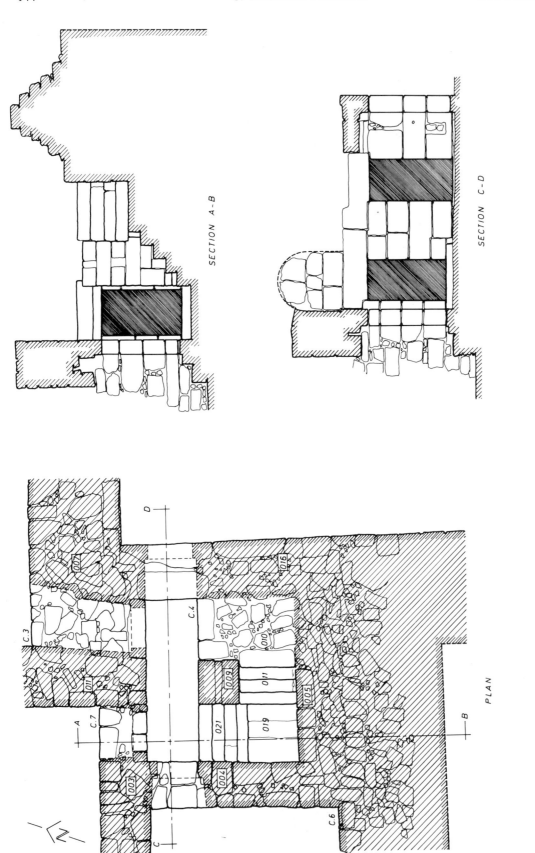

SECTION A - B

SECTION C - D

PLAN

ARCHITECTS: BERT DE VRIES and ERIC GREEN

Fig. 12. Plan and elevations of the staircase in the northwest angle tower (C.4).

Fig. 13. Northeastern room (C.3) of the angle tower, view from the south. Note the engaged arch springers that carried the roof of the first story.

been found built into the walls of these rooms, however, as at Qaṣr Bshīr. This suggests that even if these two ground floor rooms did function as stables in some period, this was not a purpose intended originally. The roofs of these two rooms apparently collapsed in the 551 earthquake. But some limited evidence of Umayyad occupation (late seventh or early eighth century) was recovered near their still-intact doorways. The much smaller southwest room, however, apparently remained roofed and was in use intermittently in the Islamic period, as evidenced by several domestic installations.

The most striking evidence of this early Islamic reoccupation was an inscribed stone found near the doorway of the southeast room (C.3). Several drawings of horsemen and other figures appear to be fitted around the Arabic inscriptions (fig. 15). Preliminary analysis by Vincent A. Clark identified two distinct inscriptions. The upper text consists of six lines and is the complete text of Sura 112 from the *Koran*, commonly found on tomb-stones. The text appears to be early because the letter forms are undotted and some have archaic features. The lower text, also Arabic, is enigmatic and requires further study. The stone was found among the tumble debris within the doorway and was clearly not *in situ*. If it represents a tombstone from a nearby burial, it suggests that use of the ruined fortress as a cemetery began in the early Islamic era, earlier than previously supposed.

Beneath the tumbled walls and roofing arches of the 551 earthquake was evidence of Byzantine and Late Roman occupation in these rooms. Foundations were reached only in a restricted probe in the northwest room, however, requiring further excavation next season.

The projecting semicircular angle tower fits neatly into the typology of Roman fortifications of the late third and fourth centuries, as noted previously (for parallels from several parts of the Empire, Parker and Lander 1982: 191, n. 17; Parker 1985: 13; 1986a: 69–72).

Fig. 14. Double Bedouin burial from the angle tower. Note the glass bottle just above the meter stick.

The Church

Among the buildings within the fortress is a rectangular structure in the northwest quadrant near the north gate with an apse on its eastern end (fig. 16). This building, tentatively identified as a church from its surface architectural features, was investigated through a series of trenches (J.1–7), and its identity confirmed. Other principal goals were to date the church, articulate its plan, and recover its occupational history. Since Diocletian launched the last great persecution of Christianity in the Empire and systematically purged Christians from the army, the church could not have been built when the fortress was constructed ca. 290–300. But how much later was it erected? Its date provides evidence for the vexing problem of the conversion of the Roman army from paganism to Christianity (MacMullen 1984: 41–44). Further, since the church was clearly secondary in date, what occupied this space originally? Because sacred places tend to remain sacred, even after a change in religion, would an earlier pagan structure of some sort be found beneath the church?

The church measures ca. 24 × 13 m, including the narthex on its western end (fig. 17). The church was basilical in plan, with the nave divided into three aisles by east–west arches carried by columns. Somewhat surprisingly, the only entrance into the church from the exterior was via a door in the north wall of the narthex. The narthex was

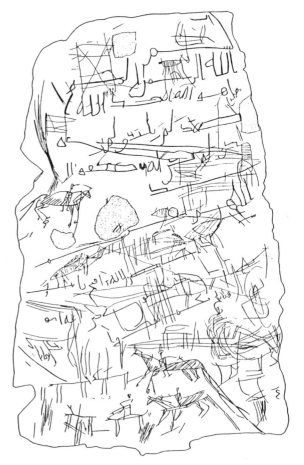

Fig. 15. Drawing of the inscribed stone from the entrance of the southeastern room (C.3) of the angle tower. (Drawing by Denise Hoffman.)

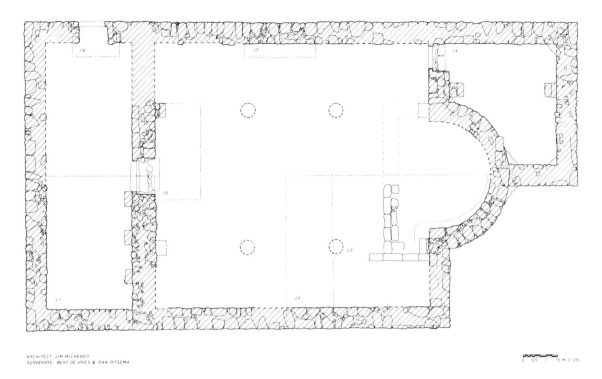

ARCHITECT JIM MICHENER
SURVEYORS BERT DE VRIES & DAN RITSEMA

0 05 1   15 M (1.25)

Fig. 16. Plan of the Lejjūn church in the early sixth century.

Fig. 17. General view of Lejjūn church apse and portion of nave, view from northwest. Upright meter stick rests on *synthronon* or bench in apse.

Fig. 18. Narthex of the church, view from south. Note arch springers to right and fallen roof beams above the meter stick, which rests below floor level on sterile soil. Function of the stone basin to left is undetermined.

roofed by parallel limestone arches and slabs (fig. 18). A second door in the east wall of the narthex gave access into the nave. The church was erected in the late fifth century, based on pottery and coins from its foundations. Major refurbishings occurred by the early sixth century. These included laying new floors of oil shale pavers, rebuilding the doorways at a higher level, constructing a new chancel screen of carved oil shale, and adding a *synthronon*, or deacon's bench, in the apse. An additional room, probably a sacristy, was located on the northeast corner of the building (fig. 19). The sacristy was connected by a doorway with the north side aisle of the nave. The sacristy yielded considerable artifactual material apparently sealed by the 551 earthquake. This included several large storage jars and a ceramic multinozzled oil lamp. The lamp was incised with "trees of life" surmounted by birds in full relief (fig. 20).

This church is small, quite poor, and rather shoddy, even by the relatively modest standards of Transjordan. There was no evidence that marble, mosaics or frescoes were used. Beneath the church were extensive wall foundations of an earlier structure, probably contemporary with the foundation of the fortress. But there is no evidence that these foundations in fact represent an earlier pagan sanctuary. They may be the remains of Late Roman barracks.

In any event, it seems clear that a significant portion of the garrison was Christianized by the end of the fifth century. Other traces of Christianity include a few lamps inscribed with Christian crosses and a cross inscribed on a building stone found within the collapsed northwest angle tower. How long paganism survived among the soldiers is problematic. There is some evidence to suggest that the cult of the standards was maintained in the legionary shrine (*aedes*) into the early sixth century. There also is evidence of deeply devout pagans in the local area. At Areopolis (modern Rabba, ca. 12 km west of Lejjūn), pagans reportedly rioted ca. 385 when the imperial authorities attempted to close or destroy their temples (Jones 1964: 167, 943, with full references).

Soundings of Khirbet el-Fityān

The *castellum* of Khirbet el-Fityān is located 1.5 km northwest of Lejjūn. It sits atop the steep northern bank of the Wadi Lejjūn and commands the best view of the surrounding topography in the entire region. Initial survey in 1976 yielded pottery of the Iron II, Early Roman (Nabataean), Late Roman, Early Byzantine, and Late Ottoman periods (Parker 1976: 24; 1986a: 74–79). The fort probably served as the central hub of a complex observation and communication network, tested in 1982 (Parker 1985: 16–19). Soundings of Fityān were conducted in 1980. These included excavation of the main gateway (D.1) and two adjacent

barrack rooms (D.2–3) (Parker 1982: 11–16, figs. 12–15). These soundings established that the barracks were built directly on bedrock during Stratum VI (ca. 300) and were contemporary with the construction of the legionary fortress in the valley below. Given the proximity of Fityān to the legionary fortress, the former was probably garrisoned by a detachment of IV *Martia*, as advanced originally by Brünnow and Domaszewski (1905: 38). The soundings also suggested that the *castellum* was abandoned by the end of the fifth century, i.e., at least a half century before the legionary base.

Although the barracks were now securely dated, the date of the enclosure wall of the fort remained undetermined. Earlier pottery, including Early Bronze, Iron Age, and Early Roman (Nabataean), had appeared in the soundings, though always mixed with later material. Thus a trench (D.4)

Fig. 19. The sacristy of the church, view from the east. Note the exterior wall of the apse, upper left. Entrance from nave, upper right. Flat-lying stones served as foundation for paved floor. One paver remains *in situ* at right end of meter stick.

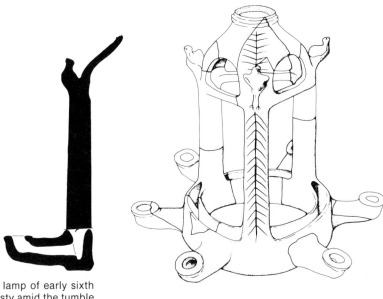

Fig. 20. Drawing of the ceramic ring lamp of early sixth century date. It was found in the sacristy amid the tumble of the 551 earthquake. (Drawing by Denise Hoffman.)

was laid out this season to section the west wall of the fort and determine its date. Unfortunately, very little artifactual material appeared in the sounding of the enclosure wall. The few sherds recovered from the foundations dated to the Iron Age. Therefore it appears that the Romans, although clearing the enclosed area of the fort to bedrock before constructing their barracks, may have simply built their enclosure wall atop an earlier Moabite foundation.

Soundings of Qaṣr Bshīr

Located 15 km northeast of Lejjūn, Qaṣr Bshīr is one of the best preserved *castella* of the Roman Empire (figs. 21, 22). The fort, ca. 56 m square, is a classic Diocletianic *quadriburgium* securely dated by its *in situ* Latin building inscription of 293–305 (figs. 23–24). Its ancient name was *castra Praetorii Mobeni*. The fort was presumably garrisoned by an auxiliary unit. Surface pottery collected in 1976 suggested it was abandoned by the end of the fifth century (Parker 1976: 24). Thus this fort, contemporary with Lejjūn, offers important evidence about the major military buildup in this sector. Two small soundings (H.1–2) conducted in 1982 revealed something of its occupational history, including evidence of some limited Umayyad occupation from one probe. The discovery of

apparent mangers in most ground floor rooms strongly suggested that Qaṣr Bshīr was designed for a cavalry unit (Parker 1985: 15–16; 1986a: 53–55, fig. 21).

More extensive soundings were undertaken in 1985. The goals were to obtain artifactual material for comparison with the legionary fortress, to recover a complete stratigraphic profile of the fort, and to learn more about its garrison. Soundings were laid out to examine the courtyard (H.6), a stable (H.3), and a cistern (H.4) within the courtyard. A structure in the *vicus* outside the fort was also investigated (H.5). In addition, a new plan of the *castellum* was drawn, superseding that of Domaszewski (fig. 22).

The results affirmed the stratigraphic history outlined above, with the primary occupation in the fourth and fifth centuries. Of the ground floor rooms, 23 were designed as stables, with three mangers in each to accommodate at least 69 horses or camels (fig. 25). The soldiers were housed in the second story of the rooms built against the enclosure wall. The room directly opposite the main gateway probably served as the *principia*. It lacks both mangers and a second story, instead having a high ceiling over the ground floor and an anteroom that projects into the courtyard. Further evidence of limited Umayyad reoccupation also appeared, although again confined to small areas.

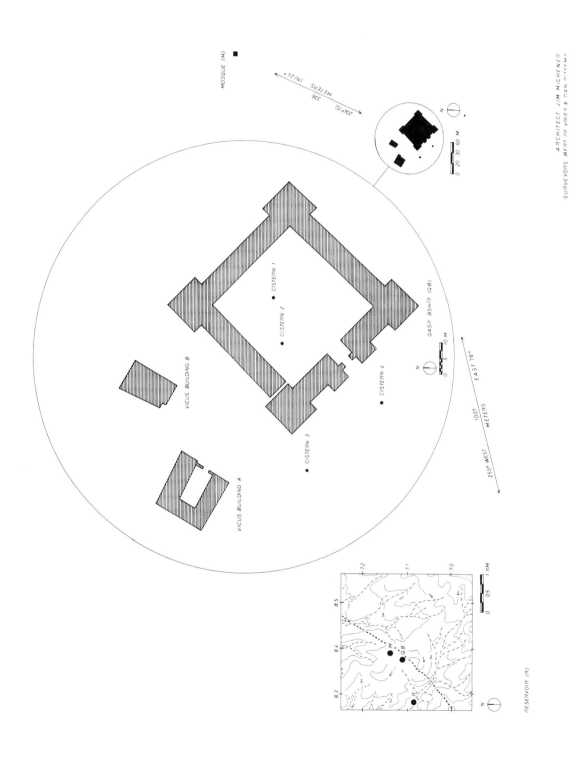

Fig. 21. Map of Qaṣr Bshir and its environs.

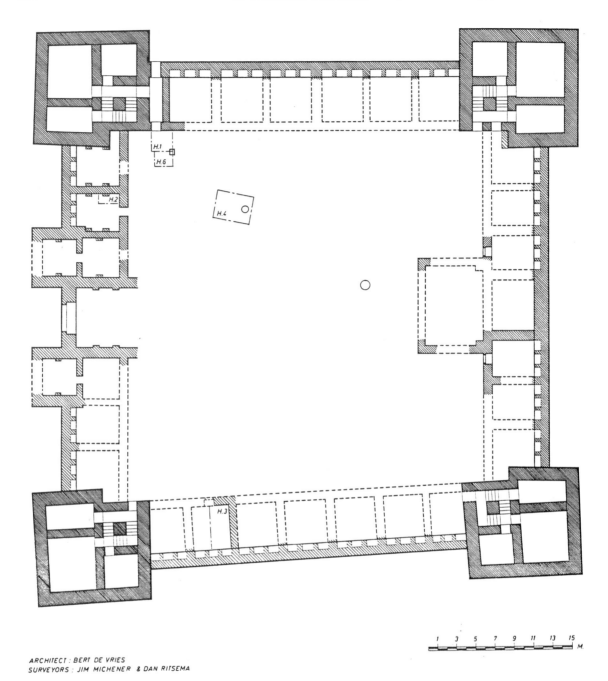

ARCHITECT : BERT DE VRIES
SURVEYORS : JIM MICHENER & DAN RITSEMA

Fig. 22. Plan of Qaṣr Bshīr.

THE SURVEY OF THE LIMES ZONE

From its inception the project has sought the most comprehensive picture of the region through the conduct of two parallel surveys: a survey of the *limes* zone itself and a survey of the desert fringe east of the frontier. In addition, close communication has been maintained with two other surveys working in adjacent areas. The region west of the upper Mūjib was surveyed by the Central Moab Survey between 1978 and 1982 (Miller 1979: 43–52). The adjacent region south of the Wadi el-Ḥasā has been surveyed by a third project (MacDonald 1982; 1984a; 1984b; MacDonald, Banning, and Pavlish 1980; MacDonald, Rollefson, and Roller 1982; MacDonald *et al.*

Fig. 23. Main gate of Qaṣr Bshīr, a typical Diocletianic *quadriburgium*, view from southwest. Latin building inscription of A.D. 293–305 is *in situ* on lintel, though not visible in this photo. Note the projecting interval towers that flank the gate.

Fig. 24. West angle tower of Qaṣr Bshīr, view from southwest. Note the interior doorways of the second and third stories.

1983). The three projects have therefore covered an entire section of the Transjordanian plateau from the edge of the Dead Sea escarpment to the eastern desert. The projects are also sharing their results to obtain the broadest perspective of this region: central Moab and northern Edom.

The goal of the survey of the *limes* zone is to identify and examine all sites between the modern Desert Highway and the upper Wadi Mūjib. Given the overall project objectives, particular emphasis was placed on locating Roman/Byzantine sites (both military and civilian) that functioned within the military frontier (fig. 26). But all sites of all periods encountered were recorded. A substantial portion of the fortified frontier zone was surveyed in 1982, with 130 sites visited (Parker 1985: 16–18; 1986a: 82–84). In 1985 additional sectors of the *limes* zone were surveyed and another 150 sites were recorded. Thus a total of 280 sites of the *limes* zone have been investigated. Although most of the *limes* zone within the region outlined above has been covered, a few gaps remain to be filled in the next season. Virtually all the sites visited are new additions to the emerging archaeological map

Fig. 25. The mangers built into the enclosure wall (H.3), view from northwest. Three such mangers were built into the back wall of nearly all the ground floor rooms, which served as stables. The soldiers lived above their mounts in rooms of second story.

of Transjordan. Considerable use was made of aerial photographs in locating and interpreting sites. The results must not be regarded as exhaustive, but may be regarded as a representative sample of a majority of sites in the region.

The surveyed region was generally bounded by the Desert Highway to the east, the Wadi es-Su‘eida to the north and the Wadi ed-Dabba to the west. Both wadis are part of the upper Mūjib catchment. A few sites slightly beyond these parameters were also visited.

This region served not only as a frontier of the Roman Empire, of course, but also of the Moabite and Nabataean Kingdoms. Each constructed a system of fortified posts in the upper Wadi Mūjib and its tributaries. Each apparently followed a somewhat different strategy, as suggested by the deployment of their posts. The degree of potential divergent uses of the region was limited by topography, climate, and resources, and must not be overstressed. But these varying strategies were probably based upon different kinds of exploitation of the region, necessitating variations in settlement patterns and security arrangements. Thus the evidence permits a comparison among the successive frontier arrangements.

Although all three frontiers followed the same general line, it appears on preliminary analysis that the Nabataean frontier was advanced farthest east. This era also apparently witnessed the greatest number of sites occupied within the frontier zone. The outer edge of the Moabite and Roman frontier zones appears to have been located somewhat to the west. As pointed out long ago by Nelson Glueck, many of the ubiquitous watchtowers were originally constructed in the Iron Age or Early Roman (Nabataean) periods and reused by the Romans. Other towers, such as Qaṣr Abū Rukba, appear to be Roman foundations (figs. 27–28). The feasibility of rapid transmission of signals among the network of posts was demonstrated by an experiment in 1982 (Parker 1985: 18–19).

In sum, considerable evidence of occupation was found from the Palaeolithic (to 35,000 B.C.), Chalcolithic/Early Bronze Age (4500–2200 B.C.), Iron Age (1200–539 B.C.), Early Roman (63 B.C.–A.D. 135), and Late Roman/Early Byzantine periods (A.D. 135–500). There was minimal evidence of occupation of the region in the Neolithic (8500–4500 B.C.), Middle and Late Bronze (2200–1200 B.C.), and Late Byzantine and Islamic periods (A.D. 500–1918).

THE SURVEY OF THE DESERT FRINGE

The region designated as the desert fringe (east of the modern Desert Highway) clearly lies beyond the Roman/Byzantine military frontier zone. Much of the surveyed region is drained by the Wadi el-Hafīrah and its tributaries, which drain towards el-Qatrana to the northwest. The wadi is

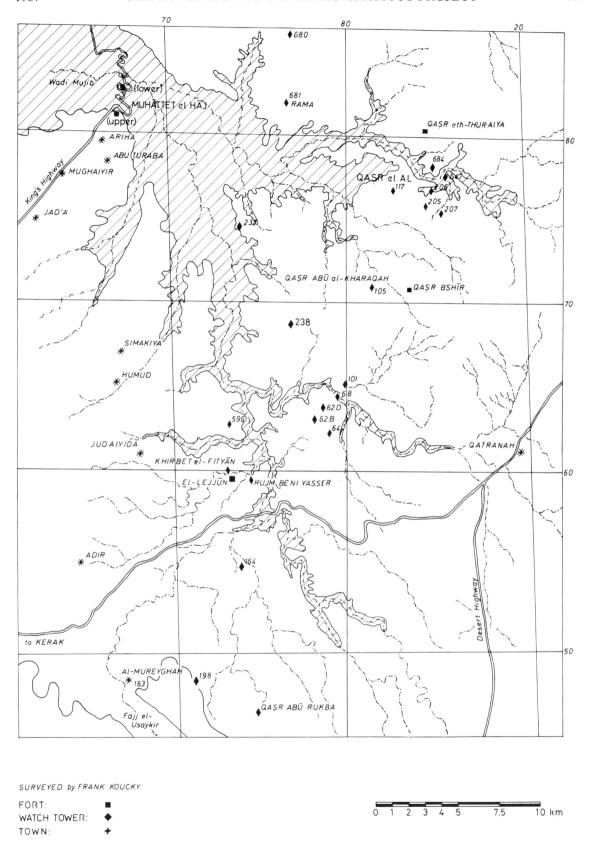

SURVEYED by FRANK KOUCKY

FORT: ■
WATCH TOWER: ◆
TOWN: ✳

0 1 2 3 4 5   7.5   10 km

Fig. 26. Map of the Roman *limes* zone. Note the concentration of watchposts guarding the eastern entrances of the wadis north and south of Qaṣr Bshīr.

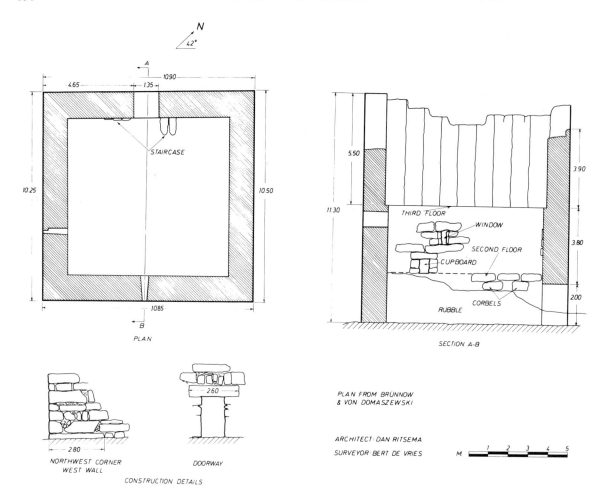

Fig. 27. Plan and elevation of Qaṣr Abū Rukba, a typical Roman watchtower of the frontier zone.

bounded by high rocky hills and empties into the Qaᶜ el-Hafīrah mudflats (elevation ca. 810 m) near Qatrana. South of the wadi is Jebel el-Mutarammil, which reaches an elevation of 952 m. The goals were to obtain evidence of Roman/Byzantine military activity (such as outlying watchposts) and evidence of nomadic activity (such as campsites and inscriptions).

Portions of the desert fringe up to 15 km east of el-Qatrana were sampled in 1980. Some 50 sites were recorded (Parker 1982: 18–19). Another 57 sites were visited in 1985, for a total of 107 sites surveyed from the desert fringe. The method employed was essentially a vehicle survey with some limited reconnaissance on foot. The results should be considered as no more than a representative sample of the archaeological resources of the region.

Not surprisingly, sites were considerably less substantial and much more widely scattered than in the frontier zone to the west. The great majority of sites were simple campsites utilized in several periods, presumably by nomads or seminomads. There was considerable evidence of human activity in the Palaeolithic period. Evidence of Nabataean presence was also substantial. The Nabataeans manned several outposts overlooking the wadis, no doubt to monitor nomadic movements. Two of these sites found near Qatrana in 1980 probably also served the Romans in this fashion. One (No. 16) was apparently a reused Nabataean post; the other (No. 20) may have been constructed by the Romans during the fourth century military build-up. Both monitored movement through the Wadi el-Hafīrah. No such additional outlying watchposts were found in 1985, however, suggesting

Fig. 28. General view of Qaṣr Abū Rukba, view from northwest.

that this region may have simply been patrolled, either by regular Roman forces based in the fortified posts to the west or perhaps by *foederati*. A few more Thamudic inscriptions were found both in the desert fringe and in the *limes* zone. A few dozen of these useful but problematic texts have now been recorded by the project. They indicate the passage of the Thamudic tribes through the area in their seasonal migrations.

The best represented periods of occupation were Palaeolithic, Chalcolithic/Early Bronze, Early Roman (Nabataean), and Late Roman/Early Byzantine.

HISTORICAL CONCLUSIONS

The third season of the *Limes Arabicus* Project has provided more detailed evidence about the Roman fortified frontier east of the Dead Sea. Some preliminary observations may be offered at this stage. A substantial military buildup in this

sector ca. 300 may now be regarded as proven. It may be viewed as part of an overall policy of strengthening and reorganizing the entire eastern frontier. It may especially be compared to similar buildups along the Syrian frontier, where the *Strata Diocletiana* was established (Poidebard 1934: 27–94; van Berchem 1952: 10–17), and in northern Transjordan, were the northwestern outlet of the Wadi Sirḥān was refortified (Kennedy 1982: 183–86; Kennedy and MacAdam 1985; Parker 1980: 871–73; 1986a: 15–36; 1986b; Speidel 1987). Each of these frontier sectors clearly emerges as a defense in depth. The reasons for such a massive investment of military and financial resources from an empire only just recovering from the turmoil of the third century are clear. Some reconstruction of the imperial defenses was mandated in any case after the Sassanid and Palmyrene invasions of the East. But the Saracen tribes posed another threat, in 290, which required the presence of the Emperor Diocletian himself on a campaign in Syria.

Tribes of the Arabian peninsula, tempted by the weakened condition of the imperial defenses and suffering from the "bedouinization" of Arabia (Caskel 1954: 36–46), migrated toward Roman territory. Unless controlled, they posed a threat to the local sedentary population.[4] The military capabilities of the Arabs were further enhanced by a technological development—the North Arabian camel saddle. The implications of this military technology were so great, in one scholar's view, that control of the north Arabian Desert by the commercial Arabs of Petra and Palmyra was replaced in the third century by anarchy among the desert tribes (Bulliet 1975: 90–105). Finally, one must not exclude the possibility of microfluctuations in the environment. Literary sources suggest that droughts of only a few years duration could have enormous consequences on the border between the desert and the sown, as traditional water sources in the desert dried out and forced large numbers of nomads toward the better-watered districts inhabited by the sedentary population. A good example from a later period is preserved in a Syriac letter of A.D. 485, in which a two-year drought led to massive tribal migrations and devastating nomadic raids on both sides of the Perso-Roman frontier in Mesopotamia (Trimingham 1979: 151; Parker 1986a: 150).

East of the Dead Sea, the evidence suggests that major nomadic pressure was being exerted through the Wadi Mūjib approaches to this frontier sector. The Roman response to this threat involved reconstruction of the regional road system to facilitate movement of troops and supplies, construction of new forts, reoccupation and refurbishing of older Moabite/Nabataean fortifications, and the introduction of new military forces (Parker 1986a: 135–43).

The most important new evidence obtained this season was the discovery of the 50 percent reduction of the legion at Lejjūn by the late fourth century. The abandonment of some forts by the late fifth century was already known, but the reduction by half of the largest military unit in this sector less than a century after the Diocletianic buildup was not.

What can explain this reduction? Two possible explanations immediately spring to mind. Zosimus (2.34) asserts that Constantine weakened the frontier forces (limitanei) in order to strengthen the mobile field army (comitatenses) kept behind the frontiers. It is possible that two cohorts of legio

IV Martia were withdrawn from Lejjūn at this time, between 324 (when Constantine conquered the eastern half of the Empire by defeating Licinius) and 337. Another possibility is that half the legion may have been withdrawn for Julian's Persian expedition in 363 and never returned to Lejjūn. Unfortunately the literary sources that detail this campaign, such as Ammianus Marcellinus, do not provide a detailed breakdown of Julian's expeditionary force to prove or disprove this suggestion.

The numismatic evidence from the excavated barracks in the northeastern quadrant of Lejjūn (Area K) seems to support the latter alternative. The three precisely datable coins all postdate the death of Constantine I in 337 but antedate Julian's campaign of 363. It is tempting to suppose that a vexillation of IV Martia was transferred to Syria, where Julian massed his forces, in late 362 or early 363. The ill-fated expedition set out on March 5, 363 (Ammiannus Marcellinus 23.2.6). Thus the barracks at Lejjūn that housed these troops would have been empty during the earthquake of May 19, 363. Julian was killed in Mesopotamia on June 26 while the Roman army was already in retreat. By that time the reconstruction program at Lejjūn was underway and it perhaps was already clear that the vexillation of IV Martia would not return. Therefore, only four blocks of barracks were built in place of the former eight. The ruined barracks in the northeastern quadrant of the fortress were cleared to their foundations but never rebuilt.[5]

It must be stressed that this explanation is merely the most likely scenario based on the available evidence. Other explanations are also possible. In any case, following the earthquake of 363 the new barracks erected in the fortress remained in use throughout the remainder of the legionary occupation.

The argument that most fortifications in this sector were abandoned by the early sixth century was strengthened this season by new evidence. None of the surveyed military sites of the Roman limes zone yielded any Late Byzantine (i.e., sixth or early seventh century) pottery, as noted in previous seasons. The abandonments of those four forts excavated thus far appear to have occurred peaceably, implying the demobilization or transfer of the garrisons according to a definite imperial policy and confirming assertions in the literary evidence (Procopius, Anecdota 24.12–14; Bellum

Persicum 1.17.45–48). A similar phenomenon has been observed for the Syrian frontier south of the Euphrates (Liebeschuetz 1977: 487–99). Primary responsibility for the defense of the southeastern frontier, from the Euphrates to the Red Sea, was transferred to the Ghassānids and their Arab *foederati*. The garrison at Lejjūn was probably demobilized ca. 530. Therefore the final two decades of its occupation probably reflect a squatter occupation of the fortress, perhaps by demobilized soldiers and their families, ended by the 551 earthquake.

The abandonment of the *limes* meant a decrease in security. This explains the relative paucity of sites occupied in the local region in the Late Byzantine (sixth and early seventh centuries) period. The abandonment of the *limes* also contributed to the success of the Muslim Arab invasion of the early seventh century.

ACKNOWLEDGMENTS

The third season of the *Limes Arabicus* Project was conducted between June 8 and July 31, 1985 under a permit granted by the Department of Antiquities of Jordan. The project is sponsored by North Carolina State University and is affiliated with the American Center of Oriental Research (ACOR) in Amman. Principal funding for the 1985 season again was provided by the National Endowment for the Humanities. Additional funding was provided by the Dumbarton Oaks Center for Byzantine Studies, the National Geographic Society, the North Carolina State University Foundation, the NCSU Faculty Professional Development Fund, student contributions, and a number of private donors. The Department of Antiquities also provided important logistical assistance. The author is deeply grateful to all these organizations and individuals for their support.

Special thanks are due to Adnan Hadidi, Director of the Department of Antiquities, and David W. McCreery, Director of ACOR, for invaluable advice and assistance.

Senior staff in the field in 1985 included John Wilson Betlyon, numismatist and camp administrator; Vincent A. Clark, team leader of the desert survey and Semitic epigrapher; Patricia Crawford, palaeobotanist; Bert De Vries, architect/surveyor; Eric Green, photographer; Jennifer C. Groot, objects specialist; Denise Hoffman, draftsperson; Frank L. Koucky, geologist and director of the survey; S. Thomas Parker, director, stratigrapher, and ceramicist; and Michael Toplyn, faunal analyst. Area supervisors were Anne E. Haeckl (Area A—the Lejjūn *principia*), Jennifer Groot (Areas B and K—the Lejjūn barracks), Andrea Lain (Area C—the Lejjūn fortifications), Robert Schick (Area J—the Lejjūn church), and Vincent A. Clark (Area H—Qaṣr Bshīr). Nabil Beqaᵓin again ably served as department representative.

Square supervisors were Lynn Boone, Susan Downey, Julie Ferguson, Timothy Ferrell, Victoria Godwin, Nelson Harris, Eric Lapp, Kathleen Mitchell, Jane O'Brien, Janice Scilipoti, Patricia Seabolt, Michelle Stevens, Michael Strickland, Carolyn Tesari, Laurie Tiede, Anne Undeland, and Louise Zimmer. James Michener and Daniel Ritsema were assistant architect/surveyors. Julie Ferguson and Patricia Seabolt also served on the survey. Victoria Godwin also acted as pottery and glass registrar.

NOTES

[1]For a detailed examination of the Arabian frontier and its history, Parker 1986a.

[2]For a more detailed overview of the fortress, Parker and Lander 1982: 185–210; Parker 1986a: 58–72.

[3]Cf. coin nos. 31, 37, 39 in the numismatic appendix below.

[4]For a recent discussion of the Arabs in the first through fourth centuries, Shahîd 1984a; 1984b.

[5]For recent detailed discussions of Julian's Persian campaign with extensive bibliography, Bowersock 1978: 106–19; Shahîd 1984b: 107–37.

BIBLIOGRAPHY

van Berchem, D.
    1952   *L'armée de Dioclétien et la reforme constantinienne*. Paris: Geuthner.
Bowersock, G. W.
    1978   *Julian the Apostate*. Cambridge, MA: Harvard.

Brünnow, R., and von Domaszewski, A.
    1904–09 *Die Provincia Arabia*. 3 vols. Strasburg: Trübner.
Bulliet, R.
    1975   *The Camel and the Wheel*. Cambridge, MA: Harvard.

Caskel, W.
   1954   The Bedouinization of Arabia. Pp. 36–46 in
           Studies in Islamic Cultural History, G. E.
           von Grunebaum, ed. Memoirs of the Ameri-
           can Anthropological Association 76. Men-
           shasha, WI: George Banta.
Fellmann, R.
   1976   Le 'Camp de Dioclétien' à Palmyre et l'archi-
           tecture militaire du Bas-Empire. Pp. 173–91
           in *Mélanges d'histoire ancienne et archéologie
           offerts à Paul Collart*. P. Ducrey *et al.*, eds.
           Cahiers archéologie Romande 5. Lausanne:
           Boccard.
Fink, R. O.
   1971   *Roman Military Records on Papyrus*. Ameri-
           can Philological Association Monographs 26.
           Cleveland: Case Western Reserve.
Johnson, A.
   1983   *Roman Forts*. New York: St. Martins.
Johnson, S.
   1983   *Late Roman Fortifications*. London: Batsford.
Jones, A. H. M.
   1964   *The Later Roman Empire*. 2 vols. Oxford:
           Blackwells.
Kennedy, D. L.
   1982   *Archaeological Explorations on the Roman
           Frontier in North-East Jordan*. British
           Archaeology Reports International Series
           134. Oxford: British Archaeological Reports.
Kennedy, D. L., and MacAdam, H. I.
   1985   Latin Inscriptions from the Azraq Oasis,
           Jordan. *Zeitschrift für Papyrologie und Epig-
           raphik* 60: 97–107.
Kolbe, H.-G.
   1974   Die Inschrift am Torbau der *Principia* im
           Legionslager von Lambaesis. *Mitteilungen
           des deutschen archäologischen Instituts, röm-
           ische Abteilung* 81: 281–300.
Lander, J.
   1984   *Roman Stone Fortifications. Variation and
           Change from the First Century* A.D *to the
           Fourth*. British Archaeology Reports Inter-
           national Series 206. Oxford: British Archaeo-
           logical Reports.
Liebeschuetz, W.
   1977   The Defences of Syria in the Sixth Century.
           Pp. 487–99 in *Studien zu den Militärgrenzen
           Roms II*. Cologne: Rheinland.
Luttwak, E. N.
   1976   *The Grand Strategy of the Roman Empire
           from the First Century* A.D *to the Third*.
           Baltimore: Johns Hopkins.
MacDonald, B.
   1982   The Wadi el-Ḥasā Survey 1979 and Previous
           Archaeological Work in Southern Jordan.
           *Bulletin of the American Schools of Oriental
           Research* 245: 35–52.

1984a   A Nabataean and/or Roman Military
         Monitoring Zone Along the South Bank of
         the Wadi el Ḥasā in Southern Jordan. *Classi-
         cal Views/Échos du Monde Classique* 27.3:
         219–34.
1984b   The Wadi el-Hasa Archaeological Survey.
         Pp. 113–28 in *The Answers Lie Below: Essays
         in Honor of Lawrence Edward Toombs*, ed.
         H. O. Thompson. Lanham, MD: University
         Press of America.
MacDonald, B.; Banning, E. B.; and Pavlish, L. A.
   1980   The Wadi el Hasa Survey, 1979. *Annual of
           the Department of Antiquities of Jordan* 24:
           169–83.
MacDonald, B.; Rollefson, G.; and Roller, D. W.
   1982   The Wadi el Hasa Survey 1981. A Prelimi-
           nary Report. *Annual of the Department of
           Antiquities of Jordan* 26: 117–31.
MacDonald, B. *et al.*
   1983   The Wadi el Hasa Survey 1982: A Prelimi-
           nary Report. *Annual of the Department of
           Antiquities of Jordan* 27: 311–23.
MacMullen, R.
   1984   *Christianizing the Roman Empire*. A.D *100–
           400*. New Haven: Yale.
Miller, J. M.
   1979   Survey of Central Moab. *Bulletin of the
           American Schools of Oriental Research* 234:
           43–52.
Parker, S. T.
   1976   Archaeological Survey of the *Limes Arabi-
           cus*: A Preliminary Report. *Annual of the
           Department of Antiquities of Jordan* 21:
           19–31.
   1980   Towards a History of the *Limes Arabicus*.
           Pp. 865–78 in *Roman Frontier Studies 1979*,
           eds. W. S. Hansen and L. J. F. Keppie.
           British Archaeological Reports International
           Series 71. Oxford: British Archaeological
           Reports.
   1982   Preliminary Report on the 1980 Season of
           the Central *Limes Arabicus* Project. *Bulletin
           of the American Schools of Oriental Research*
           247: 1–26.
   1983   The Central *Limes Arabicus* Project: The
           1982 Campaign. *Annual of the Department
           of Antiquities of Jordan* 27: 213–30.
   1985   Preliminary Report on the 1982 Season of
           the Central *Limes Arabicus* Project. *Bulletin
           of the American Schools of Oriental Research
           Supplement* 23: 1–34.
1986a   *Romans and Saracens: A History of the
         Arabian Frontier*. ASOR Dissertation Series
         6. Winona Lake, IN: Eisenbrauns.
1986b   A Tetrarchic Milestone from Roman Arabia.
         Zeitschrift für Papyrologie und Epigraphik
         62: 256–58.

Parker, S. T., and Lander, J.
1982   *Legio* IV *Martia* and the Legionary Camp at el-Lejjūn. *Byzantinische Forschungen* 8: 185–210.

Poidebard, A.
1934   *La trace de Rome dans le désert de Syrie.* 2 vols. Paris: Geuthner.

Rakob, F., and Storz, S.
1974   Die Principia des römischen Legionslagers während der Prinzipätszeit. *Mitteilungen des deutschen archäologischen Instituts, römische Abteilung* 81: 253–80.

Russell, K. W.
1980   The Earthquake of May 19, A.D. 363. *Bulletin of the American Schools of Oriental Research* 238: 47–64.

1985   The Earthquake Chronology of Palestine and Northwest Arabia from the 2nd through the Mid-8th Century A.D. *Bulletin of the American Schools of Oriental Research* 260: 37–59.

Shahîd, I.
1984a   *Rome and the Arabs. A Prolegomenon to the Study of Byzantium and the Arabs.* Washington: Dumbarton Oaks.

1984b   *Byzantium and the Arabs in the Fourth Century.* Dumbarton Oaks Monographs. Washington: Dumbarton Oaks.

Speidel, M. P.
1987   The Roman Road to Dumata (Jawf in Saudi Arabia) and The Frontier Strategy of *Praetensione Colligare. Historia* 36.

Trimingham, J. S.
1979   *Christianity Among the Arabs in Pre-Islamic Times.* London: Longman.

APPENDIX

Coins from the 1985 Season of the Limes Arabicus Project

JOHN WILSON BETLYON
Smith College

The third season of the *Limes Arabicus* Project yielded a total of 95 coins, many of which were heavily encrusted or mineralized from many years in the calcareous soils of the region. The coins were cleaned in the laboratories of Smith College using electrolytic reduction in a solution of sodium carbonate ($NaCO_3$). Varying strengths of the solution were employed to speed the conservation process (6%–8%) or retard the process (3%). Generally recommended current densities of 2 amp/dm^2 were increased to remove the most difficult mineralized deposits. All coins were also bathed in a 10% solution of sulfuric acid (H_2SO_4) in the field, which softened the encrustation. Sulfuric acid is not usually used for this purpose because of its extremely caustic properties. However, no alternate acid was available in Jordan at the time. Great care was exercised throughout the conservation process to insure the thorough cleaning of the coins and their greatest possible preservation.

Coins from the third season fall into the following categories:

Late Roman	13
Early Byzantine	41
Late Byzantine	19
Mamlūk	1
Ottoman	1
Uncertain, unidentifiable	20
TOTAL	95

A catalogue of the coins follows, listing obverse and reverse types, metal, weight, diameter, object number, location in the field (area.square:locus), and die orientation, when discernible. The mint and date of a coin follow, when known.

Unless otherwise noted, all coins are struck from bronze.

I. LATE ROMAN

    1. OBV: IMP.CM.AVR.PROBVS.P.AVG; bust to r., radiate, dr., cuir.

    ↑ REV: CLEMENTIA.T-EMP; emperor stg. r., receiving Victory from Jupiter, stg. l. holding scepter; below, E/XX[I].

    Antoninianus 3.94 g, 23 mm

    Object #675, C.7:017 (Mint of Antiochia, ca. A.D. 280)

    Webb 1933: 120, no. 924.

This coin is the oldest yet found at el-Lejjūn. It predates slightly the proposed date for the construction of the fortress, which apparently occurred during the reign of Diocletian. This specific coin is well worn and is representative of the large output of the Antiochian mint in the late third century (Webb 1933: 15). It was probably acquired in normal commercial activity by legionnaires and brought to Lejjūn early in the life of the garrison. Unfortunately, the stratigraphic context is Late

Byzantine, and sheds no light on this particular find. It is an *antoninianus*, predating Diocletian's edict that altered the monetary system, ca. A.D. 293–294.

2. OBV: FL.VAL.CONSTANTIVS.NOB.C[AES]; radiate bust to r.

↓ REV: CONCORDIA.MILITVM; prince stg. r. in military dress, receiving small Victory from Jupiter, stg. l., leaning on scepter. In exergue, mint mark ANT; and */H, the *officina* designation.

Half *follis* 3.53 g, 21 mm

Object #611, C.3:022 (Mint of Antiochia, A.D. 296)

Sutherland 1973: 621, no. 61a.

This coin is apparently a unique example. It is the only coin struck on these types from Antiochia with the *officina* H. It was struck when Constantius I held the rank of Caesar.

3. OBV: IMP[CMA.MA]XIMIANVS.PF.AVG; radiate bust to r.

↑ REV: CONCORDIA.MILITVM; prince stg. r., in military dress, receiving small Victory on globe from Jupiter stg. l., leaning on scepter. No legible mint mark.

Half *follis* 2.31 g, 20–22 mm

Object #707, A.6:004 (Mint of Alexandria (?), ca. A.D. 296–297)

Sutherland 1973: 667, no. 46b.

4. OBV: IMP.C.SEVERVS.PF.AVG; radiate bust to r.

↑ REV: CONCORDIA.MILITVM; prince stg. r., in military dress, receiving small Victory on globe from Jupiter, stg. l., leaning on scepter. In exergue, [A]LE; A between figures is *officina* designation.

Half *follis* 3.02 g, 19–21 mm

Object #568, B.5:015 (Mint of Alexandria, A.D. 306–307)

Sutherland 1973: 675, no. 84.

5. OBV: GAL.VAL.MAXIMI[NVS.NOB.CAESS]; radiate bust to r.

↑ REV: CON[CORDIA].MI-LITVM; and like no. 4 above. In exergue, ALE; no *officina* designation legible.

Half *follis* 2.67 g, 20 mm

Object #558, B.1:061 (Mint of Alexandria, A.D. 306–307)

Sutherland 1973: 675, no. 85.

6. OBV: GAL.VAL.MAXIMINVS.NOB.CA[ESS]; laur., cuir. bust to r. flan shows excessive wear.

↑ REV: GENIO.CA-ESARIS; Genius stg. l., modius on head. Worn.

Follis 5.12 g, 25 mm

Object #637, A.2:142 (Mint of Antiochia, ca. A.D. 307–308)

Sutherland 1973: 627, no. 81.

7. OBV: Completely mineralized; fragmentary.

REV: Mineralized; fragmentary; mint mark ANT in exergue.

Half *follis* 2.69 g, 23 mm

Object #634, H.5:008, Qaṣr Bshīr (Mint of Antiochia, ca. A.D. 310–325)

8. OBV: IMP.LIC.LICINVIS.PF.AVG; laur., cuir. bust to r.

↓ REV: IOVI.CONSERVATO-RI.AVGG.NN; Jupiter stg. l., chlamys l. shoulder, leaning on scepter, Victory on globe in r. hand; eagle with wreath to l., below. In exergue ANT; *officina* designation, ΔI.

Follis 3.36 g, 22–23 mm

Object #664, A.3:104 (Mint of Antiochia, A.D. 315–316)

Brunn 1966: 678, no. 17.

This coin (no. 8) is an issue of Licinius I when he held the title and powers of Augustus. Most of these coins represent typical issues struck in quantity in the East. Example no. 3 is a very common issue of Maximianus Hercules, and is known from sites throughout the eastern Mediterranean. It is a type struck in a number of mints and is part of the typical legionnaire's pay package. Example no. 4 was struck by Severus, as Augustus; the CONCORDIA.MILITVM types were usually associated with the army, and emphasized the emperor's relationship with his military forces. Coins 5 and 6 are issues of Galerius Maximianus as Caesar. All of these coins are *folles* issued under the reform of the monetary system initiated by Diocletian. The *follis* first weighed as much as 10 g, but was reduced in weight in only a few years to 5 g and then 3 g.

9. OBV: CONSTANTINVS].NOB.CAES; laur., dr., cuir. bust to l.
    REV: IOVI.CONS-E]RVA[TORI.CAESS; Jupiter stg. l., chlamys across l. shoulder,
         leaning on scepter, holding Victory on globe. In exergue, SM[N]; *officina* designa-
         tion B.
    Follis 2.71 g, 19–20 mm
    Object #626, J.3:059 (Mint of Nicomedia, A.D. 317–320)
    Bruun 1966: 604, no. 30.

10. OBV: IMP.LICINIVS.AVG; laur., dr. bust to r.
    REV: DN.LICINI.AVGVSTI around VOT/XX in two lines, inside laurel wreath.
    Follis 2.34 g, 18–19 mm
    Object #640, J.3:066 (Mint of Siscia, ca. A.D. 320–321)
    Bruun 1966: 444, no. 160.

This coin was struck while Licinius I held the office of Augustus. The last two coins come from mints some distance from el-Lejjūn. These coins may have come to Arabia with troops transferred to Lejjūn from the West. In any event, this period in the fourth century was still a time when interchange with the West was a common occurrence.

11. OBV: IMP.C[..]MAXIMIANVS.AVG; radiate bust to r.
    REV: Emperor stg. r., receiving Victory from Jupiter stg. l.; no inscriptions legible;
         partially mineralized.
    Follis 4.15 g, 22–23 mm
    Object #728, B.1:098 (ca. A.D. 304–305)

12. OBV: Laur., dr. bust to r.; inscription illegible; frag.
    REV: IOVI.CONS[ERVATORI]; Jupiter stg. l., well worn. No legible mint mark;
         fragmentary.
    Half *follis* 1.99 g, 21–23 mm
    Object #631, J.2:016

13. OBV: Completely mineralized.
    REV: Completely mineralized.
    Follis 3.63 g, 21–22 mm
    Object #474, B.4:034

These coins of the early fourth century bear no mint marks, making more specific attribution impossible. All of the coins are made of bronze, and are the small change of their day. These examples come from the reigns of Maximian Herculius as Augustus (296–305), Licinius I (308–324), Maximinus (305–313), and Constantine the Great (306–337). The Late Roman coins show certain occupation and use of the fortress area beginning late in the third century or early in the fourth century A.D. This numismatic evidence is in keeping with the ceramic record from the site and with epigraphic and literary sources which document Diocletian's program of fortification east of the *via nova Traiana*.

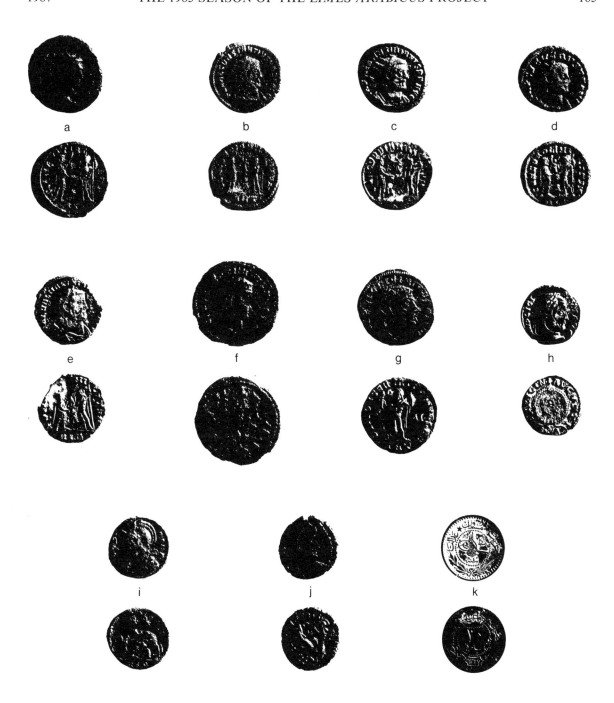

Fig. 29. Coins from the 1985 season from Lejjūn (all at 1:1):
   a. Bronze *antoninianus* of Probus, struck at Antioch, A.D. 280 (#1 in the numismatic appendix).
   b. Bronze half *follis* of Constantius I (as Caesar), struck at Antioch, A.D. 296 (#2).
   c. Bronze half *follis* of Maximianus Hercules, A.D. 286–297 (#3).
   d. Bronze half *follis* of Severus, struck at Alexandria, A.D. 306–307 (#4).
   e. Bronze half *follis* of Galerius Maximinus (as Caesar), struck at Alexandria, A.D. 306–307 (#5).
   f. Bronze *follis* of Galerius Maximinus (as Caesar), A.D. 307–308 (#6).
   g. Bronze *follis* of Licinius, struck at Antioch, A.D. 315–316 (#8).
   h. Bronze *follis* of Licinius, struck at Siscia, A.D. 320–321 (#10).
   i. Bronze commemorative medal honoring Constantine I, struck at Rome by Constans, A.D. 337–340 (#29).
   j. Bronze *follis* of Constantius II, A.D. 347–355 (#36).
   k. Nickel 1/4 piaster of Muhammed V, struck at Constantinople in 1327 A.H. (A.D. 1913, #75).

II. EARLY BYZANTINE

Almost 44 percent of the coins found in 1985 were from the Early Byzantine period. Once again, as in earlier seasons, this category includes the most coins which is to be expected. Most of the occupation of the site was within the Early Byzantine period.

14. OBV: CONSTAN]TINVS.AVG; diad., dr. bust to r.
↑   REV: PR]OVIDENTIAE.AVGG; camp gate with two turrets; star above; single entry with no doors; variable size of stones in wall. In exergue, SMA]NTA.
     Follis (AE 2) 2.99 g, 20–21 mm
     Object #674, H.5:009, Qaṣr Bshīr (Mint of Antiochia, A.D. 327–328)
     Bruun 1966: 691, no. 78.

15. OBV: Diad., dr. bust to r.; inscriptions illegible.
↓   REV: PROVIDEN]TIAE.CAESS; camp gate as in no. 15 above; S]MANT in exergue.
     Follis (AE 2) 2.06 g, 19–20 mm
     Object #710, C.3:042 (Mint of Antiochia, ca. A.D. 328–329)

Both of these coins were struck by Constantine the Great. The second is from the same time period as the first, although it represents a somewhat later series (note the slightly smaller size). Already, Diocletian's *folles* were becoming smaller because of unchecked inflation which was weakening the economy.

16. OBV: Helmeted bust to r., no inscription legible.
↓   REV: Victory stg. l., r. foot on prow, holding scepter; leaning on shield. No inscription legible.
     Follis (AE 3) 2.27 g, 15–16 mm
     Object #566, B.1:059 (Mint of Constantinople, A.D. 330–332)
     Brunn 1966: 214–17, nos. 515, 548.

This specimen is a common commemorative medal struck late in Constantine the Great's reign. It celebrates Constantine's years on the throne and his establishment of the new capital in the East. The reverse often is without any inscription; but the obverse normally reads, CONSTANTINOPOLIS.

17. OBV: CON]STANTINVS.MAX.AVG; diad., dr. bust to r.; worn, partially mineralized surface.
↓   REV: GLORIA.EXERCITVS (well worn); two soldiers stg. either side of two standards; SMANA in exergue.
     Follis (AE 2) 2.37 g, 19–21 mm
     Object #589, J.1:020 (Mint of Antiochia, A.D. 335)
     Bruun 1966: 693, no. 86.

18. OBV: CONSTA[NTINVS.MAX.AVG]; diad., dr. bust to r.; worn.
↓   REV: GLO[RIA].EXER[CITVS]; two soldiers stg. either side of two standards; SMANA in exergue.
     Follis (AE 3) 2.37 g, 18–19 mm
     Object #709, C.3:044 (Mint of Antiochia, A.D. 335)
     Bruun 1966: 693, no. 86.

Both of these coins were struck by Constantine II holding the power of Caesar. Both represent very common types, as is obvious below.

19. OBV: CONSTANTINVS.[. . . . .]; bust to r.
   REV: Two soldiers stg. either side of two standards; no mint mark or ethnic legible.
   ↘ *Follis* (AE 3) 2.58 g, 18–19 mm
   Object #560, A.3:062 (ca. A.D. 330–340)

20. OBV: Bust to r.; detail and ethnic worn.
   REV: Two soldiers stg. either side of two standards; no mint mark or ethnic legible.
   ↙ *Follis* (AE 3) 1.41 g, 17 mm
   Object #619, J.1:028 (ca. A.D. 330–340)

21. OBV: Same as 20 above.
   REV: Same as 20 above.
   ↖ *Follis* (AE 4) 1.39 g, 14 mm
   Object #665, A.3:108 (ca. A.D. 330–340)

22. OBV: Bust to r., inscription off flan.
   REV: Two soldiers either side of single standard; no mint mark or ethnic legible.
   ↘ *Follis* (AE 3) 1.24 g, 16–18 mm
   Object #639, C.3:022 (ca. A.D. 330–340)

23. OBV: Bust to r., surface damaged by mineralization.
   REV: Two soldiers stg. either side of single standard.
   ↗ *Follis* (AE 3) 1.66 g, 16–18 mm
   Object #635, J.3:066 (ca. A.D. 330–340)

24. OBV: Same as 23.
   REV: Same as 23.
   ↘ *Follis* (AE 4) 1.41 g, 15–16 mm
   Object #641, J.3:066 (ca. A.D. 330–340)

25. OBV: Same as 23.
   REV: Same as 23.
   ↓ *Follis* (AE 4) 1.64 g, 15–16 mm
   Object #643, H.5:007, Qaṣr Bshīr (ca. A.D. 330–340)

26. OBV: Same as 23.
   REV: Same as 23.
   ↗ *Follis* (AE 4) 1.58 g, 14 mm
   Object #671, C.3:024 (ca. A.D. 330–340)

27. OBV: [. . . . . . .]IVS.PF.AVG; bust to r.
   REV: Same as 23.
   ↓ *Follis* (AE 3) 2.56 g, 16–18 mm
   Object #673, A.3:113 (ca. A.D. 330–340)

28. OBV: Same as 23.
   REV: Same as 23.
   ↓ *Follis* (AE 4) 0.94 g, 14–15 mm
   Object #699, A.3:103 (014 extension) (ca. A.D. 330–340)

This group of coins represents very common issues from the second quarter of the fourth century. They were struck by rulers from the family of Constantine the Great, and were issued in abundance by the principal imperial mints. With the passage of time, inflation continued to reduce the size of the *aes* denominations. The coins shrunk from diameters of ca. 21 mm to only 14 mm. Some of this change is the development of smaller denominations within the same series, although inflation accounts for most of this change.

29. OBV: VRBS.ROMA.[BEATA]; helmeted bust to l.
    REV: She-wolf suckling Romulus and Remus; above, * *; below, R ⚘ P.
    Commemorative medal 2.48 g, 17–18 mm
    Object #612, J.1:022 (Mint of Rome, A.D. 337–340)
    Kent 1981: 250, no. 39.

This medal was struck by Constans to honor his father, Constantine the Great. A series of these medals was struck in Rome in the period just after A.D. 330. It purposefully had no reverse ethnic, although the mint mark for Rome is clearly visible below the type.

30. OBV: DV.CONST[ANTINVS.PF.AVGG]; bust to r.; flan worn.
    REV: No legend; emperor in quadriga, hand of god reaches towards him; in exergue
        SMA[LA].
    Follis (AE 4) 1.48 g, 14 mm
    Object #713, H.5:014, Qaṣr Bshīr (Mint of Alexandria, ca. A.D. 337–340)
    Kent 1981: 539, no. 4.

This special coin, struck under the authority of Constantine II, also honored Constantine the Great. Its presence in the auxiliary *castellum* at Qaṣr Bshīr indicates that it was also occupied in this period.

31. OBV: Bust to r.; inscription illegible.
    REV: Emperor, stg., with globe in r. hand, holding spear in l.; no inscription legible.
    Follis (AE 4) 1.83 g, 14 mm
    Object #636, K.1:001 (ca. A.D. 335–350)

32. OBV: Bust to r., inscription illegible; worn.
    REV: Soldier spearing fallen horseman; no inscription legible.
    Follis (AE 3) 2.05 g, 16–17 mm
    Object #711, C.7:020 (ca. A.D. 347–355)

These coins were often struck by Constantius II and were common in the mid-fourth century throughout the empire.

33. OBV: [. . . .]CAE[. . .]; bust to r.; worn.
    REV: Jupiter, stg. l.; worn; no inscription; detail illegible.
    Follis (AE 4) 1.17 g, 12–13 mm
    Object #695, B.1:130 (ca. A.D. 340–355)

34. OBV: Bust to r., worn; inscription off flan.
    REV: Victory walking to l., holding wreath and palm branch; flan worn.
    Follis (AE 3) 1.73 g, 14–15 mm
    Object #638, A.6:003 (ca. A.D. 337–347)

35. OBV: Veiled bust to r.; inscription illegible.
    REV: Emperor stg. r., in quadriga; no inscription legible.
    Follis (AE 3)1.49 g, 15 mm
    Object #633, C.3:024 (ca. A.D. 337–347)
    Cf. Kent 1981: 514–15, 539.

Example no. 35 is one of the types dedicated to the deified Constans. A great many such coins were struck at Nicomedia, Antiochia, and Constantinople. The lack of clear inscriptions on the coin flan, however, makes more precise attribution impossible.

36. OBV: [. . .]TIVS.PF.AVG; bust, dr., cuir., to r.
↓   REV: FEL.T]EMP.RE[PARATIO]; helmeted soldier to l., shield on l. arm, spearing
        fallen horseman, shield on ground to r., enemy clutching neck of fallen horse.
        Officina S.
    Follis (AE 3) 4.36 g, 18–19 mm
    Object #730, C.7:017 (A.D. 347–355)
    Cf. Kent 1981: 523, nos. 141, 541.

37. OBV: CONSTAN]TINVS.PF.AVG; bust, dr., cuir., to r.
↓   REV: FEL.TEMP.RE]PARATIO; and as 36 above.
    Follis (AE 3) 2.90 g, 16–18 mm
    Object #715, K.2:002 (ca. A.D. 347–350)

38. OBV: Bust to r., inscription illegible.
↓   REV: Helmeted soldier, spearing fallen horseman who clutches neck of fallen horse. No
        detail or inscriptions visible.
    Follis (AE 3) 3.14 g, 17–18 mm
    Object #551, A.2:096 (ca. A.D. 347–355)

Two of these coins, nos. 36 and 37, were probably struck in Antioch or Alexandria, from which many of these coins came. This military type was struck by Constantius II and Constans following the death of Constantine the Great. The reverse inscription, FEL.TEMP.REPARATIO, was used with several different types and signified the universal rule of Rome, protecting the civilized world from the perils of barbarism.

39. OBV: [. . . . .]CONS[. . . .]; bust, dr., cuir., to r.
↓   REV: SPES.[REPVBL]ICAE; emperor helmeted in military dress, stg. r., holding globe
        and spear; below, mint mark R * P.
    Follis (AE 4) 1.99 g, 15 mm
    Object #714, K.2:002 (Mint of Rome, ca. A.D. 355–361)
    Kent 1981: 279, no. 320.

This coin was struck by Constantius II. It is one of several dominant military types which are found in great numbers at the site. The types may have been minted specifically as specie to pay the army.

40. OBV: Completely mineralized.
↓   REV: Emperor, facing, seated on throne inside bistyle temple, holding globe and spear.
    Follis (AE 2) 4.79 g, 20 mm
    Object #562, C.7:002 (ca. A.D. 367–375)

This type is unknown in bronze, although it is similar to silver issues of the mint of Antiochia from the reigns of Valentinian I, Valens, and Gratian. It is a large bronze denomination, common to the fourth century, which may have been struck only in this province for some special purpose. There is precedent for such *aes* strikings in the provincial mints. The coin is worn and poorly preserved (especially the obverse), making more certain attribution impossible.

41. OBV: Bust to r.
↑   REV: [SALVS.REPVBLICAE]; Victory advancing l., carrying trophy, dragging captive;
        mint mark illegible.
    Follis (AE 4) 0.96 g, 13 mm
    Object #553, B.1:000

42. OBV: Same as 41.
   REV: Same as 41.
↑ *Follis* (AE 4) 2.04 g, 13–14 mm
   Object #696, Survey Site 680B

43. OBV: DN[. . . . . . .]AVG; bust to r.; well worn.
   REV: Victory advancing l., dragging captive; inscription illegible.
↘ *Follis* (AE 4) 1.64 g, 12–14 mm
   Object #705, Surface find at Lejjūn.

These three coins are typical issues of the late fourth century. They were struck at many mints in the period ca. A.D. 378–392, during the reigns of Valentinian II, Theodosius I, and Arcadius (cf. Pearce 1951: 292–93). The size and weight of the coins continued to shrink. It was only a matter of time until these coins would be so small and so worthless that the populace would refuse to use them.

44. OBV: Bust to r., inscription illegible.
   REV: Laurel wreath with cross inside.
↓ *Follis* (AE 3) 1.64 g, 15–16 mm
   Object #603, A.2:096 (A.D. 402–450)

This coin is similar to several already known from Lejjūn from the previous two seasons. It is from the reign of Theodosius II, who erected a monument adorned with a large cross in Constantinople, which he commemorated in his coinage on more than one occasion (cf. Whitting 1973: 113; and Thompson 1954: 61–62).

45. OBV: Completely mineralized.
   REV: Laurel wreath surrounding VOT/XX/ . . . in several lines.
   Follis (AE 4) fragmentary, 15–16 mm
   Object #554, A.2:093 (A.D. 340–360)

The following coins may be attributed to the Early Byzantine period by virtue of their size and/or distinguishing marks on their flans. In each case, mineralization of the metal has occurred to some extent, resulting in the partial or complete loss of definition in the coin types.

46.	Object #607	C.6:010 Wreath(?)	early fifth century
47.	Object #618	A.3:079 Bust to r.	ca. A.D. 355–385
48.	Object #627	J.3:027 Victory to l.	ca. A.D. 375–423
49.	Object #628	J.3:059 AE 4	fourth/fifth centuries
50.	Object #629	B.6:004 AE 4 (frag.)	fourth/fifth centuries
51.	Object #663	A.3:101 AE 3/4	fourth/fifth centuries
52.	Object #712	C.6:045 AE 3	fourth/fifth centuries
53.	Object #727	J.4:018 AE 4	fifth century
54.	Object #733	C.6:043 Bust to r.	late fourth century

III. LATE BYZANTINE

55. OBV: Bust. dr., cuir., to r.
   REV: Completely mineralized.
   Nummus 0.48 g, 9–10 mm
   Object #565, B.1:124 (Mint of Constantinople, ca. A.D. 491–498)
   Bellinger 1966: no. 15.

56. OBV: Bust to r.
↑   REV: Large Є faintly visible.
↑   *Pentanummium* 0.85 g, 10–11 mm
    Object #732, C.6:038 (Mint of Antiochia, A.D. 491–518)
    Bellinger, 1966: no. 49.

These two coins are among the earliest in the Late Byzantine series, coming from the reign of Anastasius I in the late fifth and early sixth centuries. The mint of Antiochia produced a great many *pentanummia* such as the one found this season. Several similar coins have come from excavations in earlier seasons in other areas of the fortress.

57. OBV: Emperor's bust, facing; partially off flan; frag.
↑   REV: Large K ; worn; frag. and partially off flan.
↑   Half *follis* 4.23 g, 15–18 mm
    Object #552, B.1:118)A.D. 518–538)

Coin no. 57 is a half *follis* of the early sixth century, probably from the reign of Justinian I or Justin I. The coin has been cut; approximately half the flan has been removed for some reason. The expected diameter of the complete coin is ca. 22–25 mm, and its weight 7.2–8.5 g. This type dates to the decades following A.D. 518 (Bates 1971: 47 nos. 308–9).

58. OBV: Bust to r.; inscription illegible.
↗   REV: Large X ; inscription illegible.
↗   *Decanummium* 1.13 g, 12–13 mm
    Object #570, Surface (NE area of fortress) (A.D. 527–565)

59. OBV: Bust to r.; inscription illegible.
↗   REV: Large X ; wreath border.
↗   *Decanummium* 0.83 g, 11–12 mm
    Object #556, C.3:005 (A.D. 527–565)

Both of the *decanummia* are from the reign of Justinian I, and date after A.D. 527. There are no discernible markings that would enable us to date or place these coins more precisely. Coins like these were struck in the first half of the sixth century at a number of mints (Morrisson 1970: nos. 21–23).

60. OBV: Completely mineralized.
    REV: Large A .
    Nummus 0.77 g, 9–11 mm
    Object #615, J.1:016 (A.D. 527–565)
    Bellinger 1966: no. 309.

61. OBV: Same as 60.
    REV: Same as 60.
    Nummus 0.73 g, 10–11 mm
    Object #630, J.1:030

62. OBV: Same as 60.
    REV: Same as 60.
    Nummus 0.90 g, 10–11 mm
    Object #708, C.3:044

63. OBV: Same as 60.
    REV: Same as 60.
    Nummus 0.98 g, 8–9 mm
    Object #731, C.7:017

Nummia with the monogram Ⱥ were struck by Justinian I in the second quarter of the sixth century. Undoubtedly these coins are to be associated with the final occupation of the fortress before the major earthquake of A.D. 551. Although such coins were struck until A.D. 565, these examples probably date from earlier in Justinian's reign. The dating of these specific types is unresolved, and needs further study (Bates 1971: 9–10). These small coins cannot be dated more precisely. They may have been used within the fortress before the garrison was transferred or demobilized ca. A.D. 530; or they may come from a later occupation which preceded the 551 earthquake. *Nummia* were still circulating in this part of the sixth century; within two decades public confidence in these small denominations had been lost.

The following coins are attributable to the Late Byzantine period because of some identifying characteristic or their size and weight. Explanatory information accompanies the listing.

64.	Object #602	B.5:015 *decanummium*	early sixth century
65.	Object #567	J.2:007 *pentanummium*	early sixth century
66.	Object #564	B.1:061 *nummus*	fifth/sixth centuries
67.	Object #557	J.2:007 *nummus*	fifth/sixth centuries
68.	Object #609	C.6:010 half-*follis*	early sixth century
69.	Object #614	J.1:016 *nummus* (frag.)	fifth/sixth centuries
70.	Object #616	J.1:016 *nummus* (frag.)	fifth/sixth centuries
71.	Object #704	B.1:146 *pentanummium*	early sixth century
72.	Object #706	C.6:038 *decanummium* (?)	early sixth century
73.	Object #726	J.4:017 *nummus*	fifth/sixth centuries

These coins meet the size and weight requirements for the listed denominations in the early Late Byzantine period at el-Lejjūn. They were probably struck under the authority of Anastasius I, Justin I, and Justinian I.

The Late Byzantine corpus from the site confirms arguments by the principal investigator that the earthquake of A.D. 551 probably destroyed much of the fortress. A small group of people may have lived in the ruins for awhile, but the coins lead us to believe that such an occupation would have been short lived, at best.

IV. ISLAMIC: MAMLŪK

74. OBV: Partially off flan; evidence of Mamlūk-style heraldry; no legible inscriptions.
    REV: Large rosette.
    AE 3.26 g, 15 mm
    Object #613, Survey Site 611, Qatrana Fort.

The rosette is a common Mamlūk design, here employed over the entire reverse of the coin as a blazon, or heraldic coat-of-arms. The flan is very worn, showing some evidence of mineralization, as well. The coin probably dates to the fourteenth or fifteenth centuries A.D. (cf. Balog 1977: 201 no. 68).

V. ISLAMIC: OTTOMAN

75. OBV: *Tughra* of Muhammad V, with olive branch and sheaf of wheat below; year Ɛ = 4.
    REV: (10) *parah* (in Arabic); around denominational designation, *zuriba el-rubuᵓ ghirsh fi-qustentīnīyah*; ١٣٢٧ (1327 A.H. or A.D. 1909).
    Nickel 10 Parah, or 1/4 piastre, 2.58 g, 18 mm
    Object #725, Survey Site 689B.
    Nicol, el-Nabarawy, and Bacharach 1982: 141, similar to nos. 4454 and 4455 (from the mint of Cairo).

This coin is in excellent condition, showing very little sign of wear or weathering. The *tughra* is stylized in the usual Ottoman form, so that this particular coin must be attributed by date rather than by the name of the sultan. This issue was struck in the fourth year of Muhammad V's reign, or A.D. 1913. The date on the reverse is the year of Muhammad V's accession to the throne; the date on the obverse indicates the regnal year when this particular coin was struck within his reign.

VI. UNCERTAIN AND UNIDENTIFIABLE

Some coins were either too fragmentary to be read or were completely lost to mineralization and corrosion.[1]

CONCLUSIONS

The coins from the third season of excavations were predominantly from the Late Roman, Early Byzantine, and Late Byzantine periods. As excavation moved into deeper levels, fewer late coins were found. Of special interest is the early coin of Probus, which probably was minted before the foundation of the fortress under Diocletian.

The coins document an occupational history of the legionary fortress at el-Lejjūn which began in the late third or early fourth centuries. Fifth century use of the fortress is certainly assumed because of ceramic remains. However, so few bronze coins were struck in this period that we have no adequate numismatic evidence to corroborate late fifth century activity. No occupation is documented after the early- to mid-sixth century, except at sites in the vicinity of the fortress, and in the burial areas (dug intrusively into Area C, the northwestern corner tower of the fortress).

ACKNOWLEDGMENTS

The writer would like to thank Nina Jorgenson, Katherine Schneider, and Karen Ruthman, all students in the Chemistry Department of Smith College, Northampton, Massachusetts, for their assistance in cleaning the coins.

Research on these coins was made possible in the summer of 1986 by a research grant from the American Philosophical Society and a Mellon Grant in the Humanities administered by Smith College.

NOTE

[1]The unidentifiable coins are listed here by object number, area, and locus.

				481	A.1:086	559	B.4:068
				575	B.1:138	608	C.6:010
601	J.1:020	569	A.3:074	617	J.1:016	632	J.2:016
563	B.5:007	724	J.4:010	642	J.3:074	662	C.3:024
555	A.1:082	561	A.2:099	672	A.3:113	676	B.5:040
487	B.1:114	729	H.6:007	697	A.3:107	698	A.3:107

BIBLIOGRAPHY

Balog, P.
    1977   New Considerations on Mamlūk Heraldry. *American Numismatic Society Museum Notes* 22: 183–211.

Bates, G.
    1971   *Byzantine Coins.* Archaeological Exploration of Sardis. Cambridge, MA: Harvard University.

Bellinger, A. R.
1966 *Catalogue of the Byzantine Coins in the Dumbarton Oaks Collection and the Whittemore Collection*, Vol. 1, *Anastasius I to Maurice, 491-602*, A. R. Bellinger and P. Grierson, eds. Washington, DC: Dumbarton Oaks Center for Byzantine Studies.

Bruun, P. M.
1966 *The Roman Imperial Coinage*. Vol. 7. *Constantine and Licinius*. London: Spink and Sons.

Kent, J. P. C.
1981 *The Roman Imperial Coinage*. Vol. 8. *The Family of Constantine*. London: Spink and Sons.

Morrisson, C.
1970 *Catalogue des Monnaies byzantines de la Bibliothèque Nationale*. Paris: Imprimèrie nationale.

Nicol, N. D.; el-Nabarawy, R.; Bacharach, J. L.
1982 *Catalogue of the Islamic Coins, Glass Weights, Dies and Medals in the Egyptian National Library, Cairo*. American Research Center in Egypt. Malibu, CA: Undena.

Pearce, J. W. E.
1951 *The Roman Imperial Coinage*. Vol. 9. *Valentinian I to Theodosius I*. London: Spink and Sons.

Sutherland, C. H. V.
1973 *The Roman Imperial Coinage*. Vol. 6. *Diocletian to Maximinus*. London: Spink and Sons.

Thompson, M.
1954 *The Athenian Agora 2: The Coins*. Princeton: American School of Classical Studies at Athens.

Webb, P. H.
1933 *The Roman Imperial Coinage*. Vol. 5, Part 2. *Probus to Diocletian*. London: Spink and Sons.

Whitting, P. D.
1973 *Byzantine Coins*. New York: G. P. Putnam's Sons.

Glass from the
North Theater Byzantine Church,
and Soundings
at Jerash, Jordan, 1982–1983

Glass from the North Theater Byzantine Church, and Soundings at Jerash, Jordan, 1982–1983

Glass from the North Theater Byzantine Church, and Soundings at Jerash, Jordan, 1982–1983

Glass from the
North Theater Byzantine Church,
and Soundings
at Jerash, Jordan, 1982–1983

Glass from the North Theater Byzantine Church, and Soundings at Jerash, Jordan, 1982–1983

Glass from the North Theater Byzantine Church, and Soundings at Jerash, Jordan, 1982–1983

Carol Meyer
Oriental Institute
University of Chicago
Chicago, IL 60637

The corpus of glass treated here ranges from Roman through Mamluk and later, but the bulk of the corpus is from the Byzantine and Umayyad periods. Most was recovered from fill and reuse levels in a Roman theater and from a Byzantine church that remained in use into early Islamic times. The corpus is not merely a large (263 items illustrated), carefully excavated one; the stratigraphy and dating are also briefly discussed. Comparanda for individual forms are given, primarily from dated Near Eastern contexts, but also from the Mediterranean basin and beyond. The corpus is intended as a reference for excavators dealing with Near Eastern glass of ca. A.D. 350–750, with the expectation that it may be used not only for identifying single items, but eventually for group and regional studies.

The material presented here should not be considered the Jerash corpus but a corpus. It comes from the North Theater, the Church of Bishop Isaiah, and soundings of the ACOR team of the Jerash International Project.[1] The glass ranges from Roman through Mamluk and later periods, although most of the corpus is Byzantine and Umayyad, fourth through mid-eighth centuries. Although this corpus is not a controlled sample of all glass from the ancient city, it does represent a detailed analysis of all the diagnostic glass recovered from the ACOR trenches. The study is intended to present a large, excavated, and carefully dated glass corpus; that future work by others may modify our understanding of the corpus is expected and hoped for in a promising field of research.

The glass from the general Syro-Palestinian area in the middle of the first millennium A.D. is at best spottily published. Some reports are inadequate or outdated; others, such as Khirbat al-Karak (Delougaz and Haines 1960), are thorough but treat a much more limited corpus. In other studies glass vessels or artifacts are only dated within a vague range of centuries. Thus the glass, which numerically may be the second most abundant category of artifacts after potsherds, loses value as a clue to dating. The present corpus, which comes from loci dated by coins, pottery, lamps, stratigraphy, and construction history, should improve the dating of the glass of the first eight centuries A.D.

It is difficult to detect regional differences in the glass industry. After the invention of glass-blowing about the middle of the first century B.C. (Grose 1977; 1984) the technology spread rapidly throughout the Roman Empire. Over the decades, however, differences might have been expected to develop between provinces. The two most extensive corpora for the Near East are from Karanis, Egypt (Harden 1936) and Sardis, Turkey (von Saldern 1980); geographically Jerash, in Jordan, lies between them. Although the three corpora are not temporally coterminous, there is considerable overlap, and there are some indications of regional differences, which in turn suggest a province if not a specific point of manufacture. Unfortunately, the voluminous literature on glass in private collections or museums often has to rely on comparisons with unexcavated material without a secure provenience or date.

Jerash, ancient Gerasa, is one of the Decapolis cities; it lies 48 mountainous kilometers north of Amman in a mild, well-watered valley. A few Iron Age sherds have been recovered there, and the town is thought to have been founded in the late Hellenistic period, though the early remains—some of which lie under the south end of the site—have scarcely been sounded. Most of the monumental buildings for which Jerash is famous—the Oval Forum, South Theater, Temples of Zeus and Artemis, the colonnaded streets—were erected in the first and second centuries A.D. A second burst of construction occurred after Christianity was legalized, at the beginning of the Byzantine period.[2] Numerous churches were built, often from stones and materials robbed from Roman buildings. The city may have been in decline, but much of the site was inhabited in the Late Byzantine period and continued to be occupied after the Islamic conquest in A.D. 636. Most of the sherds and small finds in the North Theater date to the late Byzantine/Umayyad period, ca. 630–670, which may have been critical historically but whose pots and goblets cannot yet be separated typologically into Byzantine or Umayyad, much less Christian vs. Moslem. The Umayyad period, then, is considered to last from A.D. 661 to 746/7 when a major earthquake toppled much of what was left of Jerash. Some people continued to live in Jerash through the Mamluk and later periods up to modern times, but the remains are much more scanty.

More background information on the excavations and methodology is given here than is usual for a glass report because it is not clear when the final publication will appear, although the preliminary reports have appeared (Zayadine 1986). Figure 1 shows the location of the trenches in the North Theater.[3] The ACOR team was allotted the inside of the theater—seats, orchestra, stage, and scaene—which was excavated with trenches JNT-B-I to VIII (*J*erash *N*orth *T*heater-Area *B*-Trench *I*). The British team excavated the exterior of the theater and the internal passages, the JNT-A trenches. They ceded to the ACOR team the

vaulted audience parodos (JNT-B-VII) and the western approach corridor (JNT-A-XIV), which were contiguous with JNT-B trenches. The Australian team excavated the Portico, JNT-C. The glass from the British trenches will be published with that from the Australian trenches.

The North Theater was built in two stages, the first dating to ca. A.D. 165/6. The original building, which included the lower cavea, was an odeon that seems to have served also as a bouleuterion or assembly hall for the representatives of the tribes or political units within Jerash. Later, ca. A.D. 230, the upper cavea and a new scaenae frons were added. Much later, after the theater went out of use, some walls were constructed in the Byzantine period in the lower part of the theater and inside the stage. For the profiles and further details, see the report in Clark (1986). Many cut blocks were robbed for other buildings. Then the whole lower cavea was filled with tumbled blocks, probably earthquake damage, and soft gray soil. In the Umayyad period this was leveled off enough to permit reuse of some of the interior vaults, such as JNT-B-VII (see fig. 4), and installation of a series of pottery kilns.[4] The kilns seem to have been destroyed by further block tumble, perhaps the earthquake of A.D. 746/7, and thereafter the use of the theater area was sporadic; only the upper cavea remained above ground.

The North Theater was built on a hillside, and the open half-bowl that is the cavea looks to the north. Uphill to the west (Area F), a Byzantine church with three apses and elegant mosaic floors was built by one Bishop Isaiah. The church is supported in part by a terrace wall, and the depth of the strata beneath it is as yet unknown. The church was built in the middle of the sixth century, during the reign of Justinian the Great, and remained in use in the Umayyad period. Some of the best-preserved glass vessels came from the church, and most of them seem to be Umayyad in date. Baur (1938: 518) dated most of the glass in the Byzantine churches to the fourth and fifth centuries because the forms are thought to be less pleasing than those of the Roman period. It seems likely that most of the glass in the ruins of the Bishop Isaiah church belong to the time of its destruction, not its construction, hence the discrepancy in dates used here versus those in the earlier study.

Two small soundings (Area A) were sunk on a terrace northwest of the North Theater, on the

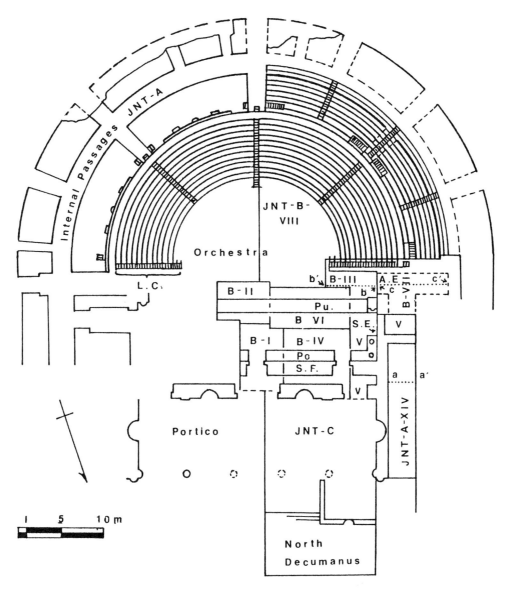

Fig. 1. Jerash North Theater with approximate location of trenches JNT-B-I to VIII and profiles (a–a', b'–b, c–c'). Based on S. M. Balderstone and J. L. Cowherd.

A.E. = Audience Entrance Arch (Parodos), L.C. = Lower Cavea, Po. = Podium, Pu. = Pulpitum, S.E. = Stage Entrance Arch, S.F. = Scaenae Frons.

site of the proposed new housing. The purpose of the trenches was to ensure that no important remains would be damaged. No structures came to light but a few small finds, including glass, were recovered. The last sounding, Area E, lay west and uphill from the theater and church. The Area E trench was an attempt to locate the edge of the North Decumanus. Some walls and artifacts were found, but the Decumanus was not.

Part of the surface layer of the lower cavea of the North Theater was scraped off before excava-

tions began, but thereafter careful stratigraphic control was maintained in the trenches there and in other areas. The recording system was that used at Tell el-Ḥesi, with a few modifications for the demands of the site. All categories of finds were saved, from marble sculpture to olive pits, although relatively few loci could be screened. All the glass was kept, bagged and labeled. The supervisor was known to want glass and other small finds, even bone splinters, and the workmen were quite meticulous. Although some uncertainty is

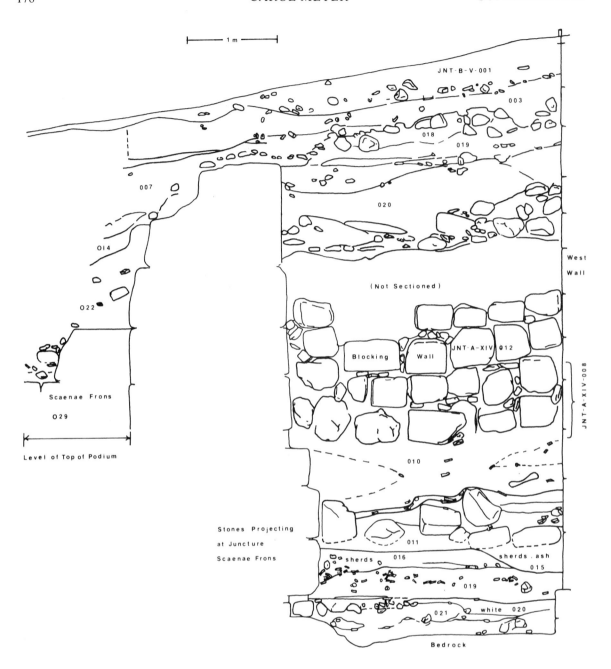

Fig. 2 (a–a'). Early Byzantine and Roman fill in the west corridor. JNT-A-XIV plus west end of JNT-B-V (top).

bound to remain, at least 75 percent of the glass was recovered, and all of this was cleaned, counted, and tabulated. Body sherds were then discarded but all rims, bases, and other diagnostic pieces were kept and selected ones drawn, a total of about 300 items.

Relatively few complete forms were recovered. Four vessels—a lamp, a shallow bowl, and two goblets—were complete from rim to base and a few more forms were reconstructible on paper. None of the glass except some from the Church of Bishop Isaiah was in primary context. On the other hand, most of the glass probably was not deposited far from its point of use and breakage, i.e., most of it was probably tossed down from the dwellings above, within the North Theater or

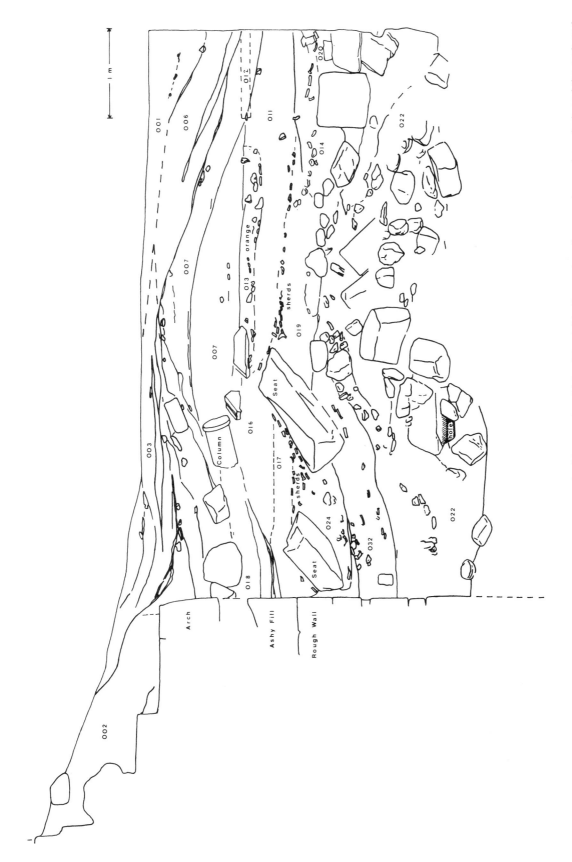

Fig. 3 (b′–b). Late Byzantine/Umayyad and later fill outside the west audience entrance (parodos), and the arch and rough wall beneath. JNT-B-III, facing north.

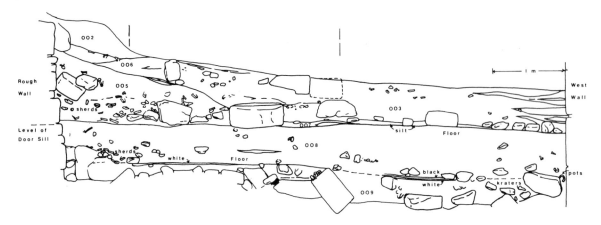

Fig. 4 (c–c'). Fill and floors inside the entrance vault, facing south. JNT-B-VII.

uphill, or possibly even from repairs or recon-struction on the Church of Bishop Isaiah. Fur-thermore, the glass almost certainly represents domestic (or possibly church) debris, not grave goods. Many, if not the majority, of the published, intact glass vessels of the fourth to eighth cen-turies from the Near East have no clear pro-venience but were probably looted from tombs. In particular such collections include large numbers of perfume flasks and kohl jars, types poorly represented in this Jerash corpus. It is possible that most of the Byzantine and Umayyad glass without archaeological context published to date is not an accurate representation of the varieties of glass in use in daily life.

Much of the value of the Jerash corpus lies in its being carefully dated; the basis of the chrono-logical scheme therefore should be presented in further detail. The names of the periods and their dividing points are historical labels and events; these include the accession of Constantine in 324, the Battle of Yarmouk in 636, and the earthquake of 746/7. There is no reason to think that the Battle of Yarmouk or the accession of a new emperor had any immediate effect on the Jerash pottery or glass corpora. The dates merely delimit the blocks of time within which the various types of vessels were developed, became popular, and fell out of use. Predecessors, heirlooms, and frag-ments redeposited in later levels may be expected. A statistical summary of the distribution of the types over time has been drawn up but is too bulky to include here.

To assign dates to levels or objects from Jerash, each layer or soil unit such as a pit or sherd pocket was given a locus designation, e.g., JNT-B-III-002. The loci were recorded and described in the field notebooks, daily plans, and locus summary sheets, but their layering is usually most easily seen on the profiles (figs. 2, 3, 4). Sherds and small finds in a locus were saved and labeled. The diagnostic potsherds—rims, bases, special fea-tures or decorations—were sorted and dated by Vincent Clark. The pottery dating is based on comparisons to corpora from other sites such as Pella and on internal evidence such as coins. The pottery from Jerash will be the subject of studies by members of the excavation teams and cannot be presented here. Again there are problems such as early examples of a type or intrusive sherds; rodent holes were especially conspicuous in the upper levels. Nevertheless, far more work has been done on the chronology of Palestinian pot-tery than on the glass. Julian Bowsher dated all the coins and is continuing research on them and on the inscriptions from the North Theater. Some types of ceramic lamps can also provide dates.

All of these dating indicators for a given locus may be tabulated—sherds, coins, lamps, strati-graphic position. Table 1 presents the dating evi-dence for all the loci that yielded glass. On such a basis a locus can be given a broad date, e.g., JNT-B-VII-008 as Umayyad. The latest dating evidence is usually taken for the locus date unless it can be shown convincingly that the lone Ottoman sherd, for instance, is intrusive in a Late Byzantine/ Umayyad level.

The designation Late Byzantine/Early Umayyad (LByz/Um) is an important one because many potsherds in this corpus cannot be distinguished as either latest Byzantine or earliest Umayyad. Nor is there any reason to think that any pottery definable as "Umayyad" would be imposed immediately. Even purely Islamic coinage was slow to appear. Therefore Late Byzantine/Early Umayyad is given an arbitrary range of A.D. 630–670, overlapping slightly into the Umayyad dates, 661–747.

Although almost all the glass is fragmentary, the form, such as rim or base diameter, can often be reconstructed. Unfortunately the tiniest fragments often come from the best-dated loci, and the largest pieces from the least informative loci, such as cavea clearance. This report therefore contains a large number of references, without attempting to be exhaustive, to gain a) some idea of the whole vessel shapes, b) some clues as to their distribution around the eastern Mediterranean basin, and c) the reported dates at other sites, even if the dates do not always coincide with those at Jerash.

No good evidence for glass manufacture was found at Jerash; the cakes of colored glass in the "Glass Court," probably for tesserae, have not been shown conclusively to be Jerash products (Baur 1938: 517–18). In the Late Byzantine/Early Umayyad and later fill of the lower cavea of the theater numerous lumps of glass, some quite large and some with scum on the top, and a warped goblet base (fig. 8:Z) were recovered. The amount of glass and the extreme thinness of much of it make it unlikely that the glass was transported far, if it was produced at another center.

Where such a center or centers may have been located is as yet unknown. Particularly after the invention of glassblowing, workshops were probably set up in many cities; in some cases it would have been more reasonable to import a glassworker than the glass itself in quantity. For the Syro-Palestinian area, Weinberg reports six deformed fragments of Roman period molded bowls at Hagoshrim in upper Galilee, which suggest a nearby factory (Weinberg 1973: 38–39). Two possible glass centers have been reported near Haifa, Jalamet el-Asafna, and one near Kafr Jasif, east of Acre. The latter site dates to the fifth or perhaps the sixth century A.D. Although no actual kiln was found, much kiln debris was; the furnace(s) may have produced basic glass for glassworkers elsewhere to finish (Philippe 1970: 60–62; Weinberg, in press). Glass melt, masses of glass fragments including wasters, and a small chamber full of burnt earth and charcoal (but no furnace)

may point to the existence of a fourth or fifth century workshop at Samaria (Crowfoot 1957: 404–5). According to literary sources Hebron was producing glass before the ninth century. Tyre is mentioned as manufacturing beads in the seventh and tenth centuries, exporting glass in the 12th century, and making high quality glass in the 13th century (Riis and Poulsen 1957: 31). Haynes (1948: 51) suggests, however, that the early Crusades at the end of the 11th century may have checked glass production at Tyre, Hebron, and elsewhere. Glass production is reported in Akko, Tripoli, and Antioch in the 12th and 13th centuries, in a new town named Armanaz settled after the Crusades (1268–1291), and in Aleppo in the 13th and 15th centuries. Damascus was especially famous for its enameled glass in the 14th century, until Tamerlane ravaged Syria and reportedly took the most skillful glass masters to his capital at Samarkand ca. 1400 (Riis and Poulsen 1957: 31).

Egypt has a most ancient history of glassworking. For the Roman period Alexandria is often mentioned as producing luxury glass and perhaps bottles for shipping valuable liquids. Diospolis Magna near Coptos may also have been making glass (Charlesworth 1924: 31). A notice, as yet unconfirmed (ARCE Newsletter 1958: 2), on the Polish excavation at Athribis/Benha reports two cylindrical furnaces of the second to fourth centuries used for glass. At Alexandria buildings dated to the fifth to the early seventh century have yielded debris from the manufacture of beads and green and deep blue glass, and pieces of glass furnaces but not the actual structures (Rodziewicz 1979: 198–205; 1984: 240–43). Written sources mention blue and green alexandrine glass in the seventh century, painted vessels in the 11th century, and exports to England in the 14th century. Transparent glass was manufactured at Fustat from the 11th until the 14th century (Riis and Poulsen 1957: 31–32).

Farther afield, Iraq is known to have produced glass from the ninth to the 14th centuries, some exported as far as Spain, although the center of glassmaking apparently shifted. Glassworkers were moved from Basra to Samarra in the ninth century (Riis and Poulsen 1957: 31–32) when the latter was the capital (A.D. 838 to 883; Lamm 1931: 362). Later Baghdad, in the tenth and 12th centuries, and Qâdisîyâ on the Tigris, in the 12th and 13th centuries, became glass centers (Riis and Poulsen 1957: 32). Persia also produced glass,

TABLE 1. Dating Evidence for Loci with Glass

Locus	Sherd Date	Other Dating Evidence	Locus	Sherd Date	Other Dating Evidence
AREA A - TRENCH I			011	LByz/Um	Coin, early fourth century
			012	LByz/Um	
001	Modern		013	LByz/Um	
002	Modern	Coin, Justinian I, 527–565	014	LByz/Um	Coin, Umayyad, early eighth century; lamps, Jerash type
003	EByz				
005	EByz		015	LByz/Um	
006	EByz/LRom	Lamp, second century A.D.	016	LByz/Um	
007	EByz/LRom		017	LByz/Um	Coin, LByz, 518–602
			018	LByz/Um (or later)	
AREA A - TRENCH II			019	LByz/Um	
			020	LByz/Um	
001	Umayyad	Lamps, LRom/EByz	021	Mamluk	
002	LByz		022	LByz/Um	
003	LByz		023	LByz/Um-Ott	Lamp, seventh–eighth century or later
004	LByz				
005	LByz		024	LByz/Um	Lamp, Umayyad
006	LByz	Lamp, ERom	025	LByz/Um	
007	LByz		026	LByz/Um-Ott	Coin, Dinar, 894; lamp, Mamluk/Ottoman?
NORTH THEATER - TRENCH B I			027	LByz/Um	
			028	LByz/Um	Coin, Umayyad, copy of LByz follis, late seventh century
001	Modern	Two coins, third century B.C., eighth century A.D.			
			029	LByz/Um-Ott	
002	Ottoman	Coin, Umayyad	030	LByz/Um	Coins, Anastasius, 491–498?, and late fourth century
004	(LByz/Um) Um				
006	(LByz/Um) Um		031	LByz/Um	Coin, LByz, illegible, 498–538
008	Mamluk		032	LByz/Um	
009	Mamluk		**NORTH THEATER - TRENCH B IV**		
010	Mamluk				
NORTH THEATER - TRENCH B II			008	(LByz/Um)	Lamp, Umayyad, Jerash type, LByz/Um
			009	Umayyad	Lamp, Umayyad "bi Jerash"
001	Modern	Lamps, Umayyad or later?	011	Umayyad	
002	Ottoman		012	Umayyad	
008	Ottoman		013	Umayyad	
009	Ottoman		016	Umayyad	
011	Ottoman	Coin, Byz, illegible, early sixth century	017	Umayyad	
			018	Umayyad	Lamp, Umayyad
012	Umayyad	Lamp, Um	021	Umayyad	Coin, late second to early third century
013	Umayyad	Lamp, Jerash type, LByz/Um			
017	Mamluk?	Lamp, LByz	022	LRom/Ebyz	Coins, Licinius II, 311–324, others fourth century
018	Mamluk				
025	LByz	Coins, one second century; others mostly second, fourth centuries	**NORTH THEATER - TRENCH B V**		
			001	LByz/Um-Ott	
026	EByz		002	LByz/Um-Mam	
028	EByz	Coins, second–fourth century (mostly last half fourth century)	003	LByz/Um-Mam	
			004	LByz/Um-Mam	
			005	LByz/Um	
029	EByz	Coins, few second, third century; most fourth century; latest, first half fifth century	006	LByz/Um-Mam	Lamp, Abbasid/Fatimid
			007	LByz/Um-Ott	
			008	LByz/Um-Mam	
			009	LByz/Um-Ott	
NORTH THEATER - TRENCH B III			010	LByz/Um-Ott	
			011	LByz	
001	LByz/Um–Ott[a]		012	LByz/Um-Ott	
002	LByz/Um–Mam		013	LByz/Um-Mam	
003	LByz/Um–Mam		014	LByz/Um	
004	LByz/Um	Lamp, Jerash type, LByz/Um	015	LByz/Um	
005	LByz/Um		016	LByz/Um	
006	LByz/Um		017	LByz/Um	
007	LByz/Um	Lamp, Jerash type, LByz/Um	018	LByz/Um-Abb	
008	LByz/Um (or later)		019	LByz/Um	
009	LByz/Um	Lamps, Jerash type, LByz/Um			
010	LByz				

[a] Indicates that most of the sherds are LByz/Um but that there is enough later material to show later activity or disturbance.

TABLE 1, *continued*

Locus	Sherd Date	Other Dating Evidence
020	LByz/Um	
021	LByz/Um	
022	LByz/Um	
023	LByz/Um	
024	LByz/Um	
025	LByz/Um-Mam	Coin, Justin II, 568–569
026	LByz/Um-Mam	
027	LByz/Um	
028	LByz/Um	
029	LByz/Um	Coin, Theodosius, 388–392
030	LByz/Um	
031	LByz/Um	Three coins, EByz, late fourth century; Byz, illegible; Anastasius I, 498–512
032	LByz	
033	LByz/Um	
034	LByz/Um	Coin, probably Justinian I, 527–565
035	LByz/Um	
036	LByz/Um	
037	LByz/Um	Coin, mid-fourth century

NORTH THEATER - TRENCH B VI

Locus	Sherd Date	Other Dating Evidence
006	EByz	Coins; statuary
007	EByz	
010	EByz	Coins, all second half fourth century
011	EByz	Coins, two third century; through fourth century; one second quarter fifth century
014	EByz	
015	EByz	Two coins, late fourth century

NORTH THEATER - TRENCH B VII

Locus	Sherd Date	Other Dating Evidence
001	(Robber hole)	
002	LByz/Um-Ott	
003	LByz/Um-Mod	Three coins, Constantius?, 341–346; Justin II, 569–570; Theodosius I?, 383–390
004	LByz/Um-Abb	
005	LByz/Um-Ott	Two coins, Constans, 341–346; Umayyad, 700–750
006	LByz/Um-Ott	Coin, Theodosius I, 388–392
008	LByz/Um	
009	LByz/Um	

NORTH THEATER - TRENCH A XIV

Locus	Sherd Date	Other Dating Evidence
004	Byzantine	
005	Byzantine	
006	EByz	
007	Byzantine	
008	EByz	
009	LByz/Um	
010	EByz	Four coins, Nabataean, Aretas IV, 1–2 or 5–6 A.D.; Roman, third century; LRom/EByz, first half fourth century; Valentinian II (?), 375–392
011	EByz	
012	EByz	Coin, late fourth century
013	EByz	
014	EByz	

Locus	Sherd Date	Other Dating Evidence
015	EByz	
016	EByz	Two coins, Constans, 333–337; Constantius, 354–361
017	EByz	
018	EByz	
019	EByz	Coin, Constantius I, 310–324
020	LRom	
021	LRom	

AREA E - TRENCH I

Locus	Sherd Date	Other Dating Evidence
008	LByz	
010	Rom/Byz	
012	Rom/Byz	
013	LByz	

AREA F - BISHOP ISAIAH CHURCH

Trench and Locus	Sherd Date	Other Dating Evidence
I-001	Mamluk	Mamluk occupation
II-001	Mamluk	Surface
IV-003	Umayyad	
V-001	Umayyad	
002	Umayyad	Coin, EByz, 393–423
VI-002	Umayyad	Coin, LByz, 567/8
VII-001	Mamluk	Occupation
002	Mamluk	
003	Mamluk	Occupation
VIIA-001	Mamluk	
VIII-002	Umayyad	
003	Umayyad	
007	LByz	
008	LByz	
009	LByz	
010	LByz	
011	LByz	
IX-002	Umayyad	
003	Umayyad	Two coins, Umayyad
X-003	Umayyad	
XI-002	Umayyad	
XII-002	Umayyad	
003	Umayyad	
XIII-001	Umayyad	
002	Umayyad	Coin, Umayyad
XIV-002	Umayyad	East exterior wall collapse debris
XV-002	LByz	Coin, sixth century
003	LByz	Two coins, EByz, 383–392; and sixth century
005	LByz	Coin, sixth century
006	LByz	
007	LByz	
008	LByz	Lamp, fifth to sixth century
009	LByz	
010	LRom	
XVI-002	Umayyad	Two coins, EByz, 383–392; and Umayyad
003	Umayyad	Coin, Umayyad; lamp, eighth century
005	Umayyad	
007	Umayyad	
009	LByz	
012	Umayyad	

some of it luxury wares, and transparent and opaque varieties are mentioned in the sixth, seventh, and probably in the tenth centuries (Riis and Poulsen 1957: 31–32).

In spite of the mention of glassworkers such as *vitrarii* and *diatretarii* as early as Constantine the Great, glass production at Constantinople itself, the heart of the Byzantine empire, is not definitely attested until the 16th century. Although it seems reasonable to assume that the capital had a convenient source for utilitarian glass items, some at least was certainly imported from Syria-Palestine and Egypt (Philippe 1970: 17–19). At Sardis, however, there is some evidence for glass manufacture in the Byzantine period. Von Saldern points to the cullet, wasters, crucible fragments, and the "remarkable homogeneity" of the ordinary wares such as goblets, lamps, bowls, bottles, and salvers (von Saldern 1980: 36).

Still, probably the oldest glass furnaces known date to ca. A.D. 600–650; they were excavated at Torcello, Italy. Here were four furnaces—one (or two) for fritting, one (or two) for firing batches of glass in pots, and one for annealing (Harden 1971: 86). The next known actual furnace is at Corinth, Greece, dated to the 11th to 12th century (Davidson 1940: 299). Only one furnace was found there but it may have had three stories, one for the fire, one for the vat of glass being worked, and one for annealing (Davidson 1940: 302). Such an arrangement is much more fuel efficient.

Another, as yet unexplained, phenomenon is sometimes considered related to glass production. At Jerash dense deposits of broken glass, mostly lamps, dishes, bowls, wine goblets, bottles, and window glass, up to 0.25 m deep, were found in a passage north of St. Theodore's church and under a stairway leading from the cathedral's Fountain Court to the passage. Baur suggests that the fragments were collected for remelting, although no sign of a furnace was found (Baur 1938: 514–15). At Khirbat al-Karak also, heaps of broken glass were found in the east entrance room and a passage on the south side of the church; perhaps these were scraps saved for reuse (Delougaz and Haines 1960: 49). Here again there is no more evidence for glassworking than for the opposite possible explanation: that the glass, having been used in the church and broken, was still sanctified and could not be recycled, only deposited in some unused corner of the church.[5]

The following sections run in chronological order: Roman (first to early fourth centuries A.D.),

Early Byzantine (A.D. 324–491), Late Byzantine (A.D. 491–636), Late Byzantine/Umayyad (ca. A.D. 630–670), Umayyad (A.D. 661–747 or later), Mamluk (A.D. 1250–1516), and Ottoman to modern. Details on individual vessels or artifacts illustrated are given on the figure descriptions. These include color, locus, locus date (LocDt), stylistic date (StyDt), material culture number (MC#), catalogue number (Cat#), and comments. Two dates are given because it is quite possible for a glass sherd to be deposited in a locus much later than the date of its production. The catalogue number or material culture number plus the locus should enable one to retrieve further information about findspot, associated finds, date of excavation, and the like. Catalogue numbers are for the use of the excavators and other investigators; they are not the official Registration Numbers, which do not include fragments, study collections, and samples.

No attempt has been made to devise a rigid typology (such as IA1 = Goblet with stem and flat foot) because such a typology would have to be altered the minute new data become available, or new forms would have to be fitted into the typology in a Procrustean manner. Vessels are grouped by form and labeled with the shortest possible descriptive terms. Some forms or decorations may have begun in an earlier period than the one to which they are attributed here, or may continue into later periods. The evidence for these cases will be discussed individually.

ROMAN GLASS

Although the North Theater was a Roman construction, it was so thoroughly reworked and re-used that few loci can be dated so early (Loci 020 and 021 in fig. 2, for instance). Almost all of the Roman sherds were found in later contexts. Some of the glass included in the Early Byzantine or later sections may be Roman; such examples will be noted. There are so few Roman pieces between the first and early fourth centuries A.D. that they will be treated together.

Cast Vessels

Ribbed Bowl (fig. 5:A).   One fragment, a thick amber base, was found in the lower cavea of the theater. There are similar later pieces (cf. fig. 13:U), but this one's color and thickness seem more like the Roman glass.

Ribbed bowls (also called "pillar-molded" bowls) seem to have been widely distributed in the first century A.D., and their manufacture dates back to the first century B.C. (Grose 1977; 1979; 1982). Although the ribbed bowls were made by casting, a two-part or closed mold probably was not used in many cases; instead a preformed blank with ridges was heated and sagged over a simple forming mold (Grose 1984: 28). A number of ribbed bowls were found at Hagoshrim in the upper Galilee, including six deformed pieces that suggest local production (Weinberg 1973: 38–39), and more than 3,000 fragments of cast vessels are reported from Tel Anafa (Grose 1979: 54). Hesban yielded some early glass, roughly dated to the first and second centuries; these included some ribbed bowls (Goldstein 1976: 128–29), and some 40 pieces were recovered at Samaria (Crowfoot 1957: 403). Harden states that ribbed bowls were rare in Egypt, and illustrates one from Karanis (Harden 1936: 118–19, pl. 14); he mentions another from Armant (Harden 1936: 99–100). These bowls are not uncommon at Quseir al-Qadim on the Red Sea coast (16 illustrated in Roth 1979: pls. 52–58, 61, 62, 65; five in Meyer 1981: pls. 55–56; two in Meyer, unpublished). Dura-Europos yielded some ribbed bowls from ca. A.D. 1–100 (Clairmont 1963: pl. 4), and Sardis had some 15 fragments thought to have been imported from the eastern Mediterranean (von Saldern 1980: 11–12). Four bowls with ribs, one molded and three blown (*Zarte rippenschalen*), have been recovered at the Samothrace cemetery and dated to the Augustan period (Dusenbery 1967: 39, 44–45), and others came from Corinth (Davidson 1952: 94–97). It has been suggested that some ridged bowls were made at Aquilea, Italy (Calvi 1968: 70–71). Without attempting a complete list of sites from which ribbed bowls are known, they seem to have been common in Syria and the Crimea (Harden 1936: 99–100), Cyprus (Harden 1936: 99–100; Fitzwilliam Museum 1978: no. 32), and Italy (Grose 1977; 1979; 1982). One fragment has been recovered as far away as Arikamedu in east India (Wheeler 1946: 102).

Linear-Cut Bowls (fig. 5:B–F). These are another type of relatively common Roman bowl. They are mold-made, generally thick, and usually have one or more incised lines on the interior, although fig. 5:C has an exterior line. Their means of manufacture, sagging a preformed circle over or into a mold (Grose 1984: 28), and their distribution are similar to that of the ribbed bowls. A

large number are known from Hagoshrim in the Galilee in a variety of colors: aqua, colorless, yellow-green, light purple, browns, green, and olive (Weinberg 1973: 40, 42). Many more were retrieved at Samaria (Crowfoot 1957: 403). One sherd is illustrated from Pelusium, Egypt (Fontaine 1952: 79, pl. 5), and more are known from Quseir al-Qadim (Roth 1979: pl. 52; Meyer, unpublished). Clairmont (1963: pl. 4) published three from Dura-Europos, dated to the first century A.D. Von Saldern presents some nine bowls from Sardis and suggests that they may be as early as the third quarter of the first century B.C., and that the ribbed one may be slightly later (von Saldern 1980: 7–8; Grose 1977; 1979). Two bowls, probably Augustan, were recovered from the Samothrace cemetery (Dusenbery 1967: 39), and a few from Corinth where they are attributed to the second century (Davidson 1952: 93–94).

The fragments in fig. 5:C and E may be Hellenistic, of the type called Grooved Bowls (Grose 1979); if so, their presence is the more noteworthy as Hellenistic material at Jerash is scarce.

Blown Vessels

Crimped Band Bowls (fig. 5:G, H). Also called "bowls with applied fillets," these are shallow or deep bowls with two thick, tooled bands or handles on the rim. The two Jerash fragments come from the fill of an agricultural terrace (Area A–II) but have parallels at Wadi ed-Daliyeh Cave II (Weinberg and Barag 1974: 104, pl. 39:4), Carthage (Tatton-Brown 1984: 195, fig. 65), on Cyprus (Vessberg 1952: 114–16, pls. 1–2), and at Sardis. There, as at Jerash, the bowls are greenish or aqua; they are said to be common in the late first to third centuries (von Saldern 1980: 21, pl. 21; cf. also von Saldern 1974: 206–7; Isings 1957: 59).

Pinched-Sided Beaker (or indented beaker) (fig. 5:I). Only one possible example of this popular Roman type was recovered, and that was in a very late locus (JNT-B-III-002, Mamluk, but mostly Late Byzantine/Early Umayyad). The form is common from about the second half of the first century to the first half of the third century (Isings 1957: 46–47; Hayes 1975: 41) both in the east and west. Without presenting an exhaustive list, finds are reported from Egypt (Roth 1979: pls. 53, 56–59, 65; Meyer 1981: pl. 56; Meyer, unpublished); Syria, Cyprus, Gaul, Italy, and the Rhineland (von Saldern 1968: 93, pl. 51).

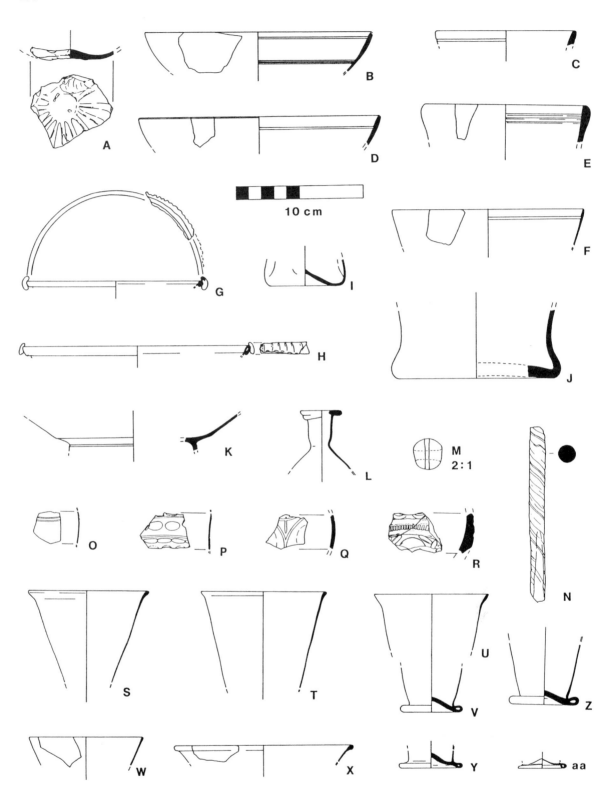

Fig. 5. Roman and Early Byzantine Glass.

Unguentarium (fig. 5:L).   Thousands of Roman unguentaria are known, the majority without provenience and probably robbed from tombs. The piece shown here is unusual for its short neck, which has a parallel of sorts in the old Jerash excavations dated to the fourth or fifth century (Baur 1938: 534), and at Samaria, similarly dated (Crowfoot 1957: 411–12). The olive color and the quality of the glass, and another small bottle from a tomb at Homs, ca. A.D. 125–250 (Hak 1965: 27–29), suggest an earlier date, and Hayes (1975: 42–45) discusses an "early" (C) type of unguentarium that is light green, of fair quality, and with a folded-in, flattened rim, which he suggests is probably Syro-Palestinian. Cooney (1976: 107) illustrates an amber flask with a wide, turned-in rim, a very narrow restriction at the neck and base angle from El-Bahnasa (Oxyrhynchus), Egypt, about the second century. Finally, a rather good comparison may be found with a flask from the Samothrace cemetery. This is bluish-green, has a concave base and a rim that was " . . . pulled out, up and flattened over top," and is dated ca. A.D. 25–50 (Dusenbery 1967: 42). There are also small piriform bottles from Morgantina, Sicily, and from sites in Italy, a type said to be abundant in the last decades of the first century B.C. (Grose 1977: 25; 1982: 28). Given the widely varying dates published, it is a pity that the Jerash piece has no better provenience.

Other Glass

Miscellaneous Bases.   The very heavy base (fig. 5:J) of clear glass with a slightly purple tint has no good provenience (lower cavea) but is tentatively attributed to the Roman period because of the quality of the glass. The incomplete base (fig. 5:K) may have been molded, but it is now obscured by a very heavy yellow to white patina with etched "wormholes"; the patina seems characteristic of early glass at Jerash. The form is closely comparable to some deep bowls with high feet from Dura-Europos, first century A.D. (Clairmont 1963: pls. 2–3), Karanis (Harden 1936: pl. 14), and Sardis (von Saldern 1980: pl. 22).

Cut Decoration.   The very thin sherd (fig. 5:O) with two incised lines is now mostly white patina, but it was found in a Late Roman locus (JNT-A-XIV-020). The more elaborate cut glass (fig. 5:P–R) was widely exported luxury ware that has been found as far away as Norway (Kisa vol. 3, 1908:

Fig. 5. Roman and Early Byzantine Glass

	Color	Locus	LocDt	StyDt	MC #	Cat #	Comments
A	Amber	Lower Cavea	–	Roman	–	1272	Ribbed bowl
B	Amber	Area F-XV-009	LByz	Roman	2	2079	Linear cut bowl
C	Clear	Area A-II-005	LByz	Roman	12	1045	Linear cut bowl
D	Clear	JNT-A-XIV-014	EByz	Roman	4	1639	Linear cut bowl
E	Clear, yellowish	JNT-B-V-007	LByz/Um	Roman	7	1416	Linear cut bowl
F	Clear	JNT-B-VII-001	Um	Roman	1	1610	Linear cut bowl
G	Lt Y-green	Area A-II-004	LByz	Roman	11	1033	Crimped band bowl
H	Lt Blue-green	Area A-II-005	LByz	Roman	12	1045	Crimped band bowl
I	Lt Blue-green	JNT-B-III-002	Mam (most LByz/Um)	Roman	14	–	Pinch-sided beaker
J	Clear, purple tint	Lower Cavea	–	Roman?	–	1096	Heavy base
K	Milky white	JNT-A-XIV-017	EByz	Roman	4	1647	Molded, thick Y to Wt patina, "wormholes"
L	Olive	Lower Cavea	–	Roman?	–	1113	Unguentarium
M	Black w/ Wt stripe	Area F-XV-010	LRoman	Roman	2	2080	Bead
N	Turquoise w/ dk stripes	Lower Cavea	–	Roman	–	1096	"Stirring rod"
O	Clear?	JNT-A-XIV-020	LRoman	Roman	3	1654	Incised, mostly Wt patina
P	Clear	JNT-A-XIV-019	EByz	Roman	3	1651	Incised, thick Wt patina w/ "wormholes"
Q	Clear	JNT-A-XIV-015	EByz	Roman	1	1640	Incised
R	Clear	Lower Cavea	–	Roman	–	–	Incised, very thick
S	Lt Blue-green	JNT-A-XIV-019	EByz	EByz	19	1653	Beaker, slightly lopsided
T	Lt Blue-green	JNT-A-XIV-016	EByz	EByz	37	1646	Beaker
U	Lt Blue-green	JNT-A-XIV-008	EByz	EByz	26	1632	Beaker rim
V	Lt Blue-green	JNT-A-XIV-008	EByz	EByz	26	1632	Beaker base
W	Lt Blue	JNT-B-III-002	Mam (most LByz/Um)	EByz	14	–	Beaker rim, "stone"
X	Lt Blue	JNT-A-XIV-015	EByz	EByz	10	1641	Beaker rim
Y	Lt Blue	Area A-II-002	LByz	EByz	8	1014	Beaker base
Z	Lt Blue-green	JNT A-XIV-019	EByz	EByz	8	1652	Beaker, pontil scar
aa	Lt Blue-green	JNT-A-XIV-013	EByz	EByz	4	1638	V. thin, beaker?

907) and India (Raschke 1978: 632–34). Egypt is believed to have been a major center if not the center of production for such luxury wares, although Harden (1964: 22) suggested that the cut glass found in Syria may actually have been Mesopotamian. Cut glass has been excavated at Karanis (Harden 1936: 86, pl. 13) and Quseir al-Qadim in Egypt (Roth 1979: pls. 55–56, 60, 64; Meyer 1981: pls. 55–56; Meyer, unpublished). According to Hayes (1975: 132) the plain or faceted colorless Egyptian vessels date to the first century A.D., and the elaborate cut designs, including figures, are characteristic of the second century. On the other hand, a number of cut glass vessels from Dura-Europos have been dated somewhat later, ca. A.D. 100–256 (Clairmont 1963: pls. 7–8). A number of cut fragments, of late first and third century date, have been excavated at Sardis (von Saldern 1980: 15–17), and a colorless cut glass bowl from the second century, at Corinth (Davidson 1952: 93–95). Unfortunately the Jerash pieces come from Early Byzantine or undated loci and cannot contribute to the debate as to where or in which century the cut glass may have been manufactured.

Beads (fig. 5:M).   Individual beads seem to be rare or infrequently reported. The bead shown in fig. 5:M, however, did come from a Late Roman locus (Area F-XV-010).

Stirring Rods (fig. 5:N).   Neither of the two segments recovered at Jerash has a good provenience (lower cavea only). The unpublished fragment is blue-green, twisted, and only 2.5 cm long. The use of "stirring rods" remains speculative. They have been called "stirring rods," "kohl sticks,"[6] and "dipping rods." Complete rods may terminate in a loop, knob, disk, spoon, or even a bird (von Saldern 1980: 33–34). A few even have a glass spindle whorl on the shaft (Vessberg 1952: 152–53; Corning Museum of Glass 1982: 42). Glass rods have also been used as architectural ornament, bordering tesserae on a pilaster fragment (Goldstein 1979: 263). Stirring rods are generally considered early or mid-Roman (von Saldern 1980: 33–34; Fitzwilliam Museum 1978: 50; Isings 1957: 94–95); the dated examples from Araq el-Emir (Lapp 1983: fig. 20), Homs (Hak 1965: 34), Karanis (Harden 1936: 285–86, pl. 21), Sardis (von Saldern 1980: 33–34), and the Samothrace cemetery (Dusenbery 1967: 49) would fall into the first to third century range.

So far the "snake-thread" decoration said to be characteristic of third to fourth century Romano-Syrian glass (Harden 1964: 23) is absent from this and from Baur's (1938) corpus. Nor was any millefiore or similar luxury glass recovered.

EARLY BYZANTINE (A.D. 324–491)

It has been said that the bulk of Romano-Syrian glass, with a wide variety of forms and decorations, was produced in the third and fourth centuries (Harden 1964: 23) and that the volume declined around A.D. 400 due to the troubles in the west that disrupted the markets (Haynes 1948: 34). In this corpus, however, Byzantine glass is more generously represented, given that very few Roman deposits were excavated. Von Saldern states that "glass made about the middle of the first millennium A.D. was part of an international style that transcended national and geographical boundaries. Influenced particularly by the Syrian-Palestinian convention of forms, fabrics, and modes of decoration popular about A.D. 400, ordinary glass found (and made) in Palestine, Asia Minor, Greece, and Italy is close in date and appearance" (von Saldern 1980: 37).

Given the sparcity of excavated, published glass from the eastern Mediterranean dating to the Byzantine period, it is difficult to investigate the questions of decline in quantity, fewer forms of vessels, or interregional homogeneity. It may be said, however, that the Jerash Byzantine glass is relatively abundant and diverse, and that it includes many new forms, though few of these are the attention-getting luxury wares.

What seems to be standardized is the color of the glass; almost all the Byzantine, Late Byzantine/Umayyad, and Umayyad glass is light blue, blue-green, or green. This agrees with Harden's observation (1971: 80) that after the fourth century almost all glass is green, blue-green, yellow, brown, or deep blue, and that only the dark blue would have required the intentional addition of a colorant, copper. Even the last three colors are uncommon at Jerash, although olive green was apparently popular at Sardis (Hanfmann 1959: 52). Much of the Byzantine glass is extremely thin. If there is even a moderately thick layer of patina or decomposition, virtually no glass may remain, which may explain the poor preservation and hence poor publication of some of the glass. The molded or cut Roman glass vessels tend to be much thicker. Also, some of the Byzantine glass—especially the windowpanes—has a distinctive black surface that curls and flakes off like paper ash. A similar phenomenon has been noted at Sardis (Hanfmann 1959: 52).

Most of the Early Byzantine glass here comes from the soundings in Areas A and E, and North Theater trenches JNT-B-II, Loci 028 and 029, and JNT-B-VI-014, and above all from the western approach corridor JNT-A-XIV. Here debris of the Early Byzantine period was dumped over the remnant Late Roman surface to a depth of at least 3.25 m (see fig. 2). Some of this debris may have come from the Byzantine church uphill in Area F.

Beaker (fig. 5:S–U, W–X). These are simple, conical beakers usually with slightly thickened, flaring rims and egg-shell thin bodies. Two (fig. 5:S, T) could nevertheless be reconstructed to about two-thirds of their heights. One large rim and body fragment and a base (fig. 5:U–V) were found so close together that they are probably parts of the same vessel, and similar bases may have terminated the beakers. The walls are so thin that it is not surprising that they broke, and that no beakers survived intact from rim to base. Many of the fragments of simple, thickened rims may belong to such beakers. Some of the delicate, flaring rims in the Mezad Tamar corpus, late third to early seventh century (Erdmann 1977: 132, pl. 6) might have been broken off beakers. A few delicate rims, possibly beakers, are published from Araq el-Emir (Lapp 1983: figs. 19:12 and 20:10), one from Wadi ed-Daliyeh Cave II (Weinberg and Barag 1974: 104, pl. 39:7), and a number from Carthage, where they are fairly common from the fifth century on (Tatton-Brown 1984: 19, fig. 66).

Beaker Bases (fig. 5:Y, Z, aa; fig. 6:A, B). Assuming that the looped-out base mentioned above does belong to a beaker, the following examples may be tentatively labeled "beaker bases." One of them (fig. 5:aa) is very thin; fig. 6:A and B are unusual both for their color, yellow-green and yellowish, and for their flatness. Most of the beaker bases are slightly kicked up. Several very similar bases are reported from Mezad Tamar, late third to early seventh century (Erdmann 1977: 114, pl. 1); several from Araq el-Emir are published, with dates ranging from ca. A.D. 100–150 to 335 or later (Lapp 1983: fig. 19:7, 13, 14, and fig. 24:22); and at least two are known from Dibon (Tushingham 1972: fig. 13). There are a couple of comparable bases at Sardis, one that is eggshell thin and said to resemble first to third

century bases (von Saldern 1980: 22–23, pl. 21), and a second dated to the late Roman or Early Byzantine period, third to sixth century (von Saldern 1980: 63, pl. 24). Similar bases at Carthage are dated to the late fifth to seventh century (Tatton-Brown 1984: 197, fig. 65).

Trailed Beaker (fig. 6:C). This is one of the most attractive pieces of glass found in the theater. It is yellow-green with a dark blue trailed-on decoration of open diamonds. More fragments of the trailed ornament were found, so there probably was a second band lower on the body. The ground rim is found on other vessels of the period. Comparative pieces are few. A similar vessel apparently with some applied decoration was listed with the Roman glass at Sardis but was recovered from an early Byzantine locus (von Saldern 1980: 31, pl. 22). A Byzantine goblet with a chain or diamond decoration, two small handles, a high stem, and a flat foot was found at Sucidava, Romania (Tudor 1965: 118).

Ground Rim Vessels (fig. 6:D–F). These probably had round bottoms but are distinguished by their smoothly ground, beveled rims. An exceptionally fine cup with a round bottom and incised CHI-RHO monogram was excavated by the British team (Clark et al. 1986). A series of similar cups, at least two of which were decorated, are reported from Mezad Tamar, late third to early seventh century (Erdmann 1977: 106, 127–28, pl. 5), and others from Carthage (Tatton-Brown 1984: 197, fig. 65).

Bent, Looped-Rim Vessels (fig. 6:G–J). Many of the Jerash vessels have rims that are folded in or out, leaving an air space (a loop in cross-section), but this group of vessels is distinguished by an angle in the rather deep loop. Fortunately all the Jerash examples come from dated Early Byzantine or Early Byzantine/Roman loci; comparative material is scanty. Two possible parallel pieces are reported from Araq el-Emir (Lapp 1983: figs. 23:3, 24:5). Also, a dark blue vessel with a folded-out rim comes from Egypt; the bowl rests on a thick stem and a flat foot. It has no provenience, but is dated to the fourth century (Cooney 1976: 106). Four possible parallels are some bowls in the Fitzwilliam Museum, also from Egypt, said to be fourth or fifth century (Fitzwilliam Museum 1978: 47–48, 55); they rest on a stemmed foot or pedestal base.

Shallow Bowl (fig. 6:K). This is a simple form and so is hard to date. Similar forms have been

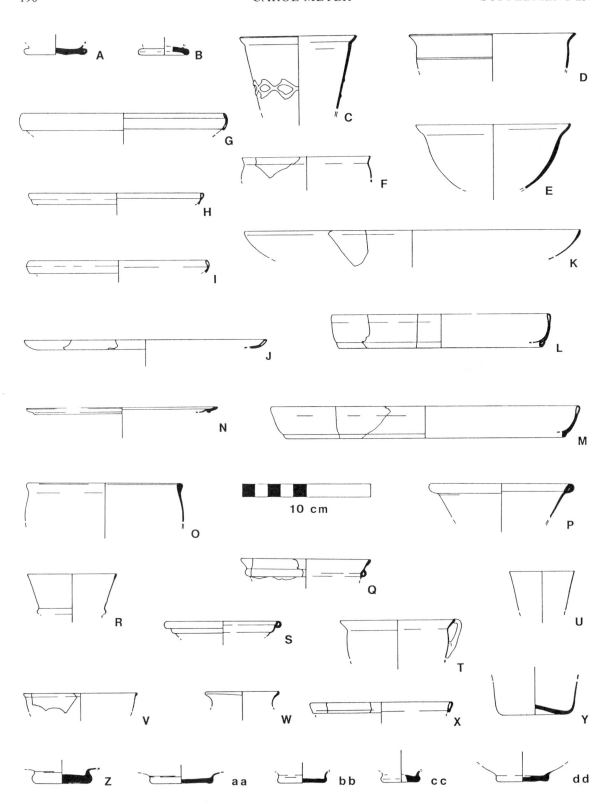

Fig. 6. Early Byzantine Glass.

published from Dura-Europos, first century (Clairmont 1963: pl. 4), from Sardis, Early Imperial Roman (von Saldern 1980: 31–32, pl. 22), and from Meẓad Tamar, late third to early seventh century (Erdmann 1977: 132, pl. 6). This example may therefore be Roman, although it has an Early Byzantine findspot.

Dishes with Looped Rim and Base (fig. 6:L, M). To form this type of dish or shallow bowl the entire upper half of the vessel was folded out and down, and the edge turned out and up to make a ring base; if there ever was a foot it is not preserved in these pieces. The vessels are quite distinct from the Roman cylindrical dishes whose rims and bases are two separate loops (Davidson 1952: 99–100; Isings 1957: 62–63; Meyer, unpublished). All three Jerash examples come from loci dated to the late fourth or fifth century. An olive green bowl like these is illustrated in Harden (1936: 71, pl. 12); three comparative pieces are cited. One is said to come from Tyre, a second was excavated at Jerash in 1929, and a third was a complete bowl from a sarcophagus found at Köln-Müngersdorf and dated to ca. 370.

Miscellaneous Rims (fig. 6:N–X). Little can be said about these rims, nor can many parallels be found. The clear, thin glass rim (fig. 6:N) could be a shallow dish or bowl; the closest parallel comes from Araq el-Emir, similarly dated (Lapp 1983: fig. 24:1). The bowl with a slightly incurved rim (fig. 6:O) may be compared to an Early Byzantine one from Sardis (von Saldern 1980: 62, pl. 24). The rolled-in rim (fig. 6:P) is similar to one at Meẓad Tamar, late third to early seventh century (Erdmann 1977: 125, pl. 4), and another at Araq el-Emir (Lapp 1983: fig. 24:6). The looped-out roll under the rim of fig. 6:Q has a parallel in a vessel from Wadi ed-Daliyeh Cave II (Weinberg and Barag 1974: 105, pl. 39:10), and perhaps from Hama, top layers (Riis and Poulsen 1957: 32–33). Von Saldern suggests that a bulging rim, early Byzantine, similar to fig. 6:S may have broken off a small bowl or bottle with a conical or funnel neck (von Saldern 1980: 81–82, pl. 27); note a similar rim of fifth to early seventh century date from Alexandria (Rodziewicz 1984: pl. 74). The small bowl or cup (fig. 6:T) could have had two or more handles. Finally, fig. 6:W is notable for

Fig. 6. Early Byzantine Glass

	Color	Locus	LocDt	StyDt	MC #	Cat #	Comments
A	Y-green	JNT-B-III-003	Mod (most LByz/Um)	EByz	34	1612	Beaker base?
B	Yellowish	JNT-B-II-009	Ott	EByz	48	290	Beaker base
C	Y-green w/ dk blue dec.	JNT-B-II-029	EByz	EByz	4	1657	Beaker w/ trailed dec., ground rim
D	Lt Y-green	JNT-A-XIV-011	EByz	EByz	2	1635	Ground-rim cup
E	Lt Y-green	JNT-A-XIV-008	EByz	EByz	6	1623	Ground-rim cup
F	Lt Blue-green	JNT-A-XIV-006	EByz	EByz	3	1622	Ground-rim cup
G	Lt Y-green	JNT-B-II-028	EByz	EByz	3	1656	Bent loop bowl
H	Clear	JNT-B-VI-011	EByz	EByz	4	1661	Bent loop bowl
I	Lt Blue-green	JNT-B-II-029	EByz	EByz	11	1659	Bent loop bowl
J	Lt Blue	Area E-I-012	Rom/EByz	EByz	1	2020	Bent loop bowl
K	Lt Green	JNT-A-XIV-016	EByz	EByz?	2	1642	Shallow bowl, Roman?
L	Lt Blue-green	JNT-B-II-029	EByz	EByz	4	1657	Dish, looped rim, base
M	Lt Blue	JNT-B-VI-014	EByz	EByz	3	1660	Same, Bk ashy patina
N	Clear	Area A-I-003	EByz	EByz?	–	990	Rim, pane?, or Roman?
O	Lt Y-green	JNT-A-XIV-016	EByz	EByz	22	1644	Incurved rim bowl
P	Lt Y-green	JNT-B-VI-014	EByz	EByz	3	1660	Thick rim, impurities
Q	Lt Y-green	JNT-A-XIV-017	EByz	EByz	12	1649	V. thin, thick Bk patina
R	Lt Y-green	JNT-A-XIV-016	EByz	EByz	2	1642	V. thin rim, ripple
S	Lt Blue-green	JNT-A-XIV-011	EByz	EByz	32	1637	Rim w/ impurities
T	Lt Blue-green	JNT-A-XIV-008	EByz	EByz	1	1624	Two handles originally?
U	Lt Blue-green	JNT-A-XIV-008	EByz	EByz	37	1633	Rim
V	Lt Y-green	JNT-A-XIV-016	EByz	EByz	2	1642	Rim
W	Clear, purple band on lip	JNT-A-XIV-011	EByz	EByz	17	1636	Rim, impurities
X	Lt Blue	JNT-A-XIV-018	EByz	EByz	3	1650	Rim, v. thin
Y	Lt Blue-green	JNT-A-XIV-016	EByz	EByz	34	1645	Kick-up base
Z	Blue-green	JNT-A-XIV-006	EByz	EByz	14	1627	Pad base
aa	Y-green	JNT-A-XIV-019	EByz	EByz	3	1651	Pad base, molded?, v. thick patina
bb	Blue-green	JNT-A-XIV-016	EByz	EByz	16	1643	Pad base
cc	Green	JNT-B-II-009	Ott	EByz	48	290	Pad base
dd	Green	JNT-A-XIV-014	EByz	EByz	4	1639	Pad base

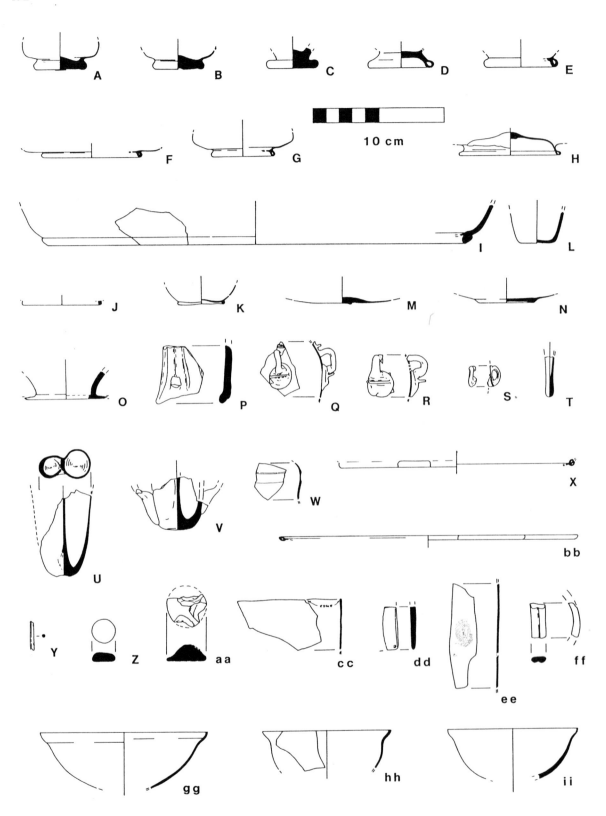

Fig. 7. Early and Late Byzantine Glass.

having an applied purple stripe on the lip. Looped-out rims such as fig. 6:X are common during the Byzantine and later periods.

Kick-Up Bases (fig. 6:Y). A variety of bases were found, but little can be said about them, except that all but one pad base (below) were recovered from Early Byzantine levels. In addition to the simple kick-up base shown here, some of the beaker and looped bases were kicked up.

Pad Bases (fig. 6:Z–dd; 7:A–C). These thick bases are common but usually have such thin walls that it is difficult or impossible to guess the complete form. Some (fig. 6:Z–cc) seem to have walls that flare out sharply, sometimes almost horizontally. One base from Sardis, loosely dated as Byzantine to Late Islamic, approaches this form (von Saldern 1980: 64–66, pl. 24). Other pad bases seem to have walls that curve up (fig. 7:A, B), as does a base from Karanis, fourth to fifth century (Harden 1936: 219, pl. 19). A close parallel

for the very thick pad base (fig. 7:C) also comes from Sardis, first to fourth century (von Saldern 1980: 22–23, pl. 21), but the best parallels for all varieties of pad bases shown on figs. 6 and 7 come from Meẓad Tamar, late third to early seventh century (Erdmann 1977: 114, pl. 1).

Looped Bases (fig. 7:D–H). These bases have little in common except that they are made by folding out the base of the vessel to make a hollow ring base. Two bases (fig. 7:D, E) have good parallels at Sardis, Early Byzantine (ca. 400–616) levels (von Saldern 1980: 66–67, pl. 25), and fig. 7:D also has a parallel at Carthage, fifth to sixth century or later (Tatton-Brown 1984: 207, fig. 68). Two others (fig. 7:G, H) resemble a flask from Kish, fifth century (Harden 1934: 134–35); their walls are eggshell thin. Both narrow and broad looped bases are illustrated among the Meẓad Tamar corpus, late third to early seventh century (Erdmann 1977: 116, pl. 2), and from

Fig. 7. Early and Late Byzantine Glass

	Color	Locus	LocDt	StyDt	MC #	Cat #	Comments
A	Lt Y-green	JNT-A-XIV-006	EByz	EByz	14	1627	Pad base, pontil scar
B	Green	JNT-A-XIV-008	EByz	EByz	11	1630	Pad base, pontil scar
C	Lt Blue	Area A-I-003	EByz	EByz	–	990	V. heavy
D	Lt Blue-green	JNT-A-XIV-016	EByz	EByz	34	1645	Looped base
E	Lt Blue-green	JNT-A-XIV-016	EByz	EByz	22	1644	Same, thin
F	Yellowish	JNT-A-XIV-006	EByz	EByz	34	1628	Looped base, Bk ashy patina
G	Lt Blue-green	JNT-A-XIV-006	EByz	EByz	36	1629	Looped base, Bk ashy patina
H	Lt Green	JNT-B-II-029	EByz	EByz	11	1659	Looped base, thin
I	Blue-green	JNT-A-XIV-015	EByz	EByz	10	1641	V. broad base
J	Lt Blue	Area E-I-012	Rom/EByz	EByz	1	2021	Ring base, popped off
K	Turquoise on clear	JNT-A-XIV-019	EByz	EByz	8	1652	Ring base, applied
L	Blue-green	JNT-A-XIV-015	EByz	EByz	1	1640	Flat base
M	Turquoise	JNT-A-XIV-019	EByz	EByz	3	1651	Base, pontil scar
N	Blue-green	JNT-A-XIV-011	EByz	EByz	17	1636	Molded? base
O	Color?	JNT-A-XIV-006	EByz	EByz	3	1622	Mostly cream to Y v. flaky patina
P	Y-green	JNT-B-II-029	EByz	EByz?	11	1659	Handle w/ "stone," Roman?
Q	Y-green	JNT-A-XIV-010	EByz	EByz	1	1634	Handle
R	Y-green	JNT-A-XIV-008	EByz	EByz	19	1631	Handle, impurities
S	Dk Blue	JNT-B-II-028	EByz	EByz	3	1656	Tiny handle from kohl jar?
T	Lt Blue-green	JNT-B-II-029	EByz	EByz	4	1657	Perfume flask?
U	Lt Blue	Lower Cavea	–	EByz	–	1099	Double kohl jar
V	Blue-green	Lower Cavea	–	EByz	–	1626	Double kohl jar
W	Lt Y-green	JNT-A-XIV-011	EByz	EByz	32	1637	Molded groove?, deeply pitted
X	Clear	Area A-I-003	EByz	EByz	–	989	Dec. loop?
Y	Green, opaque	JNT-B-VI-015	EByz	EByz	4	–	Pin? Kohl stick?
Z	Color?	JNT-B-II-029	EByz	EByz?	14	1658	Game piece, prob. Roman
aa	Y-green	JNT-B-VII-006	Ott (much LByz/Um)	EByz?	2	1615	Game piece, prob. Roman
bb	Lt Blue	JNT-A-XIV-017	EByz	EByz	6	1648	Window pane?
cc	Lt Blue-green	JNT-A-XIV-008	EByz	EByz	11	1630	Window pane
dd	Lt Y-green	JNT-B-II-011	Ott	Byz?	2	258	Window pane?
ee	Lt Blue-green	JNT-A-XIV-008	EByz	Byz	11	1630	Window pane
ff	Opaque w/ red-brown streaks	JNT-A-XIV-016	EByz	EByz?	2	1642	Bracelet
gg	Lt Y-green	JNT-A-XIV-004	LByz	LByz	13	1619	Ground-rim cup
hh	Pale green	JNT-B-V-036	LByz/Um	LByz	9	1608	Ground-rim cup
ii	Lt Blue	JNT-B-VII-005	Ott (most LByz/Um)	LByz	2	1614	Ground-rim cup

Araq el-Emir (Lapp 1983: fig. 24:11, 12).

Very Broad Base (fig. 7:I). No comparable pieces seem to be published. The method of forming it appears to be the same as for the dishes with looped rim and base.

Ring Bases (fig. 7:J, K). These are delicate rings added on to a base; fig. 7:J has popped off. Two (one not illustrated) are turquoise coils applied to thin clear or pale blue bodies.

Miscellaneous Bases (fig. 7:L–O). Figure 7:N may be mold-made, although it is difficult to be certain because of surface decomposition. The form, much less the original thickness and color, of fig. 7:O is obscured because the sherd is now almost completely reduced to a cream or yellow decomposition layer. A similar but much smaller base, dated to ca. A.D. 100–150, from Araq el-Emir may be noted (Lapp 1983: fig. 19:15).

Handles. The broad strap handle (fig. 7:P) is probably from a Roman flagon (Roth 1979: pls. 54, 58; Meyer 1981: pls. 55–56) but it was recovered from an Early Byzantine level. Two unusual little handles (fig. 7:Q, R) have projecting ridges. The only parallel found so far is from Araq el-Emir (Lapp 1983: fig. 24:31) and is probably early Byzantine. The tiny dark blue handle (fig. 7:S) is an uncommon color but may have come from a kohl jar like the one from a tomb cave near Netiv Ha-Lamed He, dated to the mid-fifth to early seventh century. The unguentarium or kohl jar is bluish-green with two tiny handles and dark blue trailed-on zigzags, scallops, and rim (Barag 1974: 13, 83).

Perfume Flask (fig. 7:T). This fragment is too small to provide much information, but it may be the tip of a tubular bottle like the ones from the Samothrace cemetery, probably Augustan (Dusenbery 1967: 43–44) or a two-handled toilet bottle reportedly found in a tomb near Bethlehem (Fitzwilliam Museum 1978: 48–49). The fragment is also the only possible candidate for one of the spindle-shaped bottles said to have been fairly common (cf. Fitzwilliam Museum 1978: 48; Tatton-Brown 1984: 205, fig. 67).

Double Kohl Tubes (fig. 7:U, V). According to Baur (1938: 513–14, 546), only two fragments of double-barreled "unguent flasks" were recovered; three more pieces were found in the recent excavations. All have a very late (Mamluk) or poor (lower cavea) provenience, but enough dated parallels are available to place them in the Early Byzantine period. Many "kohl tubes" with one or two handles and thread decoration were found in Palestinian tombs of the fourth and fifth centuries (Philippe 1970: 66), but von Saldern (1974: 231–33) dated two from the "eastern Mediterranean" (no provenience) as early as the third or fourth century. Three excavated examples from Khirbat al-Karak, one with a bronze applicator and one that was broken and reworked, are dated generally to Byzantine times (Delougaz and Haines 1960: pl. 50). Several double kohl tubes are reported at Pella from Tomb 39A, ca. 350–375 (McNicoll *et al.* 1982: 537), and two more are listed from Tomb Chamber 3 at Bethany. Both of the latter are blue with dark blue threads, and one has a bronze "kohl spoon"; such vessels are said to be "quite common in tombs of the Byzantine period" (Saller 1956: 329–30, pl. 57). Crowfoot (1957: 411, 413–14) noted several fragments and illustrated one double "kohl-tube" from Tomb 3 at Samaria, dating them to the fourth or fifth century and citing parallels from a fourth century tomb at Beit Fajjar and from other places. As some tubes have been found with a kohl-like residue or with bronze or ivory applicators, they appear to be kohl tubes rather than perfume flasks (Crowfoot 1957: 411, 413–14). Their wide mouths would also be better for kohl than for perfume. Harden notes that the "Syrian double unguentaria" are never found in the west. He lists "unguentaria" with wide, elaborate handles as one of the new forms introduced in the fifth century (or fourth? Harden 1969: 63) and the double or quadruple "unguentaria" as later (Harden 1971: 81). No double flasks are reported from Sardis, but if they are indeed kohl tubes, their absence in the west and in Turkey suggests that ladies there did not wear kohl.

Decorative Techniques (fig. 7:W, X). In general, few pieces of Byzantine glass seem to have been decorated; the trailed beaker and the applied turquoise ring bases have already been discussed. The groove on fig. 7:W appears to have been molded, but the sherd is quite thin and deeply pitted. The rim with a looped ridge below it has been mentioned; the fragment shown here on fig. 7:X (the angle of the vessel wall may be much steeper), may come from a similar vessel. Several cups (or jars?) from Meẓad Tamar display such a looped ridge (Erdmann 1977: 108, 141–42, pl. 7).

Window Glass (fig. 7:bb–ee). Window glass was abundant in JNT-A-XIV, but only four pieces are shown here. One is flat, with a rounded edge (fig. 7:cc); fig. 7:dd came from a late (Ottoman) locus but is discussed here because it has a corner with a slight depression or dimple. The sherd on fig. 7:ee is painful to look at; it bears a thumb-print. Finally, fig. 7:bb might be the edge of a small, round pane even though it is thinner than usual.

There is some debate about different methods of manufacturing window glass and when and where the techniques were developed. Three pro-cesses are in question: cast and/or roller-molded, "muff," and "crown" or "bull's-eye" glass. Cast glass would have been poured into a mold and rolled or tooled until it reached the edge of the mold. The dimple on the corner of fig. 7:dd might be a tool mark, and the fingerprint could have been picked up from a ceramic mold. Roller-molded glass, however, is said to have been com-mon in Italy and the western provinces of the Roman Empire from the first century A.D. on (Harden 1939: 91). "Muff" glass is produced by blowing a cylinder, then cutting it open and flat-tening it out. It is not easy to distinguish cast from "muff" glass, especially if the surfaces have decomposed. "Muff" glass is said to have come into use later than cast glass, ca. A.D. 300 (Boon 1966: 45). "Crown" glass is made by blowing a globe, opening it out, and then turning it until it "flashes" or spreads into a broad disk. This pro-duces a round pane that is thick in the center, thin at the edges, and fire-polished on both faces. The rims of the Jerash panes were folded over before they were flashed, probably to strengthen them; fig. 7:bb may be such a rim. Blown circular panes were in use from the fourth century on in the Eastern Roman Empire (Harden 1939: 91); they will be discussed below with the Late Byzantine/ Umayyad examples.

At Sardis the Byzantine (ca. 400–616) window-panes, by weight, were probably more abundant than the other glass (von Saldern 1980: 91–92); an estimated 1,000 panes were recovered (von Saldern 1980: 3). The glass is usually light aquamarine or olive (occasionally clear), glossy on both sides (plus a few glossy/mat) (von Saldern 1980: 91–92), and often has a black flaky surface (Hanf-mann 1959: 50, 52) like that on the Jerash panes. Hanfmann (1959: 52) considered the Sardis panes more like the Karanis roller-molded glass than Medieval Byzantine or Islamic glass. Von Saldern, however (1980: 91–92), considered them to have been made by the "muff" process. The window glass from Carthage was not catalogued but it is

usually greenish, colorless, with a black enamel-like weathering, and it is said to be the "muff" or cylinder blown type in use in the fourth century and later (Tatton-Brown 1984: 208). As indicated, it can be difficult to distinguish between the two techniques, but the evidence from Jerash supports cast and tooled panes. Panes from the Byzantine church at Shavei Zion are apparently all cast, possibly roller-molded (Barag 1967: 69–70).

Nonvessel. One thin rod segment was found, opaque lime green, ground to an approximately round cross-section (fig. 7:Y). It is much thinner than the Roman "stirring rods." Hak (1965: 34) published four yellow glass "kohl sticks," three of which have disks at the end, from tombs at Homs dated to ca. A.D. 125–250. At Sardis, a few blue or aqua rods were excavated in Roman contexts, and a couple more, one greenish, in early Byzan-tine loci (von Saldern 1980: 33–34, 90, pl. 16). Two "needles," one dark green and one blue, were found in the Samothrace cemetery with bone rods near a skull, suggesting hair ornaments (Dusen-bery 1967: 49).

The North Theater yielded two glass blobs (fig. 7:Z, aa), not stamped like weights, which were quite puzzling until the publication on the Samo-thrace cemetery was encountered. Three glass astragali, Augustan in date, and counters or game pieces of various colors were recovered there (Dusenbery 1967: 49); the counters resemble the Jerash pieces. Game counters were common at Karanis, Roman period, and elsewhere in Egypt and the west, particularly in tombs (Harden 1936: 291–92, pl. 21). Three are published from Car-thage, although they seem to come from later contexts (Tatton-Brown 1984: 209).

Finally, a short piece of a black or opaque bracelet with red-brown streaks (fig. 7:ff) was found in the western corridor of the theater. Although bracelets are not common at Early Byzantine sites, a black one with a trapezoidal cross-section has been reported from Nikertai, near Apamea (Canivet 1970: 65), and two more fragments in olive-green or blue glass come from Sardis (von Saldern 1980: 91, pl. 16).

LATE BYZANTINE (A.D. 491–636)

Most of what has been said about Early Byzan-tine glass also pertains to Late Byzantine glass. A few forms seem to be new, such as some small bottles with narrow necks, but most are the same

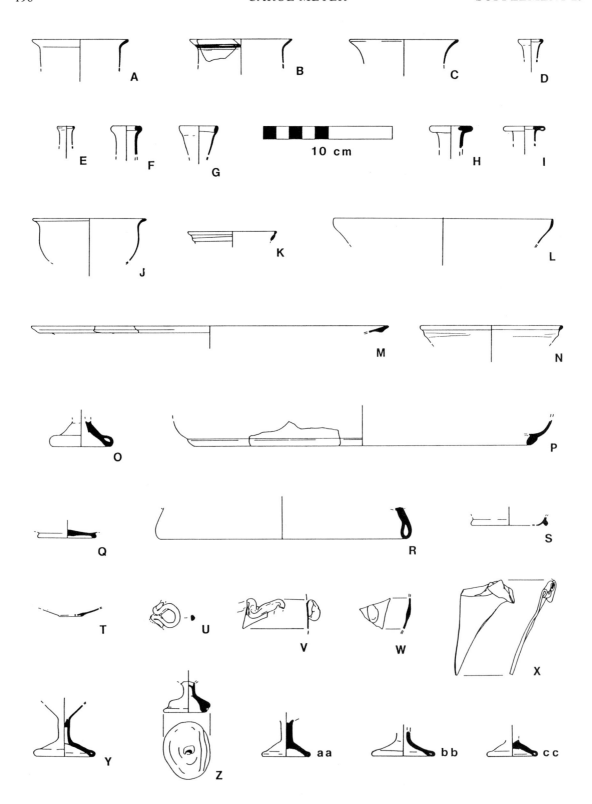

Fig. 8. Late Byzantine and Late Byzantine/Early Umayyad Glass.

as or similar to Early Byzantine pieces. Most of the glass is light green or blue. More Early than Late Byzantine loci were excavated; most of the Late Byzantine glass comes from the test trenches in Areas A and E, the church in Area F, and a few loci in JNT-A-XIV.

During these centuries, sixth and early seventh, the Byzantine Empire had numerous problems, including wars in the east against the Persians. They finally conquered Syria, and Jerash with it, and the emperor Heraclius regained the territory only a few years before the Moslem conquest. What effect this turmoil may have had on glassworking in Syria, Constantinople, or elsewhere is uncertain (Haynes 1948: 37–40). The earthquakes of ca. 550–555 probably wrought damage at Jerash as well. Harden (1964: 24) felt that the glass of the late fifth to seventh centuries displayed less "competence and verve," though much church glass was produced, including lamps, windowpanes, and drinking vessels. Decorative techniques are said to have been limited to trailed threads, cutting and engraving, and molding. Polygonal vessels are

supposedly common (Harden 1971: 81) but none were recovered during the excavations reported here. Nor is any decoration at all common, though some of the vessels in the large Late Byzantine/ Umayyad group (below) are probably Byzantine.

Ground Rim Cup (fig. 7:gg-ii). These are the same as the cups discussed above with the Early Byzantine vessels. The form and the ground rim do seem to be distinctive of the Byzantine period.

Cylindrical Beaker with Flaring Rim (fig. 8:A–C). This form appeared in the Early Byzantine corpus as well, but the best-preserved examples are from the Late Byzantine. Figure 8:B has thin, trailed purple and turquoise threads; fig. 8:C may not be Byzantine but resembles this form more closely than any other.

Unguentaria (fig. 8:D–I). These little necks may come from perfume bottles, the relative scarcity of which has been noted in this corpus. Sardis, however, produced several "miniature bottles" with folded-in rims and bodies ranging from roughly conical, to oval, to candlestick-like. One still rests in its tubular bronze casing (von Saldern

Fig. 8. Late Byzantine and Late Byzantine/Umayyad Glass

	Color	Locus	LocDt	StyDt	MC #	Cat #	Comments
A	Lt Y-green	Area E-I-010	LByz	LByz	1	2014	Cylindrical beaker, flaring rim
B	Purple, turq. threads on lt blue-green	Area F-XV-003	LByz	LByz	1	2077	Cylindrical beaker, flaring rim
C	Lt Blue	JNT-B-III-002	Mam (most LByz/Um)	LByz?	13	–	Cylindrical beaker, flaring rim
D	Lt Blue	Area A-II-002	LByz	LByz	3	1011	Unguentarium?
E	Lt Blue	Area A-II-005	LByz	LByz	17	1045	Unguentarium?
F	Lt Blue	Lower Cavea	–	LByz	–	1098	Unguentarium?
G	Lt Y-green	Area A-II-006	LByz	LByz	3	1050	Unguentarium?
H	Lt Blue	Lower Cavea	–	LByz?	–	1112	Unguentarium?
I	Lt Blue	Area F-VIIA-001	Mam	LByz?	1	2091	Unguentarium?
J	Lt Y-green	Area F-XVI-009	LByz	LByz	2	2087	Cup or lamp?
K	Lt Blue-green	JNT-B-II-025	LByz	LByz	–	1655	Folded ridge under rim
L	Lt Blue	Area A-II-005	LByz	LByz	8	1045	Bowl
M	Clear	Area E-I-010	LByz	LByz?	5	2012	Plate, Roman?
N	Lt Blue-green	Area F-VIII-009	LByz	LByz	3	2082	Ripple under rim
O	Blue-green	Area A-II-004	LByz	LByz	8	1031	Looped base
P	Lt Y-green	JNT-A-XIV-005	LByz	LByz	5	1620	V. broad base
Q	Lt Blue	Area E-I-018	LByz	LByz	5	2012	Shallow dish?
R	Lt Blue-green	Area F-XV-008	LByz	LByz	3	2078	Broad, high, looped base
S	Lt Y-green	Area A-II-005	LByz	LByz	3	1037	Ring at base angle
T	Clear	Area A-II-005	LByz	LByz?	12	1045	V. delicate
U	Lt Y-green	Area A-II-003	LByz	LByz?	2	1017	Loop, handle?
V	Lt Y-green	JNT-B-III-010	LByz?	LByz	1	–	Ruffle
W	Lt Blue w/ dk turquoise blob	Area E-I-010	LByz or earlier	LByz?	8	2018	Blob dec.
X	Blue-green	Area F-XV-008	LByz	LByz	3	2078	Rumpled window edge?
Y	Lt Blue-green	Lower Cavea	–	LByz/Um	–	1098	Goblet base, looped
Z	Lt Blue-green	Lower Cavea	–	LByz/Um	–	1099	Same, warped
aa	Lt Blue-green	JNT-B-III-004	LByz/Um	LByz/Um	6	–	Goblet base, looped
bb	Lt Blue-green	JNT-B-III-008	LByz/Um	LByz/Um	7	–	Goblet base, looped
cc	Amber	JNT-B-III-023	Ott (most LByz/Um)	LByz/Um	13	–	Goblet base, looped

1980: 78–79, pls. 15, 27). Two rims (fig. 8:H, I) are tentatively placed here, although they were retrieved from later loci. The mouths resemble Roman unguentaria, but the glass is more like Byzantine and later fabrics. Also, they seem similar to vessels from the Byzantine Tombs 4 and 7 at Khirbat al-Karak (Delougaz and Haines 1960: pl. 50), or perhaps even a pale blue-green flask from the Umayyad building (Delougaz and Haines 1960: pl. 60).

Miscellaneous Rims (fig. 8:J–N). These have nothing in common except that they were recovered from Late Byzantine levels. Figure 8:J may be a small cup or bowl, or even a hollow-stemmed lamp (see section on Late Byzantine/ Umayyad). The squashed loop under the rim of fig. 8:K is similar to the Early Byzantine rim on fig. 6:Q. The clear rim, fig. 8:M, possibly from a plate, may be Roman, judging from the quality of the glass.

Bases (fig. 8:O–T). Little can be said about these bases except that all are dated by their findspots to the Late Byzantine. The looped base (fig. 8:O) seems more like the Late Byzantine/ Early Umayyad "looped goblet bases" than the Early Byzantine looped bases. The light blue base (fig. 8:Q) resembles a base, possibly from a shallow dish, recovered at Sardis and approximately dated as Roman–Early Byzantine (von Saldern 1980: 67–68). The very broad base (fig. 8:P) is almost identical to the Early Byzantine example already discussed. The odd ring base (fig. 8:S) that seems attached to the angle rather than the bottom of the vessel has parallels at Ḥesban (S. M. Goldstein, personal communication) and at Karanis, fourth to fifth century (Harden 1936: 229, pl. 19). Finally, the base shown on fig. 8:T is exceptionally delicate.

Ring Loop Handle (fig. 8:U). This unusual little handle, if it is one and not a decorative loop, might have come from the angle of the body and neck of a squat jar like an aryballos.

Decorative Techniques (fig. 8:V, W). After the fourth century decoration was limited to molding (unattested in this Byzantine corpus), threads, and applied ornamentation (Harden 1971: 80). The thread-trailed beaker (fig. 8:B) has been noted. The ruffle shown on fig. 8:V comes from a small locus only tentatively dated as Late Byzantine, but it may have a parallel in a light green bottle with heavy green ruffles from the Clergy House at Jerash, dated ca. 500 (Baur 1938: 538–40).

Far and away the most troublesome bit is a fragment of light blue glass with a blue blob on it (fig. 8:W; the second example is not illustrated). Sherds with applied blobs have been found, although not frequently, throughout the Middle East and southern Europe. Surprisingly, none are reported from Sardis. At Corinth some pale green bowls(?) with blue blobs arranged in triangles are dated to the fourth century (Davidson 1952: 97–98). In other instances the blue prunts may have adorned lamps (Harden 1936; Corning Museum 1964: 158; von Saldern 1974: 250–51). Dates range from Roman (Quseir al-Qadim, Meyer 1981: 226) to Medieval (Samarra, Lamm 1928: 91–92).

Window Glass (fig. 8:X). This fragment may represent the rumpled edge of a round bull's-eye windowpane.

LATE BYZANTINE/UMAYYAD
(ca. A.D. 630–670)

A large portion of this corpus comes from loci dated to the Late Byzantine/Early Umayyad period. As is seen on fig. 3, which shows the cut through the fill of the west audience entrance of the North Theater, the Late Byzantine/Early Umayyad layers are thick and comprise two major stages of deposition. Locus 022 is basically stone tumble and fine gray soil, possibly windblown. Sherds, glass, and other finds there were scanty. Loci 014 and 020 may represent a leveling-off of the debris to build the kilns (Schaefer, in Zayadine 1986); the sherd pockets (013, 016, 017, 019) and other layers (006, 007, 010, 011, 012, 014, 024, 032) represent debris from and over the kiln presumably destroyed in the first half of the eighth century (by the earthquake of 746/7?). Loci 008 and 018, fill blocking the entrance to the vault, are probably later. Figure 4, the interior of the vault, closed off at the east end to make a room, shows two floors. Locus JNT-B-VII-009, below the lower floor, is Late Byzantine/Early Umayyad; 008 just above has more Umayyad sherds plus a few possible Abbasid ones. The upper floor was probably associated with the kiln, judging from the relative elevations of the various installations. The topmost fill is mainly Late Byzantine/Early Umayyad, but has enough Abbasid and later sherds to indicate that it was open until more recently. The sections through the center of the North Theater, Trenches I and II, show a sequence similar to fig. 3, but run somewhat deeper to Byzantine fill (published in Zayadine 1986).

The Late Byzantine/Early Umayyad glass corpus is generous; a few new forms such as stemmed goblets with flat feet and beaded-stem lamps appear, and other forms such as long-necked bottles become more common. Philippe (1970: 22) states that at first Early Umayyad glass was hardly differentiated from Late Byzantine and that there is nothing distinctly Arab about the glass until the eighth century, well into the Umayyad period. At present it is indeed not possible to separate Late Byzantine from Early Umayyad glass and it may be unrealistic to expect sparkling new forms of glassware to have been developed because of the Islamic Conquest, a political event. A whole new set of glass types probably did not spring up overnight, without previous trial pieces or predecessors, nor are they likely to have all died out simultaneously; the famous "battleship curve" is probably a better description of the life of a particular form. The Late Byzantine/Early Umayyad corpus will be presented as a unit here, but in some cases it may be suggested that forms with Byzantine comparisons and no Umayyad ones are more characteristic of the Byzantine period, and those that have no Byzantine parallels but do have Umayyad ones are more likely to belong to the Umayyad period.

Almost all the glass is light blue or blue-green and much of it is bubbly, with a creamy or silvery surface layer; the glass is often pitted below the patina.

Stemmed Goblet with Looped Foot (fig. 8:Y–cc). Goblets with solid or hollow stems and bases formed by looping up the hot glass are one of the commonest, or most commonly preserved, forms. These goblets may be the functional descendents of the Early Byzantine beakers; the shape of the fragile upper part (cf. fig. 11:X–Z, Umayyad) seems similar, and there are quite a few Byzantine looped bases (cf. fig. 7:D). Harden (1936: 167) reached a similar conclusion for the series of beakers and stemmed goblets at Karanis. Most of the Jerash goblets are light blue or blue-green, but there are a few green or amber examples. Figure 8:Z seems to have been looped up too vigorously and rumpled, although it still sits flat. It is one of the few indications that such vessels might have been produced at Jerash.

This type of goblet is widespread around the Mediterranean basin. At least 90 fragments of

"wine glasses" are reported from Mount Nebo (Saller 1941: 318–19, pl. 140), and some seem to have looped bases. More are published from Khirbat al-Karak, Byzantine church (Delougaz and Haines 1960: pl. 60); Ḥesban, said to be "standard third to fourth century" forms (Goldstein 1976: 130); Shavei Zion, fifth to sixth century (Barag 1967: pl. 16), and other sites throughout the Near East. Some pieces were excavated at Sardis where they are dated to the sixth and seventh centuries, perhaps as early as the fifth (von Saldern 1980: 57–58, pl. 24; Hanfmann 1959: 50, 52–53). At Invillino, a late Roman to mid-sixth century site, goblets with looped bases are thought to have been produced locally or at least in the region (Philippe 1970: 97–99).

This corpus contains fewer Umayyad stemmed goblets with looped bases, but predecessors among the Late Byzantine vessels lead to the suggestion that they tend to be earlier, i.e., Late Byzantine, rather than later, Umayyad. The excavated goblets from Khirbat al-Karak, Shavei Zion, Sardis and perhaps Invillino would support this thesis.

Stemmed Goblets with Flat Feet (fig. 9:A–D). These are also common, and there appears to be more variety in the flat feet; one is octagonal (fig. 9:B) and some, such as fig. 9:A, are tooled. In some cases the stem bulges or is beaded.

Comparable vessels are again abundant. Baur (1938: 523–27) published only this type of goblet from the earlier excavations. The "wine glasses" came mainly from St. Theodore's and the Fountain Court, and were thought to be fourth or fifth century (but this is probably too early). Some of the many "wine glass" fragments at Mount Nebo seem to have flat bases (Saller 1941: 318–19, pl. 140). A number of such bases were excavated in the Byzantine church and Tomb 4 at Khirbat al-Karak, and some even preserve the lower parts of the goblet bowls (Delougaz and Haines 1960: pls. 50, 60). Other bases are reported from Shavei Zion, fifth to sixth century (Barag 1967: pl. 16); Bethany, dated to the Byantine period (Saller 1956: 330–31); Nikertai, near Apamea, fifth and sixth centuries (Canivet 1970: 64–66); and elsewhere in the Syro-Palestinian area. The stemmed goblets from Karanis with flat, tooled bases and straight-sided bowls sometimes ornamented with threads are given as fourth and fifth centuries, and may be predecessors of goblets with spreading rims (Harden 1936: 167, pl. 16). Several goblets, at least one of which seems to have a tooled base,

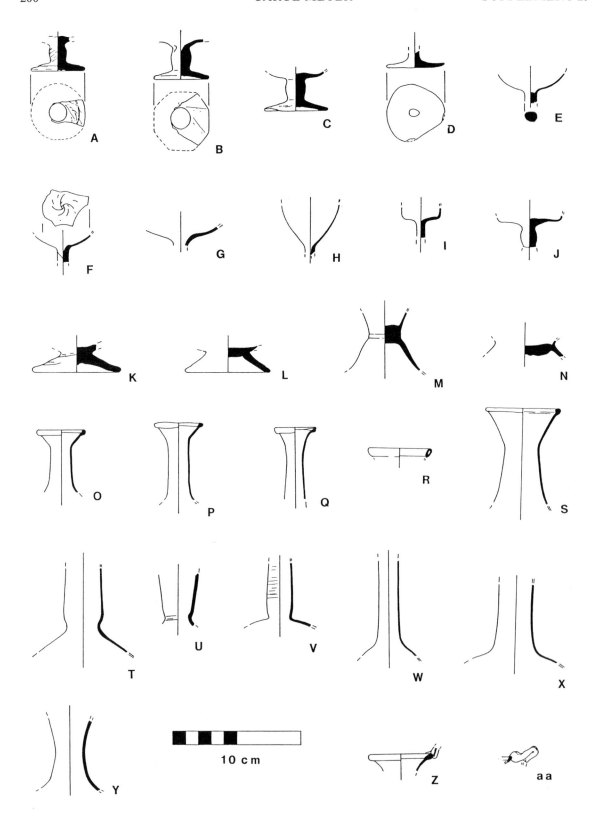

Fig. 9. Late Byzantine/Early Umayyad Glass.

were excavated at Alexandria in contexts dated from the fifth to the early seventh century (Rodziewicz 1984: pl. 73). The Damascus Museum has a complete goblet, said to be third or fourth century (Zouhdi 1964: 49). Farther afield, Cooney (1976: 106) has published a nearly complete goblet from El-Amarna, Egypt. It is pale green with a dark green thread trailed on the rim and more threads on the body; the base displays "straw marks" from crisscross tooling like fig. 9:A and B. Goblets with slender or beaded stems and somewhat higher arched feet are abundant at Carthage; 118 examples have been reported from there (Tatton-Brown 1984: 200–201, fig. 66). They occurred earliest in fifth-century contexts and peaked in the seventh century (Tatton-Brown 1984: 210–11). At Sardis goblets were one of the commonest forms, 500 or more fragments having been recovered. Von Saldern dates them to the sixth and seventh centuries but notes goblets as early as the first century A.D. Most of the Sardis wine glasses are green or light aquamarine, though some are olive or even clear (von Saldern 1980: 53–57, pl. 24).

I have labeled this shape a "goblet" or "wine glass" although some examples may have belonged

to vessels used as lamps. Baur (1938: 524–25) illustrated a reconstructed vessel, from the Fountain Court of the Jerash cathedral, with a looped-out rim and three handles like those on the usual tumbler lamps to be discussed below, and a solid stem and flat foot like the ones shown here. Such lamps are found among the new forms that appear in the fifth century (Harden 1971: 81). A lamp of this type could either sit on its flat foot or be suspended by its three handles.

Goblet bowls (fig. 9:E–J). The fragments of the lower part of the goblet bowls could have had looped or flat feet; fig. 9:J might even come from a beaded-stem lamp. Figure 9:F seems to have been twisted in the making. A few goblet bowls from the Jerash Fountain Court have been published, and more examples from St. Theodore's, the Synagogue Church, Saints Peter and Paul, and the South Tetrapylon have been noted (Baur 1938: 523, 526). Although glass from Constantinople itself seems to be either rare or strictly utilitarian—or unpublished—some pieces from Saraçhane, sixth to seventh century levels, include goblet stems (Harden 1971: 83).

Waists (fig. 9:K–N). These are very thick waists or bases and waists that might come from

Fig. 9. Late Byzantine/Early Umayyad Glass

	Color	Locus	LocDt	StyDt	MC #	Cat #	Comments
A	Green	JNT-B-III-025	LByz/Um	LByz/Um	3	–	Flat goblet foot
B	Lt Blue-green	JNT-B-III-009	LByz/Um	LByz/Um	6	–	Same, octagonal
C	Turquoise	JNT-B-Surface	–	LByz/Um	–	1618	Flat goblet foot
D	Lt Blue	Lower Cavea	–	LByz/Um	–	1274	Flat goblet foot
E	Lt Blue	JNT-B-III-014	LByz/Um	LByz/Um	22	–	Goblet bowl
F	Lt Blue	JNT-B-III-029	Ott (most LByz/Um	LByz/Um	1	–	Same, twisted
G	Lt Blue-green	JNT-B-III-002	Mam (most LByz/Um)	LByz/Um	14	–	Goblet bowl
H	Lt Blue	Lower Cavea	–	LByz/Um	–	1102	Goblet bowl
I	Lt Blue	Lower Cavea	–	LByz/Um	–	1113	Goblet bowl
J	Lt Blue	Lower Cavea	–	LByz/Um	–	1098	Goblet bowl
K	Blue-green	JNT-B-V-029	LByz/Um	LByz/Um	6	1602	Thick waist, "swirled foot"
L	Yellow-green	Area F-VII-002	Mam	LByz/Um	–	2069	Thick waist and foot
M	Blue-green	Lower Cavea	–	LByz/Um?	–	1093	Thick waist
N	Lt Green	Lower Cavea	–	LByz/Um	–	1112	Thick waist, looped
O	Lt Y-green	JNT-B-III-007	LByz/Um	LByz/Um	5	–	Bottle w/ flaring mouth, rolled-in rim
P	Lt Blue	JNT-B-IV-008	LByz/Um	LByz/Um	44	735	Same
Q	Lt Blue	JNT-B-III-021	Mam	LByz/Um	2	–	Same
R	Lt Blue-green	Lower Cavea	–	LByz/Um	–	1112	Same
S	Lt Olive	Lower Cavea	–	LByz/Um	–	1096	Same
T	Lt Blue	JNT-B-V-022	LByz/Um	LByz/Um	10	1450	Bottle neck
U	Lt Blue	JNT-B-III-011	LByz/Um	LByz/Um	12	–	Bottle neck
V	Lt Blue	JNT-B-III	–	LByz/Um	5	1597	Bottle neck, traces of threads
W	Lt Green	Lower Cavea	–	LByz/Um	–	1096	Bottle neck
X	Lt Blue-green	Lower Cavea	–	LByz/Um	–	–	Bottle neck
Y	Blue-green	Lower Cavea	–	LByz/Um	–	–	Bottle neck
Z	Lt Blue	JNT-B-III-007	LByz/Um	LByz/Um	18	–	Kohl jar
aa	Lt Blue-green	JNT-B-II-008	Ott	LByz/Um	5	241	Kohl jar

squat wine goblets or from shallow bowls. Two bases (fig. 9:K, L) are quite similar to a Byzantine/ Umayyad "wine-glass lamp" from Khirbat al-Karak (Delougaz and Haines 1960: pl. 60), a fifth or sixth century swirled or tooled base from Shavei Zion (Barag 1967: fig. 16), and a bottle-green base from Sardis, earlier than A.D. 616 (von Saldern 1980: 64–65, pl. 24). The thick waist on fig. 9:M has no good provenience but does have a parallel at Hama, probably seventh or eighth century (Riis and Poulsen 1957: 42–43), and another at Sardis, Byzantine but possibly Islamic (von Saldern 1980: 61–62, pl. 24). The last waist (fig. 9:N) may actually be a "high looped pedestal base" as discussed below. There is a thick-waisted, loop-footed Byzantine base at Sardis (von Saldern 1980: 63, pl. 24), and a goblet from Hama with a conical base that resembles the Jerash fragment in form but not color. The Syrian vessel is transparent and is dated to the eighth to tenth century by comparison to Persian glass (Riis and Poulsen 1957: 37–38). Although none of the Jerash fragments preserve any of the wall of the vessel, the waists could perhaps have come from tall goblets such as the one in the Bryan Strauss Memorial Foundation collection (no provenience). It has a tall body, trailed fillets under the rim, a short, thick stem, and a flat foot and is thought to be fifth century (Philippe 1970: 67–68).

Bottle with Flaring Mouth and Rolled-in Rim
(fig. 9:O–S). These bottles, which probably had long necks, round bodies, and kick-up bases, are distinctive forms and are fairly abundant. Some fragments were recovered from Late Byzantine loci, but most examples are Late Byzantine/Early Umayyad or Umayyad. They belong to Baur's Type M "bottles" and an example from St. Theodore's has been published (Baur 1938: 532, 539). Similar pieces were excavated from the Byzantine period Tomb 7 at Khirbat al-Karak (Delougaz and Haines 1960: pl. 50), similar rims are reported from Mezad Tamar, late third to early seventh century (Erdmann 1977: 106, 125–26, pl. 4), and at least one was recovered at Araq el-Emir (Lapp 1983: fig. 24:26). Some complete bottles reputedly come from third to fifth century tombs near Bethlehem (Fitzwilliam Museum 1978: 48), and from some Byzantine tombs at El Jish (Makhouly 1939: pl. 33). The tall bottles from Tomb E 220 at Samaria, third century, have quite early dates (Crowfoot 1957: 408–10). At Hama, some green

glass necks are given as much later, after the ninth or tenth century (Riis and Poulsen 1957: 41). Note that the handles on one example, at the angle of the tall neck and body, have ridges somewhat like the ridged Early Byzantine handles shown on fig. 7:Q, R. At Sardis there are a number of Byzantine-period (ca. 400–616) flaring rims, although most seem to be thickened rather than folded in (von Saldern 1980: 72–73, pl. 26).

These flaring-mouth bottles certainly did continue into the Umayyad period (see below) and perhaps later; the exceptionally early date of the Samaria glass might, if correct, indicate that such forms came into use much earlier.

Bottle Necks (fig. 9:T–Y). These necks probably belong to the rims just listed, or perhaps the bottles with straight rims (below). Figure 9:V preserves traces of a trailed thread decoration. Numerous long-necked bottles, some with trailed threads, were excavated at Khirbat al-Karak, some from the Byzantine Tomb 4, and some from apparently more broadly dated Byzantine/Umayyad loci (Delougaz and Haines 1960: pls. 50, 59). At Bethany, however, some long-necked bottles from Tomb 71 are reported to be as early as the second to fourth centuries (Saller 1956: 169, 328). Bottle necks are fairly common at Carthage and three of the illustrated ones (Tatton-Brown, 1984: 202–4) closely resemble the rims in fig. 9:T, X, Y; the colors (greens) are different, however. At Sardis bottles, at least some of which have tall necks, are common in the Byzantine period, ca. 400–616 (von Saldern 1980: 70–72, pl. 26). Harden lists flasks with very long necks as a new form introduced in the fifth century (Harden 1971: 81). Obviously the dating of these distinctive flasks could stand clarification. They are fairly numerous and may have potential as chronological and regional markers.

Kohl Jars (fig. 9:Z, aa). The fragments are similar to the bottles with flaring mouths and rolled-in rims but these have handle attachments. They are tentatively called "kohl jars" on the basis of their resemblance to two two-handled jars from a tomb-cave near Netiv Ha-Lamed He of the mid-fifth to early seventh century (Barag 1974: 13, 83). On this basis, they would be Late Byzantine rather than Umayyad. A similar rim and handle fragment from Mezad Tamar, late third to early seventh century (Erdmann 1977: 119, pl. 3) would support this.

Ewer (fig. 10:A). This is the only ewer or pitcher mouth in the present corpus; there is no way to know if it had a handle. Baur (1938: 522, 540) shows a trefoil rim from St. Theodore's; the handle is missing, if there ever was one. The best parallel is from the Khirbat al-Karak Byzantine church; the piece has a similar mouth and neck, plus a handle (Delougaz and Haines 1960: pl. 60). One trefoil mouth fragment from Meẓad Tamar is decorated with trailed threads (Erdmann 1977: 108, 142, pl. 8). Two greenish colorless trefoil mouths are illustrated in the Karanis corpus (Harden 1936: 243–44, pl. 19). An Early Roman (A.D. 1–100) pitcher from Dura-Europos is slightly different (Clairmont 1963: pl. 4); other published Near Eastern glass pitchers do not appear to be comparable.

Bottles with Straight Mouths (fig. 10: B–G). Some of these have barely rolled-in rims or slightly widened mouths, but none flare as sharply as the bottles with flaring mouths and rolled-in rims. The straight-mouth bottles also occur in Late Byzantine contexts and seem to correspond to some of Baur's Type M "bottles," some complete examples of which were recovered from Tombs 6 and 12 (Baur 1938: 538, 541–43). Other parallels may be found at Shavei Zion in fifth to sixth century contexts (Barag 1967: fig. 16); Meẓad Tamar, late third to early seventh centuries (Erdmann 1977: 123, 128, 138–39, pls. 4, 5, 7); and perhaps on Cyprus, third-to-fourth centuries (Vessberg 1952: 131, pl. 7). It is at Sardis, however, in the Byzantine period (ca. 400–616) that the most numerous and complete comparative pieces are found. Most of the necks are tall and slender and narrow slightly toward the body, which is usually globular or occasionally cylindrical. The few bases that are preserved are usually kicked up. The glass is generally light green or blue, and eggshell thin (von Saldern 1980: 69–71, pl. 26). It is possible that the straight-mouth bottles are more characteristic of Sardis and the flaring-mouth ones of the Syro-Palestinian area, but this suggestion needs further investigation.

Hollow-Stemmed Lamps (fig. 10:H–L). This is a very long-lived type, but only one of the lamps shown here was excavated from a well-dated locus. Fortunately it (fig. 10:H) is the most complete example; fragments of the rim and base came from a protected pocket behind one of the column bases on the podium of the scaenae frons.

Although the sherds, which are quite thin, do not join, they must belong to the same lamp.

The history of glass lamps is worth a brief review. They came into use some time after the fourth or fifth century, especially in churches and later in mosques. Eventually they replaced ceramic lamps, and remain in use in churches and shrines to this day. Whatever their precedents may have been, glass lamps seem " . . . to have reached universal popularity in the Early Byzantine period" (von Saldern 1980: 49), i.e., before A.D. 616.

Baur (1938: 521) reported several "goblet-shaped lamps with plain stem" among the thick glass deposits around St. Theodore's and the cathedral Fountain Court at Jerash. Some 107 lamp stems were found at Mount Nebo, some of which seem to be hollow (Saller 1941: 316–17, pl. 140). More lamps are reported from Bethany, and at least some of these are Byzantine (Saller 1956: 330); dozens from both the church of St. John Baptist and from the town site at Samaria (Crowfoot 1957: 414–15, 418–19); Nessana, dated to the fifth to seventh centuries (Harden 1962: 84–85); Shavei Zion, fifth to sixth century (Barag 1967: fig. 16); Ovdat, in a room annexed to a church (Philippe 1970: 77–78); Ḥesban (Goldstein 1976: 130); Dibon (Tushingham 1972: fig. 13); and other sites throughout the Near East. Two other possible parallels are illustrated among the Meẓad Tamar glass, late third to early seventh century (Erdmann 1977: 102, 117, pl. 2). Finally, hollow-stem lamps are common at Sardis in Byzantine contexts (ca. 400–616) (von Saldern 1980: 50–51), and three are published from Carthage, probably sixth century (Tatton-Brown 1984: 202, fig. 66). Some conical lamps from Karanis may resemble fig. 10:L; they are dated to the fourth to sixth century (Crowfoot and Harden 1931: pl. 28).

Stemmed, footless lamps had to sit in a holder or polycandilon. Lamm (1929: pl. 5) presented a two-lamp holder, without provenience and broadly dated to the eleventh to fifteenth century; its central pedestal allowed it to rest on a table or other surface. Most of the other polycandila are wheels pierced with holes for the lamps, the whole suspended by chains. Polycandila and chains have been recovered at Jerash both by the old excavations (Crowfoot and Harden 1931: 207) and the recent ones (in Zayadine 1986). Holders for three, four, six, eight, ten, or even sixteen lamps are known. The six-lamp polycandilon from Sardis

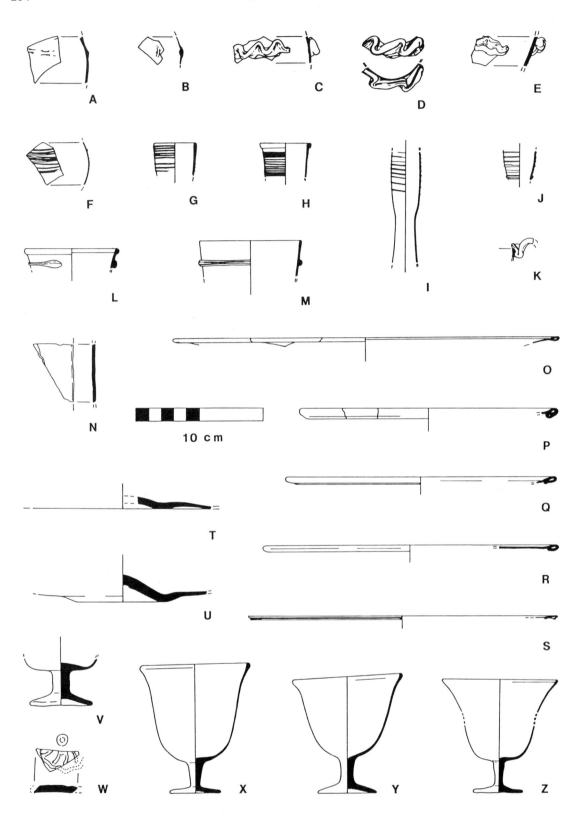

Fig. 10. Late Byzantine/Early Umayyad Glass.

is dated to the sixth to early seventh century (Philippe 1970: 78; von Saldern 1980: 50). A sixth-century poem describing St. Sophia in Constantinople mentions a silver polycandilon (Crowfoot and Harden 1931: 200; Philippe 1970: 78).

Lamps with Solid, Beaded Stems (fig. 10:M). The lamps were, judging from better-preserved pieces, bowl-shaped with a solid, beaded stem without a foot. Most of the Jerash beaded lamps were found in Umayyad or later levels, so they will be discussed in a later section.

Tumbler Lamp (fig. 10:N–Q). The most complete examples were excavated from Umayyad levels in the Bishop Isaiah church (below), but the form dates back to the end of the Byzantine period, so it will be treated here. The lamps are generally slightly flaring or tumbler-shaped; the rims are looped out and three handles run from the rim to side of the vessel. Bases are usually kicked up, but as mentioned, a few lamps may have had stems and flat feet (Baur 1938: 524–25). The old Jerash excavations recovered a great many

tumbler lamps, and handles and bases thereof, especially from the cathedral Fountain Court and St. Theodore's (Baur 1938: 520–31, 543).

As for the hollow-stemmed lamps, comparable pieces are abundant and widespread. Figure 10:Q is particularly noteworthy because the blob on the inside of the base may be a wick tube. No lamps with wick tubes are mentioned in the 1938 Jerash report,[7] but an estimated 20 are published from Mount Nebo (Saller 1941: 315–16). Others are reported from Gezer, fifth to sixth century (Crowfoot and Harden 1931: pl. 28); Samaria, from the Church of St. John Baptist (Crowfoot 1957: 418–19); Ophel, same date (Saller 1941: 316); Bethany, Byzantine, perhaps the first half of the fifth century (Saller 1956: 330); Nessana, fifth to seventh century (Harden 1962: 84); and Meẓad Tamar, late third to early seventh century (Erdmann 1977: 112–13, pl. 1). At Ḥesban, Goldstein (1976: 130) notes a wick tube from a beaker-shaped lamp that "... must be post-seventh century." Lamps with wick tubes were used from early Islamic times,

Fig. 10. Late Byzantine/Early Umayyad Glass

	Color	Locus	LocDt	StyDt	MC #	Cat #	Comments
A	Lt Blue-green	JNT-B-III-015	LByz/Um	LByz/Um	21	–	Ewer
B	Lt Blue	JNT-B-III-032	LByz/Um	LByz/Um	8	1608	Bottle w/ straight rim
C	Lt Blue	JNT-B-III-002	Mam (most LByz/Um)	LByz/Um	14	–	Bottle w/ straight rim
D	Lt Y-green	Lower Cavea	–	LByz/Um?	–	1099	Bottle w/ straight rim
E	Lt Blue-green	JNT-B-VII-003	Mod (most LByz/Um)	LByz/Um	18	1611	Bottle w/ straight rim
F	Lt Blue	JNT-B-III-007	LByz/Um	LByz/Um	5	–	Bottle w/ straight rim
G	Lt Blue	JNT-B-V-030	LByz/Um	LByz/Um	12	1604	Bottle w/ straight rim
H	Lt Y-green	JNT-B-V-029	LByz/Um	LByz/Um	24	1603	Lamp, hollow stem
I	Lt Blue	Lower Cavea	–	LByz/Um?	–	1100	Lamp, hollow stem
J	Blue-green	Lower Cavea	–	LByz/Um?	–	1098	Lamp, hollow stem
K	Yellow	JNT-B-III-005	Mam (most LByz/Um)	LByz/Um?	5	–	Lamp, hollow stem
L	Lt Blue	JNT-B-VII-003	Mod (most LByz/Um)	LByz/Um?	34	1612	Lamp, conical stem
M	Blue	JNT-B-III-007	LByz/Um	LByz/Um	5	–	Lamp, beaded stem
N	Lt Blue	JNT-B-III-011	LByz/Um	LByz/Um	7	–	Tumbler lamp
O	Blue-green	JNT-B-III-025	LByz/Um	LByz/Um	15	–	Tumbler lamp
P	Yellow-green	JNT-B-III-014	LByz/Um	LByz/Um	1	–	Tumbler lamp, handle
Q	Lt Y-green	JNT-B-V-031	LByz/Um	LByz/Um	2	1607	Tumbler lamp w/ wick tube?
R	Amber	JNT-B-III-025	LByz/Um	LByz/Um	3	–	Rim, looped out
S	Y-green?	JNT-B-III-011	LByz/Um	LByz/Um	12	–	Tall lamp rim? thick patina
T	Y-green	JNT-B-III-025	LByz/Um	LByz/Um	3	–	Bottle w/ straight rim?
U	Lt Blue?	JNT-B-III-022	LByz/Um	LByz/Um?	14	–	Thick patina, Byz? beaker?
V	Lt Blue	JNT-B-III-007	LByz/Um	LByz/Um	5	–	Rim, folded in
W	Yellow-green	JNT-B-V-037	LByz/Um	LByz/Um?	1	1609	Unguentarium? earlier?
X	Blue-green	JNT-B-III-011	LByz/Um	LByz/Um	29	–	Kick-up base
Y	Lt Blue-green	JNT-B-V-027	LByz/Um	LByz/Um	6	1601	Kick-up base
Z	V. dk amber almost opaque	JNT-B-III-030/031	LByz/Um	LByz/Um	11	–	Kick-up base, pontil scar
aa	Yellow	JNT-B-III-013	LByz/Um	LByz/Um	5	–	High looped pedestal base
bb	Blue-green	JNT-B-III-011	LByz/Um	LByz/Um	7	–	High looped pedestal base
cc	Clear	JNT-B-III-031	LByz/Um	LByz/Um?	17	1599	Ring base, Byz?
dd	Lt Blue	JNT-B-III-011	LByz/Um	LByz/Um	12	–	Handle, rim fragment
ee	Lt Blue	Lower Cavea		LByz/Um	–	1112	Handle, rim fragment

through the 12th century, and up to modern times (Saller 1941: 316; Crowfoot and Harden 1931: pls. 28, 30; Lamb 1965: 38; Riis and Poulsen 1957: 37–38).

Other, tubeless, lamps are known from widespread sites. Over a hundred lamp fragments were recovered at Mount Nebo (Saller 1941: 316, pl. 140), and a few are published from Shavei Zion (Barag 1967: fig. 16). Riis mentioned but did not illustrate fragments of probable hanging lamps from Hama, possibly fifth to ninth century in date (Riis and Poulsen 1957: 32–33). A vessel excavated at Alexandria in fifth to early seventh century context is given as a *"gobelet"* (Rodziewicz 1984: 240, pl. 73) but may actually be a lamp. Some rims and handles at Pelusium, Egypt, are probably pieces of lamps (Fontaine 1952: 79, pl. 4). Seven "bowl-shaped" lamps with three handles are reported from Carthage, the earliest dated to the sixth century (Tatton-Brown 1984: 202, fig. 66). A lamp from Paphos, Cyprus, is dated to the fifth or sixth century (Fitzwilliam Museum 1978: 54–55), and at Sardis a type of bowl-shaped lamp with handles is fairly common —or at least the handles are. Most are fifth to early seventh century (von Saldern 1980: 45–48, pls. 11, 23).

Looped-out Rims (fig. 10:R). Fragments of looped-out rims are quite common and many probably come from tumbler-shaped lamps. Figure 10:R is unusual because it is amber-colored.

Miscellaneous Rims (fig. 10:S–W). The rims shown here have nothing in common except that they were excavated from Late Byzantine/Early Umayyad loci. Figure 10:U is very thin and seems more like the Early Byzantine beakers than like anything else in the corpus. A series of delicate rims, some slightly irregular or thickened, were found at Meẓad Tamar, late third to early seventh century (Erdmann 1977: 130, 132, 137, pls. 5, 6). The rim on fig. 10:T may be from a bottle with a tall straight neck, wider than the "bottles with straight necks." A series of wide-mouthed, tall-necked bottles come from a fifth to seventh century tomb cave near Netiv Ha-Lamed He (Barag 1974: 13, 83), and similar rim fragments were found at Meẓad Tamar (Erdmann 1977: 132, 137–39, pls. 6, 7). A number of bottle rims, both straight and flaring (cf. fig. 10:U) are reported from Alexandria in fifth to early seventh century context (Rodziewicz 1984: pl. 74). Finally, Baur (1938: 521–23) illustrated some fairly tall tumbler-

shaped lamps with plain rims, a type from which the fig. 10:S rim could have come.

Kick-up Bases (fig. 10:X–Z). Kick-up bases are common and many must have belonged to bottles or tumbler lamps. The dark amber, almost opaque base (fig. 10:Z) is unusual for its color.

High, Looped Pedestal Bases (fig. 10:aa, bb). These are broader and stand higher than the Byzantine "looped bases," and may come from bowls or even lamps. There are comparable bases from Khirbat al-Karak (Delougaz and Haines 1960: pls. 59–60), Shavei Zion in fifth and sixth century contexts (Barag 1967: fig. 16), and at Meẓad Tamar, late third to early seventh century (Erdmann 1977: 116, pl. 2). Again the dates from Samaria, third to fifth centuries, for a series of bowls on tubular bases, rather like Revere bowls, seem early (Crowfoot 1957: 408, 410). Finally, we may note a three-handled lamp, possibly Syrian, sixth to eighth century, on a high pedestal base (Smith 1957: 200–210).

Miscellaneous Base (fig. 10:cc). The ring base shown here resembles the Early Byzantine bases and the fabric, clear glass, is more typical of earlier periods, so this may be Byzantine or even Roman.

Handles (fig. 10:dd, ee). Numerous fragments of handles, probably from three-handled lamps, were recovered; sometimes they are attached to segments of rims. The one on fig. 10:dd is thicker than usual, and fig. 10:ee flips up.

Nipped Decoration (fig. 11:A, B). Only two small fragments of nipped decoration were recovered, but they may be compared to several other examples, including the decoration on a squat bottle from St. Theodore's church (Baur 1938: 522, 536); a narrow-necked bottle from the Byzantine Tomb 4 at Khirbat al-Karak (Delougaz and Haines 1960: pl. 50); a pear-shaped, flaring-mouth bottle from Beth Shan, "Arab and Byzantine" levels (Fitzgerald 1931: 42); and a bottle, a chance find, from Sardis (von Saldern 1980: 20, pl. 4). The comparative materials are consistently earlier and the fragments are probably Byzantine rather than Umayyad.

Ruffles (fig. 11:C–E). This type of applied decoration seems to have been used for centuries (see Late Byzantine, Umayyad, and Mamluk sections), almost always applied to the necks of tall bottles. Baur (1938: 534–35, 543) published several bottles with ruffles from the old Jerash excavations, and as usual the dates are earlier (fourth to sixth century) than those proposed here (seventh century and later). The constriction at the bottom of the bottle necks (Baur 1938: 534, 543) is similar to that on the "bottle necks" discussed above. A virtually identical bottle was found in the Byzantine (sixth century?) monastery at Samaria (Crowfoot 1957: 418). Some bottle necks with ruffles were excavated at Khirbat al-Karak (Delougaz and Haines 1960: pl. 59), as were a number at Mount Nebo. At the latter site the pieces are dated to the eighth century by comparison to finds at a Byzantine-period synagogue near Jericho (Saller 1941: 320, pl. 141). Some bottle necks from Hama (Riis and Poulsen 1957: 60–61) and Egypt (Harden 1936; Fontaine 1952: 79, pl. 4) have ruffles also, but ruffles are absent on the Sardis vessels.

Trailed Threads (fig. 11:F–M). A few pieces with applied threads have been noted (figs. 8:B, 9:V); this is one of the most common types of decoration in this period. Thread and "vermiculate" decoration is said to be late Roman, probably Syro-Egyptian in origin (Philippe 1970: 75–76); it does not seem to have been common so early, but there is a tall neck with wound threads from Dura-Europos, dated to A.D. 100–256 (Clairmont 1963: pl. 12). Thread decoration lasted until the tenth century at least (Philippe 1970: 75–76), perhaps later as indicated by finds at Hama (Riis and Poulsen 1957: 60–61) and in Italy (Gasparetto 1979: 83).

Parallels for the thread-thin decoration are abundant. Baur published a number of tall bottle necks from the previous Jerash excavations (Baur 1938: 533–35, 545), and Harden published two long-necked bottles at Kharijh, in north Jordan, dated to the sixth century. Harden also discussed two more pieces of the same date, part of a large group from Ajlun, very close to Jerash. One has a spout and the other, a lightly ribbed body (Harden 1971: 79). Several fragments, some decorated with white, green, brown, or black in addition to the usual blue, were recovered at Mount Nebo (Saller 1941: 320–21, pl. 142). More examples were unearthed at Beth Shan, one from underneath the church (Fitzgerald 1931: 42); at Kirbat al-Karak, from the Byzantine church, Tomb 4, and other loci (Delougaz and Haines 1960: pls. 59–60); at Shavei Zion, fifth to sixth century (Barag 1967: fig. 16); and at Mezad Tamar, late third to early seventh century (Erdmann 1977: 110, 112, 143, pls. 1, 8). In general, bottles or fragments with

trailed threads are reported throughout the Near East and Cyprus, but they do not seem to have been common outside the Syro-Palestinian area. A few bottles with thread decoration are known from Alexandria from fifth to early seventh century buildings (Rodziewicz 1984: pl. 74); several also are known from Carthage, in sixth and seventh century contexts (Tatton-Brown 1984: 204–5; fig. 67). Trailed thread decoration occurs at Sardis (von Saldern 1980: 82–84, pl. 27). Strangely enough, Gasparetto (1979) published some tall, thread-trailed bottle necks from Italy, from the 13th to 15th centuries; and Lamb (1965: 36–37) reported blue and brown trailed decoration on glass vessels of the 11th to 14th centuries in Malaya.

The heavier threads or coils in fig. 11:L and M are more unusual, although a number of fragments, some possibly from bottles, were recovered at Mezad Tamar (Erdmann 1977: pls. 4–8). Lamm (1929: pl. 22) illustrated a beaker (no provenience) with a heavy trailed thread which he considered pre-Fatimid, i.e., before ca. 900. See also the bottle mouths with heavy trailed coils from Carthage, latter part of the fifth to seventh century (Tatton-Brown 1984: 204, fig. 67).

Window Glass (fig. 11:N–U). Almost all the panes are circular "crown" or "bull's-eye" type, though fig. 11:N from a late locus might indicate that a little cast glass was still in use. Fragments of the round panes, especially the very thick centers and folded rims, are among the most numerous identifiable pieces recovered. Reconstructed rim diameters are up to 24 or 30 cm. The Jerash fragments are all blues or greens, but clear panes are reported from the old excavations (Baur 1938: 546), and wine-colored, lavender, brown, yellow, red, opaque black, and purple are known from other sites such as Samaria, Beth Shan, Mount Nebo, Hama, and Samarra. Even allowing for colors that altered over the centuries, this is a considerable variety.

Cast and "muff" window panes have been discussed in the section on Early Byzantine glass. "Crown" glass was made by blowing a globe which was then attached to a pontil rod as if making any other blown vessel. The cut, open end was usually folded out, at least at Jerash, to strengthen the rim, and then the whole thing was spun until it "flashed" or opened into a disk. This left a very thick center as the "bull's-eye," a more or less dish- or bowl-like profile, and thin edges.

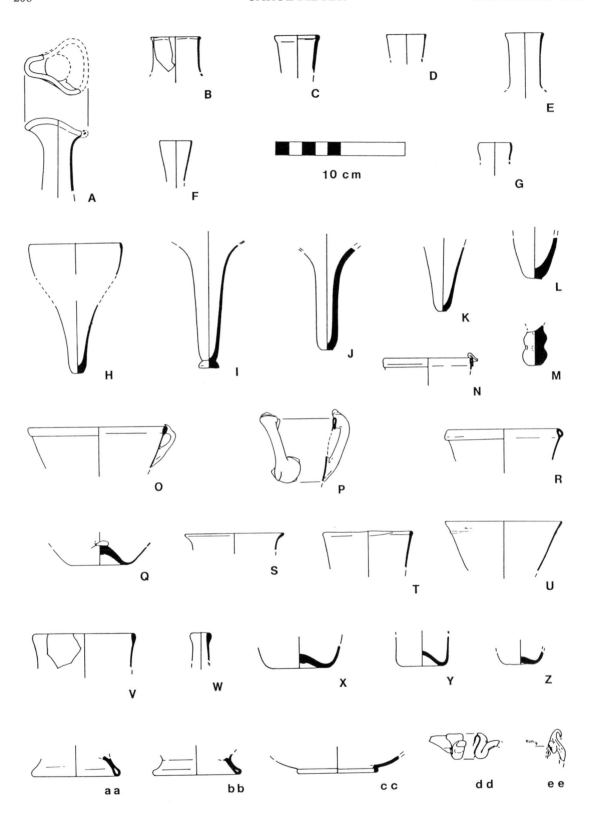

Fig. 11. Late Byzantine/Early Umayyad and Umayyad Glass.

The thin part can be cut and set as small panes but at Jerash the builders seem to have used the whole disks. They would have been translucent but not transparent; the advantage of crown glass is that it is fire-polished on both sides, economical to make, and may be quite colorful.

Crown glass is said to have been invented in the Near East about the fourth century[8] and carried from there to Italy and the west (Harden 1971: 83). At first, glass windows would have been set only in more important buildings such as churches, but from the ninth century on, houses had small panes set in plaster or stucco. Palaces such as those at Raqqa and Samarra most certainly used much colored glass; the former palace even had greenish glass floor tiles (Philippe 1970: 18). At Sardis "muff" or cast glass was used until about A.D. 616, but crown glass was employed in the Middle Byzantine (late 10th to 13th or 14th century) churches (von Saldern 1980: 91–92).

The round panes were set in a white plaster frame that held at least two, probably four or more panes (Harden 1939: 91). A little plaster still adheres to some of the Jerash panes, but by far the most informative are the window pieces from Samarra, slightly later. The glass circles set in a very thick plaster mounting (Lamm 1928: 127–28) resemble windows still to be seen in old Arab houses in Damascus, the Yemen, and elsewhere. Earlier, in the Byzantine period at Sardis, the panes were apparently held by lead strips set in plaster in a window casing (von Saldern 1980: 91–92).

Comparative material is abundant but need be only briefly reviewed. Baur (1938: 546) noted window glass with straight or curved edges, with or without bull's-eyes, from the churches, apparently both cast and crown glass. However, he seemed to take some complete panes for "dishes or shallow bowls" (Baur 1938: 528, 532), which is not too surprising given the manufacturing technique. All the window glass recovered at Mount Nebo—and there was a great deal in a variety of colors—was round (Saller 1941: 64–66). Many more round panes were found at Syro-Palestinian sites, in Iran, and in Iraq. The ninth century palaces and houses of Samarra yielded a large number of frame fragments and round, folded-rim window panes in colorless, yellow-brown, dark blue, red, violet, black, light green, green, and yellow (Lamm

Fig. 11. Late Byzantine/Early Umayyad and Umayyad Glass

	Color	Locus	LocDt	StyDt	MC #	Cat #	Comments
A	Lt Blue	JNT-B-III-007	LByz/Um	LByz/Um	18	–	Pinched dec.
B	Pale Blue	JNT-B-III-002	Mam (most LByz/Um)	LByz/Um	14	–	Pinched dec.
C	Dk Turquoise on lt blue	JNT-B-III-008	LByz/Um	LByz/Um	2	–	Ruffle
D	Turquoise on lt blue	Lower Cavea	–	LByz/Um	–	1272	Ruffle
E	Y-green on lt blue	JNT-B-V-012	Ott (most LByz/Um)	LByz/Um	15	1430	Ruffle
F	Turquoise on lt blue	JNT-B-III-025	LByz/Um	LByz/Um	3	–	Thread dec.
G	Lt Blue-green	JNT-B-III-004	LByz/Um	LByz/Um	6	–	Bottle mouth, thread dec.
H	Lt Blue	Lower Cavea	–	LByz/Um	–	–	Bottle mouth, thread dec.
I	Lt Blue	Lower Cavea	–	LByz/Um	–	1096	Bottle neck, thread dec.
J	Lt Blue	JNT-B-III-002	Mam (most LByz/Um)	LByz/Um	14	–	Bottle neck, thread dec.
K	Turquoise on lt blue	Lower Cavea	–	LByz/Um	–	1112	Rim w/ handle, thread dec.
L	Lt Blue	JNT-B-V-005	LByz/Um	LByz/Um	2	1410	Trailed dec.
M	Purple on lt blue	Lower Cavea	–	LByz/Um?	–	1152	Trailed dec.
N	Lt Blue	JNT-B-III-002	Mam (most LByz/Um)	LByz/Um?	14	–	Window pane, cast?
O	Lt Blue	JNT-B-III-002	Mam (most LByz/Um)	LByz/Um?	14	–	Window, crown glass
P	Blue-green	JNT-B-III-025	LByz/Um	LByz/Um	3	–	Window, crown glass
Q	Lt Green	Lower Cavea	–	LByz/Um?	–	1098	Window, crown glass
R	Lt Blue-green	Lower Cavea	–	LByz/Um?	–	1096	Window, crown glass
S	Lt Blue-green	JNT-B-V-031	LByz/Um	LByz/Um	1	1605	Window, crown glass
T	Blue-green	JNT-B-V-028	LByz/Um	LByz/Um	13	1463	Center of crown pane
U	Olive	Lower Cavea	–	LByz/Um?	–	1273	Center of crown pane
V	Blue	Area F-XVI-005	Um	Um	3	2086	Flat goblet base, pontil scar
W	Lt Blue	JNT-B-IV-008	Um	Um	35	733	Flat base, molded?
X	Lt Blue	Area F-XVI-003	Um	Um	2	2093	Stemmed goblet w/ flat feet
Y	Lt Blue	Area F-XVI-003	Um	Um	2	2084	Same, pontil scar
Z	Lt Blue	Area F-XVI-003	Um	Um	8	2085	Same, pontil scar

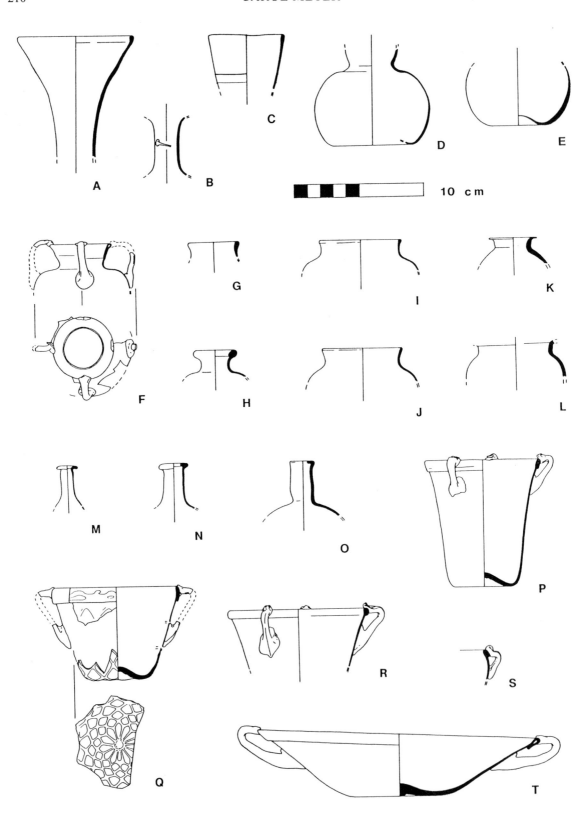

Fig. 12. Umayyad Glass.

1928: 127–28). The Middle Byzantine crown glass at Sardis has been noted; this type of glass continued to be produced in Hebron up to modern times (Harden 1971: 82–83).

UMAYYAD (A.D. 661–747 or later)

Most of the glass from the Umayyad loci is like that which has been discussed in the Late Byzantine/Early Umayyad section. Some of the Umayyad examples are much better preserved, however, especially the three goblets, a shallow bowl with two handles, a three-handled tumbler lamp, and a molded tumbler lamp that could be reconstructed from rim to base. A few forms appear for the first time in this corpus. These include the two-handled shallow bowl, a four-handled jar or bottle, and molded and marvered decoration.

Most of the Umayyad glass was recovered from the Bishop Isaiah church, which was a mid-sixth century foundation but continued in use probably until the eighth century (cf. also Philippe 1970: 50). After two centuries of use the church may well have stood in need of repairs, and indeed tiles stacked along one wall may have been intended for that purpose (Clark 1986). In any case the glass may be more accurately dated to the end of the life of the church than to its construction.

It is a little difficult to assess Philippe's statement that, . . . *si . . . le IXe siècle est l'âge d'or de la civilisation musulmane, la production verrière de la période ommeyade (660–749) semble—à en juger par le produit des fouilles—assez limitée en ce qui concerne le nombre et la diversité des formes* (Philippe 1970: 7). A respectable diversity of forms is present in this corpus, and more Umayyad pieces are undoubtedly included with the Late Byzantine/Early Umayyad group, which would obviously raise the quantity of the Umayyad glass as well. It is possible that at other sites earlier excavators quickly removed upper "late" or "Islamic" layers and cursorily treated the contents in their haste to reach lower, earlier levels; such a practice would result in fewer corpora of Umayyad and later glass and an apparent lack of diversity and quantity.

Like the Late Byzantine/Early Umayyad glass, most of this is light blue or blue-green, usually with a creamy or silvery decomposition layer. A few sherds of red, white, and blue, or red, white, and black dragged and marvered vessels, and a red, white, and blue bracelet, however, represent the most colorful and elaborate glass since the Roman period.

Stemmed Goblet with Flat Foot (fig. 11:V–Z). These are the same as the goblets discussed with the Late Byzantine/Early Umayyad glass, but three complete or almost complete ones were recovered from the Bishop Isaiah church. One of the first things noticed about these and the other relatively complete vessels is that they are lopsided; the rims are neither absolutely horizontal

---

Fig. 12. Umayyad Glass

	Color	Locus	LocDt	StyDt	MC #	Cat #	Comments
A	Lt Blue	Area F-XIII-001	Um	Um	61	2073	Bottle w/ flaring mouth
B	Lt Y-green	JNT-B-IV-021	Um	Um	7	1626	Bottle neck, start of trailed thread
C	Lt Blue	Lower Cavea	–	Um?	–	1096	Bottle mouth, trailed thread
D	Lt Blue	Area F-IV-003	Um	Um	–	2081	Bottle bottom
E	Lt Blue	Area F-XII	Um?	Um	57	2071	Bottle bottom
F	Lt Blue	Area F-XVI-003	Um	Um	8	2085	Jar w/ four handles
G	Lt Blue	JNT-B-IV-018	Um	Um	2	750	Jar mouth
H	Lt Blue	JNT-B-VII-003	Mod (most LByz/Um)	Um?	34	1612	Jar mouth
I	Lt Blue	JNT-B-II-008	Ott	Um?	46	287	Jar mouth
J	Lt Blue	JNT-B-II-009	Ott	Um?	10	245	Jar mouth
K	Clear	Area F-XII	Um?	Um?	57	2071	Jar mouth, Roman?
L	Clear	JNT-B-V-001/002	Ott (most LByz/Um)	Um?	–	1598	Jar mouth, Roman?
M	Amber	JNT-B-IV-008	Um	Um	35	733	Perfume flask?
N	Lt Blue	JNT-B-I-004	Um	Um	–	29?	Perfume flask?
O	Olive	Lower Cavea	–	Um?	–	–	Perfume flask?
P	Lt Blue-green	Area F-IX-002	Um	Um	2	2074	Tumbler lamp
Q	Lt Blue-green	Area F-XVI-007	Um	Um	1	2088	Tumbler lamp, molded
R	Lt Blue-green	Area F-XIII-001/002	Um	Um	60, 61	2073	Tumbler lamp
S	Lt Blue	JNT-B-I-004	Um	Um	–	764	Handle, rim
T	Lt Blue-green	Area F-IX-002	Um	Um	2	2075	Shallow bowl w/ two handles

nor perfectly round. Although this is not surprising in blown vessels, it does mean that the rim
fragments restored as circles may not be absolutely
accurate. One base fragment (fig. 11:W) seems to
be molded or tooled.

Bottle Rims and Neck (fig. 12:A–C). Similar
pieces have been discussed with the Late Byzan-
tine/Early Umayyad bottles. Figure 12:A is like
the bottles with flaring mouths and rolled-in rims,
apparently not an uncommon form in the Umayyad period. Figure 12:C has a straight neck, parallels for which are found among the Byzantine/
Umayyad Khirbat al-Karak glass (Delougaz and
Haines 1960: pl. 59).

Bottle Bottoms (fig. 12:D, E). Both the bottles
with straight necks and the ones with narrower
necks and flaring mouths frequently had globular
bodies and kick-up bases like these two. Baur
(1938: 541–43) published a complete bottle with a
round body from Tomb 6 in the southwest cemetery. Comparable bases are reported from Samaria,
Tomb E 220, early third century (Crowfoot 1957:
408–10; the dates again seem very early). A series
of bottles from Sardis, where they are common,
have oval or spherical bodies and are dated to the
fifth to sixth century (von Saldern 1980: 70–71, pl.
26); there is little at Sardis between ca. A.D. 616
and the late tenth century.

Four-Handled Jar (fig. 12:F). The handles or
scars of handles are quite clear; there do not seem
to be any comparable bottles or jars published.

Jar Necks (fig. 12:G–L). Only fig. 12:G and K
are from Umayyad loci; the rest are from later
deposits. The form may have continued in use for
centuries. All the jars have short necks. The
narrow-mouth jars (fig. 12:G, H) may be compared to similar but not identical shapes at
Khirbat al-Karak, from both the Byzantine church
and the Umayyad building (Delougaz and Haines
1960: pl. 60); they may also be compared, perhaps,
to a large green jar with a very restricted mouth
from Hama (Riis and Poulsen 1957: 40–41). The
wide-mouth jars (fig. 12:I, J) may have Byzantine
parallels (ca. 400–616) at Sardis (von Saldern
1980: 79–81, pl. 27). Finally, the two clear jars
(fig. 12:K, L) are distinctive both for their fabric
and thickness.

Perfume Flasks (fig. 12:M–O). These are small
vessels with tall, narrow necks but little else in
common; the label "perfume flask" is tentative.
The amber-colored fabric of fig. 12:M is unusual.
The folded-in rim (fig. 12:N) resembles the Late

Byzantine unguentaria discussed above (cf. fig.
8:F, H) and the form may well have remained in
use. Similar but greenish necks are reported from
Iran and are thought to be sixth to eighth century
(Lamm 1935: 9, pl. 9). The olive green neck (fig.
12:O) has no good provenience but is grouped
here because of its rim shape. The olive-colored
fabric also resembles the Late Byzantine/Early
Umayyad narrow neck on fig. 10:W. The rim
shape is similar to a fragment from Meẓad Tamar,
late third to early seventh century (Erdmann 1977:
123, pl. 4).

Tumbler Lamps (fig. 12:P–R). This form was
discussed with the Late Byzantine/Early Umayyad
glass, but once again the most complete examples
come from the Bishop Isaiah church. The form
appears to have come into use in Late Byzantine/
Early Umayyad times; it continued along with the
beaded-stem lamps through the Umayyad period,
and then became less common. The mold-blown
lamp (fig. 12:Q) is quite thin and could only be
reconstructed on paper from a number of fragments. It is shown as having two handles, the
number recovered, but probably actually possessed
three. A trace of the blown diamond design is
visible even under the folded-out rim. Molded
decoration will be treated further with the mold-
blown fragments below, but to date there seems to
be no good parallel for a lamp so decorated.

Handle (fig. 12:S). This may be a sherd of a
tumbler lamp although the handle seems smaller
and the rim more bowed than usual.

Two-Handled Bowl (fig. 12.T). Enough fragments of the bowl were recovered from the Area
F church to restore it from rim to base. It, like the
goblets, is lopsided. One handle is attached to the
rim and body; a second handle, actually a little
smaller, was found but the join was too tenuous
to mend. The rim was complete enough to show
that only two handles existed. The problem is that
the many dishes or shallow bowls unearthed in
the earlier excavations, especially in and around
the cathedral's Fountain Court, had three handles
(Baur 1938: 528, 530). Also, a fairly uncommon
type of lamp, a shallow bowl with three handles,
was found at Sardis in Byzantine loci, ca. 400–616
(von Saldern 1980: 45, pls. 11, 23).

Lamps with Solid, Beaded Stems (fig. 13:A–
D). These are fairly common. One fragment (fig.
10:M) was listed with the Late Byzantine/Early
Umayyad glass but again some of the best examples were excavated in the Bishop Isaiah church.

Figure 13:D seems to be a solid stem attached to a bowl that bends down rather than up, as if the stem descended from a kick-up base. Hollow-stem lamps with such bowls are reported at Nessana in the fifth to seventh century (Harden 1962: 84–85), and at Hama, dated to the 11th to 12th centuries by comparison to lamps from Al-Mina, Kouban, and Corinth (Riis and Poulsen 1957: 38–39). The ordinary beaded-stem lamps with cup-shaped bowls found by the earlier Jerash excavations were dated to the fifth to sixth century, which is probably too early. Many such lamps were recovered; about 175 stems and "a bushel of fragments" from the Fountain Court and dump north of St. Theodore's are reported, plus more from the other churches (Baur 1938: 519–21). About ten beaded lamp stems are known from Mount Nebo (Saller 1941: 317, pl. 140), two small fragments from Dibon (Tushingham 1972: fig. 13), and a hollow beaded stem, possibly tenth century, from Hama (Riis and Poulsen 1957: 50–51), though it may not even be a lamp. A report on Ḥesban lists but does not illustrate "lamps with long solid beaded stems" (Goldstein 1976: 130), but no other close parallels are evident. Beaded-stem lamps are conspicuously absent at Sardis, though there is a beaded-stem, footed goblet (von Saldern 1980: 54, pl. 12).

Thus beaded-stem lamps appear to be abundant at Jerash and quite uncommon elsewhere. The lamps, then, might have been made and used only in the Jerash area, or manufactured after sites such as Sardis (to A.D. 616) were abandoned. Only one or two hollow-stemmed lamps were retrieved by the recent excavations from Umayyad loci. It may be suggested therefore that the hollow-stemmed lamps tend to be earlier and the beaded-stem lamps later.

Incurved Rims (fig. 13:E–G).   These rims have little in common except that all curve inward and all come from Umayyad loci. Figure 13:E has a close parallel at Khirbat al-Karak, Byzantine/Umayyad (Delougaz and Haines 1960: pl. 59). The rim in fig. 13:F is similar to that of a bowl from Ḥesban (S. Goldstein, personal communication) and is reminiscent of the Early Byzantine bowl on fig. 6:O. A slightly in-curving rim like fig. 13:G is illustrated with the Meẓad Tamar corpus, late third to early seventh century (Erdmann 1977: 139, pl. 7).

Looped-in Rim (fig. 13:H).   Most of the looped rims in this corpus are folded out; this one, how-

ever, is looped inward, and so broadly as to leave a thick round rim.

Miscellaneous Bases (fig. 13:I, J).   Figure 13:I resembles in a general fashion the Early Byzantine base on fig. 7:D and the Late Byzantine base on fig. 8:O, but the amber color is unusual.

Ruffle (fig. 13:K).   This type of decoration has already been discussed. The sherd shown here, however, has a large enough diameter and enough curvature from top to bottom to suggest that it came from a bottle body rather than a neck, the usual location of ruffle decoration.

Trailed Thread Decoration (fig. 13:L).   Trailed threads seem to be used almost exclusively on the necks of tall bottles; the piece illustrated here would have been somewhat broader than usual.

Marvered Decoration (fig. 13:M–P).   The decoration is produced by trailing threads of colored glass, here red and white, on a hot vessel, in this case blue or black, dragging the surface to make a scalloped design, and rolling or marvering the whole on a slab to smooth the surface. It is a most ancient technique, employed at least since the time of Egyptian core-formed vessels. Marvered decoration was revived in the Islamic period but there are actually few closely comparable pieces. Sherds are reported from Mount Nebo, some with straight lines and at least one with a wavy or scalloped line (Saller 1941: 321, pl. 142), but it is difficult to judge from the photographs. Marvered-in threads are mentioned at Bethany (Saller 1956: 331), and Lamm (1929: pls. 29–31; 1935: 14–15, pl. 44) illustrated many pieces, some red and white or blue and white; but the proveniences—Egypt to Palestine and Iran—and dates are too vague to indicate more than the existence of other marvered vessels. The white-on-green rim sherd on fig. 13:P could be later; it has no dated findspot.

Molded Decoration (fig. 13:Q–V).   The mold-blown lamp has been noted; the other sherds shown here are too small to determine what kind of vessel they came from. Round dimples, ovals, or networks of diamonds seem to be widespread types of decoration. More or less comparable pieces may be noted from Ḥesban, Islamic period (Goldstein 1976: 131); Hama, no later than 13th century (Riis and Poulsen 1957: 51–52); Samarra, ninth century (Lamm 1928: 43–44); Egypt and Iran (Lamm 1929: pl. 9; 1931: 364, pl. 76; 1935: 11, pl. 21); Serçe Limani, early 11th century (Bass 1984); and Sardis, which yielded a mold-blown,

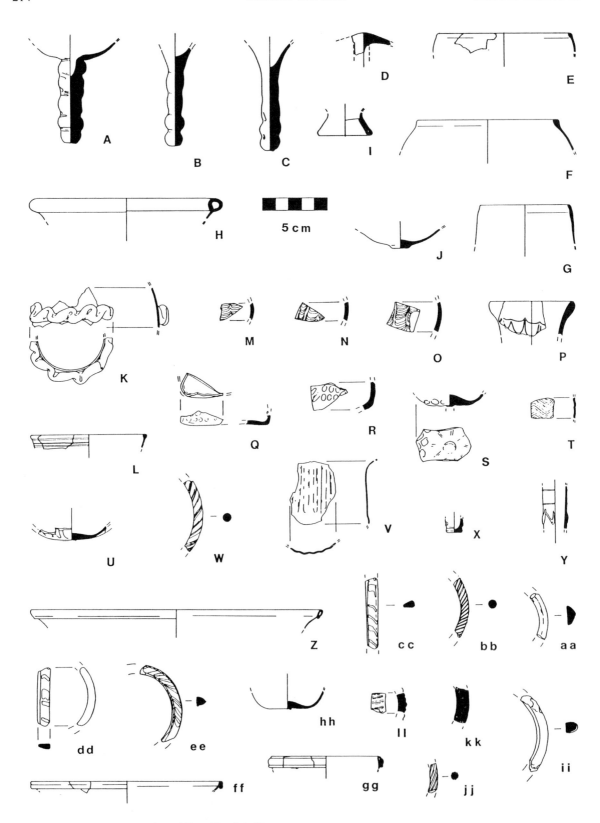

Fig. 13. Umayyad, Mamluk, and Post-Mamluk Glass.

honeycomb bottle, probably imported and probably 10th to 12th century (von Saldern 1980: 102–3, pl. 18). The single small zigzag patterned sherd (fig. 13:T) has parallels from Ḥesban, Islamic period (Goldstein 1976: 131); Egypt (Lamm 1929: pl. 11); and Corinth, 11th and 12th centuries (Davidson 1940: 311). A blown, ribbed base similar to that on fig. 13:U is found in the Carthage corpus, sixth century (Tatton-Brown 1984: 205, fig. 67). Baur (1938: 543–44) published a bottle dated to ca. 500 with ribbing similar to that on fig. 13:V, although he stated that the ribs were made with an implement while the glass was hot, rather than being blown into a mold. Other ribbed bottles are reported from Shavei Zion, fifth to sixth century (Barag 1967: fig. 16); Meẓad Tamar,

Fig. 13. Umayyad, Mamluk, and Post-Mamluk Glass

	Color	Locus	LocDt	StyDt	MC #	Cat #	Comments
A	Turquoise	Area F-XII-002	Um	Um	58	2072	Beaded-stem lamp
B	Blue	Area F-IX-003	Um	Um	8	2076	Beaded-stem lamp
C	Blue	Lower Cavea	Um	Um?	–	1273	Beaded-stem lamp
D	Lt Blue	JNT-B-III-023	Ott (most LByz/Um)	Um?	24	–	Stemmed lamp, kicked up?
E	Clear	JNT-B-IV-018	Um	Um	2	750	Incurved-rim bowl
F	Lt Blue	Area A-II-001	Um	Um	12	1008	Incurved-rim bowl
G	Lt Blue-green	Area F-XVI-003	Um	Um	2	2084	Incurved rim
H	Yellow-green	Area F-XII-002/3	Um	Um	–	2083	Bowl, rolled-in rim
I	Amber	JNT-B-IV-008	Um	Um	35	733	High looped base
J	Blue-green	JNT-B-IV-008	Um	Um	4	723	Button base
K	Lt Blue-green	JNT-B-IV-021	Um	Um	1	1625	Ruffle
L	Turquoise on lt blue	JNT-B-III-014	Um	Um	1		Rim, trailed threads
M	Red, Wt on black	Area F-XVI-012	Um	Um	1	2090	Marvered, scalloped
N	Red and Wt on blue	JNT-B-IV-008	Um	Um	11	725	Marvered, scalloped
O	Red and Wt on dk blue	JNT-B-II-002	Ott	Um	60	284	Marvered, scalloped
P	White on dk yellow-green	Lower Cavea	–	Um?	–	1099	Marvered loops, v. thick dk patina
Q	Lt Y-green	JNT-B-III-026	Ott (most LByz/Um)	Um	14	–	Molded, dimples
R	Yellow-green	Lower Cavea	–	Um	–	1112	Molded, dimples
S	Lt Y-green	JNT-B-II-009	Ott	Um	10	245	Molded, diamonds
T	Clear	JNT-B-II-009	Ott	Um	26	256	Molded, zig-zag
U	Blue	JNT-B-VII-005	Ott(most LByz/Um)	Um?	7	1613	Molded, ribs, pontil scar
V	Lt Blue	Lower Cavea	–	Um	–	1112	Molded, ribs
W	Red, Wt, Y threads on v. dk blue	Area F-VIII-002	Um	Um	3	2070	Bracelet, twisted threads
X	Emerald	JNT-B-V-002	Mam (most LByz/Um)	Mam	10	1404	Cut vial
Y	Turquoise on lt blue	JNT-B-II-011	Ott	Mam?	2	258	Bottle neck, threads, zig-zag, LByz/Um?
Z	Lt Blue	JNT-B-III-005	Mam (most LByz/Um)	Mam?	5	–	Looped-out rim, LByz/Um?
aa	Opaque	JNT-B-V-003	Mam (most LByz/Um)	Mam	7	1408	Bracelet
bb	Red, blue, Y on black	JNT-B-II-001	Mod	Mam?	15	267	Bracelet, Um?
cc	Green and red brown on red stripe on dark olive	JNT-B-V-001	Ott (most LByz/Um)	Mam	1	1400	Bracelet
dd	Y and blue on red stripe on black	Area E-I	–	Mam	3	2009	Bracelet
ee	Y and Wt twisted threads, Y and green stripes on red patches on blue	Lower Cavea	–	Mam	–	1093	Bracelet
ff	Lt Blue	JNT-B-II-011	Ott	Ott?	2	258	Rim, folded-out, LByz/Um?
gg	Lt Blue	JNT-B-V-007	Ott (most LByz/Um)	Ott?	17	1415	Folded out, up, LByz/Um?
hh	Lt Yellow	JNT-B-II-009	Ott	Ott	5	244	Base
ii	Turquoise on olive	JNT-B-V-001	Ott (most LByz/Um)	Ott?	1	1400	Bracelet
jj	Emerald	JNT-B-V-012	Ott (most LByz/Um)	Ott?	19	1427	Bracelet
kk	Dk Olive	JNT-B-I-001	Mod	Ott?	30	3	Same, fine
ll	Black?	JNT-B-II-002	Ott	Ott?	46	281	Bracelet, notched, Roman?

late third to early seventh century (Erdmann 1977: 110, 143–44, pl. 8); Hama, later than the tenth century (Riis and Poulsen 1957: 50); Alexandria, fifth to early seventh century (Rodziewicz 1984: pls. 73, 74); and Samarra, ninth century (Lamm 1928: 43).

The base on fig. 13:U is problematic; without the pontil scar it could be a Roman ribbed bowl. Some late ribbed bases are known, however, from Kish, fifth to sixth century (Harden 1934: 134–35); Egypt (Lamm 1929: pl. 9); and Susa, perhaps sixth century (Lamm 1931: 361, pl. 77). But for the mold-blown lamp, all of the molded decoration shown on fig. 13 probably would have been dated later.

Bracelet (fig. 13:W).   The color scheme, red and white (and yellow?) on blue, is the same as that of some of the marvered sherds. Goldstein notes some bracelets from Ḥesban with spiral twisting and contrasting colors trailed on (Goldstein 1976: 132). At Sardis, glass bracelets were fairly common in the Middle Byzantine period, late 10th to 13th or 14th century, and some are twisted with colored threads, although different color schemes were favored there (von Saldern 1980: 98–99, pl. 18).

MAMLUK (1250–1516)

By Mamluk times Jerash, or at least the area investigated by the ACOR team, must have been virtually abandoned. Only a few glass sherds can tentatively be attributed to the period.

Cut Base (fig. 13:X).   The small, emerald green, cut base has Mamluk parallels of a sort at Quseir al-Qadim (Whitcomb 1981: pl. 58), and an eighth to tenth century parallel at Hama (Riis and Poulsen 1957: 53).

Bottle Neck (fig. 13:Y).   The bottle neck with trailed threads and a zigzag could be Late Byzantine/Early Umayyad, Mamluk, or even Ottoman. The bulges of an elaborate bottle neck from Hama do have turquoise zigzags (Riis and Poulsen 1957: 60–61), and thread-trailed and ruffle decoration did continue in use after the Umayyad period, at least in the west. Some 13th to 15th century bottle necks from Italy are strikingly similar to the Late Byzantine/Early Umayyad examples on fig. 11 (Gasparetto 1979: 83).

Rim (fig. 13:Z).   Judging from the glass fabric, the broad rim could be Late Byzantine/Early Umayyad; the locus date (Mamluk, mostly Late Byzantine/Early Umayyad) is inconclusive.

Bracelets (fig. 13:aa–ee).   Glass bracelets are known from earlier centuries but apparently they achieve greater popularity in the Mamluk period. Bracelets do not seem to be very thoroughly studied, but parallels for the simple one on fig. 13:aa may be seen among the Sardis finds. Here plain bracelets of olive, black, or blue with flat or round cross-sections are common in Middle Byzantine loci. They may even be locally manufactured (von Saldern 1980: 98–101, pl. 18). A few bracelets were noted at Meẓad Tamar, late third to early seventh century (Erdmann 1977: 111, 144, pl. 8:932) and also at Quseir al-Qadim (Whitcomb 1981: pl. 59).

The black bracelet twisted with red, yellow, and blue threads (fig. 13:bb) might be Umayyad like the one on fig. 13:W, but is listed here because there are some later parallel pieces. Colored, twisted bracelets were excavated from Mamluk loci at Quseir al-Qadim (Whitcomb 1981: pl. 59); Sardis, 12th and 13th century reoccupation levels (Hanfmann 1959: 53–54); and Hama (Riis and Poulsen 1957: 68).

The more elaborate bracelets (fig. 13:cc and dd) with colored strips marvered on and then stripes or blobs on top of that are grouped here on the basis of parallel pieces. The most similar bracelets are those from the Mamluk occupation of Quseir al-Qadim (Whitcomb 1981: pl. 59), and the Middle Byzantine (late 10th to 13th or 14th century) levels at Sardis (von Saldern 1980: 98–100, pl. 18). The fanciest bracelet of all (fig. 13:ee) has slender rods of twisted white and yellow glass added along the edges. Several bracelets from Akhmim, thought to be Roman, have twisted cords in addition to the pressed-in colored stripes (Cooney 1976: 162), but the best parallels are at Quseir al-Qadim, Mamluk loci (Whitcomb 1981: pl. 59), and at Hama, thought to be early Islamic (Riis and Poulsen 1957: 63, 68).

OTTOMAN—MODERN

As for the Mamluk period, post-Mamluk occupation in and around the ACOR excavation area was spotty and the glass finds scanty. Much of what there is may be earlier, though this cannot yet be demonstrated.

Rims (fig. 13:ff, gg).   The fabric looks like the typical Byzantine through Umayyad glass, but no convincing parallels for the forms have yet been found, especially the rim (fig. 13:gg) that folds out, down, and back up.

Bases (fig. 13:hh). Another yellowish base was recovered, but it is not illustrated; it is kicked-up.

Bracelets (fig. 13:ii–ll). There are problems in dating the bracelets from the uppermost levels. No close comparisons are available for the turquoise-on-olive bracelet in fig. 13:ii. The two twisted bracelets (fig. 13:jj, kk) have parallels from the Roman period on (cf. von Saldern 1980: 33–34; Tatton-Brown 1984: 208, fig. 69). The notched bracelet (fig. 13:ll) may even be Roman. A black(?) bracelet whose exterior was tooled to form notches was excavated from a Roman context at Sardis (von Saldern 1980: 33–34). Twelve ribbed bracelets are reported from Cyprus, possibly second or third century A.D. (Vessberg 1952: 154, pl. 10), and five notched black bracelets are published from Karanis, Roman period (Harden 1936: 282–83, pl. 21).

CONCLUSIONS

The Jerash glass corpus may be used in several ways. It may be compared to the large glass corpora from Karanis and Sardis to gain some idea as to what they have or do not have in common and hence may provide some indication of differences among the regions or provinces. Second, a group of forms more characteristic of the Syro-Palestinian area may be sifted out, along with a group that is best attested at Jerash itself. Finally, some important shifts in the kinds of glass used over the centuries can be documented.

The groups and comparisons, or lack of them, are made with some trepidation. Nothing is easier to shoot down than a statement such as, "There is no X" or "Apparently no Y or Z remain." On the other hand, such statements can provoke response from sources missed or underutilized or unreported that can add to our knowledge of the matter.

Several points may be made about the Karanis and Sardis corpora. Most of the Karanis glass was recovered from houses, the later ones dated to the fourth and fifth centuries or roughly the Jerash Early Byzantine period. Although the Karanis corpus is large and many glass finds came from intact hoards, no statistics on how many of what type of vessel were compiled. The Sardis glass comes from shops, the gymnasium, a synagogue, and various other buildings dated to ca. 400–616, which covers both the Jerash Early Byzantine (A.D. 324 to 491) and Late Byzantine (A.D. 491 to 636) periods. Some counts are presented (von Saldern 1980: 3–4), but not enough

for statistical comparisons with Jerash. No large Umayyad glass corpora are available, but the Sardis Middle Byzantine period (late 10th to 13th or 14th century) overlaps the Jerash Mamluk period (1250–1516) and a few observations may be made on this glass.

In any case, comparisons between sites can deal only with the most distinctive or best-known types. Simple rims or kick-up bases may be quite abundant but they are so unspecialized that they could pertain to many vessel forms from different periods.

The glass fabrics characteristic of the Karanis glass are mainly green or yellow, ranging from very pale to dark (Harden 1936: 23). At Sardis the glass is generally light aquamarine or pale green, plus some "bottle" green and olive and a little colorless or pale blue (von Saldern 1980: 36). Most of the Jerash glass is light blue or blue-green, with some yellow-greens and other colors; it seems to resemble the Sardis fabrics more than the Karanis ones.

In terms of specific vessel forms, the stemmed goblets are found at all three sites. Both the flat-footed and looped-footed varieties (figs. 8:Y–cc, 9:A–D) are well represented at Jerash and Sardis, but they are not common at Karanis or elsewhere in Egypt. The Karanis goblets are usually olive, yellow, or green, not blue-green or bluish as at the other two sites, and have straight sides and sometimes thread or coil decoration. Harden (1936: 167–73) suggested that they may be the predecessors of the Syrian spreading-mouth goblets, and the successors of the earlier beakers. This agrees with the series of Early Byzantine beakers to Late Byzantine goblets observed at Jerash, although the dates seem to lag. What is peculiar to Karanis are goblets on short fat stems with turquoise, white, or colorless snake thread decoration which is quite rare in the east but well known in Europe (Harden 1936: 169).

The Karanis jars with zigzag and other trailed decoration are similarly unattested at Jerash or Sardis (Harden 1936: pl. 17). Also characteristic of Karanis and not the eastern sites is a series of deep bowls on high or ring bases, many with green, yellow, or purplish coil decoration (Harden 1936: pls. 11, 12, 14). Coil decoration is uncommon at Jerash and Sardis and the color combinations used are different.

Only two bowl forms seem to have connections to the Egyptian forms. The Jerash Early Byzantine dish with looped rim and base has parallels at

Karanis, Tyre?, and near Cologne (Harden 1936: 71). The Early Byzantine bent, looped rim vessels (fig. 6:G–J) may have parallels in Egypt, if not at Karanis.

Bottles are found at all three sites but the shapes differ. Those at Karanis are relatively short and squat. The rims are rolled-in but they differ from the Jerash rims and are often more elaborately profiled. Most of the bottles are green rather than bluish and some have a green ruffle on the shoulder, not the neck (Harden 1936: pl. 17). The Jerash bottles are generally tall or very tall like the Palestinian ones and frequently have an indent where the neck and shoulder meet, and ruffles or trailed threads on the neck. The tall vessels, though, may be later than the Karanis corpus as they do continue into the Umayyad period. At Sardis, bottles are one of the most common vessel types. The body is usually ovoid and the neck tall and slightly conical; a variant has a funnel-like upper part (von Saldern 1980: 69). At Jerash on the other hand the flaring mouths seem to be more common.

The types of lamps at the three sites present an interesting picture. Harden (1936: pl. 16) illustrated only the tall conical ones, sometimes decorated with incised horizontal lines or blue blobs, at Karanis. Such lamps are unattested at Jerash or Sardis, although both hollow stem lamps (fig. 10:H) and tumbler lamps (fig. 12:P–R) are abundant. On the other hand, the Sardis lamps shaped like a beaker with a knob at the bottom have no published, excavated parallels (von Saldern 1980: 52). The Jerash beaded stem lamps are probably too late for comparison.

Karanis seems to have yielded more decorated glass than Jerash or Sardis. As noted, colored coils and snake-threads are not uncommon. Millefiore, which is probably Roman, has been reported at Karanis and Sardis but not in this Jerash corpus. Mold-blown decoration, especially ribbing, is attested at all three sites but not in abundance. The distinctive Jerash blue trailed threads and ruffles tend to run later, Late Byzantine through Umayyad.

Window glass was not discussed in the Karanis corpus but was abundant at Jerash and Sardis. All of the Sardis Early Byzantine windowpanes were flat, thought to have been made by the "muff" process (von Saldern 1980: 91). Most of the Early and Late Byzantine panes at Jerash are flat, and such evidence as there is would indicate

that they were cast. Not until the Late Byzantine/ Early Umayyad period, early seventh century, are the round "crown" panes prevalent, and at Sardis the Middle Byzantine (late 10th to 13th or 14th century) panes are all crown glass.

The only other comparable late glass pieces are the Sardis Middle Byzantine and Jerash Mamluk bracelets, which seem to have been widespread types throughout the Near East.

Von Saldern (1980: 37) stated that the glass of the mid-first millennium A.D. was relatively homogeneous from Palestine to Asia Minor, Greece, and Italy; he did not mention Egypt. As far as the Jerash evidence goes, its glass seems more like that from Sardis than the Egyptian material. The distinctness of the province of Egypt was manifested in other ways as well. For one, Alexandria was the center of the Arian and Monophysite heresies of the fourth and fifth centuries, and all the religious and political tangles they entailed. The Egypt–Greece–Italy and other possible linkages or connections cannot be investigated here. Particularly unfortunate is the lack of any information on the glass from the capital city, Constantinople itself.

Some types of glass do, however, seem characteristic of the Syro-Palestinian area only, or of Jerash alone. It may be more reasonable to expect similarity or compatibility or interchangeability than absolute homogeneity between the glass houses of the different provinces. A concentration of certain forms in a given region or site may point to particular wants or needs of the local population, or production in the general area, or both.

The double-barreled kohl tubes are abundant in the Near East but are not found in Sardis or the west. If they are in fact kohl tubes, then they would not be needed where women did not wear kohl. The tall Late Byzantine to Umayyad bottles with flaring mouths and rolled-in rims seem to be concentrated in the Syro-Palestinian area, though the bottles with straight rims seem to be more common at Sardis. The ruffle and trailed thread decorations frequently applied to bottles have a similar distribution, but ruffled or thread-trailed bottles are occasionally reported from Egypt, Italy, and Cyprus also.

Other vessels are not well-attested outside Jerash. This could be due to the extreme fragility of some forms and a reluctance to publish fragments, to the intrinsic rarity of other forms, to their having been manufactured locally, or even to a lack of interest on the part of earlier excavators in "late" finds such as Byzantine or Umayyad glass. Whatever the case may be, the delicate, flaring Early Byzantine beakers to date have few parallels elsewhere. It is suggested, however, that they had fairly heavy looped bases, and these are reported at other sites. The fancy yellow-green beaker with a dark blue, trailed diamond pattern has no known close kin. Surprisingly, the undecorated ground-rim cups (fig. 6:D–F) and the handles with ridges (fig. 7:Q, R) are seldom reported from other sites. The delicate Early Byzantine turquoise ring bases are, thus far, unique to Jerash, although they are uncommon even there. The Byzantine cylindrical beakers with flaring rims, one with trailed thread decoration (fig. 8:A–C), have few close parallels as well. The Umayyad beaded-stem lamps are rare outside Jerash and Mount Nebo, but published excavated Umayyad glass corpora are not numerous. Three unusual Umayyad vessels—the four-handled jar, the molded tumbler lamp, and the two-handled shallow bowl (fig. 12)—may owe their uniqueness to being well-preserved examples of relatively uncommon shapes. Mold-blown decoration, at least, is by no means rare in Umayyad and later periods.

Finally, a significant change in the way glass was used can be traced. The earliest glasses were treated as imitation stone and sometimes ground or carved like stone. Opaque blue or veined glass, for instance, could serve as substitute lapis lazuli or agate, costly, perhaps, but less so than the genuine stone. Other glasses such as millefiore and marvered core-formed vessels were definitely luxury products.

Not until the Roman period was translucent glass widely used, appreciated, and experimented with. Some Roman forms were patterned after vessels in other materials such as ceramic Terra Sigillata ware (cf. fig. 5:K) or metal bowls (ribbed bowls perhaps; cf. fig. 5:A). The real revolution, however, was the invention of blown glass in the first century B.C. This allowed rapid production and encouraged the development of new shapes that could be formed easily with the new technique. Most of the Roman glassware seems to have consisted of eating and drinking vessels, flagons for storage or shipping, and unguentaria. Window glass, tesserae, and even jewelry are uncommon and glass lamps are unattested.

In the Byzantine period, few glass dishes or bowls were used; pottery and, later, glazed ceramics would have sufficed. Drinking vessels are as popular as ever though the outward form has changed; and by the early seventh century, at least, globular bottles with long necks, instead of the Roman flagons, are more common.

A major factor may have been the growth of the new churches. Whatever architectural form was adopted, the builders seemed determined not to use the classical temple plan. Churches faced east, they were smaller but more numerous, the congregation was admitted, and interior decorations and fixtures were different. Notably, glass windows and lamps became prominent; the development of crown glass panes[9] permitted more rapid manufacture than cast glass. Glass tesserae were employed for mosaics more often though they never became ubiquitous. The number of glass bottles and goblets suggests that they were used in the church services, but this is not yet proven. One brief mention, however, from the time of the persecution of Christians during the reign of Diocletian (A.D. 284–313) is relevant. A village headman in the Oxyrhynchus nome was hauled before the judge and ordered to produce the altar vessels, books, deacons, and elders. The man, Apa Epime, replied, "Presbyteros quidem non habemus. . . . Et vasa, quibus communicamur, sunt vitrea, nam nos pauperes sumus, in parvo επιγιον (=ἐποίκιον) degentes" (Harden 1936: 40; Balestri and Hyvernat 1908: 82, translated from Coptic).

Other public buildings and private homes, of course, came to use more and more glass over the decades. A large quantity of the standardized blue or green glass came to be the norm rather than the elaborate luxury wares of earlier times. After the Umayyad period, however, glass at Jerash is, apart from the gaudy bracelets, too poorly represented to add much to the history of the use of glass.

No major theoretical propositions have been addressed in this report, and it is submitted that this cannot be done until the basic, descriptive data are accessible. The present corpus is, however, the first large, detailed corpus from a Jordanian site. Work remains to be done and complementary data will undoubtedly be produced by the other teams who excavated at Jerash. Still, the purpose of this report is to present a body of comparative material that will be of use to others working on related problems.

NOTES

[1]I would like to acknowledge the role of Adnan Hadidi, Director, and of the Jordanian Department of Antiquities, which called in and funded the seven foreign teams—Polish, French, British, Australian, Italian, Spanish, and American—for the Jerash International Project. The ACOR (American Center for Oriental Research) team's excavations were carried out by Linda Jacobs, Carol Meyer, and Jerome Schaefer in the North Theater; Meyer and Schaefer in the soundings; and Vincent Clark, team leader, and Iman Oweis in the Byzantine church. Excavation began in May 1982 and was terminated unexpectedly at the end of December 1983. The other teams excavated or continue to excavate in other parts of the ancient city, in different kinds of buildings, covering different time ranges. Further thanks are due to Donald Whitcomb and David Grose for constructive criticism, and to Janet Johnson and the Oriental Institute of the University of Chicago for assistance in the publication.

[2]In this report Early Byzantine refers to A.D. 324 to 491; and Late Byzantine, A.D. 491 to 636.

[3]The most accessible map for the Jerash site is in Browning (1982: 83).

[4]Four, possibly five, kilns have been uncovered in and around the North Theater. The two within the theater are the subject of a report by Jerome Schaefer in Zayadine (1986).

[5]One may speculate whether the Medieval Church's ban on glass vessels had anything to do with the problem of disposing of broken, sanctified pieces.

[6]In practice such rods, especially the ones with knobs at the ends, would be an exceedingly awkward way to apply any cosmetic.

[7]Wicks were held at least in some cases by S-shaped bronze holders (Baur 1938: 517).

[8]The earliest crown glass cited by Harden (1939: 91) is from "Byzantine" levels at Jerash, mostly from churches. According to the evidence obtained from the recent excavations, however, the church glass and especially the crown panes are almost all seventh century or later.

[9]These were invented in the fourth century, according to Harden (1939: 91), but more likely date to the sixth or seventh century on evidence from the recent excavations.

BIBLIOGRAPHY

American Research Center in Egypt
1958   Newsletter No. 29.

Balestri, I., and Hyvernat, H., eds.
1908   *Acta Martyrum.* Corpus Scriptorum Christianorum Orientalium, Scriptores Coptici, Ser. 3, Vol. 1 (Latin). Lipsiae: Otto Harrassowitz.

Barag, D.
1967   The Glass. Pp. 65–72 in *Excavations at Shavei Zion,* by M. W. Prausnitz. Rome: Centro per le Antichità e la Storia dell'arte del Vicino Oriente.
1974   A Tomb Cave of the Byzantine Period Near Netiv ha-Lamed He. *Atiqot* 7 (Hebrew Series) 13: 81–87.

Bass, G. F.
1984   The Nature of the Serçe Limani Glass. *Journal of Glass Studies* 26: 64–69.

Baur, P. V. C.
1938   Other Glass Vessels. Pp. 513–46 in *Gerasa: City of the Decapolis,* by C. H. Kraeling. New Haven, CT: American Schools of Oriental Research.

Boon, G. C.
1966   Roman Window Glass from Wales. *Journal of Glass Studies* 8: 41–45.

Browning, I.
1982   *Jerash and the Decapolis.* London: Chatto and Windus.

Calvi, M. C.
1968   *I Vetri Romani del Museo di Aquileia.* Aquileia: Associazione Nazionale per Aquileia.

Canivet, M. T. F.
1970   Vetri del V–VI Secolo Trovati nell'Apamene (Siria). *Journal of Glass Studies* 12: 64–66.

Charlesworth, M. P.
1924   *Trade-Routes and Commerce of the Roman Empire.* Cambridge, England: Cambridge University Press.

Clairmont, C. W.
1963   *The Glass Vessels,* Vol. 4, part 5, *The Excavations at Dura-Europos.* New Haven, CT: Dura Europos Publications.

Clark, V. A.
1986   The Church of Bishop Isaiah. Pp. 303–41 in *Jerash International Project 1981–1983,* ed. F. Zayadine. Amman: Department of Antiquities.

Clark, V. A. *et al.*
1986   The Jerash North Theatre: Architecture and Archaeology 1982–1983. Pp. 205–302 in *Jerash International Project 1981–1983,* ed. F. Zayadine. Amman: Department of Antiquities.

Cooney, J. D.
1976   *Glass,* Vol. 4, *Catalogue of Egyptian Antiquities in the British Museum.* London: The British Museum.

Corning Museum
1964   Recent Acquisitions. *Journal of Glass Studies* 6: 158.

Corning Museum of Glass and American National Committee of the International Association for the History of Glass
1982   *Glass Collections in Museums in the United States and Canada.* Corning, NY: Corning Museum of Glass.

Crowfoot, G. M.
1957   Glass. Pp. 403–22 in *The Objects from Samaria*, by J. W. Crowfoot, G. M. Crowfoot, and K. M. Kenyon. London: Palestine Exploration Fund.

Crowfoot, G. M., and Harden, D. B.
1931   Early Byzantine and Later Glass Lamps. *Journal of Egyptian Archaeology* 17: 196–208.

Davidson, G. R.
1940   A Mediaeval Glass-Factory at Corinth. *American Journal of Archaeology* 44: 297–324.
1952   *The Minor Objects*, Vol. 12, *Corinth*. Princeton, NJ: The American School of Classical Studies at Athens.

Delougaz, P., and Haines, R. C.
1960   *A Byzantine Church at Khirbat al-Karak.* Oriental Institute Publications 85. Chicago, IL: University of Chicago.

Dusenbery, E. B.
1967   Ancient Glass from the Cemeteries of Samothrace. *Journal of Glass Studies* 9: 39–49.

Erdmann, E.
1977   Die Glasfunde von Meẓad Tamar (Kasr Gehainije) in Israel. *Saalburg-Jahrbuch* 34: 98–146.

Fitzgerald, G. M.
1931   *Beth-Shan Excavations 1921–1923: The Arab and Byzantine Levels.* Philadelphia, PA: University of Pennsylvania Museum.

Fitzwilliam Museum
1978   *Glass at the Fitzwilliam Museum.* Cambridge, England: Cambridge University.

Fontaine, A.-L.
1952   Enquête sur Péluse. *Bulletin de la Société d'Études historiques de l'Isthme de Suez*, 4. Cairo: Imprimerie le Scribe Egyptien S.A.E.

Gasparetto, A.
1979   Matrici e Aspetti della Vetraria Veneziana e Veneta Medievale. *Journal of Glass Studies* 21: 76–97.

Goldstein, S. M.
1976   Glass Fragments from Tell Ḥesban: A Preliminary Report. Pp. 127–32 in *Heshbon 1974: The Fourth Campaign at Tell Ḥesbân*, by R. S. Boraas and L. T. Geraty. Berrien Springs, MI: Andrews University.
1979   *Pre-Roman and Early Roman Glass in The Corning Museum of Glass.* Corning, NY: Corning Museum of Glass.

Grose, D. F.
1977   Early Blown Glass: The Western Evidence. *Journal of Glass Studies* 19: 9–29.
1979   The Syro-Palestinian Glass Industry in the Later Hellenistic Period. *Muse* 13: 54–67.
1982   The Hellenistic and Early Roman Glass from Morgantina (Serra Orlando), Sicily. *Journal of Glass Studies* 24: 20–29.
1983   The Formation of the Roman Glass Industry. *Archaeology* 36: 38–45.
1984   Glass Forming Methods in Classical Antiquity: Some Considerations. *Journal of Glass Studies* 26: 25–34.

Hak, S. A.
1965   Contribution d'une Découverte archéologique récente à l'étude de la verrerie syrienne à l'époque romaine. *Journal of Glass Studies* 7: 26–34.

Hanfmann, G. M. A.
1959   A Preliminary Note on the Glass Found at Sardis. *Journal of Glass Studies* 1: 50–54.

Harden, D. B.
1934   Glass from Kish. *Iraq* 1: 131–36.
1936   *Roman Glass from Karanis.* Ann Arbor, MI: University of Michigan.
1939   Roman Window-panes from Jerash, and Later Parallels. *Iraq* 6: 91.
1949   Tomb-Groups of Glass of Roman Date from Syria and Palestine. *Iraq* 11: 151–59.
1962   Glass. Pp. 76–91 in *Excavations at Nessana*, Vol. I, by H. Dunscombe Colt. London: British School of Archaeology in Jerusalem.
1964   Histoire de la verrerie en Syrie. *Bulletin de Journées Internationales du Verre* 3: 19–24.
1969   Ancient Glass, II: Roman. *Archaeological Journal* 126: 44–77.
1971   Ancient Glass, III: Post-Roman. *Archaeological Journal* 128: 78–117.

Hayes, J. W.
1975   *Roman and Pre-Roman Glass in the Royal Ontario Museum.* Toronto: Royal Ontario Museum.

Haynes, E. B.
1948   *Glass through the Ages.* Harmondsworth, England: Penguin Books.

Isings, C.
1957   *Roman Glass from Dated Finds.* Academiae Rheno-Traiectinae Instituto Archaeologico II. Groningen: J. B. Wolters.

Kisa, A.
1908   *Das Glas im Altertum*, Vols. 1–3. Leipzig: Karl W. Hiersemann.

Lamb, A.
1965   A Note on Glass Fragments from Dengkalan Bujang, Malaya. *Journal of Glass Studies* 7: 35–40.

Lamm, C. J.
1928   *Das Glas von Samarra*, Vol. 4, *Die Aus-grabungen von Samarra*. Berlin: Dietrich Reimer/Ernst Vohsen.
1929   *Mittelalterliche Gläser und Steinschnittar-beiten aus dem Nahen Osten*. Berlin: Dietrich Reimer/Ernst Vohsen.
1931   Les Verres trouvés à Suse. *Syria* 12: 358–67.
1935   *Glass from Iran*. London: Kegan Paul, Trench, Trubner.

Lapp, N. L., ed.
1983   *The Excavations at Araq el-Emir*, Vol. 1. Annual of the American Schools of Oriental Research 47. Cambridge, MA: American Schools of Oriental Research.

Makhouly, N.
1939   Rock-Cut Tombs at El Jīsh. *Quarterly of the Department of Antiquities in Palestine* 8: 45–50.

McNicoll, A. W. et al.
1982   A Third Season of Excavations at Pella. *Annual of the Department of Antiquities of Jordan* 21: 343–63.

Meyer, C.
1981   Roman Glass. Pp. 215–32 in *Quseir al-Qadim 1980: Preliminary Report*, by D. S. Whit-comb and J. H. Johnson. Malibu, CA: Undena.

Philippe, J.
1970   *Le Monde Byzantin dans l'histoire de la verrerie*. Bologna: Casa Editrice Prof. Ric-cardo Pàtron.

Raschke, M. G.
1978   New Studies in Roman Commerce with the East. Pp. 604–1361 in *Aufstieg und Nieder-gang der Römischen Welt*, Vol. 2, part 9:2, ed. H. Temporini. New York, NY: De Gruyter.

Riis, P. J., and Poulsen, V.
1957   *Hama: Fouilles et Recherches 1931–1938*, Vol. 4, part 2. Copenhagen: Fondation Carls-berg.

Rodziewicz, M.
1979   Un quartier d'habitation gréco-romain à Kôm el-Dikka. *Études et Travaux* 9: 169–210.
1984   *Alexandrie III*. Warsaw: Éditions scientifiques de Pologne.

Roth, A. M.
1979   Glass. Pp. 144–82 in *Quseir al-Qadim 1978: Preliminary Report*, by D. S. Whitcomb and J. H. Johnson. Cairo: American Research Center in Egypt.

von Saldern, A.
1968   *Ancient Glass in the Museum of Fine Arts, Boston*. Boston, MA: Museum of Fine Arts.
1980   *Ancient and Byzantine Glass from Sardis*. Cambridge, MA: Harvard University.

von Saldern, A. et al.
1974   *Gläser der Antike*. Mainz am Rhein: Verlag Philipp von Zabern.

Saller, S. J.
1941   *The Memorial of Moses on Mount Nebo*. Jerusalem: Franciscan Press.
1956   *Excavations at Bethany*. Jerusalem: Francis-can Press.

Smith, R. W.
1957   *Glass from the Ancient World*. Corning, NY: Corning Museum of Glass.

Tatton-Brown, V. A.
1984   The Glass. Pp. 194–212 in *Excavations at Carthage: The British Mission*, Vol. 1, pt. 1. Sheffield, England: University of Sheffield.

Tudor, D.
1965   *Sucidava: Une cité daco-romaine et byzan-tine en Dacie*. Brussels: Latomus.

Tushingham, A. D.
1972   *The Excavations at Dibon (Dhībân) in Moab*. Annual of the American Schools of Oriental Research 40. Cambridge, MA: American Schools of Oriental Research.

Vessberg, O.
1952   Roman Glass in Cyprus. Pp. 109–65 in *Opuscula Archaeologica* 7. Skrifter Utgivna av Svenska Institutet i Rom 16, No. 4. Lund: C. W. K. Gleerup.

Weinberg, G. D.
1973   Notes on Glass from Upper Galilee. *Journal of Glass Studies* 15: 35–71.
1975   A Medieval Mystery: Byzantine Glass Pro-duction. *Journal of Glass Studies* 17: 127–41.

Weinberg, G. D., and Barag, D.
1974   Glass Vessels. Pp. 103–5 in *Discoveries in the Wadi ed-Daliyeh*, eds. P. W. Lapp and N. L. Lapp. Annual of the American Schools of Oriental Research 41. Cambridge, MA: American Schools of Oriental Research.

Wheeler, R. E. M.; Ghosh, A.; and Deva, K.
1946   Arikamedu: An Indo-Roman Trading Sta-tion on the East Coast of India. *Ancient India* 2: 17–124.

Whitcomb, D. S.
1981   Islamic Glass. Pp. 233–41 in *Quseir al-Qadim 1980: Preliminary Report*, by D. S. Whit-comb and J. H. Johnson. Malibu, CA: Undena.

Zayadine, F., ed.
1986   *Jerash International Project 1981–1983*. Amman: Department of Antiquities.

Zouhdi, B.
1964   Les verres conservés au département des antiquités syriennes des époques grecque, romaine et byzantine du Musée National de Damas. *Bulletin des Journées Internationales du Verre* 3: 41–55.